Theology in the Americas

Edited by
Sergio Torres
and
John Eagleson

ORBIS BOOKS
Maryknoll, New York 10545

Copyright © 1976 by Orbis Books
Orbis Books, Maryknoll, New York 10545
Printed in the United States of America

Library of Congress Cataloging in Publication Data

Main entry under title:

Theology in the Americas.

    1. Theology, Doctrinal—History—America—
Congresses.   I. Torres, Sergio.   II. Eagleson,
John.
BT30.A5T46   230'.097   76–22545
ISBN 0-88344-479-8
ISBN 0-88344-476-3 pbk.

CONTENTS

PART II

THE CONFERENCE IN DETROIT

PART III

AFTER THE CONFERENCE

A Preface and a Conclusion

There is a certain vanity implied in writing anything at all: The writer signals that what has been written is worth the time of somebody else. But to suggest that something is worth reading twice—first as a preface and then as a conclusion—is surely to press vanity beyond all legitimate bounds. And yet I make this seemingly arrogant suggestion: Read these words initially as a way into the immensely variegated materials that follow; then after reading the materials themselves and forming your own impressions of their content, read these words again as a way of reflecting upon your impressions. You may, by that time, disagree vigorously with what follows, in which case you will find yourself in good company, since the conference at which the following papers were given abounded in disagreement. Or you may let these initial pages serve as a springboard for your own assessment, a checklist against which to test your own reactions in more detail: affirming here, questioning there, rethinking this, rejecting that.

How the Book Came to Be

The book unfolds its own story, which need not be repeated here; indeed, that story needs the detail that the book itself provides. It is enough, for the moment, to bear in mind the following: Over the past few years there has been growing up in the Third World, and particularly in Latin America, a movement called "liberation theology"—an attempt to look at the world in terms of involvement with the underprivileged and oppressed, and to find within the Christian gospel both the analytic tools and the energizing power to work for radical change in that world. The "analytic tools" have also, and often initially, involved sociological and economic analysis, frequently along Marxist lines, and the biblical and ecclesiastical resources have involved a critical stance toward institutional religion's long alliance with the status quo. Thanks to theologians of liberation, a rereading of Christian history and Christian documents has become possible, in terms of what they contribute to a new understanding of God as one who sides with the oppressed and works with them for their own liberation.[1]

The Detroit conference, papers for which comprise the bulk of the present volume, was an attempt to gather a group of Latin Americans who have been thinking and acting (and suffering) along these lines, to meet with a group of North Americans, to discuss the possible impact and influence of the Latin American experience on the North American experience. As the texts indicate, the original intent was for a small group of North American professional theologians to meet with their Latin American counterparts. When it was discovered early in the preparations that this was too exclusive, and even elitist, the North American net was considerably widened, so that although the Latin Americans present (about twenty-five) tended to be persons with extensive theological training and experience, the North Americans (about 175) finally represented a tremendous breadth as well as depth—laypersons, social workers, parish priests and blue collar workers, many from minority groups. One result of this was that the conference quickly gravitated into "special interest groups"—North American blacks, Chicanos, native Americans, Appalachians, women, Asian-Americans, and even (in a caucus that became self-conscious only by the last day) white males. Much of the volatile nature of the conference came from the fact that the various groups discovered that they had different agendas, and that the agendas often remained antithetical rather than yielding to easy synthesis. That itself was a discovery worth all the pain.

While the emerging polarities frequently threatened to tear the conference apart at the seams, they did not in fact do so, and the concluding documents below (see especially Section Fourteen) indicate the kind of postconference follow-up that is already underway in various parts of the country, in order to take the next steps in theological reflection and action. Readers may, after exposure to this volume, wish to align themselves with some of these projects.

A New Way of "Doing Theology"

But it would be a mistake if this book were to be seen merely as a report on a conference held in Detroit in August 1975. For what makes the book significant is that it represents a whole new way of doing theology.

In the past, theology has usually been done by the "experts," who, although they sometimes worked in the heat of the battle, more often worked in the relative calm and detachment of the seminary or university or monastery, using texts of the past as their basic resources, producing large and scholarly tomes of "systematic theology," replete with footnotes, foreign phrases, and intricate arguments that could conserve and interpret the past for the sake of the present. The orientation was in large measure to books, ideas, concepts, and modes of argument, rather than to human struggle, anguish, pain, and exploitation. A finished position was being sought, a restatement of "the faith once delivered to the saints," that, if not destined to be definitive forever, might at least be normative for a long time to come.

There is no point in trying to demean or put down the need for such discursive, rational, and somewhat abstract endeavor. There is, however, a point in suggesting that no matter how valuable such activity has been in the past, and might once again be in the future, it is not the crying need of the present.

The crying need of the present is for further experimentation with the sort of theologizing that the present volume represents. In it we see the "doing" of theology as a *process*—a word introduced with some hesitation, for fear it would be confused with the process-philosophy of Alfred North Whitehead. Prefacing the word with a few adjectives may help to clarify what it means in the present context.

1. The process is *an open-ended process.* It is not assumed that theology will come to fixed positions that will be securely defined and nailed down for generations of inspection. Instead, theology will involve ongoing reflection, alternating between looking at its past conclusions and reviewing them in the light of the present world seen from the standpoint of the oppressed. This will mean rethinking past conclusions, which in turn will be tested in the light of present conditions, which themselves will be subject to re-evaluation as new data come to light and as the conditions themselves change. For awhile at least, the writing of theology needs to be done in loose-leaf notebooks. New pages will continue to be needed, and some older pages will need to be replaced.

2. The process is *a corporate process.* Input will come from many sources and many disciplines. The reflection will be done by many people, and the results will be disseminated in many ways. It is crucial to the meaning of the present book that it is *not* a new theology by an individual, but the expression of a theological process engaged in by a large number of individuals, who have worked together and struggled together, and who only by going through that corporate struggle have gained some fresh insights for the next round.

3. Therefore, the process is also a *a self-correcting process.* ("Con-

flictive process" was a tempting term, save that it does not contain any inherent hope; conflicts do not always have creative outcomes, whereas acts of self-correction almost always can.) In such a process as this book exemplifies, the end result may be, as in this case it was, very different from the initial conception. Indeed, one of the great merits of the book is its total honesty on this score. Early on it was seen that the original design was "elitist," in that it did not involve a sufficiently widespread representation of different classes, points of view, backgrounds, sexes, and so forth. The complaints arose out of those involved in the process itself; they were heeded, and corrections were made. Further corrections continued to be needed all along the way, many of them within the dynamics of the week at Detroit itself, a reality to which the pages below bear ample testimony. More corrections will be needed as the process continues, particularly as the net is widened yet further to include new voices and perspectives. But the process itself makes possible such self-correction.

There is another way in which the self-correcting aspects of the process are important. Each special interest group at Detroit needed the help of other groups to get beyond some of its own biases. The Latin Americans, it turned out, had barely awakened to the fact that they had ignored the oppression of women in their own cultures; North American women took great pains to point out that deficiency. North American black theologians have given little attention to economic sources of their own oppression: Latin Americans insisted on a new degree of economic analysis. Middle-class white women were told that they may have overlooked the class dimension of their own internal struggle for womens' liberation; a black woman Marxist gave help at this point. And so on. Each group could point more skillfully to the mote in someone else's theological eye than to the beam in its own, and the corporate self-correction in these matters was immensely fruitful.[2]

4. The process is finally *an engaged process.* From start to finish (which suggests that this might appropriately have been the first point) those who "do theology" in this fashion must be doing it with their lives as well as with their minds. Theology is not so much a matter of the classroom (though it can also be that) as of the arena of human need, immersed in the stuff of politics, engaged in the struggle with the oppressed, being open to personal risks for the sake of those whom the world counts as nothing. The key word here, a word always in danger of being co-opted and defused, is *praxis.* Thinking must be engaged thinking; it must come out of *doing* and not just cogitating. As Gustavo Gutiérrez has put it, "All the political theolo-

gies, the theologies of hope, of revolution, and of liberation, are not worth one act of genuine solidarity with exploited social classes."[3] Whatever authentic theology emerges for our day will spring from genuine acts of solidarity with the exploited—an agenda that can only be disquieting to many of the readers of this book, and to which we will later return. Part of the meaning of Detroit is that (perhaps for the first time at a "theological conference") a large percentage of the participants came from just such situations. They were not "professional theologians," but ones who, through their own daily praxis, were thinking from the vantage point of solidarity with the exploited. It was a new and important and frequently shattering experience for the few "professional" North American theologians in attendance to have to live, think, speak, respond, and be challenged by those whose academic credentials were not the ordinary ones, but whose human credentials were extraordinary. (To me, the most powerful "theological" statement came from a Chicano in a small group who apologized ahead of time that he had had no "formal education.")

This is the stuff of a new theology; it will be out of this sort of mix that we will do our most important thinking and acting in the future, if we are to be faithful both to the oppressed of our world and to the God who (as a rereading of Scripture reminds us) has already indicated the divine faithfulness toward them by taking sides with them and entering into their struggle. The present book is a stage at the beginning of that present—that open-ended, corporate, self-correcting, engaged process.

Recognizing the Threats

Such a prospect is threatening. It may be more threatening to some than to others, but in varying degrees it is threatening to all. Why? Because it calls into question the implicitly held assumptions by which we govern our lives—or think we do. Even more threatening may be the discovery that the assumptions we think are normative for our lives are only a facade to hide from public (or private) scrutiny the truly normative assumptions.

At Detroit, I was part of the group that overtly, at least, seemed most threatened—the white male theologians. Every other group had reason to mistrust us: To them we were the epitome of the oppressive power structure, as seen through the eyes of women, blacks, Chicanos, native Americans, Asian-Americans, Appalachians, and so on. Even if we weren't oppressing people personally (and delegates were occasionally, though not uniformly, willing to offer that concession) we were clearly part of the group that tended to benefit most by the oppression of others.

But it is important to realize that this was by no means a reality only for white male theologians. All the groups discovered other groups to whom they were beholden only in terms of guilt or threat. The "oppressors" in one situation had reason to feel "oppressed" in other situations; the "oppressed" could always find someone who looked upon them as "oppressors."

Granting all that, it is still the case that certain readers of the present volume will feel greatly threatened by its contents. This should be acknowledged. For it is an undeniable fact that many of the structures of society that benefit people who read books like this are structures that destroy other people. Their backs and lives are broken producing the food we eat. They will never be able to stand as long as our feet are on their necks. Their exploitation seems to be necessary for our comfort. (Readers who find such imagery extreme will find ample documentation for it in the subsequent essays.)

Now unless we are callously insensitive, we cannot help being threatened by the discovery that our survival is purchased at the cost or the demise of others. And if we would like to "do something" about it, to change the world so that such conditions do not continue, we are further threatened when it turns out that all the things we are prepared to "do" are looked upon as cheap palliatives, as foredoomed-to-failure cosmetic attempts to beautify an ugly monster, as trivial evasions of the real problem. Our concepts of "help," of "charity," of "doing good," are interpreted as ways in which we can salve our consciences without changing our lives, our status, or our comfort. We may feel better, but *nothing has changed*. The conditions that brought about the evils we attempt to remedy with a little aid or a little emergency help are still the same conditions; their evil consequences may have been alleviated for a moment or two, but *nothing has changed*.

And surely it is the insistent call for radical change, endemic to these essays, that is most threatening—"radical" in the sense of going to the *radix*, the root, of things. Consequently: if an economic system based on competition can finally only grind down and destroy, then the system must go; it will not be enough to have those on top grind with a smile on their faces instead of a sneer, or give an occasional charitable loaf of bread to those to whom they deny the possibility of earning enough loaves to feed their families adequately. And yet, if it is said that "the system must go," that becomes a genuine threat, because with the disappearance of the system would go our securities, our status, our luxuries, possibly our necessities, perhaps even our lives.

Refusing the Evasions

In the light of such a threat, most of us look for ways to evade the validity of such an analysis. And there are a number of ways to evade a position as threatening as that of liberation theology:

1. A threatening position can sometimes be disposed of simply *by calling it a "fad" and those who espouse it "naive."* This is not to say that positions can be exempted from hard-nosed analysis, but in the case of liberation theology the put-down has often been a substitute for the analysis. Concern for liberation is dismissed as this year's theological kick, similar to previous flurries over "the secular city," "the death of God," "the theology of play," or whatever; those who take it seriously are naive souls who will jump on any bandwagon; for them the present one will do until the next one comes along, at which point they will desert liberation for something else.

These are cheap shots. We can be sure that the phenomenon of "liberation theology" (by whatever name) will not disappear until oppression has disappeared, and that, unfortunately, will not be for a long, long time. Concern for liberation does not arise from theologians looking for new intellectual toys; it arises from the reality of grinding poverty, the distended stomachs of starving children, the brutality of political repression, and from a recognition that the Christian gospel announces the possibility of liberation from just such evils. And even if liberation should come this side of the eschaton, we will need to ride herd on the new situation so that the oppressed, having finally gotten power, do not merely imitate those whom they have replaced. The "fad theory" of liberation theology needs to be countered by pointing out that the *real* fad these days is calling every position but one's own a fad.

2. A threatening position can sometimes be disposed of *by co-opting it.* Third World theologians are legitimately nervous as they look at what North Americans are doing with their terms. Indeed, one of the reasons for the Detroit conference was to render such co-optation less likely. As Hugo Assmann has put it:

Perhaps the first important contribution Christians can make to the process of liberation is not to add to the process of diluting the revolutionary implications that circumstances have dictated it should contain.[4]

It will be in the short-run self-interest of most people in power to try to co-opt such a movement by broadening the term "liberation" enough to defuse it of any revolutionary power. This can be done by talking, for example, about "inner liberation," liberation of the soul, liberation of the insecure, liberation from guilt, and so on, until the word "liberation" has no more political content left than simply changing-things-a-little-bit-but-not-too-much. Although white middle-class people also need certain kinds of liberation (a theme to which we shall return), there is a danger of claiming this too readily and too quickly and hence too conveniently, so that liberation from too many cocktails is somehow equated with liberation from starving to death.

To be sure, liberation theology speaks of various kinds of liberation—from sin and guilt as well as from oppressive social structures—but there is the further fact (which the co-opters usually want to hide) that personal sin and guilt cannot be privatized, but become imbedded in social structures and achieve a kind of objective reality in them. This means that it is not enough to suggest, as those who benefit from the status quo want to insist, that freeing individuals from their own hangups will automatically lead to a just society. The just society will have to incorporate just social structures, and those are not going to come into being until a lot of unjust social structures are torn down. Their tearing down is going to involve challenges to the forms of capitalism, racism, classism, imperialism, and sexism that have become imbedded in the very nature of our society.[5]

3. A threatening position can sometimes be disposed of by *keeping it at a safe distance*. We can examine oppression far away—the denial of civil rights to Spanish-speaking poor people in Santiago, Chile, for example—and never have to confront the denial of civil rights to Spanish-speaking poor in the central valley of California. We can even be romantic about urging "revolution" upon rural guerrillas in Colombia, and still remain exceedingly uptight whenever there is the slightest sign of "unrest" in Harlem or Watts. We need at this point to hear the voice of Dom Helder Camara, archbishop of Recife, Brazil:

Instead of planning to go to the Third World to try and arouse violence there, stay at home in order to help your rich countries to discover that they too are in need of a cultural revolution which will produce a new hierarchy of values, a new world vision, a global strategy of development, the revolution of mankind.[6]

Those who follow Dom Helder's first suggestion ("stay at home") do not frequently follow his second (create a "revolution" at home). We examine manifestations of injustice at a safe distance by keeping our own engagement at a minimum—theorizing, or talking, or writing prefaces to books, so that we never have to take sides in a conscious fashion. (It is necessary to add "in a conscious fashion," because the

presumed posture of neutrality is always a vote for the status quo.)
Even when we bewail the denial of civil rights in Santiago, we are
usually unwilling to face the fact that the military junta denying those
rights is in power largely because American political, economic, and
business interests gave covert support to the overthrow of a previous
regime, and give overt support to the dictatorial regime now in power.
To put it more strongly: American tax dollars, *our* tax dollars, sponsor
the torture of Chilean priests.

4. A threatening position can sometimes be disposed of *by describing
it in emotionally discrediting terms.* In the United States, this means
disposing of liberation theology by applying Marxist or communist
tags to it. It would be foolish to pretend that there is not a lot of
Marxist analysis in the way the liberation theologians look at the
world. But the important question is not, "Is liberation theology's
analysis tinged with a Marxist hue?" The important question is, "Is
the analysis true? Does it make sense of what it is describing? Do we
understand the world better when we look at it in that way?" The
descriptive power of an analysis to illumine the world of oppressed
people is at stake, not how much the analysis is or is not Marxist.

American readers should also bear in mind that Marxism does not
have a corner on descriptive analysis. The fact that "Marxists say it"
must not preclude to others the right to reach similar conclusions,
perhaps by very different routes. The cry for social justice considerably antedates Karl Marx; the promise of "liberty for the oppressed" was not only enunciated by Jesus, but borrowed by him
from the book of Isaiah. Christians cannot be asked to disavow or be
suspicious of a position of their own simply because close to two
millennia later Karl Marx happened to offer his own version of the
same truth.

Furthermore, it is descriptively inadequate to characterize liberation theology in simplistic terms as Marxist. Some liberation theologians rely heavily on Marxist analysis; others do not. Some prefer to
be called Marxist Christians, or Christian Marxists; others do not. For
almost all of them the mix varies. Rather than weigh nicely the
components of that mix, it would be more useful to start with a
recognition of the strong engagement of liberation theology with the
biblical story and the way in which the Scriptures help to corroborate
or challenge a given sociological analysis, both in providing their own
tools for analysis and by indicating a source of power by means of
which those gripped by the biblical message can be enlisted in the
struggle for change.[7] Not all liberation theologians subscribe to a
"surplus-value" theory, but almost all of them would affirm the
Exodus story or Jeremiah 22:13–16 or Isaiah 61:1–4 or Luke 4:16–30

or Matthew 25:31–46 or a host of other passages as basic resources for dealing with the world.

There are, of course, other ways to evade the challenge of liberation theology.[8] But the above are sufficient to indicate that there are always ways to evade a challenge, particularly a threatening one.

Next Steps for North Americans

Suppose, however, that one were to try to respond. How could those of us in North America begin to take seriously the challenge of the liberation theology of Latin America? Where would we go from here? What would constitute a "theology in the Americas"?

Such concerns must be explored by those who take this book seriously. What follows is only a initial set of reflections (to which the whole book and particularly its final pages is pointing) that must be clarified and verified for each reader as he or she participates in the process itself.

Perhaps the primary need is to *reconceive the question*. As the follow-up groups after Detroit have already discovered, the task is not to take Latin American theology and "apply" it to North America, or even to look for ways to find out the "meaning" of liberation theology for North America. Rather "the goal is to contribute to a new theology that emerges from the historical, social, and religious context of the North American experience" (see below, Section Fourteen)

Theology is not a set of timeless truths, no matter how much the goal of achieving such truths may have been sought by theologians in the past. It is rather a certain kind of reflection on what is going on in very specific situations—Palestine, Rome, Constantinople, Geneva, Canterbury, Copenhagen, Hell's Kitchen, Alabama, Johannesburg, Santiago, Tokyo, Recife, Nairobi, New York, or wherever. A common heritage may be drawn upon to explain or challenge what is going on in such places. But what is going on in these places will also explain or challenge that common heritage. There is a two-way street. The specific *context* will determine the specific *content* of the emerging theology. Things will need to be emphasized in a certain way in Santiago that will need to be emphasized in a different way in San Francisco. So the real question will not be: How can we "transfer" the position of Christians in Santiago to San Francisco? It will be: Observing how Christians in Santiago try to live and think authentically in *their* situation, how can we find ways to live and think authentically in *our* situation? Certain social, political, economic, and ecclesiastical dynamics contribute to how Chilean Christians see their task. Certain other social, political, economic, and ecclesiastical dynamics—very different, perhaps—will contribute to how United States Christians see their task. So the theological task is not to imitate some other situation, but to be authentically responsible in one's own situation.

This is a tall order. Here are a few considerations that might help us begin to deal with it:

1. "Theology in the Americas" must be a combination of *particularity and global vision*. We must continue to stress the need for particularity, taking with utmost seriousness the context in which theology is done. Blacks are going to have to do black theology together; women are going to have to develop feminist theology together; Chicanos are going to have to discover theological insights specifically related to their own situation; "academic" theologians are going to have to confront together the pitfalls of traditional academic theology. All this is necessary, and it will probably constitute the next step for such groups.

But sooner or later (and at least sooner, if not concurrently) such varied contextual situations will need to be related *to one another*, for none of them ultimately exists in isolation. As Detroit made clear, each group helps to deliver other groups from parochialism. Furthermore, the final Christian vision does not point to a tightly circumscribed context for some only, but to a context that is inclusive of all. Each struggle for liberation is finally related to all other struggles for liberation; differing initial agendas may help to establish self-identity and self-worth, but all agendas, if authentic, will gradually converge. The convergence must not be too rapid or some groups will be engulfed and co-opted by others. But the convergence must not be too slow, or the groups will be manipulated into competitive stances. And nothing could make the holders of power happier than to keep those without power fighting among themselves so that they cannot join forces against the common enemy that must be displaced.

The development of a North American theology, in other words, will need to go through several stages of particularization: North American blacks, Chicanos, Asian-Americans, Appalachians, women, white males, and so on, clearly have some agendas of their own. But coalitions must emerge in the process. And to the degree that common concerns and goals emerge for North Americans, those will, in turn, need to be related to theologies emerging out of Latin America, Africa, Asia, and Europe. For conclusions that North Americans begin to reach about domestic problems will need reassessment in the light of global problems. The Christian gospel is not concerned only about the emancipation of the oppressed in North

America, but about the emancipation of the oppressed in every part of the world. The dialectic between particuarity and global vision will be an ongoing one.

2. One way to keep the dialectic alive will be to recognize that *global problems must be examined in the perspective of particular situations.* The clearest example of the need for different approaches to the same problem is the issue of power. The problem of power for Third World peoples, and for minority peoples elsewhere, is very clear: They do not have enough power and they must find ways to get more; otherwise their oppression will continue unchallenged. Their theologies must deal with that need and seek to satisfy it. But the problem of power for those in the First World is very different: The United States, for example, has too much power, and it is imperative that ways be found to see that such power is shared. The problem is the same—power—but the problem must be approached in very different ways. One who has no power cannot be asked to share it; one who has too much power must not be asked to acquire more.

3. *The new theology must be grounded in a community.* If one's final loyalty is to North America or the United States, there is no reason to work for the sharing of power; indeed, the impulse would be to make that power strong enough to resist all threats. And while institutional Christianity is frequently little more than a pale reflection of its surroundings, there do exist within the church networks, remnants—what might be called "God's underground"—which can furnish the sustenance and nurture necessary to empower people to stand against the popular currents of the culture.

The fact that the community is a global community is particularly important in this context. For it is commitment to a global community that can potentially free one from the parochialism that a local context alone may nurture. One can be open to challenges to one's own perspective when they come from others within the same global community. I may have difficulty internalizing what the reality of my affluence does to people in other parts of the world; but members of the global community can point this out to me, in the context of the faith we share in common, in ways that I have to take more seriously than if I am simply the object of a diatribe from those with whom I share very little.

Allegiance to such a community can help to liberate us from other parochialisms as well. If one is middle-class, it is difficult to avoid doing theology without taking middle-class values for granted. If one's upbringing has conditioned one to believe that capitalism is the best system for the most people, a radical challenge to capitalism is difficult to internalize. To see one's communal commitment in global terms is to be at least a little closer to escape from such ideological entrapment. North American Christians might even begin to be able to understand why many Christians elsewhere are socialists.

4. If one is to contextualize theology, it will be necessary to ask not only about Latin American oppression, but about *North American oppression* as well, and even the possible "oppression" of the "oppressors." This must not be done so quickly or glibly that it falls prey to the co-optation cited earlier. But middle-class readers of this essay need to recognize that there are certain kinds of oppression, for example, from which they too need to be liberated, such as: *a)* bondage to middle-class values with their high emphasis on success-orientation, an implicit assumption that financial security is the *sine qua non* of a full life, and so on; *b)* bondage to what in 1976 might be described as "bicentennialism," the need to believe that "America is great because America is good" (as former President Eisenhower put it), that criticism of the United States is never justified, and that support should be given to a Ronald Reagan when he virtually suggests going to war over Panama or sending troops to Africa to protect American interests; *c)* bondage to the status quo, interpreted to mean that more of the same is always good, that change is always a threat, and that evil is never due to the basic structure of society but only to a few individuals who have temporarily exploited it.

Such oppressions are powerful obstacles to the achievement of justice and freedom both domestically and globally. They are destructive not only to those who are immediately subservient to them, but destructive in their impact on the lives of those who have no control over them. Vietnam is only one symbol among others of this truth. So a "theology in the Americas" must acknowledge the importance of liberation from such oppressions as these.

5. What are *the most appropriate tools* with which to work for these ends? In Latin America, as we have observed, Marxist analysis has been a particularly relevant tool for Christians and has provided a point of contact with members of the working class, many of whom are already Marxist. In North America, however, the very mention of Marx is liable to end the discussion before it gets under way. What is one to do?

Some groups have responded that one must simply bite this particular linguistic bullet, and chapters of "Christians for Socialism" are springing up in various parts of the country. Their members contend that the degree of change needed is of such magnitude that there is no way of avoiding "scandal," threat, and challenge, so the reality might as well be faced head on: Capitalism is no longer compatible with Christianity, if it ever was, and a full-scale change of direction is needed. While this position is likely to be a minority position for some time, its forthrightness is very attractive.

There are others who argue that it is better not to draw on explicitly Marxist categories. Early in the process leading to Detroit, Rosemary Ruether suggested (see document 4) that Christians in the United States will get a more significant hearing by drawing on the terms and experience of the special American heritage, so that the emotive power of the American past need not be surrendered to right-wing reactionaries. There *is* an "American past" that can be invoked in the name of a freedom that is not freedom for the few, and although this is still a minority report on that past, the appeal can be made with telling effect. (John Coleman's paper, document 10, is a good example of this approach.) Those concerned with the contextualization of "theology in the Americas" can thus appeal to such themes as "liberty and justice *for all*" as a part of an overall heritage that challenges the present reality, which is liberty and justice for *some*.

A Short Digression for "Professional" Theologians

There is indeed need for an indigenous "North American theology," based neither on overdependence upon recent Latin American theology nor upon slightly less recent European theology. But it may be that certain liberation themes can be introduced more successfully if the ties with European theology are not cut too quickly. I realize that some Latin Americans would interpret this as a retreat from radical theology into the comforting arms of a bourgeois mentality. But some interesting things happened to European theologians in their encounters with the need for radical change from which some lessons, both pro and con, might be learned by the rest of us.

The fact that Dietrich Bonhoeffer, for example, came out of a bourgeois background gives added importance to the fact that he began to move beyond that background as a result of a new solidarity with the oppressed. Commenting in 1942 on what he had learned during the previous decade, Bonhoeffer wrote to a select group of friends from similar backgrounds:

There remains an experience of incomparable value. We have for once learnt to see the great events of world history from below, from the perspective of the outcast, the suspects, the maltreated, the powerless, the oppressed, the reviled—in short from the perspective of those who suffer. . . . We have to learn that personal suffering is a more effective key, a more rewarding principle for exploring the world in thought and action than personal good fortune.[9]

Paul Tillich was deeply involved in "religious socialism" in the years just after World War I. A number of his writings from that period are available (in Tillich, *Political Expectations* [New York: Harper & Row, 1971]), and more are shortly to appear under the editorship of Franklin Sherman. It is important for those already familiar with Tillich's thought to trace again this early part of his own pilgrimage and to reflect on why he did not pursue the socialist option more vigorously in his later life.[10]

Similar concerns can be explored in the pilgrimage of Karl Barth, who became a socialist during his youthful pastorate at Safenwil, Switzerland, and always insisted on a close alignment between theology and politics, giving support to socialist regimes in Eastern Europe after World War II, at a time when his contemporaries were trumpeting an anticommunist line.[11]

Most significant in this discussion has been Jürgen Moltmann, whose theology of hope has had undeniable influence in many parts of the world where liberation theologies have come into being, and who has himself opted for a theological position that has a more radical political side to it than that of most of his European counterparts.[12]

The task is not to take ready-made theologies from Europe and graft a few liberation themes onto them. It was fear of this that led to the most explosive outbursts at Detroit. But there were some important liberation concerns expressed in the lives and thoughts of such theologians, and one can learn from their mistakes as well as their successes.

A similar exercise is worth undertaking in discerning a slow but clear "tilt to the left" in the various papal encyclicals, conciliar documents, synodical reports, and other Roman Catholic writings of the last fifteen years.[13] There are similar documents in the history of the World Council of Churches, most notably the report of the conference on Church and Society held in Geneva in 1966 ("Christians in the Social and Technical Revolutions of our Time") as well as reports of subsequent World Council conferences and assemblies.[14]

It is not being suggested that there are clear continuities between such theologies and contemporary theologies of liberation. But there are at least connections; and those who stand in the heritage of such movements have a responsibility to scrutinize them carefully before too freely casting them aside.[15]

Can "Oppressors" Do Theology Today?

It may seem as though we have managed to blunt the radical concern that must characterize a new theology and have successfully co-opted it in ways that remove its threatening character.

It is always possible for this to happen. Attention must always be directed to the danger. And there is no doubt that this preface would have been written very differently had the writer been a black or a woman or a Chicano. So let us conclude by focusing on a problem that lies behind all of these pages: Can theology today be done by those who are not oppressed? Can those who are relatively comfortable, whose daily existence is not seriously threatened, play any role in developing a "theology in the Americas"?

Notes, then, for those whom the world usually denominates "oppressors," by one of them:

1. Surely *our first task is to listen.* Those in the saddle usually insist on issuing directions for the caravan. Those with the goods and the know-how usually feel that others want only to learn from them in order to become like them. It is time to listen for awhile, to let others speak, to acknowledge that the impetus for change may well originate in quarters other than our own, and that we had better not be writing agendas for the oppressed.

One of Elie Wiesel's characters comments, "When a Jew says he is suffering, one must believe him, and when he is afraid, one must assume his fear is justified. In neither case does one have the right to doubt his word. Even if one cannot help him, one must at least believe him."[16]

This provides an excellent starting point for a new theology: When we hear the cry, "I'm hurting," we must take it seriously. And when we discover that the cry really means, "You are hurting me," we must hear it with utmost seriousness. If others say that we are hurting them, our initial assumption must be that they are correct. Even if it should turn out that they are not correct, it is important for us to know how we were being perceived. Those living in a nation with 6 percent of the world's population who are nevertheless consuming 40 percent of the world's resources had better take seriously the cry of "the wretched of the earth."

2. We must *interpret what we hear.* Consciousness-raising, conscientization, is not limited only to peasants trained by the methods of Paulo Freire. Others can be "conscienticized" as well, not least of all ourselves. I was encouraged, at the conclusion of a recent course on

"liberation theology," at how many students said in effect, "I never knew the world was that way. . . . I never realized before that people don't necessarily appreciate receiving foreign aid from us. . . . I didn't understand how much Americans are feared and hated in the Third World. . . . I always thought other countries wanted to be like us."

Of course, nothing is changed until lives begin to change as well as attitudes. But those who have come to see the world in a different way can help interpret to others why it looks that way and why we are so reluctant to see it that way. Most North American students believe that all is well in Chile, until they are exposed to first-hand Chilean accounts that have not been filtered through the State Department or the public relations officer of a large corporation with a vested interest in keeping the Chilean junta in power. Those who hear something different must share and interpret what they hear.

This creates a special responsibility to speak to constituencies that will listen to us. If middle-class Christians become aware that they themselves bear responsibility for the fact that their brothers and sisters are hurting, then they must use whatever levers of power they possess, however feeble, to introduce the possibility of change, and do this in a responsible fashion. For white middle-class Christians to advocate a violent revolution in middle America today is as futile as it is irresponsible. But we may need to point out why other Christians in other places could feel that violent revolution is their only hope, and that other options appear closed off to them because the United States is backing the most reactionary elements in their own countries. Although electoral politics no longer seems a very direct route to increased justice for the dispossessed, it can at least be a means of containing the spread of injustice—and that is quite a lot, if one is a potential victim of the spreading injustice.

3. All of this must lead toward a position in which we develop an increasing ability *to see the world through eyes other than our own.*[17] To us, the judicial system looks just; to members of minority groups it is frequently a monument to injustice. To us, police protection is usually beneficial; to members of minority groups it can be a source of terror. To us, democracy "works"; to members of minority groups it appears to spawn petty fascists who occasionally accumulate and abuse an alarming amount of power. No radical challenge to the status quo is likely to come from us when only our own interests are at stake; the system pays off too well to us. But to be enabled, through the resources of "God's underground," to see that system *in terms of what*

it does to others, to be forced toward what Bonhoeffer called "the view from below," is at least to be started on the way to disengagement from uncritical allegiance to it.

How will the possibility of such changes become more widespread? This could begin to happen in a couple of ways. North Americans might be subjected to a kind of social science analysis that would convince us, in the most hard-nosed pragmatic way, that it is in our own best interest to share some of our power and resources with the Third World, to divest ourselves of our life-and-death control over the destinies of others, realizing that if we do not, we, who are in reality a small minority of the human family, will one day have such power and control taken from us, forcibly if necessary, since outrage against us will finally pass the boiling point. A time might come, in other words, when altruism and long-range self-interest coincided.

That would be an argument, and an important one, in the courts of power. But there would be another stance as well for the Christian remnant to propose and seek to embody—a recognition that Christian faith also talks about the fact that servanthood, voluntarily assumed, can be a vehicle for justice (cf. Isaiah 42), and that self-denial, curiously and paradoxically, can be a way to fulfillment. That will not be the message to those presently destitute and powerless; it will be an important ingredient in any witness the Christian community offers to those already too powerful.

The "Abrahamic Venture"

All of which will surely sound naive. Who indeed, is likely to make "one act of genuine solidarity with exploited social classes" (to quote Gustavo Gutiérrez again), when he or she already has comfort and security? Who is going to engage in the "self-emptying" that such a decision would involve?

Here is where we must finally go beyond social analysis, no matter how acute, and noble words, no matter how finely honed. For this is a matter of willingness to subject oneself, at risk, to the power of the gospel—a gospel that emphasizes turning around, "conversion," a fresh start, a letting-go, and a recognition that this finally comes by grace—not to be attained but only received. Simply to wait passively for grace to come will mean an ongoing consenting to present injustice; but to give up hope in its coming at all will mean consigning ourselves to despair and thereby also settling for injustice.

Our true hope surely lies in aligning ourselves with what Dom Helder Camara has called "the Abrahamic minorities," those groups here and there who have taken the risk of trying to embody the power of justice and love, those, like Abraham, who "hope against hope," willing to venture forth not knowing where they are going, taking their cue from the fact that "the protests of the poor are the voice of God."[18] At the time Abraham went forth, he had no assurance that his choice to leave security had been a wise one. Only later, in retrospect, was it clear that Abraham was all the time under the providence of God. Nor will any advance assurances be guaranteed to Abraham's children. But something of the Abrahamic quality will have to invest the lives of those who take on the task of liberation today. The degree of our ability to respond will not finally rest on the soundness of our analysis, though that is important, but on the extent of our willingness to risk our security on behalf of the insecurities of others.

ROBERT McAFEE BROWN

NOTES

1. For a full development of the methodology and themes of liberation theology see the essay below, document 3 by Phillip Berryman.

2. For making this point in an earlier published report on the conference, I was accused by Fr. Andrew Greeley, in one of his typically acerbic columns, of being a "Nazi." The point about mutual self-correction seems important enough to repeat, however, and I am willing to leave any judgments about my Nazi mentality to readers who may be less than fully captivated by Fr. Greeley's frantic prose.

3. Gustavo Gutiérrez, *A Theology of Liberation*, trans. Caridad Inda and John Eagleson (Maryknoll, New York: Orbis Books, 1973), p. 308.

4. Hugo Assmann, *Theology for a Nomad Church*, trans. Paul Burns (Maryknoll, New York: Orbis Books, 1976), p. 129.

5. It is encouraging that groups that were formerly unimpressed by this fact, the so-called "conservative evangelicals," are beginning to include this social dimension in their analysis. See especially Jim Wallis, *Agenda for Biblical People* (New York: Harper and Row, 1976).

6. Helder Camara, *Church and Colonialism*, trans. William McSweeney (Denville, New Jersey: Dimension Books, 1969), p. 111. The same point is made more stridently by Ivan Illich in *The Church, Change, and Development* (New York: Herder and Herder, 1970), pp. 45–53.

7. An excellent tool for exploring the biblical analysis is José Porfirio Miranda, *Marx and the Bible*, trans. John Eagleson (Maryknoll, New York: Orbis Books, 1974).

8. I have extended the discussion in *Is Faith Obsolete?* (Philadelphia: Westminster, 1974), pp. 125–29.

9. Dietrich Bonhoeffer, *Letters and Papers from Prison*, expanded edition (New York: Macmillan, 1971), "After Ten Years," p. 17. On the whole issue of the substantive contribution of Bonhoeffer's theology to the theology of liberation, see the fascinating

essay by Julio de Santa Ana, "The Influence of Bonhoeffer on the Theology of Liberation," *Ecumenical Review*, April 1976, pp. 188–97. This is a treatment of Bonhoeffer's impact on the Protestant ISAL group in Latin America. On the other side, Gustavo Gutiérrez has noted that while Bonhoeffer was concerned about ministry to the "nonbeliever," the real task in Latin America today is ministry to the "nonperson."

10. Much help is given in the definitive biography of Tillich: Pauck and Pauck, *Paul Tillich: His Life and Thought*, vol. 1 (New York: Harper & Row, 1976), esp. chap. 3.

11. The roots of Barth's position are helpfully explored in George Hunsinger, ed., *Karl Barth and Radical Politics* (Philadelphia: Westminster, 1976).

12. Moltmann has been both appreciated and attacked by Latin Americans. Cf. *inter alia*, Rubem Alves, *A Theology of Human Hope* (Washington, D.C.: Corpus Books, 1969); Hugo Assmann, *Opresión-Liberación: Desafío a los cristianos* (Montevideo: Tierra Nueva, 1971); Assmann, *Theology for a Nomad Church* (Maryknoll, New York: Orbis Books, 1976); José Míguez Bonino, *Doing Theology in a Revolutionary Situation* (Philadelphia: Fortress Press, 1975). Moltmann has responded to comments about him in the latter book in, "On Latin American Liberation Theology: An Open Letter to José Míguez Bonino," in *Christianity and Crisis*, March 29, 1976, pp. 57–63.

13. A convenient collection of these documents is found in *The Gospel of Peace and Justice: Catholic Social Teaching since Pope John*, presented by Joseph Gremillion (Maryknoll, New York: Orbis Books, 1976).

14. Paul Bock, *In Search of a Responsible World Society* (Philadelphia: Westminster, 1974), offers a brief historical treatment of these and other themes in recent World Council history, updating the pioneer work by Fr. Edward Duff, S.J., *The Social Thought of the World Council of Churches* (New York: Association Press, 1956).

15. As an exercise to test this proposal, I suggest reading the following Roman Catholic documents in their chronological order to see if one cannot be "radicalized" in the process: *Gaudium et Spes* (1965), *Populorum Progressio* (1967), the Medellín documents on "Peace" and "Justice" (1968), *Octogesima Adveniens* (1971), and the declaration of "Christians for Socialism" (1972).

16. Elie Wiesel, *The Oath* (New York: Random House, 1973), p. 214.

17. I have developed some of the implications of this concern and the need to move beyond it in more detail in "Who Is This Jesus Christ Who Frees and Unites?" *The Ecumenical Review*, January 1976, pp. 6–21.

18. Helder Camara, *The Desert is Fertile*, trans. Dinah Livingstone (Maryknoll, New York: Orbis Books, 1974), p. 13.

I

The Preparation
of the Conference

A Different Kind
of Conference

The original intention of the planners of the "Theology in the Americas: 1975" conference was to invite a group of Latin American theologians, representing the theology of liberation, to dialogue with North American theologians concerning the content and methodology of this new theological current.

It was hoped that such a dialogue would help both groups: the Latin Americans to understand the complex reality of the U.S.; the North American theologians to initiate a process of evaluation of the American reality from the viewpoint of the poor and the oppressed.

These plans, however, were soon to change completely. The site of the conference was changed from San Antonio to Detroit. This change was a symbol: The conference should not focus on the Latin American reality but on the situation in the U.S. Moreover, it was decided to invite not only academic theologians but also Christian activists committed to social change. The planners realized that their contribution was indispensable to this new manner of theological reflection.

The process began with the organization of reflection groups throughout the U.S. The groups were to reflect upon their own experience of faith and action and to study various documents sent out by the organizing committee. Two documents, included here, were prepared by the Research Coordination Team of the Center of Concern in Washington, D.C.

Preparation Document No. 1 invites the groups to consider the history of the United States and to evaluate the role of religion within that history.

Preparation Document No. 2 describes the three phases of the methodology of the reflection groups: description of the situation, religious meditation on the situation, return to the situation.

Background Readings

In recent years an abundant literature has appeared regarding the theology of liberation. The organizing committee proposed five documents to the participants as background reading and immediate preparation for the meetings.

Of the five, we include here only Phillip Berryman's "Latin American Liberation Theology" (first published in Theological Studies, *September 1973), a fine synthesis describing the antecedents and stages of liberation theology. For this volume Berryman has updated his original article with a substantial appendix entitled "Doing Theology in a (Counter-) Revolutionary Situation."*

Also recommended to the participants was "Reflections on Liberation Theology," by Robert McAfee Brown (included in Is Faith Obsolete? *[Philadelphia: Westminster, 1974], pp. 269–82). A North American reflection on the meaning of liberation for the U.S., the essay applies the biblical categories of the Exodus to the present U.S. reality. If God is on the side of the oppressed, God is not on the side of the oppressor. U.S. Christians are therefore called to evaluate their interpretation of American history and to examine their prophetic role within today's confrontation between rich countries and poor countries.*

Brazilian social scientist Helio Jaguaribe is the author of the third document recommended by the committee: "Trends in the United States" (taken from Political Development: A General Theory and a Latin American Case Study *[New York: Harper & Row, 1975], pp. 538–55). Jaguaribe analyzes the difficulties Americans have in admitting their country is the seat of an empire and describes the options open to the U.S. with regard to its empire.*

The fourth document was Andrew Levison's, "The Working-Class Majority" (New Yorker, September 2, 1974). It deals with the important question of whether the working class can be a factor of social change in the U.S. today and whether it can be in solidarity with the workers and the oppressed of other countries.

Finally the text of the United Nations "Declaration on the Establishment of a New International Economic Order" was circulated. This New Order will be on the agenda of all countries, rich and poor, in the coming decades. The document provides an admirable synthesis of the new convergence of forces in the

Third World. It poses challenges to the developed nations and raises hopes for the poor ones.

The First Reactions

Reactions to the planners' initiatives were not long in coming. Speaking from their own experience the members of the reflection groups offered their critiques and contributions.

The reactions of the groups are described in "A Theological Quest: Synthesis of the First Stage of Theology in the Americas" (see below document 17).

Of the various reactions and criticisms, the most important were the following:

First, the organizers were accused of trying to impose a foreign model of analysis and theological reflection on the reality of the United States.

Second, some said that the analysis of U.S. history and the present situation contained in the documents was very superficial and negative. It was necessary, they said, to indicate a positive alternative.

Third, and perhaps most important, it was suggested that there is a need to find within the religious values of American history an inspiration and a language that would enable North Americans to respond to the Latin American challenge and to express in their own categories a projection toward the future.

Documents 4-9 reflect these discussions and criticisms. They show how the process was fashioned as new people contributed their knowledge and experience.

At the same time, however, these documents show that—notwithstanding the intentions of the organizers—the process had an elitist character, for the opinions of well-known theologians were taken into greater account than those of ordinary Christians.

1

Preparation Document No. 1
An Explanation of the Process

INTRODUCTION

Plans are underway for a meeting between church people (theologians, policy planners, social scientists, pastoralists, activists, etc.) from North and South America in Detroit, from August 17 to 24, 1975. The participants will grapple with the question of how theology is done today, against the backdrop of clashes between networks of domination and forces of liberation, in both domestic and international society. To be more pointed, the participants will be asking what meaning does the Latin American theology of liberation have for the contemporary United States.

In addition to the conference itself, there will be a period of preparation and a period of follow-up. The preparation period will engage reflection groups across the country. For the most part, these will be of two kinds: (1) scholars and students from theological communities; and (2) grassroots groupings of pastoralists and activists. The nature of the postconference period has not yet been worked out, but it will deepen the searching and experimentation of the conference and its preparation period.

Before explaining the structure of the preparation period and the conference, it may be helpful to review the background and genesis of the project.

BACKGROUND

The American Empire

Latin America, as the events of Chile bring home, forces United States Christians to face the fact of the American empire. Despite the myth that the nations to the south are of little interest, the U.S.A. remains deeply involved in their economic, political, and cultural life. A firm fact of national life, the American empire in Latin America, as well as in the Orient, has been neither unplanned nor benevolent.

From as early as the Monroe Doctrine and Manifest Destiny, the commercial-military designs of expanding U.S. capitalism were imperialist. The foundations for its overseas empire were laid in three decisive steps: (1) the seizure of Mexican territories, which provided a platform for southward and eastward expansion (as well as supplying a rural proletariat for business farming from the Mexican/Indian peoples who had their communal lands stolen from them); (2) the seizure of Puerto Rico, Cuba, and the Philippines as commercial-military stepping stones to Latin and Asian resources and markets; (3) the carving of Panama out of Colombia and the construction of the Panama Canal, opening a commercial-military link between the two coasts.

Guaranteed strategic footholds both in the South and in the East, the United States began a series of overt military interventions in Latin America and the Orient in support of its commercial interests. This policy of overt military intervention continued unchecked even in the recent cases of Guatemala and Santo Domingo. With the fiasco of the Bay of Pigs invasion and the quagmire of Vietnam, however, experiments began around a more covert, sophisticated interventionism ("low profile").

By the time of the Alliance for Progress under Kennedy, U.S. economic penetration could count on the allegiance of domestic comprador classes to provide police and military support for U.S. interests. (These forces, of course, continued to be trained, equipped, and financed from the U.S.A.) In turn, through external control of economic life by the post-World War II international financial institutions (World Bank, International Monetary Fund, Inter-American Development Bank), as well as through the control of U.S. based institutions of finance and credit, U.S. economic interests wielded great power over satellite economies, namely the power of creating anarchy. The military coup in Chile in 1973 confirmed the viability of this new policy. In addition, the expansion of U.S. cultural programs (e.g., CIA support of certain media and student movements, U.S. marketing of satellite television, the shaping of educational institutions by major U.S. universities and foundations, and even the extensive U.S. missionary presence) helped create a sympathetic consciousness in the new urban middle classes, thus legitimating the neocolonialist penetration at least for those classes as well as for the comprador elites.

In recent decades, however, external resistance to the empire has grown. From its twin thrusts into Latin America and Asia came Vietnam and Chile, revealing each in its own way the fundamental iniquity of the imperial enterprise. On both flanks, the empire met serious challenge. Also, although Africa has been the weakest imperial front (except for the pillage of its population in slave times), the failure of U.S. financed repression in the Portuguese colonies constitutes yet a third exterior challenge to the empire's viability.

Further, the hegemony of U.S. capital is being undercut both by the united front of Third World nations and by the economic cracks in the Atlantic Treaty. In the first case, raw material-producing nations of the Third World have forged a powerful coalition in the United Nations' *Declaration on a New International Economic Order.* The political and economic unity of these nations, as shown at recent international conferences, continually marginalizes the United States in the international community. In the second case, both Canada and the European Community are choosing their own paths in the face of the energy crisis of the industrialized West. The result is that the United States cannot any longer count on its Western allies, as was the case in the Cold War.

Within the United States, the seat of the empire, severe strains are also showing up. Basically these are rooted in the contradictions of an economic base whose international interests operate against its domestic interests. In the two earlier phases of the American empire (extrication of raw materials and markets for finished goods), the revenues of the empire supported American affluence. Today however, in its third phase (export platform), the empire is a drain on the U.S. people.

This happens in several ways. First, the shifting of substantial portions of its productive base to foreign export platforms creates unemployment at home and competes with U.S. workers. The attractiveness of cheap and unorganized labor, proximity to raw materials and energy resources, and lack of ecological restrictions are converting U.S. capital into a massive runaway shop. Second, the policy decision at the top level of the U.S. to move toward energy independence, requiring massive capital accumulation, is being forcibly financed by the bottom and middle income sectors of the society through price gouging, reduction of wages by inflation, and regressive taxation. Thirdly, the costs of maintaining the empire's colossal military and intelligence apparatus throughout the world (and at home), as well as the cost of its social and ecological destructiveness, are being borne by these same middle and bottom sectors.

While this tendency is just beginning, its thrust suggests further aggravation of the bitter suffering felt by the bottom sectors of U.S. society, the end of relative affluence for the middle sectors, and the deepening isolation in privilege and power for the top sectors. The resulting social climate will probably be volatile, with the political system forced into an authoritarian-military model and the old cultural system breaking down.

Together these international and domestic strains mark the end of the mythology of the American Dream. With the hegemony of U.S. capital undercut in the international community and the closing out of upward mobility within domestic society (and probably its replacement by downward mobility), the United States will no longer appear divinely chosen as number one in the world, nor as the source of bounty to its own people and the world. The international and domestic crises, therefore, converge in the cracking structures of the American empire.

Yet the empire will not collapse smoothly. Its international and domestic thrashings could be very dangerous to the human family. Already, in the international community, we see how food and starvation are being used as political and economic weapons to preserve at least some elements of the old hegemony, and how discussion of triage and the life-boat ethic are quickly replacing the mythology of American beneficence. In turn, at home racist scapegoating of national minorities may surface in the desperate clash over scarce resources between the have-nots and have-littles.

The Role of Religion

U.S. Christians have been deeply involved both in the creation of the American empire and in radical challenges to it.

The naive religious vision of American innocence supported the original imperialist thrust (as well as internal oppression of genocide against native Americans, enslavement of Africans, and oppression of the immigrant working class). At this early stage, legitimation came from the established Protestant traditions and garbed itself in claims to a new Exodus from European corruption. The nineteenth-century victories of the young empire over European commercial and military forces in the new world were seen as a messianic extension of the kingdom of God.

Later, when American capitalism consolidated itself in a corporate partnership with expanded government bureaucracy, Catholicism joined the legitimation process. In the tension of the Cold War, it was precisely Catholic allegiance which gave the U.S. such strength in the formerly Catholic colonies of Asia and Latin America.

But Christian communities also produced resistance to the iniquity of the American experience. In particular, black Christianity, although it also served as a vehicle of alienation, nurtured cultural and political defense. The same occurred for Mexican-Indian Christianity under the symbol of Our Lady of Guadalupe. From within the dominant white churches, critical strains also emerged. As American capitalism grew more exploitative of its own people, white Protestantism produced the Social Gospel and even a Christian socialist movement. In turn, white immigrant Catholicism went hand-in-hand with the labor movement and urban political organizing.

Subsiding in the post-World War II prosperity, the critical swell erupted again in the sixties. Optimistic activists tried to "open up the system" and make it work in favor of the underprivileged. The New Frontier, the Alliance for Progress, and the War against Poverty all attempted to make the empire more workable both domestically and internationally. By the end of the decade, however, as poverty continued to grow at home and abroad, as repression put down unsatisfied expectations, and as the war raged unchecked, a spirit of national disillusion settled upon the land. The empire would not yield justice.

In an inarticulate way, it became clear that the problem ran deeper than reforms of existing structures and institutions. No mere expansion of opportunity or appeal to good will would bring the justice sought for. The iniquity was rooted in the very foundations of American economic, political, and cultural life. The great American myth, to which white, English-speaking Christianity had given its allegiance, had turned into a bad dream.

The Religious Voice of Latin America

From its parched desert, there remain many creative fonts to which the American religious experience can turn for drink. Among these fonts, we wish to engage one in this particular process, in no way rejecting others. It is the voice of the *theology of liberation* from Latin America.

The new theology is marked by two radical departures from the dominant Western styles of theologizing. First, *social science* is included as an indispensable stage in the theologizing process. Second, thought is linked directly with action in a framework of *praxis.* (As a result, the theologizing usually occurs outside academic circles.) The progressive result has been living theology ever more radical in its option for the oppressed.

Structurally, the model takes its departure from concrete experience and breaks down into three moments:

1. *Analysis of the situation,* as lived by the reflectors, with stress on concrete immersion in the life of the oppressed and on the use of critical scientific resources. Here the value-free model of social science is rejected, as well as the possibility of objectivity. Instead commitment and insertion replace detachment and objectivity. The influence of the Marxian scientific tradition has been strong here.

2. *Religious meditation on the situation.* Under the guidance of the Spirit, the theologizers return to the richness of the biblical heritage and to the tradition of the church to find what fresh synthesis of symbols and messages speak creatively in the present moment. Their scrutiny has led to stress on the mosaic or liberation themes from the Hebrew Bible and to a reading of Jesus' gospel very much in this light.

3. *Return to experience.* Under the guidance of the scientific analysis and the religious meditation, the theologizing community returns to critically informed action. This return will generate fresh experience, which in turn will require fresh reflection in the framework of praxis.

Engagement with this voice has been underway for many years, both in the Catholic and Protestant communities. We recall many activities of the National Council of Churches and the United States Catholic Conference, their mission sections and their Latin American sections. Perhaps the most dramatic forum of exchange was the ten years of conferences held by the Catholic Inter-American Cooperation Program (CICOP), which provided the first major U.S. platform for the theology.

In Catholic circles, the new theology received official recognition in the Medellín Conference (1968) of the Latin American hierarchy. Later, it became the basic model for the document on justice from the International Synod of Roman Catholic bishops in Rome (1971). Names of Catholic liberation theologians like Gustavo Gutiérrez, Hugo Assmann, Juan Luis Segundo, and (by extension) Paulo Freire soon became well known in U.S. theological communities.

In Protestant circles, creation of ISAL (*Iglesia y Sociedad en América Latina*) seemed to symbolize the new theology, and names like José Míguez Bonino and Rubem Alves surfaced as its major articulators.

Interest in the new theology has been stimulated in part by the political exile of many of its practitioners from Latin America. It has also been stimulated by a growing sense that the traditional theologies simply are inadequate foundations for creative and critical grappling with the pervasive crisis of the West.

THE CONFERENCE AND PROCESS

Sensing this interest and feeling that the time was ripe for a major engagement with the new theology, concerned Catholics and Protestants organized a planning committee in 1974. Very quickly they secured the sponsorship of the Division of Latin America of the United States Catholic Conference and of the Latin American Working Group within the National Council of Churches. In addition, several theologians both from the United States and from Latin America have become theological sponsors.

In suggesting that U.S. Christians point their search for guidance at least in part toward the Latin American theology of liberation, the call is not made for a formal academic examination of its methodology. Rather it is proposed that together with Latin Christians, mature in the new theologizing process, U.S. Christians reflect critically on distinct experiences of the American empire in order to return more creatively and consciously to ongoing social practice.

It is also proposed that the reflection be done with the full support of the scientific and religious traditions, even though both are internally complex and even contain contradictory strains. Which strains prove most resourceful will have to be decided operationally (rather than by an a priori formal methodology) by the experienced and prayerful judgments of those participating in the process.

The model of the conference, therefore, will be *experience challenging experience, in an environment of scientific and religious reflection.* . . .

[There follows a description of the structure of the preparation period and of the conference itself, which we have omitted here.]

2

Preparation Document No. 2
Guidelines for Reflection Groups

In preparation for the Detroit conference, reflection groups across the country will be contributing to the process. These groups will be of three kinds: (1) major reflection groups, seated in significant theological clusters; (2) special reflection groups, dealing with particular themes in the American experience (e.g., women, native Americans, blacks, Mexican-Americans, Puerto Ricans, Orientals, white ethnics, Appalachians, etc.); and (3) general reflection groups, arising where there are enough interested persons to form a working group. All three kinds will receive the same materials, but their tasks will vary somewhat. The first and second kinds will rely heavily on their ongoing work or interests to serve as guides for reflecting on the material. The following will serve as guidelines for the general reflection groups and for the other two kinds insofar as they participate in the general reflection process.

What Is a Reflection Group?

Wherever there are several persons interested in the questions of the process and the conference, they are encouraged to form a working group as part of the process. . . . The group will receive from the national office information on the materials being discussed in the project. The group is asked to obtain these materials either from a library or from the regional coordinator and to schedule a series of meetings to discuss them critically. The frequency of these meetings can be worked out by each group. The fruit of the groups' reflections should then be returned to the *research coordination team* at the Center of Concern. Working documents for the conference will be drawn up in first draft from these responses and others, and will be returned to the groups for further criticism.

What Will Be Discussed?

The task of the conference is not to conduct a detached formal examination of the methodology of the theology of liberation, but rather to create an opportunity, for those who are already sympathetic, to pursue in critical and constructive fashion the question of its significance within the North American experience. Of course in such a process the question of methodology must also be dealt with, but from within the praxis of this new theologizing model. The total process represents, then, an experimental (critical and constructive) appropriation of the methodology in the North American context.

Given the framework of praxis, the process will take its point of departure from our concrete experience of North American history and pass through three moments:

1. Describing our situation
2. Religious meditation on the situation
3. Return to the situation

Describing Our Situation

Attempts will be made to locate our personal/social histories within the outlines of a structural synthesis of the unity of the North American experience. We will try to gather those threads of history first into three regional structures (economic life, political life, and cultural life) and then into a structural totality.

Obviously such a task can be approached only with the foreknowledge that it will be marked by major inadequacies, both methodological and empirical. Nonetheless, we would still like to proceed, guided by our shared operational judgments, *toward* an articulation of the totality of the North American socio-historical experience.

At the present moment, the core theme for examination that we recommend to the process is "The American Empire: Its Domestic and International Integration." Growing recognition of the fact of the empire and of its related domestic and international injustices provides, we feel, the best unifying point for our reflection.

Since our reflections proceed experimentally within the project of the theology of liberation, the *dialectic of oppression/liberation* (injustice/justice) constitutes the guiding thread which leads us through the analysis and synthesis of reflection on our experience.

The phenomena of oppression/liberation should be approached in three ascending stages:

1. Issues: the listing of multiple and as yet fragmented issues which are the first phenomena for critical consciousness. These in turn may be grouped into four categories or zones of the oppression/liberation dialectic, namely *ecological, sexual, racial,* and *class.*

2. Regional structures: the integration of multiple issues into functional institutions and structures in social life, namely the economic region (production and reproduction of material base of common life), the political region (norms and force in ordering of common life), and the cultural region (values and meanings, both rational and meta-rational, embedded in common life). These regional structures must be grasped both on their organizational axis (synchronic) and on their genetic or historical axis (diachronic).

While the economic and political regions constitute the indispensable background for our understanding, the cultural region is the foreground of our concern, for it is here that religious phenomena primarily appear.

In terms of institutional life, culture turns our attention to the arts, religion, education, and the media. In terms of the inner life of consciousness and the subconscious, culture turns us to the structures of logic, language, symbol, ritual, and myth.

While religion lives formally in specifically religious institutions, it also exists in more pervasive form throughout all social institutions as civil religion and within humanity's psychic life. Ideally, attention would be paid to all these aspects.

Note here that religious phenomena are being considered precisely as foreground social phenomena against the background of other general social phenomena. The examination of religious phenomena still remains within our task of "describing the situation" (objective and subjective) and does not yet bring us into religious reflection in the narrower sense of the term. That task marks the second moment of the methodology, all of whose moments together constitute a religious reflection broadly speaking (the theologizing process).

3. Structural totality: the integration of all three structural regions into the single story of the unified socio-historical experience.

In summary then, the task of the first moment will be to move in three successive stages to a simple yet profound *telling of the story* of the American empire in both its international and domestic faces. Whatever the reflection groups can contribute to this process, either by way of original contributions or by criticism of the contributions of others, will be somehow taken up into the process of the conference. . . .

Religious Meditation on the Situation

In the second moment of our reflection, we turn to the richness of the living religious tradition, both to the Hebrew and Christian writings of the Bible and to the ongoing life of the churches.

While this turn enables us greatly to transcend the North American experience, it is dialectically bound up with the use of human science in the first moment, for the past expression of religious tradition comes to us only from and through human history. The revelation is in every case historically mediated. The disclosure of the divine mystery is not, therefore, automatically more accessible to us in tradition than in the present history. Our interpretive approach to the contemporary situation and to the heritage of the religious tradition are both marked by a concern for science and scholarship, but neither can escape the fact that fundamental value options, reflecting the fruit of ongoing discernment, shape their approach.

The differences between the first and second moments, therefore, are only nuances. The first turns to a more narrow horizon (the experience of the American empire), while the second turns to a much broader one (the Jewish and Christian traditions). Granted that for most of us the latter is peculiarly privileged, it still does not lessen the single and frightening task of hearing the voice of the Living God in present and past history.

In turning to the religious tradition, we seek to discern which resources and what synthesis of those resources will prove most liberating or life-bearing for contemporary history. In the present development of the Latin American theology of liberation, great attention has been paid to the Mosaic themes of conflict, exodus, and promise within human history and to the search and struggle for human universality growing out of historical particulars, rather than to harmony, arrival, and fulfillment or to an abstract human universality which transcends or even crushes particular histories.

In the case of Latin America, since the oppressive situation was perceived as one of structural domination (the social science theory of domination/dependence between imperialist metropole and colonized satellite), the redeeming action was one which sought to shatter the internal consciousness and external structures of domination. Liberation of the dominated is its expression.

In the case of North America, at least for the dominant culture in the United States, the same situation can be perceived, but from the side of the dominators. For the dominant culture, therefore, the message of a liberating theology must not be one of rising up, but of falling down—down into the commonality of the human experience.

North America, however, like Latin America is internally complex. There, one also finds internal elites of domination tied to the elites of the external metropole. Here, one also finds internal sectors of oppressed, organically linked to the oppressed there. Similarly both here and there, one finds ambiguous middle sectors, some of whom live a schizophrenia between their objective situation and their internal consciousness. These sectors are often referred to as the middle classes. In a situation of upward mobility, they link themselves psychologically (and politically) to the elites. In a situation of downward mobility, however (which may characterize the future of North America), they may either link themselves psychologically with the oppressed, or else fall victims to the crassest of manipulation against the oppressed.

In thinking through the significance of the theology of liberation for the North American experience, it must, therefore, be first asked what it says to the social experience as a whole, but then secondly it must be asked what it says to each sector within the internal complexity.

Return to the Situation

Since the overall framework is one of praxis, the working groups should be sure to pursue their work on that model. Their reflection on the situation in the first moment should proceed as much from their own practical experience (local, regional, national, international) as from the documents. The religious meditation should be the fruit of their own religious experience as well as of the study of scholarly works. Finally, the recommended actions should be ones which make sense in their own situation as well as for the broader community. As has been already mentioned, the process is to be a critical and constructive grappling with our own experience, not simply a formal academic exercise. While study and scholarship will be respected, the articulation of our living experience is privileged.

The reflection in its third moment prepares to return to the situation and must now propose actions for those sectors of the religious community to which it can effectively speak. This in turn, when put into effect, will alter at least in part the former socio-historical experience, generating thereby fresh experience and calling in turn at a future moment for further reflection within the ongoing circle of praxis.

Conclusion

Within this overall process, there are many questions which inevitably will arise. There will be questions about the analysis of the empire, of its fact, of the shape of its international and domestic faces and their interaction, about which religious phenomena really appear, about how the tradition can be retrieved most creatively, and about the very methodology which we are experimentally entering into. We ask that you share all these questions with us, as well as your answers to them.

In addition, we ask that you share with us any resource materials or other thoughts of substance or process which you feel would benefit the experience. Even what is written here is only proposed to the working groups. It is open to challenge and revision, within the limitations set down upon us by the time line and our resources.

3

Latin American
Liberation Theology

by Phillip E. Berryman

I discovered Christianity as a life centered totally on love of neighbor. . . . It was later that I understood that in Colombia you can't bring about this love simply by beneficence. There was needed a whole change of political, economic, and social structures. These changes demanded a revolution. That love was intimately bound up with revolution.[1]

The words are those of Camilo Torres. His thought includes many elements of a liberation theology *in nuce:* It arises out of a revolutionary praxis; it is centered not on the church but on society; it involves socio-economic analysis.[2] When Camilo Torres joined the guerrillas, Vatican II was nearing conclusion. Theologians in Latin America, by and large, were simply following the conciliar discussions. Theology and "social doctrine" were still separate matters. Since that time there has arisen a "theology of liberation." In this article we propose to survey this theology, relating it to its social and ecclesial context.[3]

A word about the situation of the Latin American theologian. He generally returned from his studies in Europe to find that his theology had hardly prepared him for the kind of work he would be assigned. His theology had no relation to the life or religiosity of the popular majorities. As a member of the Catholic elite, he would look to Europe to keep up with pastoral and theological developments. If he should want to continue to work in theology, he would have no theological establishment, no research libraries, no audience for his output.[4]

Vatican II advocated an "opening to the world" which from Europe appeared to be a world of technological progress, though threatened with dangers. From Latin America it appears as a world of oppression. This became more obvious as the first Decade of Development brought increased dependence for the poor countries, as Chile's Revolution in Liberty did not solve fundamental problems, as Brazil and other countries were militarized. Latin American economists and sociologists began to reject the conceptual frameworks of the rich world and to look for instruments more adequate to the task.[5] A number of groups of Christians, and in particular priests, began to denounce structural oppression.[6] It became clear that Latin American Christians were moving away from European postconciliar concerns.[7]

Medellín

The Latin American church consciously expressed its own identity with the Second General Conference of the Latin American Episcopate (CELAM), held in the city of Medellín, Colombia, in August-September 1968. Though it was eclipsed by the visit of the pope to the Eucharistic Congress in Bogotá, this two-week meeting was as important for the continent as the Council was for the church at large. It was indeed a continental meeting of the episcopate to apply the Council to Latin America. A number of meetings and official declarations prepared the way for Medellín; we may single out *Populorum Progressio* and the *Letter of Sixteen Bishops of the Third World*. Of course, its antecedents were not simply intraecclesiastical: One should cite the general atmosphere of 1968, the Paris May, the proliferation of political and revolutionary theologies, the radicalization of Latin American social scientists. During the months preceding Medellín there circulated a base-document in order to gather opinions. In the meeting itself, 150 bishops and 100 *periti* elaborated sixteen documents which were intended as authoritative orientations for the church.[8]

One notes from the beginning a strong assertion of identity:

As Latin American men, we share the history of our people. The past shapes us definitively as Latin Americans, the present places us in a decisive conjuncture, and the future demands a creative task of us in the development process. . . . The church, as part of the Latin American essence, in spite of its limitations has lived with our peoples the process of colonization, liberation, and organization. . . . As Christians, we believe that this historic stage of Latin America is intimately bound up with salvation history.[9]

The Medellín documents follow a structure which can be expressed as reality—theological principles—pastoral options. This is evident in the documents as a whole[10] and in each particular document. Such a structure seeks to situate the church and theology in the human reality, specifically the reality of oppression and liberation, and in effect says that pastoral work and church structures are to be in function of this human reality. Medellín seeks to integrate the perspectives of social sciences, theology, ethics, and pastoral reflection.

There is a consistent striving to overcome dualisms:

Without falling into confusions or simplistic identifications, there ought always to be made manifest the profound unity which exists between the salvific project of God realized in Christ and the aspirations of man; between salvation history and human history; between the church, People of God, and temporal communities; between God's revealing action and man's experience; between supernatural gifts and charisms and human values.[11]

The bishops set out to interpret the "signs of the times," which are a theological locus and a summons from God. It is well known that the redacting committees for Vatican II's *Gaudium et Spes* encountered serious difficulties in determining and interpreting these signs. In effect, they chose only the most general signs—change, transformation, progress—in a framework of apparent ideological neutrality. Medellín declares that in Latin America these signs are expressed above all in the social order.

However, to interpret any social reality one needs an analytic framework. Even apparently "neutral" and "objective" social sciences conceal an ideological option in their choice of categories of interpretation.[12] The bishops, recognizing that one's viewpoint is conditioned, offer a typology of three attitudes: traditionalist, developmentalist, revolutionary. "Traditionalists. . . show little or no social consciousness, have a bourgeois mentality, and hence do not question social structures."[13] Developmentalists, with their technological mentality, are concerned about the means of production, put more emphasis on economic than on social progress, and see the solution of marginality as the "integration" of people into society as producers and consumers.[14]

Revolutionaries question the socio-economic structure. They want it to be radically changed, in objectives as well as in means. For them, the people are or ought to be the subject of this change, so that they participate in decisions for the ordering of the whole social process.[15]

The very use of the term "developmentalist" in an implicitly pejorative sense indicates the sympathies of the bishops. They realize, along with Latin American intellectuals, that the present course of "modernization"-with-stability is leading toward increasing dependence, cultural mimetism, and permanent underdevelopment. Significantly, they define the revolutionaries in terms not of violence but of the people participating in the process of change as subject rather than as object.

Not without inconsistencies, the Medellín documents generally employ "revolutionary" rather than "developmentalistic" categories. The document on peace is noteworthy for what it denounces. It speaks of "dominant" and "oppressed" sectors and exposes the former's facile use of "anticommunism" to repress legitimate reactions.[16] The bishops are even clearer in their denunciation of the international system of dependence of these countries "on an economic power around which they gravitate. As a consequence our nations frequently are not owners of their goods nor masters of their economic decisions."[17] They denounce the distortion of international trade brought about by increasingly disfavorable commercial terms, the drain-off of resources, tax evasion, increasing indebtedness, and "international monopolies and the international imperialism of money."[18]

One of the clearest examples of the line taken is the reversal of meaning given to the term "violence":

If the Christian believes in the fecundity of peace in order to arrive at justice, he also believes that justice is an unavoidable condition for peace. He cannot but see that Latin America finds itself in many places in a situation that can be called *institutionalized violence*, whereby for lack of structures in industry and farming, in the national and international economy, in cultural and political life "whole populations lacking basic necessities live in such a dependence that it impedes all initiative and responsibility, as well as all possibility of cultural promotion and participation in social and political life." Such a situation demands *global, bold, urgent* and *profoundly renovating transformations*.[19]

Thus the fundamental violence is that of those who maintain their privileges and power at the expense of the majorities. The bishops criticize the liberal capitalist system with its "erroneous conception of the right of ownership of the means of production" and yet feel obliged to condemn Marxism;[20] they seem to exhort to some kind of *via media* without specifying what it could be.

The bishops speak of a "liberating education" as "that which makes the student a subject of his own development."[21] The rejection of developmentalism appears in the following disjunctive:

The task of the education of these brothers of ours ["marginal" populations] does not consist properly in incorporating them in the cultural structures which exist around them and which can also be oppressive, but in something much deeper. It consists in capacitating them so that they themselves, as authors of their own progress, develop a cultural world in a creative and original way, in accordance with their own riches and which may be fruit of their own efforts.[22]

Following this basic thrust, the Medellín documents begin a major reinterpretation of the chief symbols of the Christian faith. Catechesis

today must assume totally the anguish and hopes of today's man in order to offer him the possibilities of a full liberation, the riches of integral salvation in Christ the Lord. Hence it should be faithful to the transmission of the biblical message, not only in its intellectual content, but also in its reality incarnate in the life events of man today.

Historical situations and authentically human aspirations form an indispensable part of catechesis; they ought to be interpreted seriously, within the present context, in the light of the lived experiences of the People of Israel, of Christ, of the ecclesial community in which the Spirit of the risen Christ lives and operates continually.[23]

In various places the bishops give a paschal interpretation of liberation:

As all liberation is already an anticipation of full redemption in Christ, the church in Latin America feels itself particularly solidary with every educative effort which tends to liberate our peoples. The paschal Christ, "image of the invisible God," is the goal which God's design sets for man's development, so that "we may all attain the stature of the perfect man."[24]

The bishops project their aspirations for the church:

May there be presented ever more clearly in Latin America the countenance of a church authentically poor, missionary and paschal, freed from all temporal power and boldly committed to the liberation of the whole man and of all men.[25]

The second part of the conclusions is called "Evangelization and Growth of the Faith." One of the signs of the abandonment of an inferiority complex vis-à-vis Europe is the recognition of the religiosity of the majorities of the people as a genuine expression of faith, even though it does not follow the norms of the church. Instead of a pastoral practice of attempting to bring people into conformity with official Catholicism, it urges respect for popular religiosity and a policy of recognizing its values and purifying its defects. The two key words are "evangelization" and "base-community." The need for an "evangelization of the baptized" is recognized.[26] The base-community is conceived of as a homogeneous group small enough to permit brotherly personal relationships. "It is the initial cell of ecclesial structuring, focal point of evangelization, and at present a primordial factor of human promotion and development."[27]

There emerges a more integral concept of pastoral work in the sense that "conscientization" is to be integrated into pastoral plans,[28] and one of the pastoral lines laid down by the document on peace is as follows: "To make our preaching, catechesis, and liturgy take into account the social and communitarian dimension of Christianity, forming men committed to the construction and building up of a world of peace."[29] Many of the documents end up with series of recommendations or commitments of the church: to denounce injustice, awaken a consciousness of injustice, defend the rights of the poor, set up a liberating education, make the family a "domestic church," give more importance to youth, study popular religiosity, etc. It is insisted that the church as such cannot take specific political options, the particular case being priests, whose duty it is to form laymen. "But in the economic and social order, and principally in the political order, where different concrete options are presented, neither decision nor leadership nor the structuring of solutions pertains to the priest."[30] In regard to political powers, the bishops delineate the church's stance as one of dialogue and collaboration as well as of criticism and denunciation where necessary.

The final section treats of lay movements, priests, religious, and church structures. Particularly noteworthy is the document on the poverty of the church, which, besides seeing poverty as a lack of material goods and as spiritual poverty, speaks of "poverty as commitment, which assumes, voluntarily and out of love, the condition of the needy of this world in order to give witness to the evil which it represents and spiritual freedom in the face of possessions, . . . "[31] following the example of Christ. The church is urged to solidarity with the poor in their struggle and their problems, in the denunciation of injustice and oppression.

It would be difficult to exaggerate the importance of Medellín, at least for the "liberationist" sectors of the church, for which it undoubtedly is more meaningful than Vatican II. The Council in its central preoccupations (the church, liturgy, authority, ecumenism, revelation) and in its ideologically conditioned view of the modern world in terms of "progress" reflects a "developmentalist" mentality in the sense described above. Medellín is concerned with the participation of the church and of Christians in the liberation of man.

How explain such a progressive stance in ecclesiastical documents? Perhaps we may attribute it to the groundwork done by the CELAM specialists, to the tendency of episcopal conferences to choose their more "intellectual" members as delegates to such a meeting, to the activity of the *periti* at Medellín, and to the general climate of 1968. Certainly many bishops are more ready to sign broad proclamations than to commit themselves to liberation in concrete struggles at the local level.

We must not overlook the limitations of Medellín. Although it adopts the dependence framework of interpretation, it is rather more descriptive than analytical and does not arrive at the mechanisms of oppression, for which it lacks adequate instruments of analysis. It is notably silent on how its ambitious aims are to be realized in society at large and in the church itself. Its theology will need to be developed. In any case, it has served to give a green light to creative minorities all over the continent whose participation in the liberation struggle has led to a radicalization of the themes presented in Medellín.

Christians as Protagonists: Experience of Conflict

Latin American liberation theology arises out of an experience: the discovery of institutionalized violence and the dimensions of oppression. There is often a gradual process of radicalization: One begins at the local level, for example in a cooperative, and enters into conflict with the local power structure; gradually it becomes more evident that the oppressive system is national and international. This growing awareness brings changes in one's options from the strictly pastoral toward the political.

The situation of violence is more or less known by way of the press. One has heard of tortures in Brazil, of rightist paramilitary groups operating in Guatemala, the Dominican Republic, and other places, of controlled presses and phone-tapping and omnipresent spying, of thousands of political prisoners being kept under arbitrary arrest (to mention some examples). This violence is not something accidental, which could be eliminated with more modern techniques; it is part and parcel of a repressive system. The significant thing here is that Christians in groups and individually have been involved in conflict: Priests have been incarcerated; convents and monasteries and bishops' residences have been watched and searched; a group of thirty priests in Belo Horizonte, Brazil, writes a circular protesting the killing of a student in a demonstration, and they are denounced and interrogated;[32] priests of the Third World Movement in Argentina have been imprisoned for defending the workers' right to strike; in Teoponte, Bolivia, Nestor Paz dies as a guerrilla leaving behind a diary filled with notes to his sweetheart and reflections on the gospel;[33] Santiago, Chile, becomes a refuge point for hundreds of Christians exiled from Brazil, Bolivia, and other countries.

This conflictive situation at times affects the church as institution, as exemplified in the case of Paraguay, where in the absence of other social forces capable of standing up to the dictatorship of General Alfredo Stroessner, the church has come to be looked upon as a symbol of resistance. In 1969 the government was persecuting Christian student groups which had protested the torture of political prisoners. This eventually led to the expulsion of Fr. Pedro Oliva and the suspension of the magazine *Comunidad*. In the conflict the hierarchy sided with the students and proceeded from the specific question to a wider denunciation:

Many of the present political leaders have a disincarnate and purely "religious" image of the church: They identify it with the hierarchy and pretend to exclude it from all participation in the process of change under the pretext that it "ought not to get involved in politics." And they attribute to the church merely the inoffensive mission of "pacifying without denouncing," of covering with the mantle of "spiritual unity" the profound social differences which divide the country and to dedicate themselves to purely "assistencial" activities which would not affect present sociopolitical structures.[34]

Paraguay is somewhat of an exception in that the church as institution was clearly defined, at least for a couple of years. In many other cases the hierarchy divides and does not define itself clearly. Sometimes the bishops collaborate with the authorities in expelling troublesome priests. In two cases in recent years the killing of priests has led to confrontation. In mid-1969 Henrique Pereira Neto, a student chaplain in Recife, was taken by the Death Squadron (paramilitary group), tortured, shot, mutilated, and hung. The clergy of Rio de Janeiro wrote:

He died by the violence of the dominant class which has put the country into mourning, with the extermination of students and true leaders of the people. Peace is not reducible just to the absence of war. . . . It is the fruit of justice. In Brazil, where a minority controls all political and economic power, there is no peace nor justice. There does not exist the possibility of fulfilling the single law of love for neighbor except by the struggle for the transformation of Brazilian society.[35]

In spite of police intimidation, seven thousand people arrived for the funeral. Similarly in 1971 Hector Gallego, a Colombian priest working for *campesinos* in the Santa Fe district in Panama, disappeared. He had previously had nonviolent confrontations with the local landowners and authorities. The government's efforts to prevent a serious investigation provoked a confrontation with the church which lasted several months.

This experience of conflict—at first glance not a theological theme—is a primary datum for liberation theology. Christians have come to see "the world as conflict," in Hugo Assmann's phrase.[36] This separates them from the North Atlantic postconciliar notion of a reconciliation with the world. Simply to be reconciled to this world is to accept complicity in oppression. When the church comes to take on the preoccupations of the world, it finds a divided world, a "rich world and a poor world, with opposed interests because the wealth of one and the poverty of the other are correlatives."[37]

Various Latin American authors have made theirs the views expressed by Giulio Girardi:

To be converted to the poor is to make a choice of some against others, of the oppressed against the oppressors, of the poor against the rich: One cannot sincerely be with the oppressed without enlisting against the oppressors. Now to put yourself against the oppressors is to make a class choice, of one class against another. And it is a choice which divides the church and brings the struggle into its own life, because many of the rich, the great majority of them, are Christians.[38]

This kind of language is foreign to Christians. The bulk of hierarchy and clergy continue to maintain a supraclass line. To many Christians, nevertheless, the situation is increasingly obvious. Says Gustavo Gutiérrez: "It is undeniable that the class struggle poses problems to the universality of Christian love and the unity of the church. But any consideration of the subject must start from two elemental points: the class struggle is a fact, and neutrality in this matter is impossible."[39] Actually the vocabulary of Medellín itself implicitly leads to an acceptance of the reality of class struggle, at least in terms of international mechanisms of oppression: imperialism, colonialism, international monopolies, oppression-liberation. Fear is expressed that acceptance of class struggle will divide the church. But, replies Gutiérrez, "In a radically divided world, the function of the ecclesial community is to struggle against the profound causes of the division among men."[40]

Though detractors of liberation theology like to portray it as a "theology of violence," little theological writing treats of the theme *ex professo*. Common positions can be summarized under four headings.

1. *Institutionalized violence.* Medellín here introduces a profound change in perspective—indeed, the first development since the just-

war theory. The "first violence," that practiced routinely by the power structure, is usually perfectly legal; it takes place in the haciendas and factories, banks and government ministries, the White House or Pentagon (e.g., Nixon's toast to the president of Brazil: "As Brazil goes, so should Latin America"). It is what gives the upper 5 percent control over half the wealth, and the lower 35 percent of the people 5 percent of the wealth.

2. *Counterviolence.* The "second violence" is revolutionary, that practiced in order to take power and establish a just order. Ethically here the traditional principles of self-defense are invoked. One must observe, however, that for the foreseeable future Cuban-style revolutions are impossible. The possible legitimation of guerrilla tactics, urban or peasant, would seem to be more of the order of (symbolic) "resistance" than of effective take-over.

3. *Repressive violence.* This is the violence used by the system to put down any uprising by the oppressed. As a result of Vietnam it is more technologized and hence another "accident" like Cuba is highly unlikely. As examples of the U.S. involvement we may point out the forty thousand Latin American military men trained in the Panama Canal Zone since the Rio Pact (1947), the maintenance of over three hundred U.S. experts in sixteen Latin American countries as well as mobile training teams, U.S. participation in the hunting down of Che Guevara and the leaders of the Tupamaro movement.

4. *Active nonviolence.* It is a fact that nonviolent techniques are used by students, workers, and peasants around the continent. Helder Camara speaks of the "violence of the peaceful" and proposes a continental coordinated nonviolent movement. Similar proposals exist in Uruguay. Nonviolence has not reached the ideological level of a Martin Luther King. Theologians favor it, and some such as Morelli integrate it into their theology.[41]

A Politicized Theology

In recent years there has appeared a European political theology which may be described as a corrective to a privatized, intimistic Christianity and as a suggestion that the church should be a critical force in society. Liberation theology accepts in principle the orientation of Metz and others, but it seeks to be more rooted in analysis of concrete situations and has become politicized in practice.

It would be well to survey the kind of praxis out of which this theology arises. The work may be with peasants, workers, or students. It might be pastoral work in a parish, for example, with a liberation orientation which eventually leads to taking a stand in conflictive situations. It might be a local development project, such as a cooperative. In recent years many have worked at "conscientization," inspired by Paulo Freire.[42] Such a line tends to lead toward organization and politicization. Some Christians operate consciously with an ideology and a methodology of nonviolence, though in Latin America it tends to be nondoctrinaire. Admittedly, many are sceptical of the practicality of nonviolent methods, since Latin American countries do not have the Anglo-Saxon tradition of respect of law and the stakes are higher than, for example, the independence of India. Another level of work is direct participation in political parties and movements. This is particularly the case in Chile, as well as in Argentina, where the Third World priests have opted for *peronismo*, not as an ideological program but as a practical vehicle for the taking of power by the people. Finally, there must be added the participation of Christians and even a few priests in movements of armed struggle, which for the moment have a value more symbolic than effective.

Situations vary enormously from country to country. In some countries the society has undertaken a global revolutionary project: most obviously Cuba; Chile for the moment (though the taking of some political power does not establish a socialist state); and Peru in the sense that there is a process of vigorous national affirmation. In these situations Christians have taken a basically positive stand, though in the case of Cuba the participation of Christians has been slight for historical reasons. In many countries the situation is nonrevolutionary and repressive: most notably Brazil, Ecuador, Bolivia, and Central America. There is no foreseeable breakthrough, and the combination of forcible repression, absorption of potential protest through upward mobility, and the manipulation of the masses (e.g., through soccer games, propaganda in Brazil) makes for a fundamentally nonrevolutionary situation. In Brazil the game plan calls for continued economic growth, a growing sphere of influence in the continent, a kind of subimperialism under the tutelage of the U.S., and certainly a further distancing of rich from poor. Unfortunately, the scheme seems viable at least for the foreseeable future. In a number of other countries one can find signs of a prerevolutionary situation: forces at work in society give hope of some kind of breakthrough, e.g., Argentina, Uruguay, Colombia.

Experience has led Christians to break away from the European conception of the church-world relationship. Gustavo Gutiérrez has traced an evolution of four conceptions with their corresponding types of pastoral approach.[43] In the "Christendom Mentality," where the secular lacks true autonomy, there will be a kind of Christian politics aimed at maintaining the church's position in society. Such an approach still prevails where the day-to-day business of the church is sacramentalization. A first alternative was the "New Christendom," identified with Maritain, which, recognizing the demise of Christendom and the value of liberal reforms and institutions, seeks to establish a society based on Christian principles. Signs of this approach are Christian Democrat parties, Christian unions, and specialized Catholic Action. Here the autonomy of the secular is affirmed over against clericalist pretensions. Subsequently there has appeared a further step which Gutiérrez calls the "distinction of planes," typified by Congar and Chenu. The church has a double mission, evangelization and the animation of the temporal order, but it does not have the mission of building up the world. The pastoral practice associated with this position can be called that aimed at "maturity in the faith"; concretely it may involve Bible groups, formation of base-communities, intimate liturgies, the formation of lay ministers. One of the signs of this mentality is the clear distinction between priest and layman, the former dedicating himself to tasks of the church's specific mission.

At this point it is clear that we have arrived at the position of Vatican II, which undoubtedly was an advance inasmuch as it liberated the church, at least in theory, from particular kinds of regimes and opened it to others. From being concretely identified with conservative regimes the church comes to see itself as apolitical. But experience in Latin America is leading some to question this position. For example, groups of workers and students in Brazil in the early sixties, following the pattern of French Catholic Action's *revision de vie*, found themselves increasingly impelled to political options as groups, whereas in theory political options, being a contingent question, should be left to each individual. Political radicalization in some cases leads to an abandonment of Christian groups and a crisis of faith. In any case, the image of a church which does not intervene in the temporal order comes to be seen as an idealist abstraction. In the concrete one's options are not infinite, and some of them at least are clearly in favor of an oppressive status quo. "Concretely, in Latin America the distinction of planes model has the effect of concealing the real political option of a large sector of the Church—that is, support of the established order."[44] Gutiérrez ironically notes that the distinction-of-planes position, battle flag of the progressives some years back, is now in the service of the status quo. The pastoral practice characteristic of the position of conscious political commitment he calls "prophetic."

The ILADES crisis[45] illustrates many aspects of the question and is one of the places of origin of liberation theology. The Institute was opened in 1966 under sponsorship of CELAM, the Jesuits, and Cardinal Silva of Santiago, with financing from German Catholics, both to promote the church's social doctrine and to do research. The founders were quite identified with the Christian Democratic party; President Frei was also involved. At the time there seemed to be a common language among the Christian Democrats, the bishops' pastoral letters, Catholic Action, and ILADES, and undoubtedly this alliance had helped Frei in 1964. Soon, however, ILADES began to polarize into two groups, a minority headed up by French Jesuit Pierre Bigo and a majority around Chilean Jesuit Gonzalo Arroyo. The Bigo group finally prevailed because of the backing of church authorities and Adveniat, so that the Arroyo group resigned.

The divergent explanations of the crisis are illustrative of the issues. The Bigo group alleged that from 1966 to 1969 the Institute had shifted from pastoral to political functions, that it was increasingly Marxist-infiltrated, and that accordingly it had lost both scientific objectivity and its original Christian orientation. The Arroyo group saw the conflict as basically between developmentalistic and revolutionary Christians. They defended the use of Marxist categories as more adequate instruments of analysis for the situation of dependence and domination of Latin America. They insisted that any social scientist is ideologically committed; hence they renounced a false neutrality and saw their scientific work as part of the work of liberation, so that their objectivity was that of participants, not of spectators. They vigorously maintained that they had not lost a Christian orientation but had abandoned a certain kind of Christian orientation which really had masked the ideology of Christian Democracy. ILADES had been political from the beginning, but in the midsixties, when the bulk of the Chilean church was Christian Democrat, few noticed its partisan character. By 1970 Christians voted left, right, and center, though the image of the church's affiliation with Christian Democracy remains.

The position of Vatican II (distinction of planes) was reaffirmed at Medellín: The church has no "technical solutions or infallible remedies."[46] But Medellín speaks of prophetic denunciation and calls for changes that are "global, daring, urgent, and profoundly renovating." How will these revolutionary changes be brought about if not by the organization of the majorities in order to take power? Must not this take place through a political party, movement, or coalition? Moreover, to denounce abuses in the concrete is to take a controversial position. If it is the government that is perpetrating them, the church will be considered "opposition" if it denounces them. Simply to denounce abuses does not go to the roots of the situation; e.g., in Brazil it is not enough simply to protest tortures. Why are there more than twelve thousand political prisoners? What is the whole mechanism of oppression? Criticism must be directed to the global "historical project" of Brazilian society.[47]

Some episcopates seem more willing to accept the political dimension of their actions. The Peruvian bishops in their presynodal document state: "The presence and the action of the church have inevitable political implications, since one cannot evangelize without a commitment in the struggle against the system of domination." They treat of the attempt at liberation and recuperation "of our natural resources, the repatriation of capital, control of currencies, agrarian reform, educational reform, and support for popular mobilization."[48] They propose to denounce in the synod the "pseudoneutrality of banks," to criticize so-called aid and the fomenting of the arms race in Latin America. On other occasions they have made pronouncements on the nationalization of the International Petroleum Company and the thesis of 200-mile jurisdiction over coastal waters. Undoubtedly it is easier for the Peruvian bishops to make these political statements when they are in accord with the nationalistic thrust of the government. In the repressive countries the bishops will at most condemn the worst excesses. In Brazil one notes a fluctuation between criticism and accommodation. Most recently, however, a number of bishops of the northeast have condemned not only the excesses such as torture but the "Brazilian miracle" as such.

The two points of view have reached perhaps their clearest confrontation in Chile. Early in 1971 the bishops released a long working document called "Gospel, Politics, and Socialisms."[49] Beginning with some general points on the gospel and the church, they speak of the Chilean church in the midst of rapid social changes. But the church's only official and fundamental option is for the gospel of the risen Christ: The church cannot opt for any one human group, although it prefers the service of the poor. It is true that Chile is faced with a choice between capitalism and socialism, but there are many kinds of capitalism (more or less socialized) and many kinds of socialism (more or less rigid). All are ambiguous, as are the men who lead them. It is up to technicians to judge them, not the church. They go on to warn that the specific kind of socialism being presented to Chile is Marxist; they warn against its dangers: statism and atheism. They are insistent that both capitalism and Marxism fall into "economicism." They insist that while all Christians can participate in politics, those responsible for pastoral work should not publicly proclaim their options. They close urging that the gospel concept of man and society should inspire Christians to commitment.

In their reply [50] a priest group actively committed in the transition to socialism called *Los Ochenta* (the "eighty") recognizes the bishops' letter as an invitation to dialogue. In spite of good intentions, the bishops do not analyze sufficiently either capitalism or socialism. The former they condemn in its excesses, without any penetration into its mechanisms. In regard to the latter, they do not analyze the present project of the Unidad Popular in Chile, nor do they study the evolution of the workers' movement in Chile; hence, for example, they warn against the dangers of anti-Christian Marxism, ignoring the fact that in Chile the working-class movement has not been hostile to the Christian faith.

The bishops postulate the "political independence of the church" and say that the church does not incline to any particular option. The priests answer that, as a matter of fact, the church has always participated in politics, in words and actions. Most recently its position is reformist, favoring "popular promotion." But in Chile the poor means the working class. In spite of what is said, the document does incline toward a specific option, a "Christian humanism" which is a modernized form of the liberal ideology of capitalism.

In ultimate analysis Christians are permitted only to "humanize" socialism, established without their collaboration, since socialism, being dehumanizing, will always need correctives. The political option which the document proposes is, hence, that of reforming any system whatsoever, but not that of making a revolutionary change in a system.[51]

Since capitalism still exists in Chile, the concrete option being offered is that of "humanizing" it: In the concrete, the bishops seem to be arguing for Christian Democracy. This becomes clearer when they present certain values as evangelical: equality of opportunities, creative initiative, opposition, political pluralism, freedom of thought and expression, dignity and freedom, socialization, participation in goods and activities. These expressions are characteristic of bourgeois society, which in practice denies precisely these things to its working classes. The document concludes with remarks on the bishops' understanding of the gospel.

Pablo Richard makes a penetrating criticism of the predominant attitudes of Christians in an article titled "Socialist Rationality and the Historical Verification of Christianity."[52] He notes the present search for an identity in Catholic theology and for a "universal Christian specificity." He makes a distinction between two spheres, a fundamental option for Jesus Christ, for gospel values, man, and society on which all Christians are in agreement. These values must be incarnated. However, in the sphere of particular options one must leave room for pluralism. Richard criticizes this position as an "ideological inversion" of social reality and political consciousness. It presents the gospel values as having an autonomous existence, as "subjects" which modify human existence, which appears as "object." Systems of production are relativized; what matters is that evangelical values be present. This has the effect of identifying Christianity with the dominant bourgeois ideology. A socialist rationality, by contrast, is one which interprets social reality in the measure in which it transforms it. Man finds his meaning in social praxis, not in an antecedent model of what "should be." It is not a question of evangelical values giving meaning, but rather that man in his social praxis finds meaning in evangelical values.

It is not the "gospel values" which upon incarnating themselves transform man and society, but it is rather man as historical subject who transforms social reality in the measure in which he struggles to overcome all alienation and oppression. Man is creative subject of his history and not the object of a world of values which "ought to be" incarnated. Only by taking off from praxis and not from the "gospel" will theology be able to overcome this inversion of subject-object, in which the ideological character of Christianity is rooted, and which deeply impedes Christians from taking up the social praxis of liberation.[53]

It has been suggested that liberation theology can be seen as an overcoming of the Marxist critique of religion by way of a new theological praxis.[54] Juan Luis Segundo indicates how Medellín has taken over elements of Marxist analysis which then "by their own right enter to form part of theology."[55] The theologians did not set out to become Marxists; for some it was mediated by contact with Paulo Freire and "conscientization," for others by reading of economists and sociologists or by contact with political activists. In any case, it is the reality itself which impels Christians to go back to Marx. Many Christians have found that Marxism is not only a system of thought but "a synthesis of reasons for living, a mobilizing doctrine." More significantly, Marxism today is not simply the position of the "other," heard out with sympathy, but is becoming the body of categories with which one lives his political commitment. Not so much an "external encounter," it is for many "a way of relating with oneself, a new way of thinking and living one's faith."[56]

Gustavo Gutiérrez has traced the different ways in which Marxism and Christianity have been, and are, related.[57] Among the "uncommitted" he finds two types of relationship: "total rejection" and "humanist dialogue." The first considers these as two global ways of life which are incompatible, though this can be attenuated by the recognition that Marxism contains some elements of truth. The "humanist dialogue" relationship typical of Garaudy and the European Christian-Marxist encounter is inspired by the "young Marx" rather than by Marx the economist-political strategist. One can indeed trace theological motifs in the philosopher Marx back through Hegel, Luther, and the Bible. Unfortunately, one ends up with a situation of "tragic lovers," separated by the abyss between theistic and atheistic humanism. Furthermore, in Latin America the tendency is to accept the position of Althusser that Marxism is not a humanism but a science and that strictly speaking even the concept of "alienation" is pre-Marxist! In any case, Gutiérrez suggests that something of this position should be retained.

Moving to the types of relationship among those "committed," he first distinguishes the "search for parallels,"[58] e.g., between the classless society and "neither Jew nor Greek," between the "New Man" of St. Paul and of Che Guevara, between sin and alienation. The danger of this kind of relationship is that Christianity may be reduced to being a revolutionary doctrine and that Marxism will lose its scientific character to revert to utopian socialism. The most frequent type of relationship today is what Gutiérrez calls "dualism": Marxism is science and Christianity is faith. Though this solves a number of problems and facilitates things for Christians, upon examination Marxism seems to be more than a science in view of its capacity to mobilize people.[59]

Gutiérrez moves beyond these classifications with his distinction of two levels of political action. One level is that of science, including a science of history; the other is that of utopia, which is a work of the imagination. A merely "scientific" political action would lack mobilizing force. Ideology, by contrast, is the relation lived with the world. It is largely unconscious inasmuch as it is not at the rational and spiritual level.[60] Faith and science meet at the level of utopia; hence in the concrete man they are not simply juxtaposed dualistically. In this fashion Gutiérrez believes he saves something of the value of the "humanist dialogue" and the "search for parallels" (both at the level of utopia) while maintaining the Althusserian position that Marxism is a science. Both Christianity and Marxism are still highly ideologized in the sense of being nonrational and not yet lucid, and both need to be less religious. In this sense Marxism is just beginning its secularization crisis.

We have mentioned how class struggle has become increasingly thematic in liberation theology. Ronaldo Muñoz finds that even the social doctrine of the church is accepting Marxist categories. He makes some significant remarks on ethics:

> I think that we Christians can accept in general the Marxist conception that what is ethically good is what is proven efficacious for the proletariat in revolutionary praxis, . . . a cause which is definitely identified with the cause of man. Such a conception, it seems to me, . . . is a good antidote against the degradation of Christian ethics to an individualistic morality of pure intentions.

Still, he proposes two correctives:

> (1) the primacy of the human person above any institution or program, religious or political, present or future; because the absolute of God's demand incarnates itself. . . in man, in each concrete human person, above every religious, social, or political barrier; (2) the unpostponable urgency of truth and justice above every convenience of class or opportunism of the moment; because these are characteristics which God's love has shown in historical action. . . . [61]

These warnings are not out of place in view of what has been done in the name of Marxism.

It should be clear that liberation theology does not see in the "social doctrine" of the hierarchy something which must be accepted as binding without question. It is put into historical context and its relationship with real options is revealed (e.g., papal attitude to revolution in Russia and Mexico, acceptance of fascist dictatorships, subsequent tendencies toward Christian democracy). It is further criticized as being a naive mixture of a particular kind of social analysis and a particular understanding of Christianity presented as a teaching of principles above specific political options.[62] Current church documents (Medellín, Letter to Cardinal Roy, synodal document on justice) certainly represent an advance, but even so they continue to manifest an attitude of observers rather than participants in the struggle and are still lacking an adequate analytical instrumentality.

A sign of the radicalization of the "liberation" movement is the meeting of "Christians for Socialism" in Santiago, Chile, in April 1972. Most of the principal thinkers here cited were present, along with 450 delegates from all of Latin America (though repressive conditions limited the delegations of some countries to exiles). There was a general rejection of "third ways" between capitalism and socialism, and an acceptance of Marxism as an analytical and revolutionary method. Particular stress was put on the task of unmasking ideological elements in present Christianity, e.g., the notion that class struggle is incompatible with Christian unity. It is affirmed that we are coming to "a new reading of the Bible and Christian tradition, it poses the basic concepts and symbols of Christianity anew, in such a way that they do not hamper Christians in their commitment to the revolutionary process but rather help them to shoulder these commitments in a creative way."[63]

Liberation Ecclesiology

As in other questions, Camilo Torres's intuition on the church anticipated later positions:

When we succeed in changing the structure of political power and the church is poor, that will help us change the structure of the Catholic church.

In the present age it is necessary to demonstrate that the church does not depend on the capitalist system and that Christianity has enough vigor to Christianize a socialist society.[64]

Initially Latin Americans simply received the conciliar ecclesiological themes, but there soon dawned the realization that in theology and pastoral reflection the countries of the "periphery" were importing from the (European) "center" just as in all other spheres of culture. Hence there appeared an anti-European reaction and a search for a more indigenous ecclesiology. One highly polemical example is the essay of a Uruguayan layman, Alberto Methol Ferre, "Church and Opulent Society: A Critique of Suenens from Latin America." He sees the effect of Suenens's modernizing recommendations as a strengthening of the North Atlantic rich churches at the expense of the poor churches of the periphery. He finds evidence of Suenens's neocapitalist mentality in his narrow intrachurch focus and his concern for birth control (just like McNamara!).[65]

Not all Latin American theologians would go along with the argument in detail, but most would subscribe to the central insight: The European progressive church acts as though it were the voice of the universal church, and not rather the ecclesiastical expression of the dominant North Atlantic nations. Liberation theology is no longer content to repeat conciliar ecclesiology, which, if it has abandoned scholastic abstractions, tends to fall into salvation-history abstractions. We could say that Latin Americans are looking for a functional theology in the sense that, having abandoned an inferiority complex vis-à-vis Europe, they are examining their own ecclesial situation with a view to ascertaining its own possibilities and options.

Already the Medellín documents are an evidence of this orientation, inasmuch as they situate the church and its mission in the context of "human promotion." Medellín also speaks of the church as "happening" in the world, in the human task, in history.[66] Writes Gutiérrez:

As a sacramental community, the Church should signify in its own internal structure the salvation whose fulfillment it announces. Its organization ought to serve this task. As a sign of the liberation of man and history, the Church itself in its concrete existence ought to be a place of liberation. A sign should be clear and understandable. If we conceive of the Church as a sacrament of the salvation of the world, then it has all the more obligation to manifest in its visible structures the message that it bears. Since the Church is not an end in itself, it finds its meaning in its capacity to signify the reality in function of which it exists. Outside of this reality the Church is nothing; because of it the Church is always provisional; and it is towards the fulfillment of this reality that the Church is oriented: this reality is the Kingdom of God which has already begun in history. The break with an unjust social order and the search for new ecclesial structures—in which the most dynamic sectors of the Christian community are engaged—have their basis in this ecclesiological perspective. We are moving towards forms of presence and structure of the Church the radical newness of which can barely be discerned on the basis of our present experience.[67]

In Latin America the world in which the Christian community must live and celebrate its eschatological hope is the world of social revolution; the Church's task must be defined in relation to this. Its fidelity to the Gospel leaves it no alternative: the Church must be the visible sign of the presence of the Lord within the aspiration for liberation and the struggle for a more human and just society. Only in this way will the message of love which the Church bears be made credible and efficacious.[68]

There is, then, a theological primacy of human liberation over intrachurch reform. This is one of the clearest examples of a break with the European matrix, inasmuch as European theology has maintained an ecclesiocentric focus (as exemplified in *Handbuch der Pastoraltheologie*). Of course, it is only a minority that has arrived at this position. In regard to the Latin American church, Hugo Assmann states that the greatest discrepancy is not between preconciliar traditionalists and postconciliar reformists: "The really profound discrepancy, which threatens to become an abyss, is that which exists between intrachurch reformers, nourished on North Atlantic theological progressivisms, and Christians impelled by and committed to the fundamental challenges of the liberation process."[69]

Assmann takes liberation theology primarily as that of small groups of radicalized Christians who are actively participating in the struggle (he himself is exiled from Brazil and had to leave Bolivia when the Torres government was overthrown). He speaks of reflection on faith operating on a strategic-tactical level, and goes on to say:

Theologically, these Christians have effectively brought about a shifting of the primary referential axis of their faith, which is no longer a body of doctrine nor the axis of worship (both important but, we would almost say, complementary), but is clearly the pole represented by the historic process of liberation. This evidently involves a new vision of their ecclesiality and submits the most central categories of traditional theology to revision. What is most evident is that the prophetic element of Christianity—prophecy was denunciation and praxis—has acquired for them a prevalence over institutional elements.[70]

The Christians to which Assmann refers are only a tiny minority of Latin American Catholics. Their experience is indeed the main reference point of liberation theology. But what of the masses—does this theology have anything to say to them? There is a line of thinking which seeks to relate to the pastoral practice of the church. In the first place, it accepts the reality of Latin American Catholicism: Over against a small minority of revolutionary Christians, and a somewhat larger number of bourgeois Catholics (corresponding to the urban middle classes and to the 5–10 percent of practicing Catholics with orientations running from Tridentine to postconciliar), the great majority are immersed in popular Catholicism. This traditional religiosity is part of the popular culture: It does not depend on the church for its transmission and is virtually unaffected by the "changes" except such as touch them, e.g., the Vatican's eliminating certain saints. These people are occasional clients of the church but it cannot be said that there exists a dialogue.

The Christian revolutionaries are not in contact with the majorities of these people. And those who opt for a pastoral practice of small communities of faith will of necessity still not be in contact. Segundo Galilea has dedicated a great deal of reflection to reconciling pastoral and liberationist lines of thought. He summarized his viewpoint in an interview:

Evangelization has two great challenges at these moments in Latin America. The first challenge is the problem of the repatriation or reformulation of the faith in a society in rapid change which is taking on a revolutionary consciousness. Preaching, catechesis, and, in general, Christian formation have not been prepared for this. A sharp challenge emerges. . . : to succeed in reformulating the faith so that it survives in the atmosphere of social change, even in Marxist atmospheres; not only survive but actually be a valid dialogue partner who will have something of his own to contribute. . . .

The second challenge I see at the level of. . . popular Catholicism. The question is how to recuperate Christian values which are in the depths of popular Catholicism wrapped up in alienating attitudes, feelings, customs, and rites. How to purify what is Christian so that it may come to be a liberating force which will take its place with authenticity in the process of liberation. A grave challenge, because of the difficulty of the task and because of its utter importance for the Latin American church, given the great proportion of Christians who are in this popular Catholicism.[71]

In the same paragraph in which he called religion the "opium of the people," Marx described it as a "protest" against the conditions of oppression. The intuition of Latin American pastoralists is that this dimension of protest is recuperable.

We have presented these two strains of reflection, the revolutionary and the pastoral, as though they were quite separated. In practice there is often a convergence. Often a pastoral team working at evangelization with peasants or barrio dwellers is radicalized by events and reflection, so that what begins as biblical circles evolves toward some kind of confrontation with the power structure. Similarly, any kind of conscientization which touches major points of the culture must eventually get to a conscientization of religiosity. In a number of places there have been Holy Week dramas of the Passion with present-day references; there have been protest Masses; in Nicaragua, where the Somoza dictatorship runs the country like a family business, Christian student groups have occupied churches in protest, with the tacit approval of the hierarchy; in Panama people came in silent procession from different directions, ostensibly to observe the feast of Our Lady of Mt. Carmel, but really to celebrate a protest Mass over the government's silencing of the investigation of the disappearance of Fr. Hector Gallego. It must be mentioned that the liberation thrust of pastoral work is easily more verbal than real, and that in any case it has not moved the majority of clergy and hierarchy.[72]

The liberation context affects the ministerial question. To the progressive elements of the Latin American clergy the preoccupations of North Atlantic priests seem narcissistic. Priest groups have become protagonists in the struggle for liberation. It is sometimes charged that this is due to a crisis in the properly priestly dimension of their lives and that they fill up the vacuum with the revolution. They energetically reject this accusation, declaring rather that they are rediscovering their priesthood in new dimensions. In this sense the late Bishop Gerardo Valencia Cano observed:

I understood that the vocation to evangelize the poor contains in itself the duty to denounce the injustices, the hypocrisies, of those who load the rest with heavy burdens and themselves don't touch them with one finger. Thus I understand my priesthood. . . . I don't confuse priesthood and politics; but I know that at this moment which a Christian nation like Colombia is living the priest ought to be by vocation the leaven for the change that we hope for, and that his word and his action, courageously evangelical, have to be light for the marginal and a warning alarm for those in power.[73]

For some, the inclination is undoubtedly to see the church in a small community of faith (of elite or of popular classes) and largely to prescind from the institutional church. Still, sociological realism demands that one accept the real political weight of the church and try to break its relationship with the system of domination. This does not mean that the whole church will swing to the left; it means rather that there be signs, both symbolic and real, of breaking off from the power structure and that there be created a space for a liberating Christianity.[74] An important task is seen in the *desbloqueo ideológico*, a freeing of Christian symbols from their ideological use and making them available for the liberation struggle.[75]

The Protestant experience is quite different in that it represents a minority in the dominant Catholic culture and hence does not tend to feel the same responsibility toward the whole society. Radicalized Protestants share a common language and viewpoint with their Catholic counterparts, more than with fellow Protestants whether of the traditional churches or the sects. Indeed, Protestant theologians and intellectuals have contributed far out of proportion to their numbers, and ISAL[76] groups, for example, have been one of the major focal points of the Christian left.[77] They agree in general that the primary "ecumenical" task is not the reunion of churches but the liberation of man. The unity of the church and of the churches is, in a certain sense, subordinate to the unity of mankind. Inasmuch as the class struggle is present in the churches, the true unity of the churches can come only by overcoming the oppression of classes (and indeed, nations).[78]

Liberation and the Meaning of Christian Symbols

In this essay we have dedicated much space to apparently nontheological matters. Our intention has been to situate liberation theology in its context, for its value comes not so much from new "discoveries" in doctrine or ethics as from a new relationship to the social context of oppression-liberation in Latin America. Indeed, it thus makes theological issues out of apparently "profane" realities. But this praxis leads to a kind of radical questioning of the very meaning of Christianity. In this connection Comblin has some incisive comments in an offensively simple article originally directed to a European public. He observes that the first thesis of liberation theology is that Christianity is charity—which means action. It is not what he says that saves a man but what he does. "Now one finds that European theology is interested in what is to be believed, even in what is to be said. Its object is the doctrine of Christ, and it seems to forget his action."[79] The true knowledge of God, however, is in action. But the Bible does not tell us what is to be the concrete content of love today. Biblical theology can establish what the New Testament documents meant to the communities that produced them; the study of tradition can show what has been the understanding of Christianity and the concrete forms of charity in different periods; but no biblical or historical science can show what they must mean now. This requires a reading of the "signs of the times" and needs the discernment of the Spirit. The intuition in Latin America is that today Christian love demands liberation. This is not to be taken as the total meaning of Christianity for all time. It is, however, the urgent task for our generation.

In our era it is essential to pass from a microcharity to a macrocharity. In the pretechnical era human activity is limited largely to personal relationships or to small groups. But in our technical society a great part of human activity is collective, and indeed, involuntary and unconscious. If charity is limited to the small group, it leaves out the greater part of human activity, especially collective violence and injustice: today you can kill at a distance. This transformation goes to the very essence of Christianity. If charity does not mean anything at these collective levels, Christianity has nothing to say to man today.[80]

In the conflictive Latin American situation, traditional Christian symbols are not neutral. They are part of the culture and folklore (e.g., popular songs make analogies of love with the *pasión* and *calvario* of Christ). Symbols being essentially plastic, they can be employed both in the service of the status quo and of liberation. The president of Colombia dedicates his country to the Sacred Heart in 1969 and provokes a protest from the Golconda priests over the "theological thesis of the president."[81] In Santa Cruz, Bolivia, an anticommunist crusade is preached with a procession of 40,000 people. Four days later a well-organized rightist coup originates in Santa Cruz.[82] On the other hand, Bishop Enrique Argelelli praises a strike of state employees as a "salvific event," a proof of the gospel that the people has learned from its infancy.[83] Assmann dedicates a whole study to the use being made of religion in the schools; in effect, religion is used as legitimating the dictatorship and its program of dependent capitalist development.[84]

No generation of Christians after the first century can share the original horizon of understanding of the biblical symbols. Each must reinterpret them according to its own horizon of understanding—in our present case, the horizon of oppression-liberation. It is not the theologians, in the first place, who will discover this reinterpretation with their science, but rather Christians themselves, in particular those with greater depth. The original form of liberation theology is often a group reflection or meditation, a sermon, a mimeographed flyer.[85] This theology is not particularly original in terms of what it says about the biblical themes. In most cases it is dependent on European scholarship, at least reductively. Its originality comes from its way of relating these themes to practice—more accurately, its interpretation of praxis in terms of the biblical symbols.

Juan Luis Segundo observes that the Christian moved to political liberation finds himself with the same concepts of God, sin, sacraments, and belonging-to-the-church which correspond to a theology of ultraterrestrial salvation. Theology is functioning as ideology (in the pejorative sense); he finds European theologians naive when they hold that theology can have no ideologizing function since it is concerned with revelation. He points out that ideology is largely unconscious (Althusser) and that theology has to work with the elements of a given culture.[86]

European theology tends simply to oppose faith and ideology. It will point to the "demonic" qualities of ideology. From its nonconflictive world vision it tends to see ideologies as a series of isms, a somewhat idealist perspective.[87] In Latin America "ideology" has the positive sense of an ideology of struggle in an ethico-political sense as well as the negative sense of a legitimation of an oppressive status quo. One of the tasks of liberation theology is seen as that of exposing the ideological use of Christian symbols to mask reality, e.g., invoking Christian unity against the reality of class struggle, identifying bourgeois values as Christian, defending "Western Christian civiliza-tion," etc. On the other hand, one can say that there is a search for a Christian ideology in the sense of a motivating force for social revolution.[88]

Following Mannheim's terminology, Rubem Alves asks about "The Ideological Function and the Utopian Possibilities of Latin American Protestantism."[89] Protestantism arose as a form of utopia breaking with the medieval world in the name of Christian freedom. Similarly it arrived in Latin America in a utopian form as bearer of the values of modernization: liberty, equality, and fraternity. Catholi-cism functioned ideologically legitimating and sacralizing domina-tion. With its stress on discipline, Protestantism was a utopian force which affirmed the freedom of man to build his own world and dominate his time. Today this same individualism functions ideologi-cally: The ethic of individual conversion and of self-discipline leaves the world as it is and is not an ethic of transformation of the world. Individualism is understood dualistically and not dialectically. There is, however, a new utopian thought as expressed in Medellín and with which some Protestants, similarly utopian, agree: "There is strong indication that the Latin American crisis is leading some to reinterpret the symbols of their faith but in the utopian or messianic-prophetic direction of the Old Testament."[90] Utopian and ideological interpre-tations divide Protestants as well as Catholics internally, but by the same token they provide areas of ecumenical unity.

One of the most emphatic emphases of liberation theology is the unitary vision of creation and redemption, of salvation history and human history. Here one notes a reaction against a certain abstract *Heilsgeschichte* theology deriving from Cullmann and mediated to Latin America by Liégé and others. Hernández asks "what it means that Jesus is Lord of history; it means that the goods of the earth, all the goods of the earth, are a bond of union among men and that these goods do not limit man to a brotherhood here and now but a brother-hood open to a future."[91] He draws the conclusion that the People of God, which is to reveal this to the world, before pronouncing its word has to assume a liberating commitment in the world.

In Latin American countries a minority of 5–10 percent generally controls half the wealth, whereas the lower third of the population may receive only 5 percent of the wealth. Similarly the United States, with 6 percent of the world's population, uses 40 percent of its raw materials. Evidently, in the concrete the goods of the earth are not the bond of union among men. From the developmentalistic point of view the lordship of Christ is manifest in the triumphs of technology.

Liberation theology insists that this lordship demands the socialization of the means of production in the service of all.

Gutiérrez treats at some length the relationship between creation and salvation, noting the lack of a profound and lucid theology of salvation.[92] The Bible sees this relationship in the historical experience of the Exodus. This liberation is a political act and the beginning of the construction of a just and fraternal society. The work of Christ, a new creation, is situated in this line. Gutiérrez then takes up the theme of the Promise and its "partial realizations" in history.

At this point he arrives at a problem which, while not peculiar to liberation theology, is of particular importance to it, the apparent "spiritualization" of the Old Testament in the New Testament: The temporal redemption of Israel points to a spiritual redemption of all men. He quotes Grelot, who says that the object of the promises is the "permanent *spiritual* drama of humanity, which touches directly on the mystery of sin, suffering, and salvation"; these texts have only "an accidental relationship with *political* history."[93] But, insists Gutiérrez, the "hidden" sense is intrahistoric:

The grace-sin conflict, the coming of the Kingdom, and the expectation of the parousia are. . . necessarily and inevitably historical, temporal, earthly, social, and material realities. . . .Peace, justice, love, and freedom are not private realities; they are not only internal attitudes. They are social realities, implying a historical liberation. A poorly understood spiritualization has often made us forget the human consequences of the eschatological promises and the power to transform unjust social structures which they imply.[94]

Liberation theology emphasizes the collective nature of sin. Medellín speaks of a "situation of sin" and calls for a prophetic denunciation of the sin which makes people poor.[95] Gutiérrez points out how this differentiates liberation theology from optimistic theologies of progress, which are somewhat embarrassed by sin. He quotes approvingly José María González-Ruiz's term, the "hamartiosphere," and continues:

Sin is evident in oppressive structures, in the exploitation of man by man, in the domination and slavery of peoples, races, and social classes. Sin appears, therefore, as the fundamental alienation, the root of a situation of injustice and exploitation. It cannot be encountered in itself, but only in concrete instances, in particular alienations.[96]

As a consequence, we must say that liberation from sin cannot be direct but must be mediated through political and historical liberation. Medellín states that Christ comes "to liberate all men from all the slaveries to which sin has them subject: ignorance, hunger, misery, and oppression—in one word, the injustice and hate which have their origin in human selfishness."[97] How relate these aspects? Is there not a danger of some kind of "concordism" between biblical and political languages? Gutiérrez insists repeatedly that liberation is a single process which has different levels of meaning:

economic, social, and political liberation; liberation which leads to the creation of a new man in a society of solidarity; and liberation from sin and entrance into communion with God and with all men.

The first corresponds to the level of scientific rationality which supports real and effective transforming political action; the second stands at the level of utopia, of historical projections; . . . the third is on the level of faith.[98]

The key to understanding the relationship between economic-political liberation and liberation from sin is the second level, utopia. A utopian project is to be realized in history. It corresponds to man's progressive taking of his destiny in his hands. More concretely: The revolutionary conceives of a society where men can be more brotherly and truly responsible authors of their own lives. This utopian project demands an economic and political liberation: the taking of power by the people and the socialization of the means of production, the abolition of class privileges, and an organization of the economy in function of the majorities. All this is essential but insufficient: These things alone could lead to other abuses. Needed is the creation of the New Man who lives for others (Che Guevara). This utopian liberation is the object of the cultural revolution. As sin is a historic reality, liberation from sin is mediated through historic utopias. The Christian believes in faith that neither sin nor liberation is merely intrahistoric and awaits the definitive liberation. He is aware that in its depths the kingdom is a gift (not added on after man's efforts but present gratuitously from the beginning). This seemingly speculative framework finds interesting confirmation in an essay of Sergio Arce, who reflects on the situation of the Christian revolutionary from the midst of the Cuban experience.[99]

Two focal points of liberation theology's reflection are the Exodus and Christ. In regard to the Exodus one sees it as a paradigm for the interpretation of the life of the People of God. "The Exodus gives the community the measure of the hopes it can have for the future," says Alves.[100] It is seen as political act, leaving the security of the "happy slave," the pedagogy of the desert, a permanent attitude of noninstallation. Alves sees the symbol "People of God" as giving a pattern of "social organization defined by hope in which life and freedom can be found together."[101] The majority of liberation theologians treat the

Exodus at some length, some simply presenting the conclusions of biblical scholars, others making applications of considerable ingenuity. What the present writer finds disconcerting is the lack of a hermeneutical principle which would explain with clarity and vigor in precisely what way the original Exodus relates to the present liberation.

Assmann observes that there is lacking a Latin American Christology. One finds an all-purpose, supra-situational Christology and one that is ideologically functionalized. Vatican II's Christology is either "ecclesiastical" or a vague "Christ-acting-in-the-world" which can be ambiguous.[102] Presumably, he envisions a Christology which would seek to detect where and how Christ is present in the conflictive reality of the world. Comblin protests against the "iconization" of Jesus, that is, the tendency to see in Jesus' life not so much a series of human actions as a series of illustrations of theological themes, and ultimately the tendency to replace the imitation of Christ by worship of him. He calls for a deiconization and proceeds to some reflections on the actions of Jesus.[103] Certainly there is a strong movement to utilize the revolutionary elements in the life of Jesus, his conflicts with established authorities, his poverty, preaching of brotherhood, of conversion, his self-image as Isaian liberator (Luke 4).

Gutiérrez, in his treatment of "Jesus and the political world," surveys recent publications, especially Cullmann. He questions the latter's contention that Jesus is not concerned about structural transformation but only about individual conversion in view of the coming kingdom. Instead of counterposing individual conversion to revolution, Jesus goes deeper and establishes a permanent principle of revolution. "By freeing us from sin, Jesus attacks the roots of an unjust order. For Jesus, the liberation of the Jewish people was only one aspect of a universal, permanent revolution; far from showing no interest in this liberation, Jesus rather placed it on a deeper level, with far-reaching consequences."[104] Once again, the present writer basically sympathizes but would like to see a more explicit hermeneutics which would take up the differences in our horizon of understanding which permit, and even demand, a political reading of the gospel which in its original form did not treat of social structures.[105]

Participation in the struggle for liberation implies a rethinking of the meaning of Christian life. One example is conversion, which is taken not simply in an individual but in a social sense. Conversion means conversion to "the least of my brothers." Conversion as discovery of the other as person contains the dynamism of human development of persons and of peoples. "The community of the converted, a church, precisely as such, ought to commit itself to the needs of the people as a nation,"[106] says Bishop Candido Padim of Brazil, who unites in a reflection on conversion the conversion of the church and its participation in conscientization and a criticism of the actual forms of "development" imposed on the peoples of the Third World.

Another theme being rediscovered is that of poverty. It is not simply material poverty, nor simply the poverty of the *anawim* or of spiritual childhood, but a poverty of protest and effective solidarity with the poor.

Theology: In What Sense?

Our purpose has been to mediate something of Latin American liberation theology to the North American theological community. Undoubtedly, in some ways it has seemed more journalism than theology, due to our conviction that this theology is best understood in context. We have been quoting and summarizing the thought of some of the principal theologians with little critical comment. In this final section we would like to situate it as theology.

Is this theology? The question may be legitimately asked. It is not a direct study of the Bible or of tradition; it claims no new discovery of what revelation communicated *in illo tempore*. There are many non-theological elements and it becomes impossible to find a dividing line. It is theology inasmuch as it seeks to give a theological reading of the signs of the times and to decipher the concrete content of God's will for us.

In literary form also it is not what we have come to expect from theologians. The most organic work is Gutiérrez's *A Theology of Liberation*. Alves's *Theology of Human Hope*, while ostensibly a Third World theology, really has twentieth-century Protestant theology as its interlocutor and was written as a thesis in a U.S. university. Assmann's book is a collection of aggressive essays that are rather pointers toward where a theology might be developed than theology proper. The greater part of the material is in the form of magazine articles, mimeographed notes, manifestos, or anthologies of such. There is no Latin American Moltmann. Nor would it make too much sense: Moltmann opens his *Theology of Hope* by situating it in the whole stream of theological debate in Germany; in Latin America there are few academic interlocutors. The properly theological elements here give the impression of a certain eclecticism, and one does not have the feeling that they revolve around a center, as for example in the theology which utilizes transcendental philosophy. Or to the extent that there is a center, it is the common experience of participation in the liberation struggle and a common interpretation from the social sciences. Some may feel that this is more a spirituality than a theology, but there have been periods when the two were inseparable.

The liberation theologians have themselves been trained in academic theology and have come to break with some of its conventions and viewpoints, somewhat violently, as the following paragraph from Assmann evidences:

A fundamental inclination to idealism in the form in which Karl Marx criticized it and ultimately the consequent incapacity of a historic realism would be characteristic defects of the theology of the rich world. Its questions do not take off from the real in its conflictive density; they idealize reality; certain theologies, as that of the "death of God," are an apolitical accommodation to the pragmatism of man in consumer societies; the theological theme of secularization in Europe and the U.S.A. is centered almost exclusively on the desacralization brought by the arrival of technique within the relationship man-nature and minimizes the primordial (political) aspect of the relation man-nature-man, man-domination mechanisms, "powers and dominations." To radicalize the political aspect of the theme of "secularization," illegitimating the "order" and the subjugating powers of man, would be the situational contribution of a theology of liberation which takes off from the reality of the dominated peoples.[107]

Assmann finds the theologians of the rich world insensitive to oppression and hence reactionary. He asks whether an international meeting of theologians would be able to come to agreement on the ten most serious problems facing mankind—and doubts that they would. "The exegetic and theological progressivisms of the rich world, with few exceptions, revolve around points of no importance in the face of the world's most serious problems."[108]

To work on a theology of liberation, one must be a person of the Third World. Paulo Freire suggests that the Third World, as utopian and prophetic of the world that is emerging, can be an inspiration for theology. The metropolises of the world, whose future is to maintain their status of metropolis, are thereby impeded from being utopian. To be a Third World person is to renounce the power structures and establishments, and to be with the "wretched of the earth" with authentic love.[109] One can wonder whether all theologians should be Third World people.

These theologians would all be in agreement in applying Marx's last thesis on Feuerbach to theology: They want a theology not only to interpret the world but to change it. With his usual aggressiveness Assmann says: "There is no more flight to a verbal world decked with ontological considerations that reflect man's inability to deal with the real problems."[110] The notion of a realm of truth independent of verification in history is abandoned. Assmann speaks of "praxeology"; Alves defines truth as "the name given by a historic community to those historic acts which were, are, and will be efficacious for the liberation of man."[111] More sober and circumspect is Gutiérrez when he sees theology as critical reflection on praxis in society and in the church, without ceasing to be "wisdom" and rational knowledge, its more classical forms.[112] It is our opinion that while the general intuition of truth-in-praxis is significant, the attempts of these theologians to express it fall easily into verbal overkill.

A praxis-oriented theology needs the analytical tools of the social sciences. Again, we have not come across any truly lucid explanation of the relationship between social sciences and theology.[113] Perhaps it could be along these lines: We are seeking the concrete content of charity for our situation. It is a distinguishing note of the technical age that our world is constituted by many relationships which are beyond immediate contact. The social sciences bring this world into some rational coherence. To begin to be conscious agents of our own destiny, we need the understanding brought by social science. The choice of an analytical instrumentality is already an option, since the social sciences are not neutral. Those forms of sociology which postulate the permanence of the status quo with only accidental modifications (cf. Parsons, *The Social System*) are obviously unsuited. We need an instrumentality which interprets oppression and is oriented toward liberation—fundamentally Marxism in some form. We find that Camilo Torres exemplifies much of this. In fact, he can be considered a kind of Teilhard for Latin America, his intuitions being political rather than cosmological.

One of the major responsibilities of Christians is to study more scientifically how (sociological) Christianity as superstructure functions ideologically in maintaining domination. At the same time, Christian symbols must be freed to serve in the liberation of man. This task is of prime importance for theologians.

There is a feeling that liberation theology is a "theology of the event." In this sense the analogy is with prophecy: As the prophets interpreted contemporary events in the light of the founding events of Israel, Exodus, and Covenant, so the theology of the event seeks to interpret present events in the light of Israel, Christ, and the Promises.[114] It is for this reason that many of the documents are occasional documents, reactions to particular situations. Liberation theology does not seek to be another department of theology, nor to join the various theologies that appeared as regularly as spring fashions during the sixties. While it does have certain characteristic preoccupations, it is at the same time a reflection on the perennial Christian themes from within the experience of participation in liberation struggles.

Perhaps a word is in order to correct possible overly romantic images of theologian-revolutionaries. In the greater part of the continent the climate is not prerevolutionary. There is rather a combination of violent repression, adroit manipulation, absorption of protest, propaganda, and general domestication of mind and spirit. Certainly there are left groups, but in many cases their importance is more that of symbolic resistance. Christians may be sensitized by liberation theology, but in the lack of a revolutionary project it becomes theology more of exile than of exodus.

Although this theological intuition has some official status as a result of Medellín there is no guarantee that it will not be "corrected." Recent events in CELAM and in the mood of the hierarchy give the impression that liberation theology may be marginated out to the left by a more "centrist" type of thinking more in line with the inclinations of the bulk of the hierarchy.[115]

What does all this suggest to practicing theologians in the U.S.? Somewhat at random, we close with some questions and intuitions.

1. *Third World theology*. There would seem to be some affinity with black theology. Chicano Christian groups are consciously looking into Latin American theology for insights. One can ask: Does not some kind of effective solidarity with the Third World offer a clue to the meaning of Christian poverty today?

2. *Ecclesiocentrism*. Liberation theology is convinced that church renewal cannot be sought independently of the struggle for liberation. Does not the charge of ecclesiocentrism ring true for much of post-conciliar activity and theology?

3. *Critique of social reality*. Are not the theologians often fiddling while the world burns? What will Christ's judgment be on the theologians of our century? As an example, to what extent has Vietnam influenced the theological problematic (granting that many theologians, like their liberal colleagues, have done their part in marches, etc.)?

4. *Man as agent*. Liberation theology is not so much interested in the Promethean astronaut as in the majorities in the human family: To what extent can men become free agents taking responsible decisions in solidarity with others and "ruling the earth"? Does not this view from below offer some hints for a theological critique of society?

5. *Critique of capitalism.* In a poor world the U.S. is overdeveloped, consumes much more than its share of the world's resources, uses its military might to maintain its privileges, and still is acutely aware that it has not attained the "good life." Radical analysis reveals that these injustices are structural. Is there not room for a theological critique of capitalism? (If the idea puzzles, amuses, or shocks, might not this be an indication of an ideologically immersed consciousness?)

6. *Politicized theology.* Does not the apolitical stance of the church mask a complicity with an oppressive world system? In what way does the theological profession serve the poor and oppressed, who are the majority of mankind?

7. *Methodology.* Does the common pattern of reflection in liberation theology suggest something: analysis of the reality, theological reflection, commitments? Implicitly the Marxist theory of infra- and super-structure is accepted inasmuch as the economic reality is seen as a kind of base which conditions superstructural elements, including religion and theology. Could a theological critique be made of the U.S. "historic project"—not simply President Nixon's successive "game plans" but including other elements? Could meetings of theological societies center on this type of analysis? It would be entering into the contingent, but so did He whose life theologians have spoken of as a "scandal of particularity."

Appendix

DOING THEOLOGY IN A
(COUNTER-) REVOLUTIONARY SITUATION:
LATIN AMERICAN LIBERATION THEOLOGY
IN THE MID-SEVENTIES

Significantly the foregoing article appeared in September 1973 as a military coup was overthrowing the Popular Unity government in Chile: Over ten thousand people were killed and many tens of thousands more were jailed, tortured, fired from their jobs, or forced into exile. Since then Chile is once more at the service of transnational corporations, its economy has been "corrected" (with the help of Milton Friedman and Chicago-trained economists), while workers and peasants have lost all their former gains and live under terror.

What happened in Chile is the most brutal example of the overall process in Latin America in the mid-1970s. The previous article deals with the origins or liberation theology (LT) in Latin America from Camilo Torres and Medellín up through the Christians for Socialism meeting in 1972. Here I would like to survey more recent events and literature, particularly in the light of new conditions.[116]

In Latin America the seemingly revolutionary effervescence of the 1960s lasted until the early 1970s.

The Popular Assembly in Bolivia, the victory of the Popular Unity and progress of the Allende government in Chile, the increasing stability of the revolutionary military government in Peru, the formation and advance of the Broad Front in Uruguay, the development of the Peronist movement in Argentina, the formation of the M.A.S. [Movement toward Socialism] in Venezuela, the direction of the Torrijos government in Panama, the new definition of the government in Honduras, the reaffirmation of alignment with the Third World on the part of the Echeverría government in Mexico, etc., were some of the signs . . . which announced a different era in Latin America. It was the "time of illusions."[117]

Since then there have been rightist military coups in Bolivia, Chile, Uruguay, and Argentina. More than two-thirds of Latin America lives under military rule, and even where civilian government remains (Mexico, Colombia, Venezuela, and Costa Rica) the army and police are at work, e.g., long periods of a "state of siege" in Colombia. Peru's process seems to have levelled off.

The *Cristianismo y Sociedad* analysis quoted above states that the Latin American left made a basic miscalculation: It interpreted the vigor of popular movements as a sign of the weakness of capitalism; in fact, however, the economies of various nations were passing into the control of international capital with the result that there is a "new constellation of power (international capital, military sectors, and technocracy)."[118] The authors state that the left must move from the era of illusions to a time of realism.

In a word, it would seem that the most immediate "sign of the times" in Latin America at this point is not revolution but counter-revolution.[119]

Institutionally the Catholic church seems to have moved back from some of its post-Medellín positions. After the election of Bishop Alfonso López Trujillo as secretary general of CELAM there was a "housecleaning" in the CELAM institutes of liturgy, catechesis, and pastoral theology. These institutes had been training hundreds of priests and religious and some laypeople and served as a platform for the elaboration of liberation thinking in the church. The four institutes were reduced to one, which was located in Colombia where it could be watched closely. LT has not been repudiated—the hierarchy could hardly contradict its own documents—but liberation vocabulary is used in a more generic and less directly political sense, as we shall discuss below. Actually the situation from 1968 to the end of 1972 was anomalous: On the basis of the Medellín documents and spurred on by events, progressive elements in the church had become increasingly radicalized to the point of clearly opting for socialism. What is surprising is that the conservative forces in the hierarchy delayed so long in organizing a countercoup, since LT did not represent the real thinking of the bulk of the bishops.

While the institutional church may have swung back to the right (or to the center) the issues raised by LT will not go away. In particular the "colonial fascist" regimes which prevail over the greater part of the continent frequently find themselves in conflict with the church, typically when priests or religious are persecuted or killed but also where there is widespread violation of human rights. Thus it is quite possible that the institutional church is being forced into a confrontation which it does not choose but which it may not be able to avoid.

The earlier article sought to present LT to the North American theological community. At the time it was prepared the literature was largely in the form of essays and manifestos; Gutiérrez's *Theology of Liberation* was the only organic theological study; little material had appeared in English translation. It seemed important to stress the originating experience of conflict and the praxis framework.

Today LT is well known in theological circles—even to the point of provoking backlash (Greeley, Novak, Hartford Statement). Here I will take a somewhat different approach, surveying a number of writings in more detail, and will seek to chart out emerging areas of discussion as well as the particular emphases of various thinkers.

It strikes me that we can mark out two basic directions in LT: reflection on praxis and the reinterpretation of Christian faith. The former seeks to illuminate praxis, to articulate various political and pastoral options (analysis from social sciences, Marxism, class struggle, ideology, etc.) The latter is concerned with this question: For those committed to the struggle for liberation what do the basic elements of Christianity come to mean: faith, love, God, Jesus Christ, church, sacraments, etc.?

The above is not intended as an airtight division—it is clearly fundamental that ethics and doctrine are not separated in LT—but rather as a handy way to group some recent writings. First, however, I will consider three publications which deal with both aspects.

Míguez Bonino, Concilium, CELAM

Doing Theology in a Revolutionary Situation by José Míguez Bonino presents an excellent if brief overview of the major issues in LT.[120] (The title reflects the author's preference for speaking of a theology *for*, or *in the context of*, liberation.) The first half ranges over the events which have produced LT. Chapter 4 is a particularly lucid commentary on the work of Segundo, Gera, Gutiérrez, Assmann, and Alves.

Míguez's own perspectives are offered under the four headings of the second part: "Hermeneutics, Truth, and Praxis," "Love, Reconciliation, and Class Struggle," "Kingdom of God, Utopia, and Historical Engagement," and "Church, People, and Avant-Garde." While I find the whole discussion worthwhile, I will single out a few points.

Regarding the use of Marxism, Míguez advocates a middle position between two common but unacceptable extremes: On the one hand some Christians committed to liberation refuse to make use of Marxist categories and consequently have to fall back on moral categories or ethical principles "which, lacking a rigorous historical mediation, not infrequently end up in frustration, inability to act or different forms of reformism."[121] At the opposite end, some embrace Marxism with religious fervor and surrender the historical contents of the Christian faith. For Míguez, Marxism is a hypothesis which has been borne out in fact and is the best existing framework for analysis and action. If it is such, he concludes, Marxism becomes the *"unavoidable historical mediation* of Christian obedience."[122]

Scripture reading must be engaged (i.e., you don't first find the truth and then apply it). Yet Míguez opposes shortcuts, e.g., direct political conclusions (revolutionary or pacifist) from Jesus' relations to the Zealots. Instead, we must go through two mediations, the reading of the direction of the biblical text (liberation, righteousness, shalom, the poor, love)[123] and the rational reading of the possibilities of our present situation.

Míguez notes suggestively that Marx's categories are based on work (class struggle is based on relations of production) while classical Christian anthropology has been concerned with intellectual, moral, or spiritual qualities or with the person's relation to God, neighbor, and self. Thus Marxism has been considered "materialistic." Christians from such an idealist viewpoint have seen Marxism as materialistic. Yet work is integral to a biblical view of humanity; hence Marxism may supply a needed corrective for Christian anthropology.

Taking up the theme of the "two histories," Míguez states that it is not enough to say that humanity's strivings in history are "images" of the future kingdom: Today's actions are building the kingdom. Nor is it sufficient simply to state that there is but one history. He suggests that the Pauline notion of the body (earthly and glorified) may offer a clue to the continuity and discontinuity. There is a tension between what will be permanent (love) and what is of the flesh.

Again this short and simply written book offers an excellent overview of many issues in LT.[124]

In 1974 *Concilium* dedicated a whole number to Latin American LT.[125] We will cite some of the articles in connection with their authors' viewpoints below.

Another composite work *Liberación: Diálogos en el CELAM*[126] is interesting not only for its contents but for the light it sheds on the counteroffensive within CELAM. Ostensibly it is simply a collection of presentations given at a meeting of the CELAM theological reflection team in late 1973, along with transcripts of debate and dialogue.

Why would Bishop Alfonso López Trujillo, who is considered to be the spearhead of the counteroffensive against LT, have such a book published? A close examination of the contents offers one clue: Only four of the contributors may be considered wholehearted proponents of LT (Gutiérrez, Gera, Methol Ferre, and Bishop Samuel Ruiz); the rest either question the basis of LT from the viewpoint of theology (López), social science (López, Poblete, Bigo) or Scripture (Mejía, who says flatly that the current notion of liberation does not come from the Bible[127]) or stress shortcomings, dangers, or excesses (Marins, Kloppenburg) or simply arrange biblical data with no reference to the concrete process of liberation (Pironio, Galvez, and Roxo). (In all, the essays which are clearly LT comprise 142 pages, while those which criticize, using liberation language with no political reference, amount to 202 pages!)

Thus the strategy is not simply to attack LT. It is rather to insist that "there are various tendencies and currents in the theology of liberation."[128] Thus the line of those who recognize class struggle and see socialism as necessary become simply one variety of LT. When a biblical language of liberation is used without reference to any concrete historical task, it sounds progressive and Latin American yet remains innocuous.

Certainly there are important differences between the chief proponents of LT (e.g., some stress class struggle while others propose a "people's struggle"). Progress demands mutual debate and criticism. Yet I would submit that the basic division comes not over theories about liberation but over a basic option for liberation as a historical project, the building of a nonexploitative social order, and especially "taking sides" in real struggle with all its risks.

López and others wish to establish a "pluralism" of LTs. Hence it would seem by design that he did not include in this book a series of twenty-nine propositions drawn up at that same meeting to summarize the consensus of the participants for they show broad areas of agreement in spite of very significant differences. To cite a few examples:

2. Faith and the proclamation of the gospel are intrinsically related to politics.

3. There is an intrinsic relationship between socio-political, economic, and cultural liberation, and the salvation of Jesus Christ.

5. There are collective forms of dependence: social groups, social classes,. races, nations. The process of liberation should bear in mind that this situation is conflictive in nature.

13. There must be a mediation between theology and positive scientific rationality. This poses methodological and philosophical problems and is important in liberation theology. In this area there is a serious Christian vacuum. These questions become a pastoral necessity. Faith never uses an analysis or a rational system [*racionalidad*] without giving it a new direction.

14. Marxist analysis has a strict relationship with its philosophical categories. Hence assuming its valid elements means revising all its categories.[129]

The fact that this book has a "hidden agenda" does not make it less interesting. Many of the contributions are quite worthwhile; even some of the critics raise important points; and the transcripts of debates give a fine example of debate in the church. (Can we imagine the U.S. Catholic Conference officially sponsoring and publishing a serene discussion of Marxism in the U.S. context?)

Pastoral and Political Praxis

Events in Latin America continue to propel the church hierarchy into having to take some kind of stand vis-à-vis power structures and governments. These declarations have become a veritable literary genre. In March 1975 the Paraguayan episcopate, which has found itself in continual conflict with the personal dictatorship of Stroessner, emitted a joint declaration with the federation of religious. Responding to accusations of "Marxism," it went on to denounce persecution of the church at the hands of the army and the official Colorado party. In Lent the bishops produced a pastoral letter around the Holy Year theme of reconciliation, weaving into it the need for conversion from social sin and in particular the temptations and problems inherent in the line of development being taken in the country.[130] The disappearance and death of two priests in Honduras at the hands of landowners provoked a whole series of reflections and statements from the hierarchy and Christian groups. Documents of this sort will usually mention the deeper structural injustices behind the specific incidents.

However, two documents released on May 6, 1973, by regional episcopal conferences in Brazil make a qualitative leap: They question the very basis of the capitalist system as it functions in Brazil.

I Have Heard the Cries of My People, produced by the bishops and

religious superiors of the Northeast, takes Exodus 3 as a leitmotiv.[131]
The bishops speak of themselves as "ministers of liberation"[132] who
must take a stand alongside their people. In the first part of the
document they cite an abundance of statistics on income, employment, malnutrition and its physical and mental effects, housing,
education, and health. They summarize Brazilian economic history
in search of an explanation, concluding that the present type of
development, "associated-dependent capitalism," must be maintained by the absolute power centered in the executive branch, massive propaganda, official terrorism, espionage, and secret police. The
Brazilian miracle is accomplished at the cost of the poor.

The lack of freedom, the violence of repression, injustices, the impoverishment of the people, and the fact that the interests of the nation are passing over
into foreign capital cannot be a sign that Brazil has found its own path to
historic achievement.[133]

The closing section weaves biblical themes with denunciation. The
church is not separate from the world; salvation comes from God,
who "breaks into the human masses . . . and goes on revealing himself in the long and complex process of human liberation."[134] Like
pharaoh, the powerful do not see the saving power in the people's
struggle. Fidelity to their mission as bishops demands an option for
God and for the people. Oppression and injustice come from international capitalism and its local allies. The situation calls for "an overall
historic project of the transformation of society."[135]

The historic process of class society and capitalist domination leads inexora-
bly toward class confrontation. Although it is a fact which becomes more
obvious every day, this confrontation is denied by the oppressors, a denial
which itself affirms it. The oppressed masses of workers, peasants, and the
many underemployed are becoming aware of it and are gradually taking on a
new liberating consciousness.

The dominated class has no other way to liberation but the long and
difficult march, already under way, toward the social ownership of the means
of production. This is the foundation for the huge historic project for the
complete transformation of present society into a new society. There it will be
possible to create the objective conditions within which the oppressed might
recover the humanity robbed from them, end the cries of their sufferings,
overcome class antagonisms, and finally win freedom.

The gospel calls us, all Christians and men of good will, to become involved
in its prophetic current.[136]

The companion document prepared by six bishops of the
Center-West is called *The Marginalization of a People: The Cry of the
Churches.*[137] It follows the same format with a looser style and perhaps

even bolder expression. The recurring image is that of a fruit tree: If the fruit is spoiled you have to examine the tree to see what is wrong; if the tree itself is bad "you pull it out. You plant another tree to bear better fruit for us to eat."

Citing statistics on employment, salaries, education, health, etc., the bishops conclude that the root of the problem in their area is land tenure which creates two classes: great landowners on the one hand and rural workers and small proprietors on the other. Present strategies of development are increasing the inequities. They too move on to criticize Brazilian capitalism and the way the state is facilitating the penetration of foreign capital.

The great majority of the people are marginalized. Yet only they can be the church. Jesus was understood by the poor because he was marginalized. The church itself, it must be admitted, has not always denounced the fact that the world was organized against the poor.

Capitalism must be overcome. It is the great wrong, the cumulative sin, the rotten root, the tree that bears the fruit we know: poverty, hunger, sickness, and death to the great majority. For this reason, the system of ownership of the means of production (of factories, of land, of commerce, of banks, of credit sources) must be overcome. . . . [The] church defends the right to property. . . . But it is the right of every human being, a right horribly disregarded and suppressed, because the majority, the immense majority, almost the totality of mankind is really deprived of this right which is, incidentally, recognized in our laws. . . .

Fear of change must be overcome. . . . We must believe in the force of the people. . . . To trust means to work at uniting the forces of the people, still weak because they are disunited. To trust is to be like Christ: The seed produces fruit only after disintegrating itself.

A different world must be created. We do not know what it should be. But we no longer have confidence in what is. We want a world in which the fruits of labor are shared by everyone. We want a world in which one works not to get rich but to provide everyone with the necessities of life: food, health, a house, education, clothing, shoes, water, and light. We want a world in which money will be at the service of men, and not man at the service of money. We want a world in which everyone can work for everybody, not a world divided in which each individual strives only for himself. We want a world in which there will be one people only, without divisions into rich and poor. We want a world in which everyone will do what he can for the good of all. . . .

We believe the new world shall be built above all by the work of those who are despised, like our people.[138]

The occasion of these documents was the tenth anniversary of *Pacem in Terris* and the twenty-fifth anniversary of the U.N. Declaration on Human Rights. What is new about these documents is that they do not simply reply to particular incidents or denounce symptoms, but seek to arrive at the underlying systemic causes of injustice, which they do not hesitate to name as capitalism. While they stop short of calling explicitly for socialism they do call for a radically different and classless society.

A raid on the office of the regional episcopal conference office in Recife resulted in the confiscation of many copies of the first document but further copies were mimeographed from those already in circulation. The printer of the second document and several of his coworkers were arrested and heavily fined.

These are examples of a certain kind of pastoral praxis in the hierarchy. For the church as a whole, the kind of praxis described in the previous article continues (conscientization, solidarity with the people, etc.) with increasing repression and few illusions that the revolution is near.

It seems to me that the original impetus for LT, coming in a period of optimism about revolutionary possibilities, encouraged a certain implicit model of liberation: seizure of state power within a given nation and its transformation through a socialist program (land reform, nationalization of resources, social control of the means of production). LT addressed itself to some basic issues such as the very notion of taking sides in a conflictive situation, class struggle, utilization of Marxist analysis, critique of "third ways" between capitalism and socialism, recognition of the ideological utilization of Christian symbols, etc.

On the local level Christians, including theologians, attempted to analyze events and actions in an ongoing way. Yet published LT does not get very far beyond the rather general concepts mentioned above. Beyond a basic legitimation of Christian participation in revolutionary struggle (although theologians such as Gustavo Gutiérrez insist that they are not "baptizing" revolution) LT does not shed much light on the actual options that Christians face.

Most works of LT, taking a political option for granted, are concerned with the consequences for faith. Gutiérrez states clearly that LT should not situate itself on the level of strategy and tactics.[139] It would seem that the underlying reason is that political action has its own "rationality" which is the proper domain of (committed) social science.

One thinker who does not accept this division of labor is Joseph Comblin. In *Théologie de la pratique révolutionnaire* he ranges widely over the operational aspects of the revolutionary struggle.[140]

Comblin's viewpoint is eclectic and he discusses a range of topics too wide even to summarize here. He differs significantly from most proponents of LT in his prodigious use of sources and his willingness to enter into detailed discussion of revolutionary theory and frequently to take polemical positions. As a theologian originally trained in Scripture he is clearly "out of his field"; evidently he thinks that his theological reflections should be anchored as concretely as possible.

Leaving aside the multiplicity of points developed by Comblin, I would like to single out two areas of special relevance to Latin America, the factor of the *nation* in revolution and his critique of the Popular Unity in Chile. Revolutionaries frequently speak as though class struggle and revolution were tautological. Comblin stresses that revolutions in the Third World must be national and are subject to ambiguity.

No revolution can really desire complete independence from the metropolis. Total emancipation is impossible because the empire is interiorized by each citizen of the dependent country. A national revolution has as its purpose the setting up of a national power capable of struggling with the metropolitan power. . . . There is a constant tension between class consciousness and national consciousness. . . . [141]

In the underdeveloped world, there cannot be any revolution except by stages, and any building up of socialism should be conceived with no dogmatism or exclusiveness, and as an imperfect process. Class struggle, since it exists first of all on a world scale, should be combined with the struggle for the formation of a nation. [142]

A national revolution is always ambiguous and the definitive step toward a new society that is just and human will not be possible until there is a radical change on a world level. In the meantime nonambiguity is impossible, and to look for purity is to be foreordained to failure. [143]

There are two alternatives for the Third World:

a national revolution led by a national movement that is unified, authoritarian, and based on popular consent and the support of all national classes, or a colonial fascism in order to maintain the Western way of life for the upper classes and a peripheric dependence on the center and to keep the popular classes downtrodden. [144]

For a number of years Comblin has stressed the importance of the factor of the nation. [145] One concludes that he sees a basic revolutionary strategy to be one of uniting the forces of a nation, accepting the necessity of a bourgeoisie in some sense while struggling that it be nationalist and not disproportionately privileged.

He is severe with the Popular Unity movement in Chile. While its sympathizers tend to focus simply on the obstacles from the U.S. and the Chilean right, Comblin insists that all factions of the U.P. misread what was happening. Rather than examine the real situation in Chile they simply dredged up various categories from the Marxist classics. Instead of uniting all of Chile, including the important middle classes, around a project of national liberation, they facilitated the work of the right by overstressing class struggle and attempting an incoherent mixture of populism and utopianism as a program.[146]

Comblin insists that the great danger, and indeed, the fact today is the tendency toward fascism. He analyzes in some detail the new type of fascist state emerging in Latin America as well as the type of confrontation of the church with these new regimes.[147] These ideas have been further developed in an essay called "The Church's New Praxis with Regard to National Security Regimes."[148]

The new military regimes mark a break with the Western political tradition. (In some ways their origin may be traced to 1947 in the U.S. when the National Security Council and the CIA were established.) In Latin America Brazil is the prototype. The traditional executive, legislative, and judicial powers are done away with for practical purposes and in its place a national security council and central intelligence agency (with different names) become the supreme organs of government.

These governments operate on a number of premises (explicit or implicit): The world is seen in geopolitical terms; the people are mobilized to build up military and economic power; the elites of the nation, and especially the military, are taken to be the agents of development; all opposition is branded as communism. The architects of this society would see the church and Christianity as their natural allies.

For some time the church did not perceive the real nature of the new regimes and at first its responses were improvised. Experience is gradually revealing the true nature of the struggle. The points of confrontation are human rights and the functioning of the existing development model. Defense of human rights is not peripheral to preaching the gospel: "It is actually the present day proclamation of the very substance of Jesus' message."[149] The gospel is a call to freedom, including freedom from the absolute power of the state and its ideology. This stance of the church is related to the very conception of God since for the totalitarian regimes the image of God is the state, law and order, while for Christianity the image of God is the person, the common person, the poor person. Similarly this new praxis invokes a Christology in which Jesus cannot be considered apart from his body, made up of people.

In criticizing the official development model the church goes to the heart: Such development is antipeople. And thus the church is fighting for its own survival since without a people there can be no church: Masses cannot be a church—"only a nation can follow Jesus Christ."[150] The church is not simply "speaking for those who have no voice" but it is to be their voice so that they can recognize it as their own and thus learn once again how to speak. This is a voice raised to confront the state, the power. The bishops thus demythologize state power.

Clearly Comblin claims to be raising to the level of a theory of the church's praxis what in fact the two regional conferences of bishops in Brazil did with their documents and what other hierarchies have done perhaps less directly. In this connection we may cite the example of the Chilean church, particularly in the Committees for Reconciliation and Peace, whose functions have been taken over by parishes since the Committees were disbanded by the government. Certainly there are signs of the confrontation Comblin speaks of but it does not seem to be a general phenomenon yet.

Segundo, Dussel, Miranda

Let us turn to consider three thinkers who have been engaged in systematic reflection on fundamental aspects of Christianity in the light of liberation.

Nowhere in his five-volume series of "theology for artisans of a new humanity"[151] does Juan Luis Segundo employ the phrase "liberation theology," although references to Medellín and its categories begin with volume 3 and become more frequent later. This series was worked out in a dialogue process with laypeople in Montevideo during the years after the Council. It is thus the result of a community effort over several years, and yet it bears much of Segundo's personal style and originality.

Although this series was elaborated before the explicit emergence of LT, its basic thrust is the same. At one point Segundo states: "The central theme of this whole series has been Christian liberty and its involvement in history. . . . "[152] Each volume deals with a theme that parallels a traditional theological tract: church, grace, God, sacraments, sin. Yet in each case this concern for liberation in history gives Segundo's vision an operational thrust; there is no separation of doctrine and ethics.

Segundo's perspective is decidedly Latin American. As part of the dominated "periphery," Latin Americans can experience the breakup of the identity between the "West" and "Christianity." Latin America may be the seedbed for a new idea of history (since it is historically Western) and a new idea of God which is closer to revelation.[153] Similarly, in Latin America, "secularization" does not mean so much the end of a religious sphere but rather the fact that "everything, absolutely everything in the church must be translated from the 'religious sphere' to the historic task."[154] Medellín is really much more radical than the "Dutch catechism."[155]

The purpose of volume 3 is to take a "critical approach to the God of Western society."[156] For example, in contrast to traditional trinitarian analogues (the mind, person-to-person love), Segundo suggests that the experience suggested by the Trinity is the experience of society.

God, the Christian God, is love. But not only or not so much a love (false love) which unites two people and separates them from the world and from time. But rather the love which builds human society in history. . . .

We do not have a solitary God, more or less paternal. . . . We have a *We-God* as every *we* on earth would like to be and strives to be. Despite all our twisted and disfigured images, the God whom Jesus revealed to us is a *society-God*.[157]

There is a real correlation between our society which exalts private property and proposes fulfillment in a completely private sphere (a house with a fence around it) and our image of God as remote and disincarnate. Conversely, as Christians strive for fulfillment in building a new society they will better appreciate an incarnate God.[158] One who chooses atheism rather than accept a God allied to capitalism may actually be adoring a God truer than our own. Is it not possible that

when we say we believe in God we are putting onto that divine name the low and selfish values of our own life, values which are not God? And thus is it not possible that when we say "I believe" we are making an act of faith in capitalism, injustice, suffering, inefficacy, selfishness?[159]

One example of the Latin American approach to secularization noted above is Segundo's treatment of the sacraments. Their efficacy "cannot be understood as the efficacy 'imputed' to a juridically valid rite":

It demands that the sacraments be historically "true": that is, efficacious with respect to man's liberation in real-life history. In other words, the sacraments will be valid and efficacious, as Christ intended, to the extent that they are a consciousness-raising and motivating celebration of man's liberative action in history. That does not reduce them to a merely human gesture. God is operative in them, but his activity consists in working through the praxis of man. Hence it condenses in the sacramental celebration where man intensifies his conscious awareness of the import and liberative force of his action.[160]

Segundo frequently makes unexpected connections, e.g., between sacraments and economic and political "rites."

Just as in the case of the sacred rite, people *attribute* an illogical efficacy to a model that is supposed to be beneficial to those "in the process of development" (e.g., the investment of foreign private capital). Just as in sacramental practice, we have a rite which actually is a cult rendered to an interested god. And the god in this case is the affluent group that offers "aid," that appears to be giving when in fact it is receiving. Just as the salvific efficacy attributed to the sacraments masks the loss of time, energy, and historical efficacity, so developmentalist aid maintains in a proletarian status the nations on the margin of the politico-economic empire. They remain instruments, not subjects of their own history.[161]

In the same fashion both the priest and the technical expert remain part of "another world" and are expected to be apolitical. There are also parallels between sacraments and the political rites of formal democracy, dictatorship and populism, e.g., a liturgical renewal which does not permit people to express their own conflicts and yearnings becomes a "liturgical populism" like political populism where charismatic figures are bridge-builders to a world of power above.[162] Without determining cause-and-effect Segundo holds that one attitude feeds the other.

Evolution and Human Guilt is Segundo's most personal contribution in this series. Basically he argues that although Christianity has traditionally been presented and understood in immobilist terms, it can best be understood in an evolutionary framework. From Teilhard de Chardin he takes the suggestion that while the physical universe is running down (entropy) there are concentrations of energy in higher and higher syntheses. Thus "love, grace, life, and God's gift make up the positive vector of evolution" while "egoism, sin, and enslavement to the world and the flesh make up the negative vector." "All sin is antievolutionary."[163] Sin is thus the facile synthesis, the easy way out, and sociologically speaking, it is the way of the mass. Love is the difficult synthesis and is proper to minorities. Thus history is a dialectical process of masses and minorities. This notion provides a basis for a recurrent theme in Segundo's writings: The church is not called to be the mass but the ferment, the creative minority.

Throughout this series Segundo takes as a starting point commonly accepted notions and images and works through them to a Christianity more at the service of liberation.

In a more recent essay Segundo, speaking explicitly of LT, raises the question of whether theology has anything to say regarding the alternative of capitalism or socialism in the Third World.[164] He notes that European (political) theology, rather than making a clear option, claims that the Christian will simply relativize any absolute or any system. Segundo, on the other hand, says that theology must be bold (as was Jesus) and find absolute salvation in fallible and ambiguous events. The eschatological aspect of Christian theology does not relativize the present but binds it to the absolute. The liberating event has a causal relationship to the kingdom—it is not simply an "image," "anticipation," etc. Thus the theologian should not take the position of a judicious observer in the middle but should clearly take on the sensitivity of the left: In the options over racism, international justice, or capitalism vs. socialism, the kingdom itself is at stake, albeit in a fragmentary fashion.[165]

I have been surveying Segundo's work without being able to use his systematic work on LT, which is soon to appear.[166] Yet his basic grounding in Scripture and what is happening in Latin America, as well as the penetration of his original, even idiosyncratic, observations should be apparent here.

One of the richest and most developed of LTs comes from Enrique Dussel, an Argentine layman, who is by profession and education a philosopher and historian. His output has been prolific[167] yet his theology keeps returning to a number of central points.[168]

It seems to me that Dussel's basic contribution is to translate into philosophical language the issues of LT. To take one example which proceeds from geopolitics to epistemology: Five centuries ago there were seven self-contained empires on the planet (Europe, the remains of the Byzantine empire, the Arabic world, India, China, the Mayan-Aztecs, and the Incas). One of these, Europe (and the North-Atlantic) succeeded in conquering the others and in becoming the Center, and defining itself as the *oekumene;* the European "world" became simply "the world."

Accordingly, European thinking is centered on the self, from Descartes's *cogito* all the way to Nietzsche. Actually Descartes's *ego cogito* was preceded by the Iberian *"Yo conquisto."* This kind of mentality sees its own world as a Totality, which for Dussel is what the Bible understands as "flesh." There is thus a linkage: Center (North Atlantic)="world"="flesh"="the system."

Now the basic biblical experience is the opposite of European thinking: It is face-to-face encounter. God comes from outside the system—in his Word, in incarnation, in Jesus, in the prophet, in the poor. The system, however, does not permit this face-to-face encounter with the other. It does not permit the other to be other but rather must reduce the other to the self's terms: domination. Thus there is a basic clash between Christianity and the system.[169]

These notions, which reappear throughout his work illustrate what I take to be Dussel's method. For him *"faith is a light that existentially exercises revealed categories."*[170] Thus faith is not so much a body of knowledge as a series of guidelines for making sense out of life. These categories include "flesh" (totality), the poor (the human outsider), God as creator and redeemer, the Word, the Spirit (outreaching modes of the divine in face-to-face encounter). Theology is an explicit and methodical use of these categories which Christians use implicitly and existentially. Dussel does not see theology as "dia-lectic," for the dialectical method can only show the contradictions of the system but cannot really go beyond it. He sees theology as "ana-lectic" since it confronts the system from the outside with the revealing Word. It then goes on to a liberating praxis that includes a historical project, which is at once a new historical order and a sign of the total liberation in the kingdom.[171]

Dussel applies these ideas systematically to ecclesiology. God founds his church from the outside in the world (flesh, system). The church, become flesh in the world, tends to fall into being identified with the closed system (self-identification with the Prince of this world, which is the sin of the church: Holy Roman Empire, Christian countries, Western Christian civilization).

But the essential nature of the church as the liberating community and institution requires it to identity itself with the oppressed so as to "break down the barriers" of the systems which have become closed by the work of sin or by injustice, whether political—at national or international level—economic, social, cultural, or sexual. The sign (*semeion* of St. John's gospel) of the church, its proclamation, can only be effected by involving the community in the movement of liberation (Hebrew—*pasah* means moving, march, or flight), to move a system which acts oppressively towards becoming a new system which acts to liberate. . . . The Eucharist . . . is a foretaste, a feast of liberation from sin. . . . [172]

To my knowledge, Dussel is the first Latin American theologian to advert to sexual oppression and the only one to give it some importance. His specific observations would offer little or nothing to the feminist movement and his impressions of feminism in the rich world seem somewhat one-dimensional, at least as he saw it in 1972.[173] It is nevertheless an important contribution to have integrated sexual liberation into his own vision and to have put it on the agenda for Latin American LT.

José Porfirio Miranda, a Mexican philosopher and Scripture scholar seems to have worked out his own ideas independently of Latin American LT. Yet his *Marx and the Bible* shows a number of affinities to Dussel's thought, although the style is very different.[174]

Miranda states that he is not looking for easy parallels between Marx and the Bible but is simply seeking to understand the Bible. In the first chapter he argues that property in the West, and in particular the private ownership of the means of production, is founded on violence and runs counter to the Scriptures and church fathers. Western culture and "Christian theology-philosophy" have upheld the social order of differentiating property.

The three core chapters, "The God of the Bible," "God's Intervention in History," and "Law and Civilization," are efforts to get at what the Bible really says, a message Western civilization has been unable to perceive. Miranda's argument is that the God revealed in the Bible is a God who wants justice between people—in fact, that is the only thing God wants. So, e.g., the message of the prophets is: I do not want cultus but interhuman justice.[175] God's only interest in intervening in history is justice. What the Bible says about sin and the law relates to civilization itself:

According to Paul sin is incarnated in social structures, in the powerful wisdom of the world, in the human civilization which forces us to act in a determined way in spite of the contrary conscience which man still has regarding what is good and what is bad. . . . Sin . . . has become structured into human civilization itself, whose most characteristic and quintessential expression is the law.[176]

God will save mankind, but he will destroy without a trace the entire old civilizing axiological and organizational structuralization of mankind. . . .

Paul wants a world without law. . . . Neither Kropotkin nor Bakunin nor Marx nor Engels made assertions against the law more powerful and subversive than those which Paul makes. . . . That sin is incarnated in civilization is demonstrated nowhere more clearly than in the fact that Western theology has missed this message of Paul, and yet this is the only thing that Paul has to say. . . .

When God raised up the outlawed Jesus, he was justifying the impious one, him whom the whole of the law and human civilization crucified for being impious. . . . The insurrection of authentic Christianity against all law and all civilization which has ever existed in history is a subversion which knows no limits.[177]

The final chapter explores affinities between faith and (Marxist) dialectics. Both aim at achieving real justice in the world.

Marx and Paul coincide in their intuition of the totality of evil: Sin and injustice form an all-comprehensive and all-pervasive organic structure. Paul calls this totality *kosmos*. Marx calls it "capitalism."[178]

The most revolutionary historical thesis, in which, in contrast with all Western ideologies, the Bible and Marx coincide, is this: Sin and evil, which were later structured into an enslaving civilizing system, are not inherent to mankind and history; they began one day through a human work and can, therefore, be eliminated.[179]

The West, and theology, have refused to see this since "there can be no news for the Greek mind which thus shows itself to be inextirpably the ideology of the status quo."[180]

Both Marx and the Bible believe people can cease being selfish and can find fulfillment in serving the neighbor. Both the Bible and Marx are opposed to the "objectivity" of Western science which separates morality as a field apart: Dialectical knowledge and biblical knowledge demand praxis.

Miranda concludes by speculating on a hope for the elimination of death. He suggests that Marx was not dialectical enough to embrace resurrection.[181] "In a world in which there is no longer oppression or enmity or mistrust or injustice, death too will disappear."[182]

Miranda adduces dense documentation from Scripture scholars, while frequently taking issue with them.

This book provoked a pamphlet of semi-rebuttal from (mainly Jesuit—Miranda is an ex-Jesuit) scripture scholars, theologians, and experts in Marxism and church social doctrine. The contributors to *Our Judgment on Marx and the Bible* generally praise Miranda's intention and concern while accusing him of one-dimensionality or reductionism.[183] The scripture scholars in particular point out strains in the Bible which militate against Miranda, e.g., Paul's preaching of subjection to civil authorities and the fact that he does not attack slavery as an institution. As will be apparent below, I find myself in substantial agreement with this critique while at the same time challenged by many individual observations of Miranda.

I indicated above that Miranda and Dussel, through their very diverse styles have interesting convergences. Miranda notes that Greek thought

involves the disappearance of the radical otherness which, falling under the power of the thinker, loses its resistance as an exterior being. . . .
In contrast, the God of the Bible must always be present as the Other.[184]

The Greek *kosmos* appears as a "totality."[185] Similarly Miranda makes a frontal attack on Western civilization: "The West or Christianity . . . either . . . or: This is the conclusion of our study."[186]

Miranda's *El ser y el mesías* is a study of St. John's gospel which again takes on Western thought and especially existentialism as interlocutor and antagonist.[187]

Concluding Personal Remarks

To this point I have been trying to report on some developments in Latin American LT and to highlight what seem to me to be significant expressions. In this closing section I would like to indicate what seem to be issues which need sharpening. In the process some of my own preferences will become clear.

To begin with the "reinterpretation of Christian faith" thrust, I find that I am frequently somewhat out of tune with some presentations. (The reader may judge whether it is a case of judgment, temperament, or basic option.) Sometimes liberation is offered as *the* key to understanding human history, the Bible, Christianity. In its most extreme form we find Miranda arguing that the only thing desired by the God of the Bible is interhuman justice.

My own perspective is rather more limited. I am most concerned about my own world and my own generation—the last third of the twentieth century—which becomes the horizon for determining my life task. As I seek to interpret my life I find that one of the most evident signs of our time is a profound crisis of Western civilization and a struggle for liberation.

However, I resist leaping from this sign of our times to erecting an overarching theory that covers all history. Let us suppose that at some future date economic exploitation is ended, there is a genuine participatory socialism, and it can truly be said that people are "subjects of their own destiny"—will this mean the coming of the definitive kingdom? that there will be no further crises (or challenges)? Is it not possible that entirely new potentialities and problems will present themselves and call for new interpretations of the human task and Christian faith which will not be covered by the rubric of "liberation"? (It should be evident that I do not accept the notion that we are still living in "prehistory" until the dawn of communism.)

By the same token an interpretation which sees "liberation" as the key to all meaning can give only a negative meaning to the greater part of human history—let alone prehistory. This strikes me as another example of Western ethnocentrism. To put it another way, "static" civilizations are not thereby devoid of meaning.

I do not intend to weaken or relativize the importance of liberation struggles. To state that liberation is not an adequate key for understanding all past history and all future development does not in the least imply that it is not essential for understanding my generation and for putting my life task into perspective.

The biblical symbols are extremely plastic. Thus today we give the exodus-pasch a social and political interpretation. Does this mean that we are finally discovering the "true" meaning of the Scriptures after nineteen centuries of subjection in the straitjacket of Greek immobilist thought? Or is it because historical conditions have reached a point where we see that a qualitatively new kind of society is possible?

It was Marx and the socialist tradition that first opened the Western imagination to transcending capitalism. Because of their work (itself deriving from medieval "heresies" and thus from the Bible) we can discover socialist and subversive motifs in the Bible. This new reading, legitimate and even necessary, does not render false all preceding readings that emerged in other contexts. The point is that the biblical symbols are plastic or—to vary the metaphor—they are seeds that contain unsuspected potentialities.

Thus today's liberation-interpretation is not a rediscovery of what the biblical authors *really* meant (*pace* Miranda). It is a discovery of what it means for us. This argument for plasticity does not mean that a racist or fascist theology would be legitimate. I am simply arguing that within the basic thrust of revelation the interpretation is open. Each generation must make its own reading for which it is responsible.

Obviously the biblical symbols have been utilized ideologically, and Christians have been slow to arrive at a socialist reading. After all, it is over a century since the Communist Manifesto.

To reiterate: I am wholeheartedly for a theology that emerges from participation in the "historic project" of our own generation, but I am loathe to leap to the conclusion that "liberation" is the key to all history. (For similar reasons, while I have always been intrigued by Teilhard de Chardin's synthesis, I find that the closer I get to the horizon of my lifetime the less light it sheds on my options.)

To indicate another preference (or prejudice): LT insists on being rooted in praxis and its exponents are involved in very concrete (and frequently dangerous) aspects of the struggle. Yet in their theological reflection they often remain on a very generic level. As pointed out above, it seems that they accept a certain division of labor: The "people" and particularly the vanguards make options, social scientists provide instruments of analysis, while they as theologians limit themselves to reflecting on what this praxis means for Christian faith. In some cases the division is even more explicit: They will not mix theology with the "science" of Marxism (recalling that the "conflict" of faith and science occurred because their boundaries were not respected). It should be clear that many do devote a great deal of time and energy to specific problems of praxis in their lives. However these specific problems do not enter their theology.

For my part, I would hope that theologians would elucidate with more clarity some of the issues involved in praxis. To take one issue mentioned by Dussel, Míguez Bonino, and Comblin: Is the basic struggle to be conceived as *class struggle* or a *people's struggle?* Some years ago the discussion did not surface. Class struggle was affirmed as a part of the creed, so to speak. Yet it is quite possible that concentration on the internal class struggle may facilitate external domination. Today some argue that the basic struggle is against external domination and that the whole *people* (in Latin America the *pueblo* is a reality) must be united. The goal for now is nation-building, which must take preference over the elimination of class differences. On the other hand, some who work with Indians or others "at the bottom," will understandably be less than enthusiastic over a strategy which seems to postpone the rectification of the most evident injustices that they experience.

Should Christians dedicate their energies toward the achievement of national independence and Latin American integration even through present governments? Or should anything short of total revolution be rejected as reformism? My whole point in raising the question in this oversimplified form is simply to indicate that I think it is a live issue for LT and should not be left wholly to outside (even revolutionary) "experts."

Similarly, I think that an urgent topic is—to rephrase Míguez Bonino—"doing theology in a *counter*-revolutionary situation." The first works of LT came out of the earlier "euphoria" of revolutionary expectation and dealt with many important long-range issues, e.g., use of Marxist categories, love and class struggle. However, it is undeniable that at present the trend (short-term?) is counter-revolution—a response to the emergence of revolutionary forces in the 1960s. More than two-thirds of Latin America is under military rule. Perhaps these regimes at first seemed accidental or transitional. However, similar regimes have shown a great staying power (corporatist states in Spain and Portugal). For some time now revolutionary groups have been reassessing their situation and recognizing that the struggle is long-term.

Comblin has performed an important service in suggesting that the new regimes are a new model of society and that the church is adopting (or will adopt) a new praxis in this kind of society. I do not intend to endorse Comblin's (seemingly gloomy) perspective but rather to indicate that the here-and-now praxis of Christians and the church is as important a task for LT as a reflection on the socialist future.

NOTES

1. Camilo Torres, *Cristianismo y revolución*, ed. Oscar Maldonado, Guitemie Olivieri, Germán Zabala (Mexico, D.F.: Era, 1970), p. 407 (interview).

2. Phillip Berryman, "Camilo Torres, Revolutionary-Theologian," *Commonweal* 96, no. 7 (April 21, 1972), pp. 164–67.

3. *Theological Studies* has published the most widely read and most influential single essay, Gustavo Gutiérrez' "Notes for a Theology of Liberation": *Theological Studies* 31 (1970), pp. 243–61.

4. Juan Luis Segundo, "Una iglesia sin teología," in *De la sociedad a la teología* (Buenos Aires: Lohlé, 1970). Segundo, a Uruguayan Jesuit, has completed a five-volume work that has emerged in a process of dialogue with organized lay groups spanning several years. The English translation is *Theology for Artisans of a New Humanity*, trans. John Drury, 5 vols. (Maryknoll, New York: Orbis Books, 1973–74). See also his *The Liberation of Theology*, trans. John Drury (Maryknoll, New York: Orbis Books, 1976).

5. Somewhat at random: Celso Furtado, Osvaldo Sunkel, Theotonio dos Santos, Anibal Pinto, Helio Jaguaribe, Antonio García, Rodolfo Stavenhagen, Fernando Henrique Cardoso. Cf. the bibliographical article by Gonzalo Arroyo, "Pensamiento latinoamericano sobre subdesarollo y dependencia," *Mensaje*, October 1968, pp. 516–17. This line of thought corresponds to the "radical analysis" of Baran-Sweezy, Magdoff, and others. Cf. CICOP conference proceedings and many Orbis books, e.g., Denis Goulet and Michael Hudson, *The Myth of Aid* (Maryknoll, New York: Orbis Books, 1971). For a very readable presentation, see Gary MacEoin, *Revolution Next Door* (New York: Holt, Rinehart and Winston, 1971).

6. Most notably, "A Letter to the Peoples of the Third World" (August 1967), in *Between Honesty and Hope: Documents from and about the Church in Latin America. Issued at Lima by the Peruvian Bishops' Commission for Social Action*, trans. John Drury (Maryknoll, New York: Maryknoll Publications, 1970), pp. 3–12. Other collections of these manifestos include *Iglesia latinoamericana: ¿Protesta o profecía?* (Avellaneda, Argentina: Búsqueda, 1969) and *Signos de liberación* (Lima: CEP, 1973).

7. One of the most lucid expressions: Lucio Gera, Guillermo Rodríguez, "Apuntes para una interpretación de la Iglesia argentina," *Víspera*, no. 15, February 1970, pp. 59–88. It should be noted that "Europe" is the reference point for the Latin American church's awareness of its own particularity; hence the frequent allusions to "European" theology in this article. Moreover, in general "church" refers to the Roman Catholic church, although the Protestant contribution to liberation theology has been extremely significant.

8. Medellín, *Conclusiones: Presencia de la Iglesia en la actual tranformación de América latina*, Segunda Conferencia General del Episcopado Latinoamericano. We will be quoting from the sixth edition (Bogotá, 1971), by document and paragraph number (English edition: *The Church in the Present-Day Transformation of Latin America in the Light of the Council*, vol. 2, *Conclusions* (Bogota: General Secretariat of Celam, 1970), distri-

buted by the Latin American Bureau of the United States Catholic Conference, Washington, D.C.

9. Ibid., "Message to the Peoples of Latin America."

10. Outline of conclusions: Human Promotion (Justice, Peace, Family and Demography, Education, Youth); Evangelization and Growth in Faith (Pastoral, Pastoral of Elites, Catechesis, Liturgy); Visible Church and Its Structures (Lay Movements, Priests, Religious, Formation of the Clergy, Poverty of the Church, *Pastoral de conjunto*, Mass Media). *Pastoral de conjunto* is difficult to translate in a single phrase: It involves planning, team pastoral work, organization, etc.

11. Medellín, *Conclusiones*, "Catechesis," no. 4.

12. For a trenchant criticism of social sciences, cf. C. Wright Mills, *The Sociological Imagination* (New York: Oxford University Press, 1959).

13. Medellín, *Conclusiones*, "Pastoral Concern for the Elites," no. 6.

14. Ibid., no. 7.

15. Ibid., no. 8. There follows an interesting correlation of the faith of these types.

16. Ibid., "Peace," no. 5.

17. Ibid., no. 6.

18. Ibid., nos. 8–10.

19. Ibid., no. 16 (emphasis added).

20. "The Latin American business system, and through it the present economy, respond to an erroneous conception of the right to property, of the means of production, and of the very purpose of the economy. . . .

"The liberal capitalist system and the temptation of the Marxist system would seem to exhaust the possibilities. . . of transforming economic structures. Both systems attack the dignity of the human person: one of them has as its presupposition the primacy of capital, its power, and its discriminatory use in function of profit; the other, though ideologically it holds for a humanism, looks rather toward collective man, and in practice is translated into a totalitarian concentration in the power of state. We must denounce the fact that Latin America seems closed in between these two options and remains dependent on one or other of the power centers which channel its economy" (Ibid., "Justice," no. 10).

21. Ibid., "Education," no. 8.

22. Ibid., no. 3.

23. Ibid., "Catechesis," no. 6.

24. Ibid., "Education," no. 9.

25. Ibid., "Youth," no. 15.

26. Ibid., "Catechesis," no. 9.

27. Ibid., "Joint Pastoral Planning," no. 10.

28. Ibid., "Justice," no. 17.

29. Ibid., "Peace," no. 24.

30. Ibid., "Priests," no. 19.

31. Ibid., "Poverty of the Church," no. 4.

32. *Noticias Aliadas* (news service based in Lima, dedicated to church and liberation in Latin America), August 18, 1971.

33. See *My Life For My Friends: The Diary of Néstor Paz, Christian* (Maryknoll, New York: Orbis Books, 1975).

34. *Noticias Aliadas*, September 10, 1969, p. 3.

35. Ibid., July 4, 1969, p. 5.

36. Hugo Assmann, *Opresión-liberación: Deasafío a los cristianos* (Montevideo: Tierra Nueva, 1971), p. 69; in English see Assmann's *Theology for a Nomad Church* (Maryknoll, New York: Orbis Books, 1976), p. 65; parts of *Opresión-liberación* are included in this English translation. Hugo Assmann, exiled from Brazil, forced to leave Bolivia, at present in Costa Rica, writes an aggressive and complicated prose. A doctor in theology, he has claimed that his most theological work is his reporting on the guerrilla action in Teoponte, Bolivia. See his *Teoponte: Experiencia guerrillera boliviana* (Caracas: Nueva Izquierda, 1971).

37. Noel Olaya, "Unidad cristiana y lucha de clases," *Cristianismo y sociedad*, nos. 24–25 (1970), p. 63. Olaya, a Colombian, has been left without assignment by the archbishop of Bogotá for several years, though he collaborates with CELAM institutes. At present he is working on anthropological investigations with Indians.

38. Quoted in ibid., p. 65.

39. Gustavo Gutiérrez, *A Theology of Liberation*, trans. Caridad Inda and John Eagleson (Maryknoll, New York: Orbis Books, 1973); first published as *Teología de la liberación. Perspectivas* (Lima: CEP, 1971). Gutiérrez here quotes a pastoral letter of the French bishops recognizing the existence of class struggle. The most recognized single theologian of liberation in Latin America, Gutiérrez works with the university and as consultant to bishops and pastoral teams in Peru.

40. Ibid., p. 278.

41. Alex Morelli, "Un ensayo teológico sobre la violencia," in *Liberación en América latina* (Bogotá, 1971), pp. 165–89, 206–08. Also Alex Morelli, *Libera a mi pueblo* (Buenos Aires: Lohlé, 1971), and special issue of *Cristianismo y sociedad*, "Crítica a la violencia en América latina" (four articles), no. 28 (1971).

42. Paulo Freire, *Pedagogy of the Oppressed* (New York: Seabury, 1971); also *Educación como práctica de la libertad* (Montevideo: Tierra Nueva, 1969). It is impossible to overstate the importance of Freire for the Christian left, especially from 1965–70. Most of the theologians here presented have close personal associations with Freire. He himself is deeply Christian. For recent positions cf. *La misión educativa de la Iglesia en América latina* (mimeo.; Santiago, 1972).

43. Gutiérrez, *Theology of Liberation*, pp. 53ff. Also in *La pastoral de la Iglesia en América Latina* (Montevideo: MIEC-JECI, 1968). This latter is a most penetrating analysis of different pastoral approaches, detecting the underlying (implicit) theology of each.

44. Gutiérrez, *Theology of Liberation*, p. 65.

45. Instituto Latinoamericano de Doctrina y Estudios Sociales; cf. article by Yves Vaillancourt, originally in *Víspera*, April 1971, reprinted in LADOC (translation service of the United States Catholic Conference) 2, 13a, December 1971.

46. Medellín, *Conclusiones*, "Message to the Peoples of Latin America."

47. Assmann, "Iglesia y proyecto histórico," in *Opresión-liberación*, pp. 167ff.

48. *Noticias Aliadas*, August 18, 1971, p. 1.

49. Reprinted in *Gamos*, Boletín de Centro de Investigación y Estudios Familiares, nos. 55 and 56.

50. "Reflexiones sobre el documento de trabajo 'Evangelio, política y socialismos' " (mimeo.).

51. Ibid., p. 11.

52. José Pablo Richard Guzmán, "Racionalidad socialista y verificación histórica del cristianismo," *Cuadernos de la realidad nacional* (Santiago, Chile) no. 12, April 1972, pp. 144–53.

53. Ibid., p. 151.

54. James Conway, *Marx and Jesus: Liberation Theology in Latin America* (New York: Carlton, 1973).

55. Segundo, "Instrumentos de la teología latinoamericana," in *Liberación en América latina*, p. 38.

56. Giulio Girardi, "Christianity and Marxism" (mimeo.).

57. "Cristianismo y marxismo" (Santiago, Chile), April 1971 (mimeo.).

58. *Búsqueda de coincidenicas* (orig.).

59. Gutiérrez observes that Althusser's structuralist version of Marxism is a kind of positivism; correspondingly, the Christian position here resembles fideism. Cf. Louis Althusser, *For Marx* (New York: Pantheon, 1970).

60. In this sense religion is at the level of ideology and is to be purified (brought to the rational and spiritual level) not only by faith but by science (Freud as well as Marx); see p. 24.

61. Ronaldo Muñoz, "Lucha de clases y evangelio" (Santiago, Chile; mimeo.) p. 12.

62. Cf. Joseph Comblin, *Théologie de la révolution*, vol. 1 (Paris: Editions Universitaires 1970), pp. 69–74, 184–205, for criticism of magisterium. Also Arnoldo Centeno, "Liberación y magisterio," in *Liberación en América latina*, pp. 131–62. Comblin, a Belgian, has worked in Chile and Brazil since the late fifties. His work has a European thoroughness but is rooted in the Latin American reality.

63. "Final Document of the Convention," in *Christians and Socialism: Documents of the Christians for Socialism Movement in Latin America*, ed. John Eagleson, trans. John Drury (Maryknoll, New York: Orbis Books, 1975), p. 174.

64. Camilo Torres, *Cristianismo y revolución*, p. 391.

65. Alberto Methol Ferre, "Iglesia y sociedad opulenta: Una crítica a Suenens desde América latina," special supplement to *Víspera*, September 1969. The greater part of the article takes up Suenens's proposals relating to collegiality, episcopal conferences, nuncios, the Curia, the pope. Behind the idea of a weakening of Roman centralism and the development of particular churches Methol Ferre sees a "formal egalitarianism in the style of the proclamations of the bourgeoisie" which would conceal "the primacy of the rich, grand, powerful local churches," by analogy with the U.N. Further evidence is Suenens's idea of seeking the advice of "heads of large businesses, management, sociologists, specialists in communications, public relations, and prospective." Citing Küng's fear that "progressive" European bishops might be outweighed by the presidents of African and Asian conferences, he points out that theological progressives can be social reactionaries—meaning Küng himself. He sincerely believes that Rome protects the poor churches of the "periphery" against the rich powerful churches of the (North Atlantic) "center."

66. Medellín, *Conclusiones*, "Lay Movements," no. 12 (Spanish: *acontecer*).

67. Gutiérrez, *Theology of Liberation*, p. 261.

68. Ibid., p. 262.

69. Hugo Assmann, "El aporte cristiano al proceso de liberación de América latina," reprinted in *Contacto* (Mexico) 8, no. 2, p. 19.

70. Ibid., p. 2.

71. Segundo Galilea interview "Crisis y renovación de la fe," *Misión abierta* (Madrid) no. 89 (September-October 1972), pp. 486–87. In the same issue, "La fe como principio crítico de promoción de la religiosidad popular," pp. 426–36. Galilea, a Chilean, has specialized in the pastoral side of these questions and has been director of CELAM's pastoral institute in Quito, recently closed. He has published numerous articles and small collections of articles. This issue of *Misión abierta* is a symposium on liberation theology and features articles by Gutiérrez, Comblin, Dussel, Segundo, etc., many of which also appear in *Fe cristiana y cambio social en América latina: Encuentro de El Escorial, 1972* (Salamanca: Sígueme, 1973).

72. For analysis of pastoral work, see Gutiérrez, *Theology of Liberation*, pp. 53ff. and *Pastoral de la Iglesia.* Also, from a sociological point of view, a typology in Ivan Vallier, "Religious Elites: Differentiations and Developments in Roman Catholicism," in *Elites in Latin America*, ed. Seymour M. Lipset and Aldo Solari (New York: Oxford University Press, 1967), further developed in Vallier, *Catholicism, Social Control, and Modernization in Latin America* (Englewood Cliffs, N.J.: Prentice-Hall, 1970).

73. *Noticias Aliadas*, May 3, 1969, p. 3.

74. Assmann, *Theology for a Nomad Church*, p. 100.

75. In this connection it is interesting to note the very frequent use of Christian symbols in protest music; also "protest Masses."

76. Iglesia y Sociedad en América Latina. In many countries, especially toward the south, ISAL ecumenical reflection (-action) groups exist.

77. We cite the review *Cristianismo y sociedad* (Montevideo) and at random some of the principal thinkers: Rubem Alves, José Míguez Bonino, Emilio Castro, Julio de Santa Ana, Richard Shaull, Sergio Arce, Christian Lalive, Leopoldo Niilus, Pierre Furter. A collection: *De la Iglesia y la sociedad* (Montevideo, 1971).

78. Olaya, "Unidad cristiana," p. 68.

79. Comblin, "El tema de la liberación en el pensamiento cristiano latinoamericano" (Santiago, Chile; mimeo.), p. 3; originally appeared in special issue "Libération, nouveau nom du salut," *Revue nouvelle*, May-June 1972.

80. Ibid., passim.

81. Words of President Pastrana: "In an era characterized by tremendous pressures and anxieties, men have always looked to God for support, because their faith in him constitutes, especially for people in misery, their only hope and perhaps their only reason for existence" *(Noticias Aliadas*, June 30, 1971, p. 11). A similar situation occurred in Argentina in 1969 when President Onganía dedicated Argentina to the Immaculate Heart of Mary *(Noticias Aliadas*, December 17, 1969).

82. *Noticias Aliadas*, October 2, 1971, p. 8.

83. Ibid., January 9, 1971.

84. Assmann, "La función legitimadora de la religión para la dictadura brasileira," *Opresión-liberación*, pp. 186–208; originally in *Perspectivas para el diálogo* (Montevideo) 5 (1970), pp. 171–81.

85. Cf. esp. Antonio Fragoso (Bishop of Crateus, Brazil), *Evangile et révolution sociale* (Paris: Cerf, 1969), for some of the most outstanding examples of liberation theology *in actu.*

86. "Liberación, fe e ideología," *Mensaje*, no. 208, May 1972, p. 249. Also in *Misión abierta*, p. 443.

87. For a good example, cf. "Die Kirche und die Herrschaft der Ideologien," *Handbuch der Pastoraltheologie*, pp. 109–202.

88. See Assmann, passim, esp. his very dense article "El cristianismo, su plusvalía ideológica y el costo social de la revolución socialista," *Cuadernos de la realidad nacional,* no. 12, April 1972, pp. 154–79.

89. "Función ideológica y posibilidades utópicas del protestantismo latino-americano," in *De la Iglesia y la sociedad,* pp. 1–21.

90. Ibid., p. 20.

91. Javier Alonso Hernández, "Esbozo para una teología de la liberación," in *Aportes para la liberación* (Bogotá, 1970), p. 46.

92. Gutiérrez, *Theology of Liberation,* p. 149; also Segundo, *De la sociedad,* pp. 77ff.

93. Gutiérrez, *Theology of Liberation,* p. 166.

94. Ibid., p. 167.

95. Medellín, *Conclusiones,* "Peace," no. 1; "Poverty of the Church," nos. 1, 5.

96. Gutiérrez, *Theology of Liberation,* pp. 175–76; see also "Cristianismo y marxismo," passim.

97. Medellín, *Conclusiones,* "Justice," no. 3.

98. Gutiérrez, *Theology of Liberation,* p. 235.

99. Sergio Arce Martínez, "Es posible una teología de la revolución?" in *De la Iglesia y la sociedad,* pp. 227–53.

100. Rubem Alves, "El pueblo de Dios y la búsqueda de un nuevo orden social," *Cristianismo y sociedad,* nos. 26–27 (1971), p. 22.

101. Ibid., p. 23.

102. Assmann, *Theology for a Nomad Church,* p. 103.

103. Comblin, *Théologie de la révolution,* 1:236.

104. Gutiérrez, *Theology of Liberation,* p. 231.

105. Cf. the widely-read essay "Pueblo oprimido: Señor de la historia," plus accompanying article "Puede el proletario hacer teología?" in Carlos Welsh, *Pastoral popular,* no. 126, pp. 32–48.

106. Dom Candido Padim.

107. Assmann, *Opresión-liberación,* pp. 56–57.

108. Assmann, "Aporte cristiano," p. 17.

109. Paulo Freire, "Carta a un joven teólogo" y "Tercer mundo y teología," *Perspectivas de diálogo* 5 (1970), pp. 301–5.

110. Assmann, *Theology for a Nomad Church,* p. 74.

111. Alves, "Apuntes para un programa de reconstrucción en la teología," *Cristianismo y sociedad,* p. 21. This essay is suggestive for the question of an epistemological breakaway which liberation theology involves, as evidenced by the crisis of traditional theological languages.

112. Gutiérrez, *Theology of Liberation,* pp. 1–19.

113. One widely circulated essay: Pedro Negre, "La significación de los cambios metodológicos de las ciencias sociales para la interpretación teológica" (mimeo.).

114. Rafael Avila, "Profecía, interpretación y reinterpretación," in *Liberación en América latina,* pp. 115–30. He raises a barrage of suggestive questions. Cf. also the contribution of Luís de Valle in the same collection.

115. Two signs of this shift: (1) the appearance of a new review edited by Roger Vekemans, S.J., *Tierra nueva* (Bogotá). Vekemans was intimately associated with the

whole Christian Democrat phase in Chile and felt obliged to leave when Allende triumphed. The first two issues of the magazine (subtitled "Estudios socio-teológicos en América latina") contains articles surveying "liberation theology" and questioning its theses. Vekemans, moreover, wrote a notorious statement distorting liberation theology as a theology of violence and of disrespect for church authority (December 1971). (2) In the CELAM elections of November 1972, Alfonso López, Auxiliary Bishop of Bogotá and intimate collaborator of Vekemans, was elected secretary general. The foreseeable consequence: the establishment of an intellectually respectable "center" position (developmentalist) and a marginalizing of liberation theology toward a minority left. On the other hand, one can recognize that the prominence given liberation thought in official circles since 1968 does not correspond to the sociological reality of the church. Liberation vocabulary will continue to be used but in a more abstract biblical-dictionary way.

116. In some cases I will be reporting on literature written or published prior to 1973.

117. "De la época de las ilusiones al tiempo del realismo," *Cristianismo y Sociedad*, no. 42 (1974), p. 13. This article was elaborated by a reflection team and is an excellent summary of the shift in perspective in recent years.

118. Ibid., p. 16.

119. In the introduction to his *Théologie de la pratique révolutionnaire*, Joseph Comblin emphasizes the shift from the 1960s to the 1970s, and he analyzes in some detail the neofascist regimes that predominate in the Third World today.

120. *Doing Theology in a Revolutionary Situation* (Philadelphia: Fortress, 1975).

121. Ibid., p. 96.

122. Ibid., p. 98 (author's emphasis).

123. Ibid., p. 108. Note the similarities with Dussel's categories below.

124. Unfortunately this book is marred with several errors of detail, e.g., dating the invasion of the Dominican Republic in 1962 (p. 29).

125. Claude Geffré and Gustavo Gutiérrez, eds., *The Mystical and Political Dimensions of the Christian Faith*, Concilium 96 (New York: Herder and Herder, 1974). Articles by Segundo Galilea, Enrique Dussel, Gustavo Gutiérrez, Leonardo Boff, Joseph Comblin, Juan Luis Segundo, Raul Vidales, Ronaldo Muñoz, José Míguez Bonino.

126. Bogotá: CELAM, 1974.

127. Ibid., pp. 304–07.

128. "Presentación," p. 14. This "pluralism" is also a major point of López's essay.

129. The conclusions are printed in full in *Contacto* (Mexico), año 11, no. 4 (August 1974). The translation here reflects the unpolished nature of what seems to have been an internal document.

130. Declaración de la Conferencia Episcopal Paraguayo y la Federación de Religiosos del Paraguay, "Sobre los acontecimientos últimos en el país"; Carta Pastoral del Episcopado Paraguayo con motivo de la Cuaresma 1975, "Sobre la necesaria conversión en la hora actual" (mimeo.).

131. "Eu ouvi os clamores do meu povo," Documento de Obispos e Superiores Religiosos do Nordeste, May 6, 1973.

132. Ibid., p. 3.

133. Ibid., p. 20.

134. Ibid., p. 26.

135. Ibid., p. 28.

136. Ibid., p. 29.

137. "Marginalização de um povo—grito das Igrejas," included in *Brasil: ¿Milagro o engaño? Dos graves denuncias* (Lima: CEP, 1973).

138. Ibid., in *¿Milagro o engaño?*, pp. 115–17.

139. *Diálogos en el CELAM*, p. 229.

140. Joseph Comblin, *Théologie de la pratique révolutionnaire* (Paris: Éditions Universitaires, 1974).

141. Ibid., p. 187.

142. Ibid., p. 212.

143. Ibid., p. 214.

144. Ibid., p. 217.

145. Comblin, *Nação e nacionalismo* (São Paulo: Duas Cidades, 1965). See also "Movimientos e ideologías en América Latina, in *Fe cristiana y cambio social en América Latina* (Salamanca: Sígueme, 1973).

146. Comblin, *Pratique révolutionnaire*, pp. 134–37, 188, 271–79.

147. Ibid., pp. 256ff., 305ff.

148. A version of this essay was published as "Latin America's Version of 'National Security,' " *America*, February 21, 1976, pp. 137–39. Another essay, "Los conceptos básicos de la ideología de seguridad nacional," has been edited and prepared for the Chilean bishops.

149. "Church's New Praxis," p. 14.

150. Ibid., p. 35.

151. Orbis Books has published all five volumes of this series: *The Community Called Church, Grace and the Human Condition, Our Idea of God, The Sacraments Today*, and *Evolution and Guilt*. We will be quoting from the Spanish editions of volumes 2 and 3 below.

152. *Sacraments Today*, p. 65.

153. *Nuestra idea de Dios*, pp. 47–51.

154. Ibid., p. 104.

155. Ibid., p. 101.

156. Ibid., p. 225.

157. Ibid., pp. 91–92.

158. Ibid., pp. 93ff.

159. Ibid., p. 228.

160. *Sacraments Today*, p. 55.

161. Ibid., p. 56.

162. Ibid., p. 58.

163. *Evolution and Guilt*, pp. 126–27.

164. "Capitalism-Socialism: A Theological Crux," in *Mystical and Political Dimensions*, Concilium 96, pp. 105–23.

165. Ibid., p. 123.

166. *The Liberation of Theology*, trans. John Drury (Maryknoll, New York: Orbis Books, 1976).

167. A partial bibliography: *Hipótesis para una historia de la Iglesia en América Latina* (Barcelona, 1967); *El humanismo semita* (Buenos Aires, 1969); *América Latina en la historia de la salvación* (Barcelona, 1972); *Historia del catolicismo popular en la Argentina* (Buenos Aires, 1970); *Para una destrucción de la ética* (Paraná, 1972); *La dialéctica hegeliana* (Mendoza, 1972); *Teología de la liberación e historia* (Buenos Aires, 1972) [published in English translation as *History and the Theology of Liberation*, trans. John Drury (Maryknoll, New York: Orbis Books, 1976)]; *Teología de la liberación y la ética* (Buenos Aires, 1974); *Método para una filosofía de la liberación* (Salamanca, 1974). We here use *Teología de la liberación y la ética*.

168. Dussel includes the Concilium essay in *Teología de la liberación y ética* and states that it is a summary of his ideas on LT.

169. *Liberación y ética*, passim, especially pp. 10–12; cf. also his Concilium article.

170. *Liberación y ética*, p. 188.

171. Ibid., pp. 193–94.

172. Concilium 96, p. 46.

173. *Liberación y ética*, pp. 113–34.

174. *Marx and the Bible*, trans. John Eagleson (Maryknoll, New York: Orbis Books, 1974).

175. Ibid., p. 56.

176. Ibid., p. 182.

177. Ibid., pp. 187–89.

178. Ibid., p. 250.

179. Ibid., p. 254.

180. Ibid., p. 255.

181. Ibid., p. 277.

182. Ibid., p. 282.

183. *Enjuiciamos a Marx y la Biblia* (Mexico, D.F.: La Buena Prensa, 1973).

184. *Marx and the Bible*, p. 65.

185. Ibid., p. 250.

186. Ibid., p. xvii.

187. To be published in English translation by Orbis Books in 1977.

4

Letter of Rosemary Ruether
to Sergio Torres
and the Planners of the Conference

Washington, D.C.
February 1975

Dear Sergio Torres:

I have received the papers for the Theology in the Americas Conference to be held next August. They are very good, as far as they go. But there is a total lack of any perspective on positive resources for the American religious tradition by which Americans might respond to the theology of liberation. This is a serious defect. In effect, the Latin Americans are to provide the "theology" and the Americans the "Devil." I will leave aside whether this is sufficiently critical of the Latin American reality, including the clerical-class context of the theologians of liberation. But, on the Americans' side, to provide only social analyses of the American empire, to be located theologically as the "Whore of Babylon," is insufficient. I have no objection to the accuracy of the criticism that is being made. What I want to raise is this: Out of what religious resources do you expect the American people to respond to this criticism if this is the *only* identity that they are given?

It is evident that the writer of the background paper for the conference has the most minimal understanding of American religious history. Its "messianic language" is seen solely in the light of self-mystification and imperialism. It is mentioned that as "capitalism became more exploitative," some social gospel did emerge. This presumably locates the first dawning of any self-criticism in the era of the 1880s. This is clearly incorrect. From its roots in the Puritan and

84

Enlightenment traditions, the American language could serve as a powerful language of internal self-criticism. This found a powerful expression from the 1830s to the Civil War, when this very "messianic language" was the language of those struggling against slavery. The criticism of this movement did not end with abolitionism, but gave birth to a wide-ranging utopian socialist movement, the women's movement, and visions of a reconstituted society. Every critical movement in American history has succeeded only when it has been able to draw on this national liberation language as a positive identity and a criticism of complacency, and has been able to wrest this language out of the hands of those who would use it only as mystification and self-sanctification. Every national language that has roots in biblical and liberal-socialist critical languages (as does the American language) has the possibility of being either a liberation language or a language of mystification. This is also true of Marxism, which, in the U.S.S.R., has become a language of mystification. This double possibility also exists for the theology of liberation. It is impossible to understand the black church, as well as black theology in America, without understanding how it draws on this same American language, but in a prophetic or liberating mode, and thus unmasks its use as a mystifying language of national power.

If Americans are expected to respond to the criticism of America posed by theology of liberation, they must also be able to find in this national language the resources to respond, by being able to recognize in the response of repentance that is called for, not merely judgment, but also the call to renew the covenant with their "truer selves"; to recognize this response as the true affirmation of their identity as a people who believe in "liberty and justice for all." *This is not a question of being less critical of America!* This is a question of giving people the positive basis of the alternate identity through which they can respond at all. If this basic psychological-historical reality is ignored in a misguided effort to be as apocalyptical as possible, the result will be that the language of liberty and justice in the American tradition will be ceded in advance to the FBI and the CIA, who will claim exclusive right to represent the "true Americans," and will use this language to convince people that great "enemies of America" are abroad in the land and new efforts of repression are necessary. In other words, the tone of this conference will repeat the mistake of the left of the later 1960s, which fed into a perfect symbiosis with the forces of repression. At the moment, thanks to Watergate, Americans are focusing on their true enemies in the Establishment. They are beginning to recognize that Americans have different interests from this leadership class. This is a time when they could be powerfully appealed to, to recognize that their own true identity should lead them to support or leave alone other people's liberation struggles, rather than to intervene on the side of repression. But this can be done only if the criticism of these policies of the American empire also draws on an alternative positive image of what America should be. If the language that comes to them from theology of liberation is only that of judgement of the Monster, and no call is given to an alternative identity that draws on their historical language of liberty, then the forces of repression have an easy time creating new paranoia and locating false enemies all over again. Only if American radicals return to the strategy of Martin Luther King, who always made his scathing judgment in the language of an alternative "dream," is there any possibility that his message will be heard, not just by a tiny alienated few, but by the larger masses of Americans.

I suggest that resources, such as Robert Bellah's *The Broken Covenant*, as well as theologians and American religious historians who can provide this dimension, be brought into this conference.

Sincerely,
Rosemary Ruether

5

Letter of Gregory Baum
to Sergio Torres

Toronto, Canada
March 1, 1975

Dear Sergio Torres:

After reading Rosemary Ruether's letter to you [see document 4], I did what I should have done a few weeks ago: I read your Preparation Document No. 1 [see above document 1]. Allow me to respond to this paper from a Canadian point of view.

1. While I agree with the approach to theological reflection outlined in the paper, I do not think that it is useful for North Americans to start reflecting on their condition with the eyes of Latin Americans. It seems to me the consciousness of a people must be raised by reflections on their own condition, on their history, on the structures of oppression to which they themselves, or at least certain groups among them, are exposed. In your paper you offer important material helping Americans to understand their own situation. But since you select this material mainly in the light of what happens in Latin America, it is not enough. Unless we discover our own enslavement, we cannot as a people reach out for a new collective existence. If you confront Americans simply with the Latin American analysis, you only make them feel guilty, you make them wish they could help others, but since they will not find the right perspective for understanding themselves, they will not find a language that can be heard by their own countrymen and hence they will remain powerless. We have to begin where we are. We must listen to Latin Americans and to their analysis, but then we must start analyzing our own history and our own situation of affluence and poverty.

2. I do not like the way in which the paper makes Latin American liberation theology the model from which we must learn. Canadians

87

are only too willing to learn from others. In Canada a thinker is not recognized unless he has made a name for himself or herself in another country. This is a heritage from the colonial days. Anglo-Canadian intellectuals used to turn to England; now they often turn to the U.S.A. For the sake of liberation they should be encouraged to be in touch with their own tradition and find in it resources of reflection and new vision.

In Canadian Protestantism, to give an example, a sophisticated and action-oriented social gospel movement extended into the thirties, a movement that transcended Reinhold Niebuhr's critical rejection of the American social gospel and reflected an extended dialogue with Marxist thought. Most Canadian theologians are not even aware of this. The last thing we need in Canada is to be told to turn to another country. What we need is confidence that important things have happened in our history and are happening now, thanks to which we are enabled to discern the structures of oppression in which we are involved.

Even in the U.S.A. there is a tendency among theologians to become excessively enthusiastic over theologies coming to them from other countries. This is found even among Protestants who are more deeply rooted in the American experience. For this reason, it seems to me, you should turn to liberation theology produced in your own country. There is the critical reflection of the blacks, of Mexican-Americans, of the women's movement, etc. And then there are American liberation thinkers. What about Rosemary Ruether? The interrelation between *theoria* and *praxis*, which is central in Latin American theology, has been with us for a long time. There are American thinkers who have made this the core of their theological reflections.

3. To move people toward liberation you must have confidence that within their experience there are resources for recognizing oppression and generating a new vision. It seems to me that Marxists, as good Hegelians, have always had this sort of confidence. Ideas are not imported; ideas are the reflection of people's experience in a social situation. We must learn from others, we must listen especially to the oppressed others; but we do this not by imitating them. We must reflect on our own experience. I do not see how Americans can look upon their social and political reality purely and simply in terms of the Evil Empire. Without necessarily objecting to your analysis, they must find a wider context for it, more faithful to their self-understanding and the vision of the new that emerges in their own

tradition. Rosemary Ruether's letter develops this point at some length.

4. Canadians, in particular, should not make the analysis of the American empire the only source of reflection. We are dependent on this empire and to a large extent owned by it, and at the same time we are willing collaborators with American foreign policy and the dominant business interests. But we also have our own internal structures of oppression, which we must study. At Canadian universities, students are often more interested in protesting against the Vietnam involvement of the United States and following American politics than in learning French and dealing with specifically Canadian issues. Canadians are very much in need of discovering the destiny written into their history, their geography, and their human experiences, and this includes the vastness of their as yet unpopulated land and the space and richness available to be shared with other people. While we must listen to Latin Americans and analyze the influence of the American empire, we must develop our own sense of independence from the United States so that we can assume a more responsible role in international affairs. We are in need of our own theology of liberation.

These are a few preliminary remarks.

With my best regards.

Yours sincerely,
Gregory Baum

6

Response of Sergio Torres
to Gregory Baum

Theology in the Americas: 1975
Maryknoll, NY 10545
April 3, 1975

Dear Gregory Baum:

Many thanks for your two letters. In spite of the fact that we have never met I see an affinity in our positions. . . .

1. I want to respond to some of the doubts you expressed about Document No. 1 [see above document 1]. I agree with what you say with respect to the starting point in analyzing the American reality. We should find instruments of analysis that start from the history, culture, and religious traditions of America. We are going to complement Document No. 1. Since the conference will present an opportunity to dialogue with Latin Americans, we wanted to present in that document a sense of how they view the American reality. We in Chile and South America have experienced some forms of oppression that come from the same national sectors, e.g., rich and powerful minorities who were denounced by the bishops at Medellín. But also we have seen how some American agencies and companies have undoubtedly intervened in the affairs of those countries.

The great difficulty with the American middle-class person is the fact that he ignores many of these activities. He doesn't feel bothered personally by them and so rejects them. Even if he does recognize them he feels powerless to change them. Our conference has felt that one way of drawing attention to the situation is to begin reflecting on the image that the U.S.A. projects in Latin America. The second step will be to study whether or not this corresponds to the reality; then we will try to reflect theologically on the conclusions and to leave open the field for a praxis of transformation and hope.

I attach for your review a paper from Fr. John Coleman, S.J., on "Civil Religion and Liberation Theology" [see below document 10] written from an American perspective, which seeks, in the rich tradition of liberty in the religious life of the U.S.A., elements that may enlighten the present situation of vacillation and doubt that many American citizens find themselves in after Watergate, CIA activities, etc.

2. The central objective of the conference will be to analyze the economic and political situation, national and international, from the point of view of revelation, utilizing biblical categories of domination-liberation found in the book of Exodus. The conference will not be held only for the purpose of listening to Latin Americans, which was the purpose of the El Escorial meeting (Madrid, 1972). Our meeting is centered on the American reality. The Latin Americans will share their experience and the criteria of their theological reflection.

3. We are studying ways of incorporating particular movements within this more global perspective. During the week in Detroit there will be a session on women's liberation and there are committees of theologians responsible for studying ways of integrating black libera- tion and Mexican-American theology. What we want to avoid is having the conference go off in too many directions and not focus deeply enough on its central objective pointed out above in no. 2.

4. I am not familiar with the Canadian reality. I spent fifteen days last summer visiting Toronto, Ottawa, and Montreal. Recently, I have been surveying the American reality. One is left stunned on seeing the division, even among Christians, between English and French Canada. At the last meeting of the planning committee in New York, Bill Smith, Secretary of the National Conference of Catholic Bishops, was present, and he expressed sentiments similar to those of your letter. We have agreed to add more people from Canada. Bill insisted in our meeting that the persons who may come should do so individually and not as representatives of institutions or Canadian Christians.

In spite of that, I believe that the Canadians who choose to come should make an effort to coordinate and prepare for their participation at the conference. I understand what you are saying with respect to the working schedule and activities. But, at the same time, it seems to me that this conference will be an opportunity to present the ideas you propose. There would be several possibilities for accomplishing it: prepare a document that we could circulate among the participants before the conference, make an intervention at the conference itself, etc. Another initiative that one could take, after finding out the names of those Canadians who will attend, is to arrange a meeting with them to prepare for their participation.

I wanted to respond to your letter sooner since I appreciated its content so much. Besides, I acknowledge the fact that you are one of the most influential theologians in North America. I believe that the conference will greatly benefit by your presence. . . .

I am anxious for the opportunity to meet you personally. I greet you fraternally.

Sergio Torres

7

Letter of Avery Dulles
to Sergio Torres

Washington, D.C.
March 14, 1975

Dear Sergio Torres:

Although I am participating in group reflections on "Theology in the Americas: 1975," I should like at this time to submit some personal reflections, inspired in part by those of Rosemary Ruether and Gregory Baum in their recent letters to you.

It seems to me that the conference as presently planned could have either of two major foci. The first would be an exposé and critique of recent Latin American liberation theology, as developed in the Latin American context, by sympathetic but discriminating North American observers. The second possible focus would be an exploration of something like an autochthonous liberation theology growing out of the North American situation. Both of these alternatives are tempting, but I doubt whether they can be successfully combined in a single conference lasting less than a week.

If the first alternative were chosen one could well focus on Phillip Berryman's article on Latin American liberation theology [see above document 3]. In my judgment this article sets forth nearly all the major points and raises nearly all the major questions that would have to be handled. Discussion groups could be organized that would address themselves to various themes taken from this article, utilizing, of course, the other available literature and the Latin American theologians personally present. I enclose some questions that I distilled from Berryman's article.

If the second alternative were chosen one could well focus on John Coleman's article on U.S. civil religion [see below document 10]. I personally found this a very enlightening and stimulating article. In combination with the letters sent to you by Rosemary Ruether and Gregory Baum, it confirmed me in my conviction that Latin American liberation theology, while probably very appropriate for the Latin American scene, cannot be imported on a wide scale to this country. Our social scene, our economic and political structures, and our national traditions are so radically different that an entirely fresh analysis has to be made.

Coleman's article makes a strong case for holding that there are valuable theological resources for a critique of the contemporary American situation in our national tradition of civil religion. At the conference this thesis could be further explored. Following the suggestion in Rosemary Ruether's letter to you, I should like to see also some examination of the resources in the "religious religion" (Coleman's term) of the United States. Besides Rosemary Ruether herself, some specialists in the history of American theology could be of help here (Robert Handy? Herbert Richardson? Martin Marty? or others?). They could perhaps prepare other position papers to be considered before or at the conference.

There would be the possibility of getting black, Spanish-speaking, and native American Indian theologians to expound what is in their traditions. I would not be opposed to this, but I feel that the brunt of the conference should deal with the confusions and tensions felt by all of us, and not simply with minority groups, important though their testimony is.

Gregory Baum's letter to you [see above document 5] seems to suggest that it would be important to have some Canadian theologians do something similar for the Canadian scene. This is probably a good idea.

Should the conference attempt to carry out a theological critique of the present socio-political and economic structures of U.S. society? I suspect that the task would prove too immense, even with strenuous preparations. On this point I think that there is merit in the suggestions, apparently not accepted by the Research Coordinating Team, that sample cases should be analyzed. If specific instances were selected, it might be possible to begin to develop analytic categories out of the actual problems faced by our society rather than too easily taking over categories developed by other people analyzing other societies. Of course one would have to be slow in generalizing from concrete cases to the "holistic" picture—but some useful beginnings could be made.

I shall have some other suggestions, but they can be included, I believe, in those of the Washington task groups of which I am a part.

I appreciate the hard work that you and your colleagues are doing, and I hope that these suggestions will prove helpful.

Sincerely yours,
Avery Dulles, S.J.

Lucubrations on Phillip Berryman, "Latin American Liberation Theology" [*see above document 3*]

Although the author is obviously sympathetic with the phenomenon he is describing, he is not uncritical. His article, a splendidly informative synthesis, raises excellent questions for discussion. Among the questions I should like to see discussed are the following:

1. To what extent is liberation theology a Latin American growth, not for export?

2. Can the church be at home with a theology of conflict and class struggle rather than a theology of reconciliation?

3. What are the theological principles governing violent action?

4. In the expression "political (or politicized) theology," what is meant by the term "political"?

5. To what extent does the church have a political mission and competence?

6. Is Christianity in possession of any doctrines or moral principles that are valid for all times and places?

7. What should be the objectives of structural reform within the church?

8. In Christianity should prophetic denunciation and praxis predominate over evangelization (doctrine) and worship?

9. Should ecumenism seek first of all to overcome social oppression?

10. Does the practice of "macrocharity" require the church to abandon political neutrality?

11. Are sin and grace inevitably bound up with social structures?

12. Can Jesus be plausibly portrayed as a liberation theologian?

13. Who are the "poor" (*anawim*) of the gospels?

14. Is there any methodology for a sound reading of the signs of the times?

15. Can a theology that is fully committed to revolutionary praxis be genuinely self-critical?

16. To what extent does the methodology of liberation theology rest on Marxian presuppositions?

8

Response of Sergio Torres
to Avery Dulles

Theology in the Americas: 1975
Maryknoll, NY 10545
April 3, 1975

Dear Fr. Avery Dulles:

Many thanks for your letter of March 14. I appreciate very much the fact that you are participating in the preparation of the conference, since you will be able to make an important contribution.

I want to take this opportunity to answer and evaluate some of the points mentioned in your letter.

1. Even when we have not explicitated it in the documents, the focus of the conference will be the second one of the points you mention. In 1972 there was a meeting in El Escorial (Madrid, 1972) organized by a Jesuit, Fr. Alvarez Bolado, who had the same goal that you pointed out. Almost the same Latin American theologians who will come to Detroit gave an explanation of the theology of liberation to the Spanish public. We intended the Detroit conference to be an analysis of the American political and economic situation in light of the biblical concepts of the Exodus, that is, domination-liberation.

Nevertheless, we believe it important—in a dialogue with Latin Americans—to begin with the image that America projects in the Third World and especially in Latin America. In Latin America we estimate that that image includes aspects misinterpreted by false liberation movements. But there are also aspects of truth. The power and affluence of Americans is not due only to recognized qualities and values of this great country, but also to historical circumstances of the past century that necessitated an international division of labor. Since then, the economies of some countries reduced themselves to producing primary materials in order to sell them cheaply to industrialized countries. In turn, they have had to buy expensive products manufactured with these same primary materials.

We hope that this starting point, namely the international policy of the United States and the action of the multinational corporations, affords us a better understanding of the internal reality. Since I arrived in this country, the gap that exists between the middle-class citizen—the honorable, idealistic, and religious worker—and some power groups who don't exhibit those virutes, has left an impression on me. In Chile and Latin America it is difficult to understand the apparent complicity of U.S. Christians with the forms of oppression overseas. From the point of view of the judgment of the God of the Exodus, I don't believe that it is sufficient to merely excuse them by saying that they didn't know. The message of the prophets enlightens one to discern the criteria of an authentic fidelity to the gospel in the present international situation for a country that, because of its leadership, has the obligation of being faithful to the rich traditions of liberty and idealism of the pilgrim, of those who fought the revolution, of those who abolished slavery, etc.

2. In the same ways as you do, I, too, appreciate Coleman's article [see below document 10] very much. I had the pleasure of meeting him in San Francisco and asked him to do this work, since he feels that in America this is a fundamentally rich theme. It will be included among the documents that the reflection groups will study in the second part of the preparation.

Nevertheless, I don't hold the same conviction as you with respect to the possibilities of a theology of liberation in the U.S.A. That is what we want to explore at the Detroit conference. I assume that everyone understands that the situation of Latin America is very different from that of the U.S. But, by being so different, they are united in a dialectical process. The Latin Americans feel themselves oppressed by an international system and by minorities in their very own countries which are allies and accomplices of the international powers. But they identify the U.S. as the head of the international system of oppression from the West. The reasons are long and complex, but Latin American social scientists have elaborated these reasons scientifically and their argumentation finds an audience among their American and European colleagues.

From this vantage point the theology of liberation stresses the duty of the Christians of Latin America and the U.S. to free themselves together from a structure of social sin that is dominating international relations while invoking fraternity and solidarity. The direction will be different in Latin America or the Third World than here in this country, but the objectives will be the same. We are all conscious today that the world is one and that the Christians of this country cannot be indifferent to what happens on other continents. Besides, many myths, such as outside help for developing countries, have been denounced here in this country.

3. We have realized that Document No. 1 [see above document 1] included the interpretation of the American reality from the Latin American point of view. Coleman's article will complete this perspective. Nevertheless, anything that we may find as an instrument of analysis in the rich religious tradition of America should serve us in interpreting the present situation of this country. What is God's judgment on my country, Chile, at this time? What is God's judgment on America? It is difficult to say. No one can be so arrogant as to play God. The prophets did not choose themselves. We have on earth a voice that expresses—in a certain sense—the voice of God. It is the voice of the poor; what they feel, what they say or cannot say reflects pain, suffering, the hope of Someone who has identified himself with those who are hungry, oppressed, naked. . . . The poor of Latin America and the Third World are accusing the leaders of America and are appealing to the Christians of this country who are called to the crucial task of living out the gospel in an affluent society. It is not enough to say, "They're wrong, the Soviets are also imperialists, the economy is somewhat complicated," unless we accept the liberal principle that there is an absolute separation between one's private faith and business or international policy.

What I mean to say is that it seems that liberation theology has ceased to be merely a Latin American product and that some of its criteria and instruments of analysis have value here in the U.S. If it is true, it will emerge from the conference.

4. The ongoing investigations into the participation of representatives of black liberation theology and others tend toward seeking a way to integrate those movements within the global perspective of liberation that we have chosen as the focus of the conference. I appreciate your observations on this point and I share them completely. We cannot speak of liberation in America without considering in some way women's or black liberation.

5. The possibility of studying particular cases as a starting point for the analysis of the American reality has not been definitely rejected. What we want to maintain, though, is a global perspective and the consideration of the interdependence between the international and domestic reality. In this sense we don't accept the suggestion that we

reject the holistic analysis. In spite of the risks we run as far as the design of the conference we still haven't made definite decisions. We want to remain faithful to the preparation process and listen to the reflection groups.

These are some reflections I have wanted to share with you with respect to your letter which I found interesting and thought-provoking.

I hope to meet you soon personally.

Fraternally,
Sergio Torres

9

Response of
Monika Hellwig
to Avery Dulles

1. To what extent is liberation theology a Latin American growth, not for export?

That seems to depend on what we understand by liberation theology. I understand the term to have two meanings, a particular one and a general one. In its particular sense, the term describes what might be called a "school of theology," i.e., a fairly well defined circle of Latin American theologians, most Catholics but some Protestants, who have been in constant dialogue with one another over a period of years, have developed a common vocabulary and frame of reference, and share some judgments about the Latin American political and economic situation.

In this narrower sense, I think, liberation theology is "not for export" but concerns us when its proponents turn to us and accuse us of theologizing in a way that gives religious sanction to grave injustices and dehumanizing oppression in the world, or even if they accuse us of a style of theology that renders such problems religiously irrelevant. In response to such accusations, I believe we must give an accounting concerning the public implications of the theology we write or teach and of the style of preaching and living that it sustains.

However, it seems that the term "liberation theology" has already assumed the broader or more general sense of any socio-critical theology. In this sense it would seem to include much of "black theology," the writings of Frederick Herzog, James Douglass, John H. Yoder, some of those of Thomas Merton, etc. As I understand it, what is common to liberation theology in this broader sense is that it begins with questions concerning the hope of Christians and the action appropriate to that hope (Moltmann's term) as those questions are prompted by the suffering of those most oppressed in the world or in a particular country today (the *am ha-aretz* of the contemporary experience). Moreover, those questions are asked in constant awareness of the responsibility for others that our modern technical capabilities and psychological, economic, and statistical knowledge have thrust upon us. It seems to me that it is neither necessary nor even possible to theologize directly from esoteric or highly specialized data or conclusions produced by the natural or social sciences as they are breaking new frontiers. But it does seem to be required that theology depart from questions asked by intelligent and conscientious citizens on the basis of what is now generally known, e.g., concerning psychological conditioning or patterns in which markets are manipulated or escape control.

In this sense of the term, it would seem that we have no right to be doing anything other than liberation theology. The strongest statement on this appears to me to be that of J. B. Metz: The symbol of the Cross as the central point of Christian faith, life, and worship demands the writing of history upside down from the point of view of the vanquished, because it is there that the unfinished agenda for the redemption of the world most clearly appears.[1]

In spite of the above, I have found difficulty coming to grips with the substance of liberation theology, because all the literature with which I am acquainted is a critique of the available presentations of systematic theology, and none of it really amounts to a new systematic theology.

2. Can the church be at home with a theology of conflict and class struggle rather than a theology of reconciliation?

I have some difficulty with the way this question is phrased. Reconciliation seems to me to imply that there is conflict and struggle that must be resolved. Talk of redemption from sin seems to me necessarily to involve conflict and struggle between powers operative in human society, and I do not see those powers operating unattached to groups of people. Therefore, a theology of reconciliation does not seem to be alternative to a theology of conflict and class struggle but identical with it. Under one title the project is described in terms of the problem, under the other in terms of the hoped for solution.

As far as I am aware, there are no liberation theology authors who wish to exclude some persons from the promised future, the immediate goal, or the ultimate goal of the redemption of mankind. But the insistence seems to be universal that class struggle is a fact in the world, created by those who are able to dominate the distribution of the world's resources and who voluntarily profit by taking advantage of others and keeping them oppressed and poor. Gutiérrez seems to express the general consensus:

> To love all men does not mean avoiding confrontations. . . . . Universal love is that which in solidarity with the oppressed seeks also to liberate the oppressors from their own power, from their ambition, and from their selfishness. . . . It must be a real and effective combat, not hate.
>   . . . In a radically divided world, the function of the ecclesial community is to struggle against the profound causes of the division among men. It is only this commitment that can make of it an authentic sign of unity.[2]

This raises the question, of course, as to what is that "effective combat" which is opposed to hate. I have assumed from the extreme caution about direct counterviolence (responding to systemic violence), and from the occasional explicit advocacy of nonviolent strategies, as well as from the enthusiastic way in which Paulo Freire's conscientization proposals have been promoted by liberation theology people, that their understanding of "effective combat" must in practice be somewhat along the lines of Gandhi, King, Dolci, Chávez. All these men, of course, took sides with one class against another and actively sought confrontation.

José María González-Ruiz (Spanish, not Latin American) locates the distinction between "effective combat" and hate in the nature of the change that is being effected or attempted. A mere effort to get the oppressed class into the oppressor position has nothing to do with genuine liberation, which occurs when the structures of society are so changed as to undo the oppression itself, not to pass it over into different hands.[3]

3. What are the theological principles governing violent action?

The following is my understanding of the implication of liberation theology with regard to violent action. I have not seen this set out explicitly anywhere.

Liberation is directed towards a full, conscious, creative participation of all human beings in the shaping of human life, human society, human history. This goal implies the absence of all violence, no matter how subtle or hidden.

The process of liberation is necessary precisely because we do not live in such a situation, but in a complex network of oppressive relationships, values, expectations, institutions. Oppression and violence are to be equated.

In a situation of oppression, anyone who can recognize that oppression is bound by the command of universal charity to act to change the situation so as to relieve the oppressed. In practice, this usually means unmasking and challenging an existing state of institutional or systemic violence. Those who profit by the systemic violence do not see it as violence but as the maintenance of law and order; therefore they see the challenge in itself as violent no matter how it is made. They feel justified in retaliating with greater violence than that which they perceive, in order to keep law and order.

This means there is no way to protest oppression other than with some counterviolence, and it is the oppressor who dictates the level of counterviolence necessary in order to be heard. Therefore, ethically the question of the legitimation of revolutionary violence must be placed in the context of self-defense (self-defense against the original systemic violence and the subsequent reactionary violence). The basic rules that govern it will be that it must be used only when all else fails, only when it can be effective, only at the minimum level that will be effective, only directly against the oppressor institutions, and without fostering hatred for the person of the oppressor.

Therefore, that action is most liberating (and most virtuous) which creatively modifies the present pattern of violence so as to diminish the total violence being done the most. But that action may itself be a violent one, and the necessary violence would then be justified, inasmuch as it diminishes the total violence.

In practice, it may be even more complicated than that. The man of conscience who honors the exigence of nonviolence in human relations in a total and uncompromising way is often not the one to initiate action on behalf of the oppressed. This has often been initiated by others who do not object to violence in itself and in all cases. Therefore a conscientious liberator must ask himself not only what is the least violent and most creative action in the situation. Out of the practical options of the present situation in which other liberators also have initiated action, and in which nothing is creative that does not unify efforts of a large number of people, he must also ask himself what compromises he must make if he is to act at all, and whether in conscience it is possible for him to act at all.

It seems to me that on this ethical level of discussion of the question there is very little disagreement until it comes to the practical assessment of the degree of violence that is actually required and can still be effective. Here more than anywhere, all authors appear to theorize out of their own praxis or lack of it. My own incomplete survey of positions suggests that those more distant from the Latin American scene are willing to condone more violence than those actually engaged in it, perhaps because they feel it ill becomes them to prescribe for others in a far more difficult situation than they face themselves.

The logic of this is very well expressed by José Díez-Alegría.[4] In addition to this, Almeri Bezerra de Melo, points out that there is almost no published Latin American discussion on the question of violence from a theological perspective, and very little from either Africa or Asia, while there is a flood of literature from Europeans and North Americans interested in Latin America.[5]

One interesting aspect of this line of argument is that it is (like the Just War theory) apt to argue itself off the drawing board altogether if it can be shown that in fact violence never does achieve the ultimate purpose of liberation, that it is by its nature self-defeating.

There is at least one liberation theologian, Alex Morelli, O.P., who seems to propose an essentially nonviolent position.[6]

All of the above reduces the discussion of violence to an ethical one. Some authors seem to suggest something closer to a theological discussion. Díez-Alegría suggests a distinction in the gospel between "principles" and "propositions" concerning questions of violence.[7] Juan Luis Segundo, Gustavo Gutiérrez, Hugo Assmann all reflect on the question as to how the process of human liberation is to be seen in relation to the coming of the promised reign of God.[8] It seems to me that that particular discussion is worth pursuing (in our reflection group's attempt to understand the Latin American theologians), because it underlies almost all the rest of the Dulles questions. I have not had time to go any further on these questions for this meeting, but intend to do so in the near future.

4. In the expression "political (or politicized) theology," what is meant by the term "political"?

The term can really only be defined with reference to J.B. Metz. Explicitly, at least Gutiérrez and Assmann have defined it that way.[9] Metz claims that "the new political theology" is not a theology of politics, but a perspective in which all theology must be done to be faithful to its purpose. That purpose is to interpret the Christian message in the context of contemporary life experience. The basic hermeneutic problem is not "how dogma stands in relation to history, but what is the relation between theory and practice," and Metz understands practice as essentially embracing the social or public sphere.[10]

Metz has given a justification for this position, which as far as I can determine, is accepted without hesitation by the Latin American liberation theologians. The understanding of the good news (of the at-handness of the kingdom) in the first Christian centuries was not private at all but essentially social, though possessed by a powerless group. That is why we so easily became involved in the Constantinian establishment, but that turned out to be a false relationship. Gradually Western consciousness asserted the autonomy of the secular and made man the measure of all things. Religious activity and theology then defended their own right to exist by moving into the private sphere, concerning themselves with the individual, his individual way of life, and his individual hopes after death. This also turns out to be a false relationship, because in fact our freedom is exercised in relation to the social or public sphere or else atrophies altogether. The most important decisions, commitments, relationships, values, and expectations never come under religious scrutiny at all but are left to the mercy of idols, if religious reflection busies itself only with individuals as individuals.[11]

Metz was attacked by German sociologists on historical grounds,[12] and Gutiérrez gives an alternate version of the historical justification.[13] However, it seems that a more forceful objection made from all sides is whether it is really a matter of social and political ethics rather than of a political theology.[14] Metz seemed at one stage on the verge of capitulation, but the Latin American theologians are adamant that, as far as they are concerned, it is a matter of theology. Assmann asserted in 1971, without qualification, "There is a political theology in Latin America today": the "theology of liberation."[15]

Assmann seems to me to get to the core of the question as to the nature of political theology and the sense of "political" in this context far better than Metz himself in anything that I have read. He suggests that the "new political theology" is possible only because we have grown to understand the political differently in our times; "political" describes a dimension of the whole of society, not only of structures of government. Democracy is not realized simply by having everyone vote in elections, but by multidimensional participation in the structuring of the society and its life and possibilities and of what the individuals within it offer one another as conditions of life and growth and self-realization. Political action is understood to be that which takes seriously the historical character of human existence, because it is aware of the implications in all human actions for the structuring of the lives and possibilities of others. A political theology therefore is understood to be one which desacralizes not only nature but every status quo in the name of the human to which we are called in Christ and which has not been achieved yet. Within a political theology there has to be a method that moves explicitly from praxis to theory, and therefore there cannot be a distinction between political ethics and political theory.[16] Assmann links this with Rahner's theology of revelation. It seems to me it is directly related to both De Lubac's and Rahner's work on nature and grace.

5. To what extent does the church have a political mission and competence?

Metz has an answer to this with which the Latin American theologians are not satisfied. Metz claims the church's political mission is and remains negative. This follows from his reading of history as sketched above. The task of the church is to protest all in the society that is contrary to the dignity and freedom of human persons as seen in the light of Christ, and therefore to protest all structures of society, whether economic or governmental or social or cultural, that hamper the humanization of persons as seen in the light of Christ. For Metz, the church stops there. It may not associate its name or its corporate identity or power with any platform or positive proposals, because that would be idolatrous—calling ultimate or sacred what is simply another human attempt to do the best thing in the circumstances.[17]

Juan Luis Segundo takes his point of departure from the fact that church and society are not mutually exclusive groups, and that we are asking a question in the first place about the responsibility of the ecclesial community as such for the restructuring of the society with which it overlaps or coincides.[18] He speaks of church as the community of those who know the secret of history from the inside because they have been granted a glimpse of what God is doing within mankind. He sees this community as necessarily responsible for creative activity within the society to structure it in redemptive ways. He raises the question whether this should be done by the society itself, constantly enlightened by the Christian vision, or by lay groups, or by hierarchic use of corporate power. He allows ample scope for the last, under the rubric of "substitutive function," because he judges that the concrete situation is extreme and leadership frequently cannot come from other than clerical sources.

Gutiérrez seems to propose a more modest role for the hierarchic intervention of the church, with his theory that theology and politics meet on the issue of the projection, definition, critique, and refinement of "utopias."

6. Is Christianity in possession of any doctrines or moral principles that are valid for all times and places?

According to my observations, although these authors constantly insist on theory arising out of praxis, they accept a fairly standard schema of the basic doctrines and moral principles of Christianity. Assmann gives a loosely assembled list of Christian doctrines along with suggestions on their interpretation.[19] He includes creation, sin, salvation, Christ as center of history, church. Later he discusses at length the relation of the reign of God and of conversion to God with what is going on in history.[20]

Segundo explores the pastoral implications of the principal doctrines of Christianity seen in the context of the world of today.[21] He is at great pains to establish continuity with church documents and papal teachings, etc.

Gutiérrez explains himself in terms of the traditional doctrines of creation, salvation, eschatology, ecclesiology, and is likewise at pains to show continuity.[22] He considers some aspects of Christology, but admits, like Assmann, that our Christology to date does not answer the questions that liberation theology is asking. The way Gutiérrez works within the framework of Catholic doctrinal traditions is to accept all the official teachings and then to draw out questions which have not been asked and establish them as valid questions though they may challenge the horizon of the customary explanations. This does not seem to be too different from the way any other Catholic theologian would operate. It is the quality and direction of the questions he introduces that make the difference.

Alex Morelli calls for a "theology of happening," a theology of the salvation history that is going on in people's lives here and now, and then immediately proceeds to supply categories and guidelines for such a theology from Scripture and tradition: liberation theme in the Hebrew Scriptures, as interpreted in church documents; the biblical doctrine of creation, as interpreted in Christian tradition; the meaning of "freedom of the sons of God" in Paul; and of the notion of the "new man" in relation to conversion from sin.[23] Only after establishing this framework does he move into discussion of social dimensions of liberation and the role the church should play in relation to them.

From such examples I infer that when these authors speak of theology as the critique of praxis, they have no intention of beginning at a primitive (historically naive) level of praxis. They assume the praxis of trying to live the implications of the gospel, in the supposition that when we do that we discover new dimensions of what that gospel means because "reality talks back to us." It seems to me that this is the conventional Catholic thesis about tradition applied very concretely in the present.

Concerning moral principles, likewise, I have found no evidence that the Latin American liberation theologians thought they could dispense with the decalogue or with the gospel rendering of the *shema*. The basic moral assumption seems to be the primacy of charity, the absolute exigence that charity be universal (i.e., totally non-exclusive), the understanding that charity requires positive creative activity to alter oppressive structures and conditions, the conviction of oneness in destiny of all mankind, and the conviction that what is ultimately the happiness and fulfillment of persons has to be learned by Christian living in the light of Christ.[24]

NOTES

1. Johannes B. Metz, "The Future in the Memory of Suffering," in *New Questions on God*, ed. Johannes B. Metz, Concilium 76 (New York: Herder and Herder, 1972), pp. 9–25.

2. Gustavo Gutiérrez, *A Theology of Liberation*, trans. Caridad Inda and John Eagleson (Maryknoll, New York: Orbis Books, 1973), pp. 275–78.

3. José María González-Ruiz, "Christianity and the Socialist Revolution," in *When All Else Fails* (Philadelphia: Pilgrim, 1970).

4. José Díez-Alegría, "A Christian View of Progress through Violence," in *Theology Meets Progress*, ed. Philip Land (Rome: Gregorian University Press, 1971), especially pp. 201–06.

5. Almeri Bezerra de Melo, "Revolution and Violence," in *When All Else Fails*.

6. See, for example, Alex Morelli, O.P., "Man Liberated from Sin and Oppression: A Theology of Liberation," in *Freedom and Unfreedom in the Americas*, 1971 CICOP Conference, ed. Thomas E. Quigley (New York: IDOC, 1971), pp. 81–95.

7. Díez-Algería, "Christian View."

8. Juan Luis Segundo, *Theology for Artisans of a New Humanity*, trans. John Drury, 5 vols. (Maryknoll, New York: Orbis Books, 1973–74); Gutiérrez, *Theology of Liberation;* Morelli, "Man Liberated"; Hugo Assmann, *Opresión-liberación: Desafío a los cristianos* (Montevideo: Tierra Nueva, 1971) and in English *Theology for a Nomad Church*, trans. Paul Burns (Maryknoll, New York: Orbis Books, 1976).

9. Gutiérrez, *Theology of Liberation;* Assmann, *Opresión-liberación*.

10. Johannes B. Metz, "The Church's Social Function in the Light of a 'Political Theology,' " in *Faith and the World of Politics*, ed. Johannes B. Metz, Concilium 36 (New York: Paulist Press, 1968), pp. 2–18.

11. Johannes B. Metz, "Politische Theologie in der Diskussion," in Helmut Peukert, ed., *Diskussion zur "politische Theologie"* (Mainz, Munich: Grunewald-Kaiser, 1969).

12. Ibid.

13. Gutiérrez, *Theology of Liberation*, chapters 4 and 5.

14. This objection is neatly summarized in Franz H. Mueller, "Social Ethics or 'Political Theology'?" *Thought*, Spring 1971, pp. 5–28.

15. Assmann, *Theology for a Nomad Church*, p. 38; cf. pp. 92ff.

16. Ibid., pp. 30ff.

17. Metz, "Church's Social Function."

18. Segundo, *Community Called Church* (Maryknoll, New York: Orbis Books, 1973), especially chapters 2 and 5.

19. Assmann, *Theology for a Nomad Church*, pp. 64–71.

20. Assmann, *Opresión-liberación*, pp. 145–66.

21. Segundo, *Theology for Artisans*.

22. Gutiérrez, *Theology of Liberation*, chapters 9–12.

23. Morelli, "Man Liberated."

24. Gutiérrez, *Theology of Liberation*, chapter 10; Morelli, "Man Liberated"; Segundo, *Grace and the Human Condition* (Maryknoll, New York: Orbis Books, 1973), chapter 4; none of these, however, is very specific.

The Reinterpretation
of American History

As seen above, Preparation Document No. 1 furnished the reflection groups with a historical interpretation of the United States and a critique of U.S. foreign policy. The reactions to the document were varied, but there was a consensus that there is a need to study the secular and religious history of the United States and that it is impossible to develop any theology based on experience without that historical background.

The organizing committee therefore requested several of the participants to write papers on the historical dimensions of the American experience.

"The American Journey" was prepared by Joseph Holland of the Center of Concern. It rapidly became one of the key documents of the process. The first mimeographed draft was circulated among the reflection groups, whose suggestions, criticisms, and commentaries were incorporated into second and third drafts. A revised, expanded version of this paper will be published separately by Orbis Books. A mimeographed copy of the third draft can be obtained from the Secretariat of Theology in the Americas, Room 1244A, 475 Riverside Drive, New York, NY 10027 (155 pp.; $1.50). A résumé of the paper is included in document 29 below.

As Holland says, the paper has three parts: "The first dealing with independence and democracy in the American foundation; the second with the period of

American expansion, both outwardly in geography and internally in productivity and in the size of the labor force (a period which covers most of American history); and third, the present period of limits and crises, with some projections of possible scenarios out of the crisis."

John Coleman prepared two papers, "Civil Religion and Liberation Theology in North America," included here, defines civil religion in general, analyzes U.S. civil religion, and discusses the possible points of contact between U.S. civil religion and the theology of liberation.

The groups' reaction to the paper varied. Some agreed that the concept of civil religion is helpful in understanding the religious history of the United States. It enables us to retrieve the best elements of the history of the country, to discover national identity, to avoid the errors of the past, and to project a new future.

Others felt that the document was overly optimistic, even ingenuous. They said that to use the concept of civil religion is to fall into the error of those who have tried to sacralize U.S. history, legitimating not only its attributes but its errors and myths as well.

Coleman's second paper, "Vision and Praxis in American Theology: Orestes Brownson, John Ryan, and John Courtney Murray," is not included here. (The paper has been published in Theological Studies, *March 1976). In it Coleman turns to historical figures who he believes can help us construct new models for interpreting the present and building the future.*

This paper and that of Frederick Herzog, "Pre-Bicentennial U.S.A. and the Liberation Process," included here, together represent an effort to interpret the Catholic and Protestant traditions. Herzog and Coleman agree that in U.S. history there is a heritage of struggle against injustice and oppression and that there can be no reformulation of U.S. theology without a recovery of those resources.

10

Civil Religion
and Liberation Theology
in North America

by John A. Coleman

I recently took part in a conversation with a Latin American theologian of liberation about the possibility of creating a liberation theology in the North American context. When the discussion turned to the topic of civil religion as a resource for projects of liberation in the United States, he smiled disarmingly and said, "Of course, I do not have a clue what this civil religion of yours is all about. We do not speak of such things."

Anyone conversant with the literature on civil religion which has grown up since Robert Bellah's celebrated essay on the topic of "Civil Religion in America" knows that to speak of civil religion is to raise a hornet's nest of unresolved problems of definition and evaluation.[1] In debates and colloquies devoted to the subject, questions range from "Does it exist anywhere except in the minds of intellectuals?" or "Is it a purely American phenomenon?" to "Is it anything more than mindless or idolatrous patriotism?" Martin Marty has suggested somewhat flippantly that "Civil religion at least existed once in a speech or two of Abraham Lincoln."[2] He also suggests that it is a sociologist's social construction of reality.

It is clear that civil religion is, nonetheless, one of the things we do speak about, if not under that rubric, then in terms of patriotism, the civil heritage, national destiny or purpose, or political and public theology. I will attempt in the following pages to address myself to civil religion under three topics:

1. What is civil religion? Problems of definition and evaluation.
2. America's civil religion.
3. The relevance of liberation theology for civil religion and of civil religion for understanding liberation theology.

The limits both of my competence and time will not allow me more than a brief suggestive analysis of each of these topics. The controversial nature of the term "civil religion" demands that I give, first, some special attention to questions of definition and evaluation.

CIVIL RELIGION:
PROBLEMS OF DEFINITION AND EVALUATION

Probably the best place to begin a discussion of civil religion is to define it simply as the religious dimension of the national political experience. Civil religion is a functional universal. Every nation has one. Each nation has to make some sense of its continuity and meaning in world history and its collective identity and vocation vis-à-vis other nations and its own citizens. What does it mean—in terms of ultimate vocation and moral identity—to be an Israeli, an American, or a Frenchman? To ask a deeply probing question about collective identity and purpose is to skirt on religious ground. In this, the religious dynamic is not unlike that operative in personal identity questions. To define the "soul" of a nation is to see it, in some sense, as before a more ultimate bar of judgment since no nation is the final repository of its own meaning. Nevertheless, questions about ultimate national identity and purpose transcend the peculiar provinces or exclusive competencies of either the state or particular world religions and churches.

If you like, civil religion is the mystic chord of communal memory (always being summoned to reinterpretation in the face of new historic tasks) which ties together both a nation's citizenry and the episodes of its history into a meaningful identity by using significant national beliefs, events, persons, places, or documents to serve as symbolic repositories of the special vocational significance of the nation-state in the light of a more ultimate or transcendent bar of judgment: ethical ideals, humanity, world history, being, the universe, or God.[3]

Presumably, ultimate values are involved as the depth dimension of all significant human behavior. If marriage and the family have nowhere been totally secularized, one would hardly expect that something as potent as the nation-state would be. The claims of one's nation upon the conscience are strong, compelling, and complex. William Butler Yeats caught this sense of the functional universality of civil religion when he stated, "One can only reach out to the universe with a gloved hand—that glove is one's nation; the only thing one knows even a little of." When national existence and history becomes a place where one has contact with more transcendent values, the nation becomes a moral and significantly religious identity.

Let us return, for a moment, to our simple starting definition: Civil religion is the religious dimension in the national political experience. I should like to underscore that word "dimension" as a way of safeguarding us from reifying the civil religion. It is not a "thing." It is an aspect of a seemingly permanent dimension in politics. Civil religion does not exhaust all religious functions. It leaves relatively untouched the contemplative, theological, and inner spiritual dimensions usually associated with the churches. Conversely, civil religion reminds us that the churches do not, also, exhaust all religious functions, nor, seemingly, can they.

Secondly, civil religion is only one of several aspects of the political realm. Of course, there is room for a nonreligious analysis of the polity. The term "civil religion" merely suggests that political analysis which restricts itself to questions of "Who gets what from whom and under what form of coercion" is blinded to an essential factor in all political life: the presence of shared restraining moral norms and collective religious ideals.

It may help us to understand civil religion if we ask whether the political or national realm has a religious dimension *only* when it is judged in the light of some separate world religious tradition or some separately institutionalized religious organization in society? Is the religious dimension in the political realm always borrowed or usurped from some other institutional context, e.g., the church, where it rightfully belongs? I think the clear answer is no.

Every authority system, as Max Weber reminds us, feels the need for symbols of legitimacy. It needs, in Peter Berger's terms, a "sacred canopy" of justification, grounding not only external obedience to its particular demands but inner assent to its rightful existence. Indeed, even tyrants must try to shore up their sheerly coercive authority with moral and religious trappings as the Nazi religious system shows us. They spin out ideologies. Unless we are radical anarchists who view all present or potential political authority as illegitimate, we will need to avoid a cynical view which sees every legitimacy system for political realms as, in all respects, a false ideology.

But, to continue the argument, systems of legitimacy are never purely rational. Nor are they grounded simply on utilitarian empirical calculation of consequences. Political authority systems are not legitimate just because they work. Every authority system relies upon nonrational symbolic "charisma." Because authority systems touch potent and ambiguous realities such as power, position, force, contingency, personal and collective destinies, it is impossible that the political realm lack—in however attenuated or disguised a form—a religious and mythic dimension. If the churches will not provide society with the "charisma" that it needs, it will either create its own or seek for it elsewhere.

Note that I am arguing that a religious dimension is intrinsic to the political or societal realm as such. If the experience of personal contingency, limit, and death lead individuals to ask ultimately religious questions even in the absence of any sustained contact with explicitly religious groups, national experiences of threat, contingency, breakdown, and possible decline and death bring collectivities to a similar religious threshold. There are collective situations which provide analogues to the "limit situations" or "peak experiences" which phenomenologists of religion point to as the locus for personal religious experience. Revolutionary beginnings, periods when national history hangs in the balance, moments of collective ferment, redefinition of national purpose, or acceptance of humiliation and defeat—these are the collective "signals of transcendence," again borrowing Peter Berger's language, which indicate the concrete points of contact between national political experience and experiences of transcendence. They are the places where we would expect political language to have a religious tinge. They are also, interestingly enough, the situations to which political theologians must point if their claims about the public character of religious language such as "the judgment of God over the nation," "providence," or "liberation theology" are to have any concrete reference and public significance.

The religious dimension of the political realm is, then, neither a borrowing from or usurping of the rightful domain of another institutional sector of society, i.e., organized religion. Most nations, to be sure, will probably employ the religious symbols which are culturally at hand to ground and interpret their political authority and national identity. It is worth remembering, however, that even when the symbols for understanding national destiny are largely borrowed from the great world religions, these borrowings usually involve creative and ad hoc applications of that symbolism to religious problems which arise not from within the religious tradition itself but from critical historical events within the national political experience. No knowledge of Islam, for example, as a world religion can help us to deduce a priori the way it will be used to ground the particular meaning and destiny of Egypt. Similarly, nothing in Catholicism understood as a world religion would lead us to understand the way it functions as a *civil* grounding for the experience of the Republic of Ireland where, as Conor Cruise O'Brien put it, "To be an Irishman is to be at least an 'honorary' Catholic."

It was precisely this understanding of an *intrinsically* religious aspect to the political or social realm which led Emile Durkheim to insist that every society in some profound sense is a moral and religious reality to its members. He also saw that every society, "in all its aspects and in every period of its history, is made possible only by a vast symbolism" of moral ideals which are never perfectly realized by given empirical states of the society.[4] This insight of Durkheim and, indeed, some analysis according to the mode of Durkheimian sociology would seem a necessary background for determining our answer to these questions: "Is there such a thing as a civil religion?" and "If there is, how should we evaluate it as a religious reality?" I have been arguing that even when a great world religion such as Christianity provides the main symbols for interpreting national purpose and destiny, civil religion remains, in Durkheim's terms, a dimension *sui generis*, irreducible to the constitutive properties of the tradition of that world religion. It is, at any rate, a dimension whose religious significance addresses itself properly to *all* those who participate in the national political realm, not merely to members of the churches.

It would be a mistake, therefore, to follow Martin Marty when he suggests that the only reason civil religions exist is because "the nation, state or society is one of the most potent repositories of symbols in the modern world and can often replace religious institutions in the minds of people."[5] Civil religion does not derive exclusively from the arrogance and potencies of nation states. Neither does it arise because of the failures of organized religions sufficiently to apply their more universal symbols to the concrete contingencies of national histories or because of the complacency of the churches in idolatrous patriotism. Neither civil religion nor patriotism is inherently idolatrous. Civil religions exist because of the empirical impossibility of a purely "secular" state. As W.H. Auden once put it, "Without a cement of blood (it must be human, it must be innocent) no secular wall will safely stand."[6]

If civil religion is a functional universal, the actual empirical state of civil religion in any given nation varies according to social or cultural context. The quality of the civil religion, its intensity or extensiveness, its relative importance to national self-identity or its primary institutional locations all vary from context to context. In some cases, the civil religion is mainly sponsored by the state as in Japanese Shinto. In other cases, such as traditional Catholicism in Latin America, the civil religion is derived from the church. Religious pluralism—either as intense conflict or in accommodation—as opposed to religious monism is an important factor to explain cases where "there actually exists alongside of and rather clearly differentiated from the churches an elaborate and well-institutionalized civil religion" with its own set of national feast days, shrines, sacred founding experiences, documents, saints, etc., as opposed to cases where church religion and civil religious functions are fused.[7] In cases of religious pluralism, the symbols of the civil religion, if they are to function as a powerful moral reference, must be both concrete enough to provide some meaningful content and direction to national identity and general enough so that civil religion does not become a serious alternative rival to particular religious groups within the nation.

The absence, in some cases, of a clear differentiation of the civil religion from the state or particular world religious traditions has blinded some observers entirely to the phenomenon of civil religion. Some, for instance, find the historic coalescence of Christianity and national identity as natural. They fail to see this coalescence for what it is: a historical accident involving a creative synthesis between Christianity and national culture where *both* elements contribute to the synthesis in a sort of creative compromise.[8] The symbolism, for example, involved in the creation of a Saint Louis or a Joan of Arc was neither purely Christian nor purely French. It was as much a symbolism of French national identity as of world Catholicism. It was as much a civil as—if I may be permited the misleading barbarism—a religious religion.

The civil religious dimension does not seem to differ, at least as a phenomenological system of beliefs, rituals, and moral codes, from other religions, although civil religions may be less intense and personal. Emile Durkheim once put this point bluntly by asking, "What essential difference is there between an assembly of Christians celebrating the principal dates of the life of Christ or of Jews remembering the exodus from Egypt or the promulgation of the decalogue, and a reunion of citizens commemorating the promulgation of a new moral or legal system or some great event in the national life."[9]

Civil religions display the dialectical tensions inherent in all religious systems. I can merely cite some of the most important of these to illustrate the main paradoxes inherent in the institutionalization of *any* religious system.

Transcendence vs. immanence: Civil religion is confronted by the paradox of transcendent reference and immanent embodiment, a tension deriving from the universal religious need to incarnate the transcendent "in symbolic forms which are themselves empirical and profane and which with repetition become prosaic and everyday in character."[10] The perennial danger is that the empirical national group becomes itself a deity instead of a carrier medium of transcendent reference "where politics operates within a set of moral norms, and both politics and morality are open to transcendent judgment."[11]

Routinization of ritual: Of course, emblems like the flag, special political institutions, national shrines, ritual days such as Memorial Day, the Fourth of July, etc., may become mere lifeless symbols devoid of any capacity to evoke significant commitments to national faith and purpose. They become prosaic and everyday, as cold and lifeless as the Christian ritual of Sunday Vespers portrayed so vividly in Ingmar Bergman's film *Winter Light*. For civil religions too the dictum holds good that they must be *semper reformanda*.

Priestly vs. prophetic functions: Again, civil religions embody the perennial tension between the priestly and prophetic functions of religion. They must find the right balance between the holiness of the is and the holiness of what ought yet to be. Like the other religions, civil religions are called upon both to comfort and to challenge, to celebrate and to call to action. At its best, however, a nation's "ideals and aspirations stand in constant judgment over the passing shenanigans of the people, reminding them of the standards by which their current practices and those of their nation are ever being judged and found wanting."[12]

Inclusion-exclusion: Civil religions face the temptation of over-emphasizing the exclusive election of their own group by refusing to open up national symbol systems and reality reference points to participation in and judgment by the wider body of humanity. Of course, civil religions are not the only religious systems mistakenly to think that outside their little church there is no salvation. There are also distinctions to be made between the general high priestly civil religion of the state and the various sub-species of the civil religion: the folk tradition of the people and the public theologies of the denominations whereby "the particular communities—be they religious, ethnic, or oriented around interest groups—can creatively refract generalized civil religion through specific prisms."[13] As these distinctions make clear some analysis of conflicting interests of subgroups in a society and of competing "civil religions" as well as analysis of the articulation or conflict between the civil religion and what Clifford Geertz has referred to as "primordial loyalties" toward intermediate groups in the society would be necessary for understanding and evaluating civil religions.

Moreover, like other religious systems, a civil religion "does not make any decision for us. It does not remove us from moral ambiguity."[14] Neither past successes nor failures are totally determinative. Americans are no more saved by Lincoln's faith than the Jewish audiences addressed by Jesus were by Abraham's. Whatever a nation's achievements and already attained ideals, it is still called upon to know "that here on earth God's work must truly be our own."[15]

Evaluation

It is impossible in advance of careful study of each case to give any straightforward answer to the evaluative question about the religious worth of civil religions. Nevertheless, the relevant criteria for discerning authentic from inauthentic civil religions would seem somewhat clear:

1. the nature and pervasiveness of the transcendent reference of judgment over the nation's acts.

2. the capability of national symbols and ritual to engender commitments to the deepest spirit and highest ideals of the nation. In this context, Emile Durkheim once suggested that "What we must above all cherish in society—that to which above all we must give ourselves—is not society in its physical aspects, but its spirit."[16] Indeed, he argued that we should be more willing to see our empirical society disappear than to betray the principles and spirit on which it was founded.

3. the presence or absence and relative strength of a prophetic strain in the civil religion.

4. the capability of civil religions to open up the symbols of national patriotism to include references to the wider human family. National patriotism, like world religions, has a profound vocation toward universalism. Somehow true patriotism must be wedded to cosmopolitanism so that our meaning as citizens of the nation is related to our vocation as citizens of the world. This is all the more incumbent in the modern world where projects of national self-sufficiency fly in the face of the growing interdependence of our world.

I would add to the above list a fifth and crucial factor for evaluating civil religions: justice. I have earlier claimed that a Durkheimian perspective in sociology seems necessary for an appreciative understanding of the concept of civil religion. Such a perspective, while realistic, forbids mere cynicism or negativity in the face of national moral and religious ideals. Although not unaware of the extent to which consensus could mask coercive injustices under the cloak of patriotic ideology, Durkheim was sensitive to the authentic consensus on moral ideals which often underlay and regulated conflicts, just as Karl Marx, in another context, uncovered the genuine conflicts masked by consensus ideologies.[17] Both Durkheim and Marx need to be read together in a creative dialogue if one wishes to evaluate a civil religion. Durkheim, correctly I think, once asserted that a commitment to justice could be the only national ideal capable of generating an *authentic* consensus in the modern world. "Just as ancient peoples needed above all a common faith to live by, so we need justice."[18] I do not hesitate to suggest, then, that a commitment to justice at home and in the nation's dealings with other countries be used as the touchstone for evaluating a nation's patriotic identity. Civil religions which *celebrate* constitutional arrangements which perpetrate national and international injustice are *merely* civil.[19] They are, in no authentic sense, religious. Such civil religions are functioning, in Marx's sense of the term, as ideologies. If we follow Durkheim's suggestion, in the modern world "this is true civil religion: to love justice and do the right."

How should a believing adherent of one of the world's religious traditions evaluate a civil religion in his midst, even an authentic one? Much will depend on the way in which he sees the civil religion. Is it an alternative rival to the church? Some religion above the other religions? Is it consonant with his own religious tradition? If his own religious tradition is open to wider human—even religious—values, simultaneous participation in his own religious tradition and his nation's civil religion will seem no more incongruent to him than ecumenism. If he can join with even nonreligious people in common enterprises, presumably he could also become a partner in a shared national identity which includes religious symbols not entirely his own. No one, I think, would suggest that the civil religious dimension exhausts all, or even the most relevant, aspects of religion. Nor do the churches exist mainly to lend institutional support to the civil religion. A division of religious functions need not imply conflict between the churches and civil religion or the eclipse of the churches.

Robert Bellah has also suggested a fairness rule for judging civil religions: One should not compare the worse strains in the civil religion to the best ones in his own. He also appeals to a principle of responsibility. "I am convinced that every nation and every people come to some form of religious self-understanding whether the critics like it or not. Rather than simply denounce what seems in any case inevitable, it seems more responsible to seek within the civil religious tradition for those critical principles which undercut the ever-present danger of national self-idolization."[20]

AMERICA'S CIVIL RELIGION

To seek within the civil religious tradition those critical principles which undercut the ever-present danger of national self-idolization and to find therein the symbols which promote national and international justice—we have here the essential program for a creative use of America's civil religion for doing liberation theology in North America.

In the aftermath of Vietnam, Watergate, CIA and ITT interference (to use a cold, neutral term for the reality of subversion of justice) in Chile, it is difficult for many Americans to find much solace in their national heritage. David O'Brien captures the mood of many when he assesses the legacy of the 1960s. If John Kennedy in his inaugural address could still speak glowingly of "those human rights to which this nation has always been committed and to which we are committed today at home and around the world," in the 1970s the phrase rings hollow in our ears.

It is hard to sustain devotion to democracy as blacks are denied it, and whites adopt it as a slogan to justify the murder of Asians. Liberty ceases to have meaning for people who hear it from the lips of men who assist in its destruction. The people seem to know democratic responsibility only as a part of a preorganizational past, and their vague sense of loss is smothered in the pillow of affluence. Unable to understand how the crisis came about, given little leadership in solving their problems, many Americans seem certain only of failure, explicitly the failure of their leadership, secretly the failure of themselves. The American dream of shaping the course of history, leading the world to material sufficiency, personal liberty, and popular government gives way to apathy and despair, to a sense of impotence and frustration before the rush of events over which men appear to have no control.[21]

I caught this mood of nostalgia for a dream gone sour when I heard Patty Andrews of the Andrews sisters sing "Where have all the good times gone?" in a Broadway musical last spring. One sensed in the audience an anxious question: Just yesterday all seemed so right, where did we stray and go wrong? Part of the answer lies in the often yawning chasm between high American ideals and actual moral performance. Part of it is to be found in the imperfection of the dream itself.

It seems that we *all* know now that the dream was somehow flawed from the beginning.[22] John Winthrop's fellow pilgrims may have seen themselves as a "city upon a hill" but there was no room in that spacious mansion for America's native Indians. The pilgrims' errand in the wilderness projected their own fears of the demons within their hearts upon the wilderness whose sheltering spaces their descendants callously destroyed and whose inhabitants they largely cheated, emasculated, or slaughtered. Long after the pilgrims' Calvinist doctrine of predestination had lost theological relevance in the church, it continued to operate as a social model for many Americans' self-understanding. An "elect" nation seemed to need to have some in their midst who were not quite saved.

Jefferson's much-praised proclamation of inalienable rights of life, liberty, and pursuit of happiness did not, until the fourteenth amendment, remove the scandal of chattel slavery from the land. By the 1840s de Tocqueville feared the shadow side of Jacksonian democracy and the cult of the common man when he wondered whether mediocrity and slavish conformity might smother America's institutional liberty and virtuous voluntarism. We know now also that too much of the American dream was shaped during America's gilded age in the post-Civil War period when the bitch goddess success replaced Thoreau's ideal of simplicity and Samuel Adams's insistence that solid virtue was the only lasting basis of a free republic. Too much of that dream was premised on false, energetic individualism, a secular legacy of the Arminian pietistic revivalist strain in American church religion. America's greatest failure, however, has been its ineffectual struggle with the moral dilemmas of industrialism and the riotous growth and unchecked independence of American corporate power. The older American doctrine of individualism has become, in large part, a liability for all but the industrial and banking interests whose disproportionate privileges it protects.

Arthur Schlesinger has termed the post-Civil War decades as "the critical period in American religion."[23] In that crucial turning point for American religion—denominational or civil—the robber barons went largely unchecked. Speaking of that period, David Wells says:

As the network of relations affecting men's lives each year became more tangled and more distended, Americans in a basic sense no longer knew who or where they were. The setting had altered beyond their power to understand it, and within an alien context they had lost themselves. In a democratic society who was master and who was servant? In the land of opportunity what was success? In a Christian nation what were the rules and who kept them? The apparent leaders were as much adrift as the followers.[24]

These questions still exercise our moral imaginations and judgments today.

In the period between the Civil War and the end of World War I, the famed "melting pot" image was tried and found seriously wanting as immigrant groups, largely Catholic and Jewish, were forced to worship at WASP cultural altars and where prolonged racism, anti-Catholicism, and anti-Semitism showed that, in America, some groups melted more easily than others. The failure of American religion—denominational and civil—in the post-Civil War epoch is tragically conspicuous in the way religious symbols were trotted out to glorify America's first noncontinental imperialistic expansion in the McKinley-Roosevelt era. Sidney Ahlstrom has characterized that period by remarking,

Kipling's words on "the white man's burden" became for a season the battle hymn of the republic. Never has patriotism, imperialism, and the religion of American Protestants stood in such fervent coalescence as during the McKinley-Roosevelt era.[25]

In reading the evidence for this period of American history we should be careful not to let the debunking spirit run riot. Through the nineteenth century and up to World War II, the American myth exercised a powerful attraction upon the minds of Europeans as well as Americans. Indeed, British conservatives such as Walter Bagehot needed to argue to the "special circumstances of the American continent" to fend off claims by Englishmen, inspired by the American example, for an extended franchise and the incorporation of the working classes into the national political life.[26]

The fusion of religion with shallow and exclusionary patriotism is a constant thread which runs through America's history from the Know-Nothings in the 1840s through the Protestant nativists at the turn of the century, Attorney General A. Mitchell Palmer's anti-red hysteria in the aftermath of World War I, and the revival of the Ku Klux Klan in the 1920s, down to McCarthyism and the Dulles cold-war rhetoric in the 1950s and the hard-hat stickers during the Vietnam War: "America, love it or leave it."

America—the righteous empire with a manifest destiny to conquer the vast continental expanses; the redeemer nation called to leave the tired Babylon of Old Europe and receive the teeming masses to its bosom; the bold adventure in freedom, as Oscar Handlin has called it, that was dynamic, optimistic, pragmatic, individualistic, moralistic, and egalitarian: perhaps it's for the best that the good times have gone!

My own mood in the face of the awful puncturing of the American dream and the painful confrontation with the often surrealistic nightmare of a multiplier-effect in national breakdown and failure is, somehow, something far less than despair about our national heritage. National failures have left some healthy scars. They have planted some seeds of hope. If no generation of Americans has lacked its prophets, ours seems not stingily blessed with those who wear the mantle of the best American spirit: Ralph Nader, Sam Ervin, John Sirica, and Justice Douglas to name but four who stand in the mainstream, not to mention Daniel Ellsberg and the brothers Berrigan. Has any generation of Americans shown as much passion for justice and distrust of the arrogancies of power without having the staff of presumed national self-righteousness to lean upon?

After Vietnam, fewer Americans believe they have a mission to make the world safe for pseudodemocracies. We have become, again, distrustful of foreign entanglements in the face of exposés of CIA activities in Latin America. We have probably buried forever the symbol of manifest destiny. After Watergate, many citizens have the same salutary distrust of those who hold inordinate power that inspired James Madison at his best in *The Federalist Papers*. Mass defections by the young who turned in the 1960s to a counterculture, environmental pollution, and an energy crisis have deeply undermined the seemingly invulnerable American myths of capitalistic expansion, the salvific consumer society, and so-called free enterprise. Indeed, Michael Harrington can persuasively assert that there is in America today an "invisible mass movement" in support of the goals of a democratic socialism.[27]

No religion is healthy which never confronts the reality of sinful failure. No religion is safe which does not include a healthy dose of doubt in its heart. In that sense, American civil religion is not dead, as some have concluded, but is healthier than ever before. However weak or imperfect the response, it is comforting that thousands of Americans refused to serve in Vietnam; that an incumbent president has been removed from office for criminal and moral failure; that serious efforts have been undertaken to end racial or sexist discrimination in our institutions; that some, at least, are prepared to celebrate national days of humiliation proclaimed by Congress. The body politic still includes pockets of health.

National failures have, further, placed us all in a period of collective choice where America's history over the next few decades hangs in a balance. In such a period of challenge and threat, we are summoned to remember (both in the sense of recall and reconstruct) our past in terms of what we collectively will to prevail in the future. We need to find today a "usable past" in order to forge a "usable future."[28] These choices of national identity and projected purpose are ultimately serious not only for the soul of America in completing the task of justice at home but for the future of most of the world as it struggles for liberation from economic neocolonialism. I fail to see how such choices can be denominated as anything less serious than religious, whatever the symbolism used to interpret them.

The future direction of America's civil religion and the reconstruction of a usable past are not merely *a* resource for doing liberation theology in North America. I would argue that they constitute the key arena of "conscientization"—to use the technical term of liberation theology—in the struggle. It should be obvious that it would be a national disaster if, at such a time, we left the civil heritage and patriotism to the yahoos.

It would be a disaster for strategic reasons. For, as Susan Sontag reminds us, ". . . probably no serious radical movement has any future in America unless it can revalidate the tarnished idea of patriotism."[29] In a similar vein, Robert Bellah criticizes the New Left movements of the 1960s for failing to make a "strong link to that deep religious and moral tradition in America that had itself never wholly surrendered to capitalist utilitarian society" with its systemic evils of competitive meritocracy, privatism, consumerism and arrogant bureaucracy." Nor did the leaders of the New Left grasp the fact that without making that link their efforts were doomed to failure. An alliance of outraged college youth and elements of the most oppressed ethnic minorities could not permanently change the direction of American society. Something much closer to the mainstream of the cultural tradition and with a potential appeal to a much larger constituency would be needed for basic change to be effected, if it can be effected at all.[30]

If the New Left has failed to create a new consensus for justice, no religious denomination in America alone nor even the whole of them in consort contain symbolic resources powerful and general enough to build, unaided, a national religious ideal capable of mobilizing common American consent. This, of course, has been true from the beginning of our history. America has never had a church culture. Radical and seemingly irreducible religious pluralism at the institutional level has meant, as John Smylie puts it, that in America, "only the nation bears universal purpose and has continuing historic meaning."[31] Thus, America came to be, in Sidney Mead's terms, "a nation with a soul of a church." If the best spirit of that soul has now departed, it seems unlikely that the churches will be able to achieve what eluded them in their heyday of public influence: a common faith for Americans to live by. It would be well for church critics of the very idea of a civil religion to remember the salutary challenge of liberation theology. The churches are called today to participate in a reality both larger and, in some respects, more important than they. For both Latin and North America this means that what is needed is the forging of new links at the cultural level between the churches and larger movements for social justice. The task at hand is the creation of a new, revitalized civil religion.

The genius and peculiar nature of America's civil religion has been that it is not essentially an idolatry. Americans have always understood the nation as under God. Its authentic spokesmen have always somehow known that, in President Lyndon Johnson's words, "God will not favor everything that we do."[32] Moreover, the civil heritage has not been antithetical to particular, denominational religions. America has been spared anticlericalism and the churches have been bulwarks of the authentic American ethos.

The peculiarly American doctrine of separation of church and state largely explains the absence of serious or sustained conflicts between the churches and the civil heritage in America. Toward the end of his *American Commonwealth*, Lord Bryce admits that in discussing the national and state governments of the United States, he

never once had occasion to avert to any ecclesiastical body or question, because with such matters government has in the United States absolutely nothing to do. Half of the wars of Europe, half the internal troubles that have vexed European states, from the monophysite controversies in the Roman Empire in the fifth century down to the Kulturkampf in the German Empire in the nineteenth, have arisen from theological differences or from the rival claims of church and state. This whole vast chapter of debate and strife has remained virtually unopened in the United States.[33]

It is the combination of the institutional arrangement of separation of church and state and the cooperation of church and state in the religious definition of America which explains the peculiar nature of

America's civil religion. For, "the fact that we have no established religion does not mean that our public life does not have a religious dimension nor that fundamental questions of our national existence are not religious questions."[34]

For those who would argue, like Sidney Ahlstrom, that our patriotic heritage is dead or at least bankrupt, I would suggest a warning reminder and a test. The reminder is that the American civil heritage, however flawed, is, in Ernst Troeltsch's sense, our fate. It is, of course, impossible to devise a phenomenological or historical test which would prove the superior place of America's among the world's civil religions. It is probably not necessary to add that no phenomenological or historical test would show a superiority of American church religious performance over the civil heritage on issues of collective justice. Our national heritage remains the most potent, if not the only, glove we have to reach out to the universe.

Out of the resources of that heritage Americans have always understood the religious significance of their vocation in world history. America, to put it bluntly, is our fate. When that fate is freely chosen and critically restructured, it can be changed from fate to destiny. The challenge of liberation theology to America's civil religion is to call it to retrieve (recall, remember, and reconstruct) its best heritage, to create a usable past for a hopeful future not only for ourselves but for the world. Bellah has suggested three tasks for the work of intellectual praxis involved in retrieving our past:

1. that we search the whole tradition from its earliest beginnings on and in its heretical byways as well as its mainstream;
2. that we subject everything we find to the most searing criticism, something that goes far beyond simply distinguishing the good tradition from the bad tradition, but a criticism that sees the seeds of the bad in the good and vice versa; and
3. that we open our search entirely beyond the ambit of our own tradition to see what we can learn from radically different traditions that may supplement blind spots in even the noblest strands of our tradition.[35]

The test I would suggest to those who argue that the civil religion is simply bankrupt is that they search the tradition themselves to find if there are any symbols, documents, persons, or episodes of history which embody principles that undercut the ever present danger of national self-idolization and promote national and international justice.

I tried this test myself recently on a Catholic friend who has been deeply involved in the praxis of social justice as a community organizer in Chicago slums and, later, as a director of Catholic social action programs. He had little difficulty citing numerous examples of Americans he would place in the national pantheon: John Winthrop, William Penn, Roger Williams, Jonathan Edwards, Samuel and John Adams, Thomas Jefferson, Andrew Jackson, William Lloyd Garrison, the normative figure of Lincoln, Eugene Debs, Susan Anthony, Justice Holmes, Clarence Darrow, Jane Addams of Hull House, Justice Brandeis, Norman Thomas, the early F.D.R., Walter Reuther, Reinhold Niebuhr, Martin Luther King, Justice Warren, and Walter Lippmann. His choices led me to reflect upon the criteria upon which individual Americans are admitted by the general culture to the pantheon of the civil heritage. It became apparent to me that the sacred heroes we choose to remember and celebrate tend to be men and women somehow associated with historic deeds of liberation either for the whole country or oppressed subgroups within the nation. We are more likely to remember today the names of Sacco-Vanzetti and to call them to mind as symbols of the miscarriage of justice than we are to celebrate Calvin Coolidge. In a similar way, fifty years from now Martin Luther King will still be remembered and his words and deeds celebrated when those of Eisenhower and Ford will be dim memories. Even those who constantly try to tame the American "gospel" of equality and justice and respect for the common person of its more radical implications cannot remove the revolutionary potential in the roster of those already in the pantheon. To call upon their names in a ritual litany of American celebration is to raise up specters who sit in mighty judgment on the passing shenanigans of the people.

My friend thought that Emerson, Hawthorne, Melville, and John Dewey from our national literature still had much to teach us. Walt Whitman was singled out for his egalitarian depiction of the inherent strength of the people and his trust in the common person. Mark Twain and Will Rogers belonged in his canon of American scriptures for the way their humor punctured the pretentions of power. Unlike Bagehot's England, the American republic was not, historically, premised on Americans being a deferential people. He suggested, further, that the photos of Dorothea Lange and the art of Winslow Homer and Edward Hopper deserved a special prominence in the temples of American politics as did, at another level, the poster art of Norman Rockwell.

My friend saw no need to rewrite the Declaration of Independence or the Bill of Rights, although he thought the Constitution should be rewritten so that it more clearly reflected the priority of the rights of people over the rights of property. In his view, the Constitution should take public cognizance of the special social power and corporate responsibilities of American corporate wealth. As a disguised "fourth" branch of government, corporate power needed to be unmasked and subjected to the checks and balances guaranteed in the constitution to the other three branches.

These reflections led him to consider the periods of American history which were somehow paradigmatic for him in approaching our own historical point in time and for giving a sense of identity to the whole of the American experience. They became his usable past. He suggested America's revolution and the early republic; the abolitionist movement; the populist movement of Senator Carl Schurz and William Jennings Bryan; the early labor movement at the turn of the century; the progressive movement, especially in its attack on the corporate trusts and its attempt at cooperatives; the early years of the New Deal; the movement for civil rights in the 1960s.

I cite these paradigms of my friend merely to illustrate how America's civil heritage might be re-examined as a resource for doing liberation theology in America. For alongside the mindless and idolatrous patriotism of the yahoos, there exists a patriotism, whose authentic credentials cannot be denied, which represents the best and most potent conscience of America. This high tradition of civil religion does not obviate the need to do realistic social, political, and economic analysis or to devise a politico-economic program for a more just America. Besides keeping our best ideals alive, we need to fight for structural reforms—most would call them in this context revolutions—which will reduce the great chasm between America's ideals and the realities of its institutional life. Not to do so would be to reduce the ideals to an ideology. A retrieval of America's best conscience would seem, however, the logical place to begin a program of conscientization as part of a liberation theology for North America. We need to learn how to make most Americans again believe in returning power to the people. To practice that heritage as liberation theology one must be willing to stand within the civil religion as a committed adherent and engage in the public arena's discourse and action, if not totally on its own terms, at least to challenge it to rise to the best of its tradition and fault it when that heritage is misrepresented to serve as a cloak over the interests of corporate power or imperialistic design. One must take part in our public rituals such as the bicentennial so that their rhetoric is less characterized by Stephen Decatur's mindless "My Country Right or Wrong" than that which the American Catholic Bishops have suggested for the bicentennial: "liberty and justice for all."

THE RELEVANCE OF LIBERATION THEOLOGY
FOR CIVIL RELIGION AND OF CIVIL RELIGION
FOR LIBERATION THEOLOGY

I am prepared to argue that, in a paradoxical way, the best strands of America's civil religion is a liberation theology and the Latin American liberation theology is an attempt to create a civil religion. The convergence of themes between America's civil religion and Latin America's liberation theology is striking. Both are political theologies addressed to the religious significance of the political realm. Both stress the relevance of the historical experience of the community as the locus for critical religious reflection—in the one case the community is the nation, in the other it is the church and a continent. Both are future oriented, premised on a pervasive hope for a more just, this-worldly future. In America's case that future has been, historically, both a *futurum* (a hope that the future will be as gracious as the past) and an *adventus* (a hope for a future that will include the breakthrough, at points, of the eschatological vision of an ideally just society). America's self-image has always included large doses of messianic expectation. While Latin America's liberation theology stresses the future mainly as revolutionary *adventus,* in the precise hope that the future will not resemble the past, one could argue that the new situation in America of awareness of national moral failure has diminished the relevance of the *futurum* and, like Latin America, led us to place a new stress on the emergence of a dramatically different future.

Each of the liberation theologies stresses praxis, the testing of any theoretical position in the crucible of historical experiment. Each includes an energetic voluntarism which insists that God's work of justice here on earth must truly be our own. Each theology has strong egalitarian strains, a distrust of elitism and aristocracy and the cult of the .common person. Each has a jaundiced eye ready to greet the pretensions of power. Both insist that the particular theologies of the church must be seen as interpretive schemes for larger historical tasks in which the church participates but which the church does not control.

Finally, for both theologies experiences of liberation are paradigmatic for participating in and interpreting not only our own period of history but the whole of the historical process. For in America we care to remember and celebrate only those episodes of our national history which are related to exodus experiences of liberation from some historic bondage: the Pilgrims' fleeing England as a release from religious discrimination; the American Revolution as a casting off of the unjust British yoke of dominion; the victory of Jefferson and, later, Jackson over the aristocratic party of Hamilton; Lincoln's emancipation of the slaves as a completion of the initial American intent of freedom and justice for all; the assimilation of Europe's teeming peasant masses as full citizens of the land; the extension of the franchise and the full incorporation of women and the working class into the American task; the movement for full civil rights for America's blacks. At least at the mythic level, America celebrates liberation and justice as of the essence of its own deepest meaning.

This convergence of themes between America's civil religion of conscience and Latin America's liberation theology is not surprising when we recall how the historical experience of Israel's exodus in the Old Testament serves as a paradigm for both. Somehow both see themselves as in the situation of a new Israel. In America's case, however, there is a strong need to recall Israel as the redeem*ed* rather than the redeem*ing* nation. As Rubem Alves reminds us, "No nation will ever fly the flag of freedom and equality for all."[36] Nor should any nation again pretend to. America needs to retrieve, as well, the moral motivation operative in Israel when its prophets reminded the people that they must do justice to the alien because "you, too, were once in bondage and an alien in a strange land." America should be reminded often of the possible ideological uses of the civil model of God in the Old Testament. As Herbert Richardson puts it, often "when America analogizes from the Old Testament—with its paradigm of the entire universe as an emerging *civitas* under the sovereignty of God—she 'discovers' a divine ratification of her own aspiration to establish a holy nation-state: one people, one government, one faith, one God. Such analogizing from the Old Testament involves America in an ideology that gives a religious sanction to the most destructive aspects of modern nationalism."[37]

The ironic, if not tragic, results of American foreign policy since World War II both for America and other lands makes abundantly clear that this danger of ideology is very close at hand. Graham Greene's quiet American in Vietnam playing god or the representative of the messiah nation is the very opposite of liberation theology. America was a gracious land to generations who went before because its inhabitants found here a new freedom which, in principle, belonged to all. It will continue to be gracious only on the same terms. Only on the condition that the civil religion be practiced as a liberation theology can we accept, unhesitatingly, America's civil heritage —our fate, in any case—as our destiny.

If America's civil religion must become a liberation theology, I would argue that America's experience of forging that civil religion might be of some use to Latin American theologians in their efforts to construct a liberation theology. As I see it, their strategies for a liberation theology involve, at one level, an attempt to create a new Latin American civil religion for a just society.

As a social scientist, I have often been puzzled, if not irritated, by the almost religious importance many Latin American theologians of liberation give to the writings and analysis of Karl Marx. At times, Marxist thought (albeit with a revisionary attempt to extrapolate a "scientific" Marx from Marx the materialist, atheistic philosopher) is identified *tout court* with social scientific analysis.[38] Such an approach does not accord with the antidogmatic stance of a social science. The insistence by some Latin American liberation theologians on the use of Marxist social science as *the* essential and indispensable tool for doing critical reflection on historical experiences of oppression and liberation becomes less mystifying, however, if we view liberation theology as a civil religion in the process of coming to be.

The Roman Catholic church in Latin American countries has witnessed, in this century, a new kind of religious competition and pluralism. Predominantly Catholic in population, Latin American countries now contain significant numbers of Protestants and, especially, the nonchurched Marxist left. The church itself can be divided into those who use Catholic symbols as an ideology to support conservative or repressive political regimes or at least take no political stance, and those who are attempting a new Catholic liberation theology related to political action for revolutionary changes in social structure. At least among Catholic theologians and leaders, a third group, mainly priests of European and North American origin, represents an as yet uncommitted middle group. Protestants in Latin America reflect somewhat similar divisions.

It is necessary, in the Latin American context, to find ways to forge symbolic links to build a viable community among the liberationists, those who are as yet neutral and, most importantly, the other large religious group of the continent: committed Marxists whose passion for justice and desire for revolutionary restructuring of society around ideal pictures of the just society is nothing short of religious. In this context, Gustavo Gutiérrez's attempt at creating a common platform around a shared Marxist-Christian utopian vision and program for a just society and his insistence on the use of Marxist social scientific analysis is a creative—if not, indeed, necessary—step in bringing about a "spirit or self-understanding of a community which gives it specific social substance."³⁹ Liberation theology in Latin America is a project which looks toward the emergence of a shared *religious* self-understanding of a political community (now in opposition) which hopes that its ideals will eventually become the national and, indeed, continental self-understanding. It intends to represent already in germ the authentic political—or civil—religious position on which to base a consensual agreement about the contours and principles of a future just society. In this situation for Latin America, Marxist thought functions not merely as a social scientific symbol system but equally as a religious point of reference. It must be taken with *religious* seriousness as one component of an emerging national community of revolution.

Ivan Vallier, one of the most astute North American sociological analysts of Latin America, has described the new theological leadership roles he sees emerging in the Latin American church. In speaking of a new kind of bishop or theologian, he says:

Instead of using their office and prestige as bases for promoting confessional goals and mobilizing commitments to sacramental participation, the stress has been on the problems of the poor, the importance of human freedom and dignity, and the sacredness of the value of social justice. In these allocations, the "Catholic" elements of religious meaning are subordinated to values and goals that are universally sacred. Political issues are implied in these endorsements, of course. [Nevertheless]. . . these values hold a charisma and legitimation on many bases other than Christian beliefs or Catholic theology. The important point is the church as a religious system articulates them in conjunction with other sponsors. . . . The solidification of symbolic linkages between religious leadership and human welfare enhances the charisma of both, helping to bring sacred meaning to the latter and secular legitimacy to the former.⁴⁰

As the church allies itself with the vigorous Marxist movement in Latin America, Catholicism gains new political relevance for the masses and Marxism inherits some of the sacred charisma of the church. For Gutiérrez, the Marxist-Christian dialogue is mutually corrective. Christian faith informs Marxist thought with a deeper ethical concern for personalism. Marxist analysis alerts Christians to the ideological uses of their faith in practice. For a sociologist, however, the problem Vallier refers to as central to the task of creating a liberation community in Latin America seems clearly a problematic at the level of what Bellah has called the civil religion.

If we in North America keep in mind this special religious situation of Latin America with its civil religious imperative to forge symbolic linkages between Christianity and Marxism, we can be freer than those in the Latin American context in "demythologizing" or "secularizing" Marxist analysis when using the Latin American liberation theology as a resource for doing liberation theology on our own continent. Just as the structures and even meaning of Christianity differ in both continents, so also does Marxism as a living political movement. In North America Marxist movements have never generated widespread religious resonance. Indeed, most explicitly Marxist groupings in America have almost always degenerated into what religious sociologists would refer to as dogmatic, sectarian groups with little impact on mainstream American life and few resources to link up with wider constituencies. The difference in the meaning of Marxism in both contexts should not be overlooked. Marx's impact on German, French, Italian, or Latin American social and sociological thought extends far beyond the explicitly socialist organizations: however, both in the Social Gospel movement as well as in the American labor movement as in American thought generally, Marxian influence has been slight and heavily filtered, even among the Christian socialists on the Social Gospel's left wing.

The above remarks are not meant as either polemical or disparaging of Marx's rightful place alongside Max Weber, Emile Durkheim, Alexis de Tocqueville, and Sigmund Freud as one of the giants of modern sociological theory and analysis. It is simply a cautionary note that for North American liberation theology Marxist analysis needs to be judged entirely in terms of the adequacy of its conceptual tools to filter and illuminate social reality and not also, as in Latin America, as an essential religious pillar to support the overarching sacred canopy of an emerging national civil religion and conscience for justice.

I should like to end this essay with a quotation from one of America's authentic spokesmen of the civil religion, Ralph Waldo Emerson. I choose it because of its appeal to the wider community of humanity as a criterion for judging our civil religion. I choose it also because it makes clear my contention that America's civil religion at its best has always seen itself as a kind of liberation theology. Emerson was addressing himself in 1854 to Daniel Webster in the great pre-Civil War political debate about the future of slavery in America. In his speech on the "Fugitive Slave Law," Emerson appeals beyond the mundane rhetoric of partisan political strife to the conscience of America. His words, and especially his criteria for choice, have relevance to North Americans today as they seek to find ways to unite their experience of America to the historic and larger struggle of the twentieth century of the oppressed peoples of the Third World:

Who doubts the power of any fluent debater to defend either of our political parties or any client in our courts? But the question which History will ask is broader. In the final hour, when he was forced by the peremptory necessity of the closing armies to take a side—did he take the part of great principles, the side of humanity and justice, or the side of abuse and oppression and chaos.[41]

NOTES

1. This essay is largely an extended, derivative footnote on Robert Bellah. Cf. besides his original essay found in *Beyond Belief* (New York: Harper & Row, 1970), pp. 168–93, the discussions of this essay in Donald R. Cutler, ed., *The Religious Situation: 1968* (Boston: Beacon, 1968), and Russel E. Richey and Donald G. Jones, eds. *American Civil Religion* (New York: Harper & Row, 1974). Bellah's most extended analysis of American civil religion is his *Broken Covenant* (New York: Seabury, 1975). Other helpful sources for analyzing America's civil religious heritage are Sidney Ahlstrom, *A Religious History of the American People* (New Haven: Yale University Press, 1973); Robert Benne and Philip Hefner, *Defining America* (Philadelphia: Fortress, 1974); Sidney Mead, *The Lively Experiment* (New York: Harper & Row, 1963). David O'Brien, *The Renewal of American Catholicism* (New York: Oxford University Press, 1973), ch. 3, "American Catholicism and American Religion," has some helpful remarks about Catholicism and the civil religion.

2. Martin E. Marty, "Two Kinds of Civil Religion," in *American Civil Religion*, p. 142.

3. Most of these summary symbols, when probed deeply, function as god-terms.

4. Emile Durkheim, *The Elementary Forms of Religious Life* (New York: Free Press, 1965), p. 264.

5. Marty, *American Civil Religion*, p. 140.

6. W.H. Auden, "Vespers," *Shield of Achilles* (New York: Random House, 1955), p. 80.

7. The citation is from Bellah, *Beyond Belief*, p. 168. I have treated some problems on viewing civil religions in a comparative perspective in "Civil Religion," *Sociological Analysis* 31 (Summer 1970).

8. For this point of non-Christian elements in Christian national cultures, cf. Ernst Troeltsch's classic, *The Social Teachings of the Christian Churches*, 2 vols. (New York: Macmillan, 1960).

9. Emile Durkheim, *Elementary Forms of Religious Life*, p. 475.

10. Thomas O'Dea, *The Sociology of Religion* (Englewood Cliffs, New Jersey: Prentice-Hall, 1966), p. 92.

11. Robert Bellah, "American Civil Religion in the 1970's" in *American Civil Religion*, p. 271.

12. Sidney E. Mead, "The Nation with the Soul of a Church," in *American Civil Religion*, p. 60.

13. Marty, *American Civil Religion*, p. 156.

14. Bellah, *Beyond Belief*, p. 186.

15. John F. Kennedy, Inaugural Address.

16. Emile Durkheim, *Sociology and Philosophy* (Glencoe, Illinois: Free Press, 1953), p. 93.

17. For Durkheim on repression and false consensus, cf. *The Division of Labor in Society* (New York: Free Press, 1933), bk. 3, ch.2, "The Forced Division of Labor."

18. Ibid., p. 388.

19. I have found an unpublished paper delivered October 27, 1974, at the annual meeting of the Society for the Scientific Study of Religion, Washington, D.C., by Sister Marie Augusta Neal of Harvard Divinity School, "Rationalization or Religion: When is Civil Religion not Religion but Merely Civil?" helpful in formulating some of these points. Neal supplies some tools for uncovering ideological uses of the civil religion.

20. Bellah, *Beyond Belief*, p. 168.

21. O'Brien, *Renewal of American Catholicism*, p. 6.

22. In his *Broken Covenant* Bellah traces the split between an emphasis on community vs. self-interest which has divided America's national soul from the beginning.

23. Arthur Schlesinger, "The Critical Period in American Religion: 1875–1900," *Proceedings of the Massachusetts Historical Society* 64 (1932–33), pp. 523–47.

24. David A. Wells, "Recent Economic Changes," in *The Nation Transformed: The Creation of Industrial Society*, ed. Sigmund Diamond (New York: Braziller, 1963), p. 41.

25. Ahlstrom, *Religious History*, p. 880.

26. Cf. Walter Bagehot, *The Collected Works of Walter Bagehot*, vol. 5, Norman St. John-Stevas, ed. (London, 1974), p. 410.

27. Michael Harrington, *Socialism* (New York: Saturday Review Press, 1972), pp. 305–31.

28. Cf. Henry Steele Commager, *The Search for a Usable Past* (New York: Knopf, 1967) and Martin E. Marty, *The Search for a Usable Future* (New York: Harper & Row, 1969).

29. Susan Sontag, *Trip to Hanoi* (New York: Farrar, Straus and Giroux, 1968), p. 82.

30. Robert Bellah, "Reflections on Reality in America," *Radical Religion*, vol. 1, nos. 3–4 (Fall 1974), p. 35.

31. John E. Smylie, "National Ethos and the Church," *Theology Today* 20 (October 1963), p. 316.

32. Lyndon B. Johnson in *U.S. Congressional Record*, House (March 15, 1965), p. 4926.

33. James Bryce, *The American Commonwealth*, vol. 2 (London: Macmillan, 1888), p. 554.

34. Bellah, "Reflections on America" p. 41.

35. Bellah, in *American Civil Religion*, p. 266.

36. Rubem A. Alves, "The Hermeneutics of the Symbol," *Theology Today* 29 (April 1972), p. 50.

37. Herbert Richardson, "Civil Religion in Theological Perspective," in *American Civil Religion*, p. 174.

38. In a personal communication, Chile's Arturo Gaete told me that he did not feel that liberation theology was necessarily tied to one kind of social analysis.

39. Alves, "The Hermeneutics of the Symbol," p. 46. It is interesting that Alves

quotes Durkheim extensively in this article, which gave me the idea that Latin American theologies of liberation are concerned with civil religions coming to be. For Gutiérrez, cf. *A Theology of Liberation* (Maryknoll, New York: Orbis, 1973).

40. Ivan Vallier, *Catholicism, Social Control and Modernization in Latin America* (Englewood Cliffs, New Jersey: Prentice-Hall, 1970), pp. 85–86.

41. R. W. Emerson, "The Fugitive Slave Law," in *Speeches and Documents in American History*, ed. Robert Birley (London, n.d.), 2:867.

11

Pre-Bicentennial U.S.A.
in the Liberation Process

by Frederick Herzog

(*Prefatory remark.* Having been asked only recently to write this paper it seems fair to me to state that I had hardly more than a week of uninterrupted work to complete it, two weeks at the most. The best I could do under the circumstances was to sketch an overview of what is happening among us in the U.S. in regard to the liberation process. Obviously I had to be selective. I can only hope that I did not leave out anything crucial as far as the Protestant perspective is concerned. If this were part of a book it probably would appear as chapter 3 at the earliest. In a first chapter I would address the new vision of Christology in terms of Christ and power. In a second chapter I would need to wrestle with the function of liberation language in the church. Only then would I be ready to turn to the liberation process. So in terms of the "assignment" I have been thrown into the middle of a stream. All I can do now is to swim—against the stream?)

"In the time that has elapsed between beginning to write this book and its publication, the theology of liberation tends to be a new 'consumer good' in the European-North American theological market."[1] Thus José Míguez Bonino begins his just published book, *Doing Theology in a Revolutionary Situation.* One of the things we need to commit ourselves to as we move toward the August 17–23, 1975, Detroit conference is the refusal to join the "consumer good" bandwagon. It is impossible to discuss liberation theology on the model of the polished graduate religion paper. This essay is written in view of 150,000 Chileans who have been thrown into prisons or concentration

139

camps since September 11, 1973, and in memory of the 20,000 who have been killed. We are here confronted with *real* suffering, partly supported by our U.S. taxes and as best we know with the compliments of the CIA. It was in this kind of horror that Latin American liberation theology was born—an emergency measure for an emergency situation.

In awareness of the Latin American terror of which the Chilean upheaval is merely one part it might well behoove us to turn silent and to listen to what we are told. But this is not what is intended by the original planners of the conference. One of the preparatory papers claims: "The model of the conference. . . will be *experience challenging experience, in an environment of scientific and religious reflection.*"[2] Very much will depend on how we understand *experience challenging experience.* We are not involved in a sheer academic exercise where we could score debating points. Obviously I cannot speak for the South American theologians. As far as we North Americans are concerned we had better understand the conference as one futher moment in the battle for corporate freedom. Unless we struggle for freedom ourselves in this process, we will be doomed to fail. We cannot do battle for the freedom of others in any honest way. It could only express a condescending paternalism of which we have had too much already. In the process of liberation we cannot do anything *for* anyone, unless we wish to fall prey to a false consciousness.[3]

It may come as a surprise to some, but the liberation process reaches also into North America. There certainly exists a liberation process in the South. Just when it began is difficult to say. In 1863, right after the slaves were set free? Did it begin only on December 1, 1955, when Mrs. Rosa Parks refused to surrender her seat in a bus in downtown Montgomery, Alabama? Did it start in Greensboro, North Carolina, in the early sixties with the sit-ins? There is no question in my mind that the Southern Christian Leadership Conference with Martin Luther King, Jr., at its helm was pulled forward by the irresistible momentum of the liberation process.[4] It so happened that whites also were drawn into it.[5] The memory of the corporate struggle is still alive and partly functions as incentive for its continuity.[6]

Whites who understand the dynamics of the freedom struggle will not sponge off the black agony in the liberation process. There is enough unfreedom to cope with in our white political and economic institutions that we will not get through with transforming them in our own lifetime.[7] We certainly do not need to do battle for the Latin Americans. Their spunk has already become legendary. One feels like appealing to St. Paul: "I thank God through Jesus Christ for all of you, because your faith is proclaimed in all the world" (Rom. 1:8).

Latin Americans have their own interpretation of the liberation process. As far as the United States is concerned, we are part of what some Latin Americans refer to (in a qualification) as a dialectical process. The U.S. is the center of an international system that oppresses the peoples on the margins of the industrialized nations. We are on top of the heap, they are at the bottom. We are "in," they are "out." There is of course something to be said for this picture. But it leaves out the fact that in the center of industrial capitalism itself the counterthrust of liberation is already at work.

So what can *experience challenging experience* mean in the end? It certainly cannot mean that we begin to parrot the Latin American analysis method: "It may seem strange to devote half of a book supposedly dealing with theology to a discussion of sociological analysis and political trends, only to arrive belatedly to the consideration of the theology that undergirds the positions taken by Christians."[8] We have almost analyzed ourselves to death already in U.S. Protestant theology—across the board from psychotherapy to sociology. The end has only been further increase of pop theologies. To replace our previous analyses (found wanting) with South American analyses (because exotic and thus intriguing) would add only one more nail to the coffin we have been so eagerly preparing for ourselves. The complaints about the dilemma of the U.S. churches have uniquely North American roots. Latin Americans may well be able to say: Our Christian commitment came first, our theology came second. I respect the commitment. But our situation is different. We white U.S. Protestant theologians often would not know how to recognize Christian commitment even if we saw it.[9]

The presupposition of this paper is that white Protestant theology in the U.S. first of all needs to recover the criterion for recognizing liberation. The introduction of any other method in the U.S. may well continue the reactionary tendencies so prevalent today. There is the "compulsive American tendency to avoid confrontation of chronic social problems."[10] The sophisticated evasion tactics of American capitalism can even use Marxist analysis as a red herring. Knowledge of our socio-economic dilemmas is widely disseminated, certainly among the intelligentsia.[11] The horror is we do not have the will to get well. How can our will change?

It is exactly with this focus in mind that I, too, wish to get out of "the realm of reformism and liberalism."[12] If only the bankruptcy of theological liberalism in white Protestant theology were understood!

In our society we often hear it said that we do not have the conceptual tools to come to grips with our dilemma: "It is now becoming clear that Western society lacks the conceptual tools to solve its most pressing problems."[13] But even if the proper conceptual tools were available, would the conceptualizing self have the will to use them properly? We dare not forget that the sixties, a period of intense revolutionary fever and vast socio-political and socio-economic analysis, lies just behind us. Many of the things that are still being said about revolution in Latin America were then also said about the United States.[14] We had to learn the hard way the difference between rhetoric and reality. "Those who talk about adventure or change and those who take actions designed to bring about drastic change, have largely if momentarily disappeared."[15] Some seem to experience their revolution vicariously by remote control, as it were, from Latin America or North Vietnam. Criticism of society is not enough.[16] Revolution as a positive alternative may loom on the horizon for some.[17] We need to decide at this point, however, whether or not we want to orient ourselves in a pipedream or in the actual liberation process. Part of the thesis of this paper is that unless we share in what is actually going on as liberation process we cannot be truthful in an exchange with Latin Americans, *experience challenging experience*.

The United States also has been confronted by the new factor that history can no longer be understood by "the traditional chronology of a personal struggle for rule," but has become "a central process. . . of a worldwide struggle to escape from the poverty and misery, and not less from the neglect and anonymity, which have heretofore constituted 'life' to a vast majority of human beings."[18] It is especially through the black struggle that the liberation process is moving on in the U.S.[19] The feminist thrust has entered a further factor. The American Indians, the Chicanos, and others have broadened the scope. Sometimes the process seems submerged, sometimes barely visible. But it is continuing in countless instances nonetheless. And it should be underscored that the struggle is not for sheer economic and political improvement, as is so often alleged by "innocent" by-standers. The goal is holistic: Freedom of body *and soul* in a renewed church and society. Many sharing in the liberation process harbor the hope that the liberation struggle will be able to unite what has so long been divided: genuine evangelical emphasis on biblical truth and social concern.

Here we white Protestants are confronted with more than sheer human possibility. With the sixties the liberal utopia for America was buried. Now we are realizing the need for radical repentance, consciousness-altering, not just consciousness-raising. Is the "central process" (Heilbroner) simply a chance assembly of historical forces? Or is it God at work in history? We can find out only by joining in the struggle.

What is more, the global issues are congealing also as local issues. It takes a long hard struggle, for example, to make a dent on the capital punishment syndrome in North Carolina.[20] There is no dispensation from responsibility for global issues here, since the fight against capital punishment is part of the global struggle for human dignity. The U.S. liberation process forces upon us action-reflection in which God's action constantly impinges on our action. Thus different from a method where theology might come as an afterthought, the U.S. liberation process demands the constant interpenetration of theology and analysis. Both go on at the same time, as it were. It is only that there is an irreversible direction of thought in this process. It is always set in motion by empowerment from God's action, which theology needs to articulate immediately lest it be misunderstood what is going on.

The importance of this emphasis is especially crucial insofar as in the U.S. attitudinal change is still being played off against structural change. The pietists are separated from the activists. We need to underline once more: We can learn from God's action that there can be no personal consciousness-alteration that does not also involve the structures in which a person exists and vice versa. The holistic understanding of liberation dare no longer escape us.

Liberal theology seemed to view the gospel as man's possibility in history. It often resulted in shallow activism and finally in cynicism. Neo-orthodoxy countered that the gospel reveals itself as man's impossibility in history. In the U.S. its result often was a strange Neo-pietism with its attendant paralysis of action. Liberation theology labors over the gospel as *God's* possibility in history. By divine empowerment human beings are made whole in the transformation of inimical structures. Thus *liberation theology is Christian theology responding to God's commission under the pressures of the global process of interdependence.*[21]

Before concluding the introduction we need to ponder the reservation that in the United States liberation theology might already be the new ideology of the oppressor, a new attractive package with novelty book market appeal. The only effective demurrer I know of is the confession that we are not talking about another human project for the betterment of society—tactics and strategies for futher humanistic amelioration of the plight of the poor—but of the divine reality of *liberation in history.* [22] If we do not witness to it, the stones will cry out.

In our attempt to witness we need to be sensitive to the fact that our deliberation is taking place at the time of the pre-bicentennial celebrations, when millions of Americans are being swamped by the commercials and pageants of official history. One example may stand for many. "American Parade" will debut this June at both Disneyland and Walt Disney World with an estimated twenty-five million people viewing the parade during a fifteen-month period until September 1976. An entirely new Disney family of characters, the "People of America," is being developed: "These larger-than-life dolls, together with hundreds of live performers, will highlight a pageant that traces America's glorious achievements and contributions to world progress. This monumental celebration promises to make history fun for old and young alike."[23] During these coming months there will be a constant tug-of-war between the creative self-critique we are attempting and "history as fun"—the national pageant that traces America's glorious achievements and contributions to world progress.

So what is our effort about? It's certainly not one more lesson in "development education." And it's surely also not self-flagellation over national sins. The past is gone; we face today. Whenever we use the word "repentance" it can only mean creative mind-change with no attendant guilt feelings or morose self-pity. What we are about is the creative self-critique that jolts us out of our individualistic privacy into corporate participation in God's liberation process. It is history as liberation, not "history as fun." As I report on this process I will try to reflect as best I can the work of my fellows who are laboring toward the same goal. To mention all the names would call for a long list. But let me say that while not constantly quoting them I am especially indebted to the contributions of Robert McAfee Brown, James H. Cone, and Harvey Cox.

The Will to Freedom in the Liberation Process

What is now happening among us in the liberation process is a first attempt to clarify the relationship between North American and South American theology. It has not been thought through on a large scale before. In many ways, it is the first experiment in theological interdependence on this continent. Thus far U.S. Protestant theology has been Europe-oriented in the main. Extremely important in the process is the new encounter between Roman Catholic and Protestant theology. It is an especially promising event in that the give-and-take is not tied to the abstract level of sheer theological talk, but based on action-reflection (coordinated over a period of about half a year in various groups throughout the United States).

Moving toward the specifically theological detail of the liberation process we need to note that the conference also comes at a time when the media and the religious pundits are hard at work at the engineering of consent toward a return to fundamental beliefs, soft-pedaling the challenges of radical discipleship. As to the latter, the near dead quiet is celebrated as return to spiritual normalcy.[24] The word of Jesus on the return of the evil spirit comes to mind: ". . . and the last state of that man becomes worse than the first" (cf. Matt. 12:43–45). In our culture, self-interest is unashamedly again pitted against self-interest. In the face of staggering inflation the trend toward "each man for himself" has increased.[25]

1. *The Divine Mandate.* Here lies the crux of liberation theology. By whose authority do we think or act? Unless there is a divine mandate for the church to act in a distinct way, we are involved in spiritual waste-motion. In Jesus Christ we are confronted with God's truth for *all* men and women. Here we learn that God is struggling with the marginals for justice to prevail among humankind. It is God's will in *Jesus Christ* we need to rediscover. A person who does not share in God's struggle easily acts as captain of his life, autonomously making decisions on his own authority in regard to the whole scale of issues that bedevil us today, increasing crime rate, drug traffic, abortion, divorce, alcoholism, etc. There is a great difference between those who sovereignly decide their own in these matters, and those who are learning humility in sharing God's humility as he struggles with the wretched of the earth for survival. When Schubert Ogden mentions the death of God theology and liberation theology in one breath and claims that these "fads came and went quickly because they didn't get hold of issues the church cared about,"[26] I need to stress that liberation theology in the South tries to get hold of the issues *God* cares about. Ogden is turning the truth upside down. It is a fact that the church does not always care about the issues God cares about. In the traditional South, the emphasis on salvation domesticates God's work. It leads to an innocuous spirituality that stands aloof from the struggle of the marginals as well as from the struggle for American national integrity. It is often little more than sheer emotionalism or pseudotherapy. We need to remember that God's activity frees human beings from their total thralldom. In the humility of God's struggle with the marginals we learn that the socio-therapeutic function of the church is subject to its socio-liberative function.

2. *The Human Blind Spot.* The white theologian in the South has

usually not stated his premises on these grounds. The blind spot came to full light when black theology appeared on the scene a decade ago. Black theology should not be subsumed under the general category of liberation theology. It is a counterwitness for us whites reminding us that the whole of U.S. Protestant theology has never taken most of the marginals seriously into account. How can brothers and sisters who have not responded to black theology in our own context be expected seriously to consider the methodology of Latin American theology? What is more, will the white male theologian who does not pay serious attention to feminist theology in this country notice what is going on among the women of Latin America?[27] Unless we in the U.S. pass through the needle's eye of the black, red, feminist, Chicano and other liberation experiences in the one America where we live, we will not enter the kingdom of liberation in *both* Americas. It is especially black theology that has witnessed to biblical empowerment in matters of liberation. Obviously there is danger that we overtax ourselves. Engagement with several methodologies at the same time tends to become counterproductive. But without paying attention to black theology we will probably also perpetuate our blindspot when we turn to Latin American liberation theology. Social deprivation and exploitation in this country and Latin America are interdependent. The Invisible Man and the Invisible Woman exist in both Americas. Because of our blindspot to exploitation we are blind all around to the causes of rising crime, the drug problem, etc.

3. *The Will to Freedom.* Here we must come to grips with our Protestant heritage. At no time in the history of Protestant thought in the U.S. have we been at the verge of a sharper incision between false past and new present. We are compelled to the most "merciless self-criticism" (Bellah). It is true that in our country "direct political power of the established churches was broken very early and radical religious languages thrived."[28] It is also true that these religious languages were soon often co-opted by society as opium for the people, so that today religious language is often used to keep the real issues of society concealed. Part of the horror in which we live today is that Protestant Christianity has widely been manipulated to share in the cover-up of success and affluence that hides the crimes of the U.S. as superpower. How can we wrench Protestant Christianity free from its Babylonian captivity? Here it becomes inevitable to draw upon the empowerment through biblical language, especially New Testament language. The language of primitive Christianity and religious language are not one and the same thing, not by a long shot. For the New Testament language incorporates us into God's act of liberation in

Christ that radically counters religion as opium for the people. But the biblical Christ is little known to the people. He is also little known in white male Protestant theology.

If anyone thinks that it is the biblical Christ who is usually preached from our pulpits on Sundays, let him take note of the critique of our secular prophets. The situation has not changed very much since Philip Wylie's assessment of the pulpiteers in *Generation of Vipers:*

These simpering or clamorous windbags preach Christ the Redeemer, Christ the meek and mild, Christ who dies for your sins, Christ who suffered agonies unparalleled, Christ the mystical, Christ the worker of miracles, . . . Christ the simple man, Christ the great academic philosopher, Christ the Tor-quemada of Jehovah, Christ the prince of peace, Christ the tolerator of adultery, Christ the bigot, the spigot, the wellspring of joy and man of sorrows, Christ the scourge of the temple, Christ the physician, Christ the know-it-all, Christ the Miss Fix-it, Christ the mineral spring, Christ the autocrat of the breakfast table, the bingo on Friday night. They never preach, teach, screech, or beseech the truth, come hell or holy water.[29]

I know what I'm talking about. I have been a parish minister myself. I'm still a preacher. We have to face the fact that there is a difference between the pulpit-Christ and the biblical Christ. A good American, John Dewey—nearly fifty years ago—gave us as good an explanation as any why there is a difference: "Nowhere in the world at any time has religion been so thoroughly respectable as with us, and so nearly totally disconnected from life. . . . The glorification of religion as setting the final seal of approval on pecuniary success, and the adoption by the churches of the latest devices of the movies and the advertiser, approach too close to the obscene."[30] As Protestants we can talk about liberation and religious language until we are blue in the face: We won't have understood our problem until we realize that white Protestant religion in the U.S. largely supplies the *active motive to more energetic struggle for pecuniary success.* So we are faced with a change from the self-destructive motive to a more creative motive. This can happen within the bounds of Protestantism only through empowerment by the biblical Christ.

As far as religious language is concerned, we arrive at a very simple proposition: *One does not need religion to create a just society.*[31] In fact, religion more often than not has been an obstacle to a just society.

The language obfuscation we are caught in is unbelievably vast. But if we want to make sense at all as Protestants in the liberation process, we need to disengage the image of the biblical Christ from white religion. This in turn might result in disengaging ourselves from our false self-image as Americans. Our self-image needs to be deideologized. There is no question about that. Because of a peculiar socio-economic development in this country a peculiar selfhood has taken shape that makes the American a peculiar kind of self.[32] Robert Jewett has stated the situation well when he writes about the American resources of the whole self in regard to the notion of good and evil:

The American stereotypes of good and evil are idolatrous belief structures, held not by superficial levels of the intellect but rather by the tenacious resources of the whole self. . . . On the intellectual level alone it is preposterous to think that such advantageous structures would give way under the mere infusion of contrary evidence. Consequently, the liberal tradition in America, hostile to theology, naive about the tenacity of belief structures, and superficial in its grasp of human nature, has been helpless in facing what it recognizes as one of the decisive components of the current national crisis.[33]

The keenest Protestant thinkers have emphatically pointed out since the sixties that liberal Protestantism is really helpless in the face of the national crisis. Do we now want to have a rerun of the sixties: activism without change? One of the great challenges of the Detroit conference is to appeal to the power that can eliminate the naiveté over belief structures and human nature. What keeps us in bondage are the tenacious resources of the American self as successful member of a superpower. So the task is to find the will to be free within the omnipotent nation-state. One can put the whole matter in terms of a simple question: What does it mean to be a Christian in a superpower? Without the gift of freedom there will be no Christian will to freedom.

4. *The Liberation Mission—Mission Impossible?* The task is so large that no single person can grasp all its dimensions. The frightening effects of the superpower empire stare us in the face most inescapably—in terms of present public consciousness in the U.S.—in the debate about the hungerbelt, food as weapon (Earl Butz), the lifeboat ethic, and "triage." A measure of rethinking is discernible in many quarters. Said Daniel Patrick Moynihan: "We are going to have to face up to the fact that we're a different people than we thought we were."[34] This pertains—in the context of our conference—also to our relationships to Latin America. Here the liberation mission seems a mission impossible. Only grace, an act of divine empowerment, can make us new. Once this happens we are not completely in a historical vacuum. There is a liberation tradition in the United States feeding the liberation process with momentum and direction. This country was conceived *also* as a refuge for the marginals of the world—the persecuted, the condemned, the poor. How-

ever romanticist it may sound today, the Statue of Liberty still reminds us of these origins: "Give me your tired, your poor, . . . the wretched refuse of your teeming shore. . . . " The struggle of the "wretched refuse" continued on this continent and initiated a liberation tradition that runs through the Shays rebellion, abolitionism, the beginnings of American socialism, the social gospel, and the early women's movement, to the civil rights movement and the anti-Vietnam War protest. Liberation theology needs to tie into this "other American tradition," at the same time allowing what happens time and again when the powerless become powerful and forget their beginnings.[35] Probably the majority of Americans live with the memory that their forebears arrived on these shores with little more than their hides to sell on the labor market. Many still live a deadly fear that the little security attained will be lost in the present cauldron of crises. We will be meeting in August in a city with one of the highest unemployment rates in this country. It is exactly in this regard that we need to draw a sharp line between the liberation tradition that evokes the will to freedom and the religion tradition that obfuscates radical freedom.[36] This leads us to the task of differentiating between civil religion and the liberation tradition.[37]

The Phony Covenant?

A just society is an ethical task. Reinhold Niebuhr reminds us of the temptation of mistaking the religious absolute for the ethical possibility: "Religion draws the bow of life so taut that it either snaps the string (defeatism) or overshoots the mark (fanaticism). The belief that the moral weaknesses of religion may be eliminated by increasing religious vitality is too simple to be true."[38] Today civil religion is often proposed as helpful lodestar in the malaise of contemporary American society. The sterling work of Robert Bellah affords a felicitous opportunity to ask in what sense civil religion might function constructively in the liberation process. At the outset, one may well agree with Bellah that civil religion may point to a "good thing,"[39] and that it may serve as "an analytical tool for the understanding of something that exists, which, like all things human, is sometimes good and sometimes bad, but which in any case is apt to be with us for a very long time."[40] Obviously civil religion exists. While many may still be uncertain as to what civil religion is all about,[41] it is also clear that it is not the same as liberation theology. At a time when Protestant theology needs to become mercilessly self-critical, the difference has to be underscored. The issue is not whether or not liberation theology might be able to agree to this or that facet of civil religion, but whether it can accept its basic premise.

It is crucial in this moment of bicentennial soul-searching to get a clear grasp of our national history. In this regard Robert Bellah's last book, *The Broken Covenant*, does us a great service. Bellah knows that "this society is a cruel and bitter one,"[42] standing in need of "a genuine cultural renewal."[43] As long as this task is viewed as working at a sober national ethics, Protestants certainly would want to have part in it. But then there is also the religious premise of the cultural renewal as a whole. Bellah views America in terms of a covenant people. The covenant was broken almost before it was made. In the genocide of the natives the Pilgrims denied the covenant. Can we live up to the covenant today?

The mixing of cultural and theological categories issues in an amalgam of ideas that invites Protestant theology to merciless self-criticism. There can be full agreement with Bellah's unwillingness to reject the past: "The recognition of the broken covenant does not mean to me the rejection of the American past."[44] Somehow for all of us a creative "reappropriation of tradition"[45] needs to take place. But for Bellah this also includes acceptance of the myth of the covenant: "The Pilgrim Fathers had a conception of the covenant and of virtue which we badly need today."[46] Whatever lines of argument Bellah follows, the covenant notion is the premise to which he returns time and again. I should like to single it out as test-case of what liberation theology in the U.S. can or cannot work with fruitfully. The question thus is not what society in general might want to do with the notion of the New England covenant. What is at stake is the integrity of Christian theology.

The goal of liberation theology is different from that of civil religion. It tries to discover Christian integrity for participation in God's liberation struggle. Civil religion presses toward general cultural renewal: "Unfortunately not only the Protestant tradition but the Catholic and Jewish traditions have undergone severe attrition in America and in their present form it is doubtful whether they can provide the basis for genuine cultural renewal."[47] For Protestant theology today it would simply be hubris to assume that its primary mandate were cultural renewal. If there is a cultural by-product, fine. But Protestant theology knows that the church cannot play Atlas for any culture.

Bellah gives as good an explanation as any for how the idea of covenant began to function in terms of a national covenant.[48] There was an inward covenant of conversion, and an outward *national* covenant to which all New Englanders were subject. For our purposes it is largely immaterial to argue with its various manifestations if it turns out that the covenant notion cannot function the same way as premise of liberation theology. Bellah seems to maintain (if I understand him rightly) that the covenant notion is still somewhat valid today. But God made his covenant with Israel once and for all for the sending of his Son as liberator within the context of this covenant people. The Christian church shares in the covenant—only through Christ (cf. Rom. 9–11). The once-and-for-allness of this covenant is one of the fundamental premises of liberation theology, as I understand it. To assume that this covenant might be extended to the American nation as a whole involves a mixing of categories. Bellah at one point introduces the Navaho conception of the white Americans as a "false people." What if those who transferred the covenant notion from Israel to the American nation were already a "false people" caught in a false theological consciousness? Any attempt in the Protestant churches today to revive the notion may well border on offering opium to the people. The broken covenant as a national covenant may have been a phony covenant to begin with. Christianity on these shores was soon made primarily a cultural factor, one ingredient of the societal matrix.

We have tried to extend what Bellah calls "merciless self-criticism"[49] one more step. I can agree with him that in regard to civil justice there is much constructive work we can do together on common sense grounds. But the Protestant theologian needs to take the church community seriously in seeking to recover the integrity of the Christian faith. It was Ernst Troeltsch who left an indelible impression on us as regards the particularity of the dynamics of each religious community: "History cannot be regarded as a process in which a universal and everywhere similar principle is confined and obscured."[50] What we meant to suggest was that *there is no way of leaping out of a particular religious community into some higher religion.* We need to acknowledge our radical historicity as human beings, our historical particularity. The primary problem for Christianity is not that religious people abuse the covenant of civil religion, but that they abuse the Christian faith, turning it into counterfeit Christianity in legitimating their power status.

I hope I will be pardoned for using a few personal illustrations. As to "people's language," it's exactly here that the shoe hurts. The abuse of Christianity may sound often very biblical—as in the defense of capital punishment on grounds of Romans 13. Wrote a North

Carolina minister this past July 21 in our local newspaper: "Capital punishment should be retained by the state for all those who deliberately and with forethought take the lives of other human beings regardless of race or economic status. In the 13th chapter of Romans, Paul makes it clear that the power of the state to use the sword against evildoers is ordained of God."[51] No questions asked about the difference between Nero's Rome and Governor Holshauser's 1975 North Carolina, and between pagans running the government in Rome and Christians in government today. Suppose there still were debatable reasons of civil justice for capital punishment, the theological problem is that many Americans feel it also needs Christian legitimation. Another illustration: Among my various speeches in North Carolina was one several years ago at a ministerial association meeting. At some point I said a word or two about the social loss resulting from wasteful capitalism in our society, something along the line of Vance Packard's *The Waste Makers.* I had hardly got through my speech when a minister rose to the occasion and blurted out: "What have you got against capitalism? Why, God himself is a capitalist!"[52] The particular historical faith is up against the distortion of its basic truths. And it cannot be changed in a general cultural renewal. Counterfeit Christianity has to be tackled head-on within the churches. The image of the biblical Christ needs to de-ideologize the false "Christian" self-image.

If we understand that the Puritans already operated with a distorted notion of selfhood, "for they had founded their new commonwealth on a great crime—the bondage and genocide of other races,"[53] it follows that from the very beginning of this nation the Christian notion of a corporate self was not part of the Christian movement in North America. The inherent individualism in the practical application of Puritan belief is still part of our dilemma today. Bellah realizes how much is at stake on this score.[54] The New Testament notion of selfhood has yet to find its way into the matrix of the Protestant experience on this continent. Not even in the social gospel was there a clear turning from the mistaken past. Says Arieli: "Yet most of the Social Gospelers, although they condemned the ruthless competitive capitalism of their times, ascribed to individualism an important historical role in the progress of humanity and maintained that it had abiding value as a regulative ideal of society and morality."[55] Protestantism in the U.S. stands at a turning as it is challenged by the liberation process. As long as the covenant reality is uncritically appropriated we will not pay attention to the sharp incision in the covenant notion experienced in the coming of Jesus Christ. The covenant was now qualified by a corporate selfhood that includes all peoples, especially the outcast. The Pilgrim fathers seemed blind to the inclusiveness of Jesus' corporate selfhood, as they applied the exclusivist covenant notion to the nation. Without acknowledgement of Christ's corporate selfhood, U.S. Protestantism will probably continue its individualistic bent.

Empire and Liberation

The pressures for global social change were initially labeled development. They were largely understood as goodwill gestures of the developed nations toward the underdeveloped ones. "Liberation" reflects the fact that people are able to take their fate into their own hands. The explication of the dynamics of this process is not the theologian's task. It is the domain of the social scientist. But at this point we also need to press for people's language, so that the issues can be dealt with intelligibly in the local church.

A significant literature within the past decade has made us more aware of the vast expansionism of our nation and the implicit imperialism, although this is nothing new as such. One finds similar analyses, for example, in Reinhold Niebuhr, *Moral Man and Immoral Society* (1932). But Niebuhr could still view the world as a conglomerate of nations managing to survive in a standoff of power. Nature red in tooth and claw allowed for a fair independence of each as each nation defended its own turf.[56] That independence and self-interest go hand in hand is a truly American view: "The selfishness of nations is proverbial. It was the dictum of George Washington that nations were not to be trusted beyond their own interest."[57] Growth of international commerce had greatly increased the interdependence of nations in Niebuhr's day, but more rapidly than the intelligence required to tackle the new situation.[58] While Niebuhr saw that the standoff might be changed under tremendous pressures, he did not as yet organize his ethics around a vision of global pressures. There is still ethical reflection around that at least roughly follows Niebuhr's basic model, for example, lifeboat ethics, trying to offer a response to the world food shortage.[59] But then there is also a new ethic emerging, orienting itself more in evolving global interdependence.[60]

The morality of an act is usually a function of our vision of reality. In a sense, the interdependencies of the life-support system called earth have been there for all to behold for a long time. Today because of technological limits we can no longer ignore them. This does not mean that we have become more ethical. It is only that today self-interest compels self-limitation.

It is perhaps here that we need new concepts the most. American myths are still interfering too much with new insight. Gibson Winter was one of the first to state the dilemma in which we are now caught: "When the Western World and later every part of the globe embarked upon the technological adventure, they set in motion the participatory process as a first step toward an interdependent world. . . . However, American folklore and institutions obstruct our vision of participatory society and limit our commitment to one world."[61] The task of theology is now to destroy those folk myths that function as halo of blind self-interest and to offer new concepts.

The *United Methodist Church Bishops' Call for Peace and the Self-Development of Peoples* (1972) is an important step in this regard. It seeks to transform the national myths. In some respects it has now been complemented by the Roman Catholic study on *Liberty and Justice for All* (1974). In the pluralism of U.S. church life there probably is no other way to develop new church orientation than through individual denominational statements. Perhaps their accumulative impact will provide us in the long run with something like the effect of the Latin American Medellín documents (1968). In any case, since a corporate theological base for Christian reflection in regard to the new vision of reality is a prerequisite, we need to pay very careful attention to what is already afoot in the churches in response to the liberation process.

Liberty and Justice for All states as premise "the unity of sacred and profane history" (David Tracy).[62] The objections to the document raised by Andrew Greeley are perhaps best understood on the background of a reality vision where sacred and profane history are still viewed as largely independent of each other.[63] Greeley makes a distinction between an old view of ethics and a new view: "Quite simply put, the 'old' social actionist believes, as he always has, in the politics of coalition building within the system. The 'new' social actionist believes in the politics of consciousness raising to overturn the system."[64] Do these polarities really reflect the new situation that Future Shock is confronting us with every day?

First of all, liberation theology in U.S. Protestantism is struggling with issues located not just *within* the system. We are now coping with agonies going much *beyond* the system. What is more, we don't have to overturn the system. Global pressures beyond our control are already in the process of overturning it. Second, the phrase "consciousness raising" is becoming more and more misleading for the American pre-bicentennial scene.[65] What Christians need to struggle with is repentance, consciousness-altering. It is unfortunate that Greeley links repentance to guilt, "public confession of guilt."[66] Are we so "psyched" by Freud that we can't think theologically straight anymore? Is not repentance a joyous thing (cf. Luke 15:10), a creative grip on common sense? The biblical Christ jolts us out of our ideologies and pipe-dreams to view the world as it is, caught up in the liberation process.

In Protestant theology itself the concepts are often still heavily determined by the "Greats." James C. Livingston observes: "While theologians like Barth, Tillich, and Bultmann have done much to revitalize the existential dimension of personal faith, they have given us little help in understanding how God does in fact act in nature and history."[67] This is where the crunch comes today in U.S. Protestantism when we try to relate theology to St. John's at the Gasstation. The Protestant "Greats" have not provided us with a clear vision of the historical process, partly because the gospel was still read by them against the foil of cultural particularities, the Swiss cosmos, European guilt neuroses, or American middle-class anxiety. Recent more radical theologies have not as yet sharply described the turning issued in by the liberation process.[68] Here pioneering efforts in the life of the churches themselves, such as the *Bishops' Call* or *Liberty and Justice for All*, carry special weight.

What breaks through in liberation theology is a new understanding of the gospel itself—God's work in history as a global process of humanizing pressures. God in Christ joins the power conflict and prevails. He does not shrink from joining it at the point of direst need. This fundamental factor lies at the core of the atonement. What went on in Jesus' public ministry is still going on in the historical process: God is prevailingly struggling in history for life abundant. He invites us to follow him, taking up our cross and joining the struggle (cf. Matt. 16:24). God is still acting to free humankind for true freedom.[69] This provides us with *a new conception of who God is*. Theology is not striving merely to raise human consciousness to the level of global consciousness. This is happening in myriads of ways apart from theological efforts anyway. What theology needs to stress is that God in Christ in the historical process constitutes a selfhood that *includes* the lowest form of humanity.

Without careful coordination with the scholarly analysis of social science all of this, of course, can become terrifyingly woolly. There is no Christian social science. But God in Christ frees us to get our facts straight, and the facts of social science as well, and to view them as part of his activity in history. It is awesomely difficult for us American middle-class people to get gripped by God's activity as liberation process. We're involved in the process on the side of the powerful—6 percent of the world's population using more than 30 percent of the world's product. In the eyes of many suffering people in the world *we* are the enemy.

The point of the liberation process is to compel us to compliance with God's will (cf. Luke 14:23). God is working out his purposes in history. He is not exclusively dependent on the Christian church: "God is able from these stones to raise children of Abraham" (Matt.3:9). But Christians can join in God's activity—that's the point of God's gift of freedom. This is what the present struggle in some U.S. churches is all about, as I perceive it. Theology needs to insist on repentance as mind-change from blind self-interest to creative self-limitation.

It is exactly at this point that we need to get the facts straight. In particular we need to join social science in its struggle to develop an ethics of these facts. Here our first step is the realization that we are confronted, in terms of the title of Denis Goulet's book, by *The Cruel Choice* (1973). More is involved than giving up patronizing attitudes of benevolently running history with handouts to the world's hungry.[70] Acknowledging the right of poor nations to run their own lives does not immediately bring sweetness and light. Will a poor nation be able to advance without aligning itself on one side of the world power blocs? Will it be able to back up its demands with economic muscle of its own? How does it satisfy consumer wants multiplying faster than its productive capacities?[71] There are countless dilemmas. One cannot get a handle on them in a sentence or two. One can only become part of the struggle to develop an ethics to which all people will subject themselves. This is a vast task, as Goulet reminds us: "I have also delineated, in tentative fashion, some governing principles and general requirements of ethical strategies in development. Three such principles are the subordination of goods to the good, the universalization of solidarity through conflict, and optimum sharing by the populace in decision-making."[72]

Ideology Criticism

Now that we have the raw data before us we need to summarize. How does one do liberation theology? (1) It begins with the empowerment of a new vision of God (*visio Dei*). Piety as one's relationship to God is now subject to God's justice embodied in Christ's corporate selfhood. Reflection on God in terms of Christ's struggle with the marginals, however, is no "answer" to religious curiosity, guaranteeing metaphysical security. The pressures emanating from the struggle shift the theological paradigm from "God the Problem"[73] to man the problem. Enlightenment preoccupation with the metaphysical gap between this world and the transcendent lies behind us. Now the modern questioner is being questioned, one question leading to another question with no final answers. (2) The new vision of God calls forth a new image of man (*imago Dei*). Even the pious human being time and again is sorely tempted by self-assertion without due consideration of corporate justice. The old view of man as this, that, or the other finished product is no longer adequate. We need to think of the person in the process of constant self-change toward a more fulfilled future (*imago futuri*). Theology has no right to legitimate the person in any status quo. (3) The human person in process introduces a new way of life, the liberation mission (*missio Dei*) among those still in bondage. It involves the rejection of theology as ideology.

For Peter L. Berger and Thomas Luckmann ideology is ideas serving as weapons for social interests.[74] This usually involves the legitimation of the present order or a desired future order. Ever since Constantine, theology has seldom been able to escape being used as such a weapon. What is more, it has been a concealed weapon. The major contribution of black theology for whites has been the jarring confrontation with this fact. Recently Major Jones and J. Deotis Roberts have once more brought this to our attention in forceful terms.[75] From the perspective of the American Indian, Vine Deloria, Jr., in recent years has made an unmistakably similar point.[76]

The difficulty for whites to see what is going on is that white theologians have understood time and again to use theology as a concealed weapon in their legitimation of power. Instead of being critical theory of the church, theology is dressed up as a socio-therapeutic answering service, promoting acceptance of acceptance, for example. Obviously theology as critical theory makes sense only if its subject offers critical leverage. God in Christ claiming us in the struggle of the marginals means that a person is never left to his or her own devices, but made accountable to the corporate selfhood of which each individual is a part (cf. Matt. 25:40). In Christ a person is always a double being, an "I" and a "we." One can show best how this overturns modernity by turning Descartes's formula, "I think, there-fore I am" (*cogito, ergo sum*) into "I have been loved, therefore we are" (*amor, ergo sumus*).[77]

Protestant theology, however, in myriads of ways has yielded to modernity. Protestant Christians haven't just been exploiters; their theology has also justified the exploitation. Friedrich Schleiermacher, the father of modern liberalism, argued that the modern preachers of the gospel no longer need, for example, the power of working miracles, since the great advantage in power and civilization of the Christian peoples over the non-Christian, almost without exception, makes such signs unnecessary.[78] One can show without great difficulty how Schleiermacher's great systematic work was also an apology for the power-and-civilization-advantage of the Christian peoples over the non-Christian. Any theology that offers itself as bearer of answers to modern man is likely to be found taking the same route. The point always was to give the power-hungry and power-mad a good conscience in their exploitation: God is on their side. All dilemmas of the approach that might be attacked are outgrowths of this basic distortion.[79]

The Euro-American history of power is a strange mixture of light and shadow. The achievements of modernity have brought innumerable benefits in education, medical care, transportation, etc. But modern industrialization has also brought countless ills. While theology time and again has pointed out dilemmas on the shadow side almost in overkill, it has not taken drastic steps to dissociate itself from the real causes of the ills.[80]

The core event of liberation for theology is found uniquely in unsung struggles at unprestigious places: "My grace is sufficient for you, for my power is made perfect in weakness" (2 Cor. 12:9). This is radical Otherness, Sacredness, not found otherwise. It is what galvanizes the liberation process for the Christian. Protestant theology usually does not point to this reality as core event. Unfortunately too often it functions as concealed weapon in the power struggle. So ideology criticism becomes inescapable. Whenever we experience the unsettling effect of God's involvement in the power struggle as a question that questions us in our American way of life we are at a radical new beginning. God is no longer the problem. We ourselves have become the problem.[81]

American Socialism

By now it has become clear that liberation theology is not a theory of merely one aspect of the theological spectrum. It is a fresh way of trying to view the theological spectrum as a whole, rearranging the priorities with action-reflection as the basic dynamic.

Action-reflection here is first of all reflection on God's action: How do I know what I think until I see what God does? Obviously we become vulnerable in this approach, for we cannot "prove" God's involvement in the survival struggle. God's presence in Christ could not be "proved" either. The most sophisticated theologians of Christ's day vehemently denied God's incarnation. And yet this was what it was all about: embodiment of divine truth, dogma in action.

Two simple steps need to be taken all the time in liberation theology: (1) developing the strictly theological theory; (2) responding to the social theory that best corresponds to the theological theory. Ideology criticism is the critical dimension of both steps.

Our task is not to develop a Christian blueprint for the social order, to build the kingdom of God on earth, or to Christianize society. First, the Christian has no promise that the present world order will turn into the kingdom of God. Second, in a pluralistic society with many faiths and social views there is no chance to Christianize the social order. And yet the truth of God's liberation will be tested in the social order as much as in the closet of prayer.

In our kind of society it is the socio-economic dimension that more than anything else determines our being and well-being. And since capitalism is its structural form, its oppressions become the focus of liberation theology. In capitalism today there is an "oppression explosion." We cannot possibly deal with all the oppressions at the same time. So we first of all need to discover the unity of the oppressions. Exploitation and denigration lie very much at the center.

Here socialism suggests itself as socio-economic option.[82] At this point the struggle in U.S. Protestant theology comes closest to the real crux of Latin American liberation theology, "the option between capitalist and socialist society" (Juan Luis Segundo).[83] Talk about liberation theology that does not involve this option cannot be serious. For it is capitalism that in Western civilization has helped to shape a way of life which contradicts the Christian faith.

Here a puzzlement may arise for some. Did we not reject ideology in theology? Did we not call for ideology criticism? The point is that theology dare not become ideology itself, the legitimation of the status quo or of social programs. But this does not mean that the Christian should shun involvement in ideological struggles. What liberation theology objects to is theology *as* ideology—usually carried as a concealed weapon. Our involvement in ideology has to be on ideology's own grounds, in terms of its rational power and logical consistency. Theology provides the compelling motive for choosing an ideology of justice. But it cannot argue the case for socialism itself.

The case is in competent hands when Michael Harrington argues it.[84] And the strongest part of Robert Bellah's *The Broken Covenant* comes where he stands up for American socialism: "I suspect that our difficulties will soon become so critical that even respected statesmen will disregard the taboos of the past and begin talking about and helping to delineate a distinctively American socialism."[85] It is exactly at this point where theology in North America today has to fish or cut bait. It needs to listen to the voices of democratic socialism in our own land. Paul H. Sherry has recently suggested that we may be approaching just such a moment in this country: "It may be . . . that we are beginning to witness a major change both in the American consciousness and perhaps socialism's ability to impact our life and thought."[86]

The situation in this regard is very much the same as with the issues of development and self-development relative to the American empire. The analysis of social science is already available. The question is whether or not the churches will respond. It ought to be understood in this context that an ethics of development and self-development can emerge fruitfully for the churches only under the overarching aegis of a new comprehensive American social theory.

There is a body of literature in the U.S., represented by Norman Birnbaum, Harold Cruse, Michael Harrington, Irving Howe, Christopher Lash, George Lichtheim, and Michael Walzer, that the churches need to pay more careful attention to. At least four issues need tackling: (1) the definite class structure in the United States; (2) social analysis issuing in political action; (3) public ownership and public planning as foci in this move; (4) a coherent strategy of the churches to meet the challenge of American socialism.

The U.S. churches at this time largely go about the business of tackling social issues apart from an overarching political concept—except for the concealed legitimation of the present political order. William A. Simpson, whose analysis has been incorporated in the preceding paragraphs, summarizes the challenges and the dilemmas with great clarity: "Social issues should be seen as occasions for meeting other institutions on a common ground of strategy and action rather than as annual themes to be programmed through our boards and agencies."[87]

What is possible here might be measured by the 1975 United Church of Christ working group report, *The Role of Transnational Business in Mass Economic Development*.[88] The document deals with basic religious perspectives on economic activity and offers a solid analysis of the place of the transnational corporations in the present system. But the church is largely still seen as a forum where business people and others professionally involved might find a better self-understanding. Meeting other institutions on a common ground of strategy and action seems not envisioned as yet. Even so, this is an important document that calls for careful response. It offers us an excellent test-case for examining the relationship between the church's thinking and American socialism.

I shall not be so naive as to suggest that a change in the political-economic system would immediately solve all the dilemmas we are facing, for example, the dilemmas of technology and ecology. There is a sober ecumenical agreement on the magnitude of our difficulties: "Ecumenical discussion of alternative social systems tends to the view that none of the contemporary social ideologies provides an image of the future that without fundamental rethinking could resolve the dilemmas of modern technological society."[89] But this is what liberation theology is all about at this point: to press for debate and to work for an alternative social system that is more just and viable.

Basic changes along lines mentioned above are contemplated even in the most unexpected quarters. A few months ago, Henry Ford II asked for more central planning: "Not the kind of central planning the Russians have, when they order the whole damned economy from a central plan. I'm talking about a federal planning organization that collects and disseminates information."[90] We need to ask: *relative to which system* would the planning be made? Who would benefit from the planning? Is Henry Ford talking only about socialism for the rich? What kind of planning makes sense *for all?* Will the planners take into account, for example, that cities like New York are going bankrupt already? Can transportation systems be developed that benefit the public, not just the transportation corporations? Once one starts asking questions relative to an alternative social system, there seems no end to them.

The global pressures of liberation hurt us most at the point where our present socio-economic system resists them. The high priority of internal change in our own country is made more urgent as we experience the interdependence of economic and political systems throughout the world. Some internal changes will benefit desired changes in Latin America. For the present there seems no other vision available as an alternative system than American socialism. Of course one can play off, for example, the ecological dimension against the social dimension. But the ecological dimension is interdependent with the dimension of justice. The question is whether we are willing to tackle the complex problems with new methods or whether we are satisfied with licking our wounds. In the tradition of American socialism there is available such a method, all the more so since it contains some of the most positive liberation language Americans can identify with. Here Christians can join with people of other faiths to do the most positive communal thing imaginable: develop a true *common*wealth. This can happen in a rationally consistent way as we learn creatively to deal with conflict. And we need not inject religious absolutes into the process.[91]

Protestant Catholicism?

For making sound decisions toward a more just society we need great clarity of mind and heart. This leads us once more to the basic theological step. The new vision of God (*visio Dei*) and the new image of the human person (*imago Dei*) issuing in the liberation mission (*missio Dei*) are dependent on the sovereign God (*regnum Dei*). Clarity of mind and heart for the Christian hinge on God alone.

How does God's sovereignty express itself in the liberation process where Catholics are involved as well as Protestants? The great division of the church seems to deny God's sovereignty. While it never will be overcome by human contriving, it is already being disregarded by God's working in history. He makes us respond *together* to the global pressures of the liberation process. In our common response we need to remember the deep Catholic commitment to God's presence in the church. But we need to recall likewise the Protestant commitment to the originative power of God in the pristine Christian word.[92] Since in the liberation process the one cannot do without the other, its ecclesiological implication is Protestant Catholicism.

1. *North American reality as the hermeneutical focus for U.S. Protestant theology.* Latin American liberation theology is very much to the point in its more Catholic perception of the significance of the concrete environment of the church. But this tendency is noticeable also in present U.S. Protestant thought.[93] It is just that here the frequent ideological sellout of Protestantism to culture makes the immediate application of the available Christian terms to the liberation process next to impossible. Might they not convey exactly the opposite of what they intend? The danger to which U.S. theology succumbed long ago José Míguez Bonino sees, as it were, only as a present possibility for Latin American liberation theology: "The text of Scripture and tradition is forced into the Procrustean bed of ideology, and the theologian who has fallen prey of this procedure is forever condemned to listen only to the echo of his own ideology."[94] The language we speak in our Protestant culture, to use a phrase by Rubem Alves, "has been remarkable for its paralyzing effect."[95] Nothing will be gained by merely substituting social science language for Christian language. Our difficulty is too deep-seated. The North American context widely makes us forget what the originative words

of the Christian faith meant. We simply plug into the currents of language rushing on around us. At no point has it become communally clear as yet that it is the originative Christian word that empowers us to share in the liberation process. We are still too much looking for empowering signals from the process itself.

2. *A new hermeneutical norm.* Obviously we cannot wait to act in society until we get our Christian words "de-polluted." But every action-reflection in the North American reality for the Protestant Christian needs accompanying language-purification. Liberation pertains also to our language. Because of the counterfeit prevalent here, we in North America as yet can hardly get, as it were, beyond the first five pages of Bonino's chapter on "Hermenutics, Truth, and Praxis."[96] In North America we cannot avoid first of all coming to grips with the empowerment the biblical word alone offers the Christian. When Gustavo Gutiérrez uses the term "self-liberation,"[97] it may well be that in Latin America there can be no misappropriation of its Christian meaning. In North America, however, the liberation process is so little noticed because much of the history of U.S. Protestantism has been tied to false self-liberation—from making the nation a covenant nation of freedom to self-acceptance in religious therapy. When Juan Luis Segundo speaks of this world becoming the new heaven of God,[98] it may well be that this is an effective way of communicating liberation in Latin America. In North America there is still the false notion of building the kingdom of God on earth,[99] which can only derail the liberation effort if we should decide to continue using this language. Crucial for us here is finding a new vision of *God's* doing the truth. Understandably also Míguez Bonino centers the Latin American needs in this regard on the fourth gospel.[100] What is distinctive here is that a new way of life is envisioned growing out of God in Christ as the way and the life (cf. John 14:6). The power of the pristine Christian word overcomes our amnesia of substantive Christian truth: *God* liberates. Obviously one need not find the hermeneutical norm in the word of the fourth gospel only. It is just that in the liberation process, as the Catholic and the Protestant principle become interdependent, *God's* doing of the truth is forcefully brought to bear on the church by the Christ of the fourth gospel. Even so, each gospel demonstrates how the word presence of God in Christ as liberator remains powerfully normative today.

3. *Consummation of the Reformation?* Perhaps Protestantism has done its isolation job and can no longer function with integrity except in interdependence with the Catholic community. For Protestant theol-

ogy in the North American situation the discovery of the new way of life depends on the rediscovery of the pristine power of the gospel. And yet the discovery is tied into the cultural context of the church, notably the socio-political dimension. It is not a disembodied gospel we are rediscovering. The liberation process calls for a new way of life transcending the American way of life as we have known it thus far, not negating what has been good and right, but freeing it for final usefulness in the human family. The crux of the struggle is that theological language be truly *theological*, appropriate to God's liberation. The self as agent remains subject to God as agent. But God acts in the dynamics of history not apart from the self as agent. So the struggle for not confusing God as agent and the self as agent continues. Neo-orthodoxy as neo-reformation theology could still widely insulate the Christian self from the struggles of history. But now God in his good time creates a new beginning in the time of liberation. The reformation is being fulfilled as theology struggles for continuing empowerment by the pristine Christian word *in* the vicissitudes of history. In the liberation struggles the theologian will seek to echo this word and not his own ideology, so that he receives a radically open mind for a radically open society.

There are three tentative conclusions of our study:

1. Protestant theology can only acknowledge God's liberation as disenthrallment from phony religious language and ideological self-deception. The mind becomes open for doing the truth: the sober use of social science in taking captive every thought in obedience to Christ. This is the spirituality of liberation. Theology here radically begins with God's mandate. In the process the theologian becomes quite vulnerable. Cynical realism and strident utopianism are excluded. He can only live by God's lowly struggle few care to search out. God's liberation process often propels us forward in seemingly invisible, painfully small steps.

2. Social science is trying to state social facts as they are. It is not free from ideological distortions. Ideology criticism needs to be applied here as much as in theology. But Christians need to join hands with social science in its struggle for a sober ethics of life together in the emerging global village. Social science cannot become theology, and theology cannot become social science. Theology stands in need of using social science for finding its way in the liberation process. But each needs to retain its own integrity. While theology will learn from social science, it is not *the* way for theology. Christ is the way.

3. God's liberation process confronts us with the interdependence of the Catholic and Protestant principle and makes us move forward

by the strengths of both traditions. God in the pristine Christian word
and God in history are seen to interact in a liberating way. In the
liberation process God is always one step ahead. But he enables us
also to take that step. Under the global pressures, the tough historical
realities override the "religious" differences of the past. We have a
common task in a world of need. The power of the *one* history of God
propels us towards oneness as Christians. Spirituality tempered by
justice is the goal.

Liberation theology thus understood remains a guerrilla in the
churches, an outsider at best. Its witness for pre-bicentennial U.S.A.
in the liberation process stands in a solid tradition of fringe efforts
trying to be true to theology's task, no matter what the price. In the
words of John C. Bennett:

What the churches do officially is less important than the many unofficial
initiatives within the Christian community that relate the gospel to the
revolutionary struggles for justice and peace among the nations. Often these
are on the fringe of the church even though they are in response to powers and
influences of which the church has been the chief bearer in history. These
initiatives should create an atmosphere in which it will be natural for the
church as church to speak and act at a moment of national decision.[101]

NOTES

The notes were originally meant to leave an opportunity for qualifications of issues
more complex than what meets the eye. But they should not turn into a second essay.
So I will study brevity more often than initially intended. It is enough for the
conference to articulate the basic dimensions of the liberation process.

1. José Míguez Bonino, *Doing Theology in a Revolutionary Situation* (Philadelphia:
Fortress, 1975), p. xix.

2. Preparatory Document no. 1, "Theology in the Americas: 1975," January 27,
1975; see above document 1.

3. I have called attention before to an important comment by Basil Moore, ed., *The
Challenge of Black Theology in South Africa* (Atlanta: John Knox, 1974): "I am prepared to
trust and stand alongside a man who is fighting for himself and his own freedom if I
know that his freedom is bound up with mine. I cannot wholeheartedly trust a man who
is fighting for me, for I fear that sooner or later he will tire of the struggle" (p. 5). See my
essay, "Responsible Theology?" in James W. McClendon, Jr., *Philosophy of Religion and
Theology: 1974* (Missoula, 1974), p. 159.

4. See Martin Luther King, Jr., *Stride Toward Freedom* (New York: Harper & Row,
1958).

5. The first use of the phrase "theology of liberation" in the South was directly
related to the death of Martin Luther King, Jr. See my article, "Theology of Liberation," *Continuum*, 7:4 (1970), pp. 515–24.

6. See Jack Phelps, "Integration in North Carolina: An Outside Agitator Looks
Back," *The Chronicle Magazine*, 70 (April 12, 1975), p. 1B. Occasionally I will be told

that white male theologians cannot do liberation theology. In "A Letter to the Sisters and Brothers in Faith and Order" responding to the November 14, 1975, Faith and Order Commission meeting in Marydale, Ky., I tried to face into the wind of the issue: "The whole point today is to conceive of liberation first of all not in human terms, but on God's terms. If only membership in race, nationality, color, or class would liberate me or entitle me to speak of liberation, I'd be poorly off indeed. But it is God who liberates. For this reason, *also a white theologian is enabled to do liberation theology. Perhaps on the lowest rung of the ladder. But woe unto me as a white if I do not witness to God's liberation!*" (F&OComm. 11/74,2).

7. There is of course need in this situation to discover currents of liberation among whites. In "Points at Issue between Black and White Theologies: Participants' Comments on the Conclusions," I tried to underscore the challenges involved in this factor: "Speaking of 'currents of liberation among whites,' it should be understood that we are not talking about mighty torrents of Mississippi or Missouri dimensions. There may be a few swift mountain streams of liberation. But it will take some 'climbing' and 'exploring' (often in wilderness territory) to find them out" (F&O BWT 11/74, 2).

8. Míguez Bonino, *Doing Theology*, p. 61.

9. How aware are Latin American theologians of the real plight of North American theology? My basic break with our predecessors has focused on the theology of Paul Tillich. See my article, "The Liberation of White Theology," *Christian Century*, 91:11 (March 20, 1974), p. 319; also Stuart Mews, "Paul Tillich and the Religious Situation of American Intellectuals," *Religion*, 2 (Autumn 1972). Mews believes that Tillich was speaking to a limited number of alienated intellectuals. A strange double-mindedness was made possible: "In Tillich's case, his theology has enabled men to rebel against the American way of life whilst affirming their allegiance to it" (p. 134). Nothing deep-rooted was called for. "The alienated intellectual is offered a religious vocabulary in which to articulate his misgivings about industrial society and yet hardly any intellectual commitment is required" (ibid.). Radical commitment in discipleship is difficult to find. "The revolutionary spirit was transferred from the political sphere to the cultural, the theological, the psychological realms" (p. 136).

10. Philip Slater, *The Pursuit of Loneliness* (Boston: Beacon, 1971), p. 12.

11. Two titles must suffice to represent a genre: Michael P. Lerner, *The New Socialist Revolution* (New York: Delacorte, 1973), and Howard Zinn, *Postwar America: 1945–1971* (Indianapolis and New York: Bobbs-Merrill, 1973).

12. José Míguez Bonino, *Doing Theology*, p. 58.

13. O.W. Markley, "New Images of Man," *New York Times*, December 16, 1974.

14. For a recent account of the theological story in this regard see Paul Lehmann, *The Transfiguration of Politics* (New York: Harper & Row, 1975).

15. Martin E. Marty, *The Fire We Can Light* (Garden City, New York: Doubleday, 1973), p. 20.

16. Ibid., p. 32.

17. Cf. Lerner, *New Socialist Revolution*.

18. Robert L. Heilbroner, *The Great Ascent* (New York: Harper & Row, 1963), p. 9.

19. One of the strengths of its most recent account, J. Deotis Roberts, *A Black Political Theology* (Philadelphia: Westminster, 1974), is the conflation of the black struggle with liberation struggles in Latin America and in the Third World in general (see, for example, p. 157).

20. See my brief account of the situation in *Christianity and Crisis* 35:6 (April 14, 1975), p. 80.

21. Not everyone will be happy with the term "interdependence." It depends very much on how one gives it content. See my "Interdependence On Spaceship Earth," *Christian Century*, 92:11 (March 26, 1975), pp. 304–07. I am aware of the many uses to which the term is put today. See Archie J. Bahm, "Organicism: The Philosophy of Interdependence," *International Philosophical Quarterly*, 7:2 (June 1967), pp. 251–84. It would take up too much space to argue the case for its distinct use in the paper. The meaning will be evident from the context, I hope.

22. One has to see this remark against the background of the distinctive positions of modern theology. For a convenient survey, see James C. Livingston, *Modern Christian Thought* (New York and London: Macmillan, 1971), pp. 301–500.

23. "1975: A Big Bicentennial Year, Too!" *Family Weekly*, April 13, 1975.

24. Reflective of the stress on return to normalcy is Kenneth A. Briggs, "Protestant Churches Are Found Returning to Fundamental Beliefs," *New York Times*, March 9, 1975.

25. George Will, "It Could Happen Here," *Durham Morning Herald*, February 4, 1975.

26. Briggs, "Protestant Churches." It is in regard to the project of process theology, represented by Schubert Ogden, and the concern for the liberation process that one of the most creative theological developments seems possible. I hope that the process theologians will take note. A merging of process thought with concerns for the liberation process seems inevitable. Promising attempts are underway already. See George V. Pixley, "Justice and Class Struggle: A Challenge for Process Theology," *Process Studies*, 4:3 (Fall 1974), pp. 159–75; Clark M. Williamson, "Whitehead as Counterrevolutionary? Toward Christian-Marxist Dialogue," *Process Studies*, 4:3 (Fall 1974), pp. 176–86.

27. All of us are indebted to the pioneering work of Rosemary Ruether, especially in regard to Latin American women. As regards the give and take between male and female theologians I found helpful the recent volume by Letty M. Russel, *Human Liberation in a Feminist Perspective* (Philadelphia: Westminster, 1974). She takes seriously the tradition out of which the white male theologian has to work. Sheila D. Collins, *A Different Heaven and Earth* (Valley Forge, Pa.: Judson, 1974), is also constructive in helping to revamp male prejudices in theology. Bibliographies on feminist theology are readily available. My concern here is to stress that it is of utmost importance for the white male theologian to hear women from the Third World. Annie Jiagge of Ghana on the First International Women's Day in New York City made a telling point. Because of the wealth of the developed countries, "we are faced with starvation and a struggle for the basic necessities. You are so concerned with equality, but you do not see the injustices of this set-up, and that's where our basic differences lie" (*New York Times*, March 9, 1975).

28. "Research Report no. 2."

29. Philip Wylie, *Generation of Vipers* (New York: Holt, Rinehart and Winston, 1942), pp. 300f.

30. John Dewey, *Individualism Old and New* (New York: Balch, 1930), p. 14.

31. Obviously this statement needs careful support by data. While the socialist societies of the Communist countries have no claim on true realization of justice, it does pay to study carefully such a review of China as that by Donald MacInnis, "The Secular Vision of a New Humanity in People's China," *Christian Century*, 92:9 (March 12, 1975), pp. 249–53.

32. Here one could quickly develop an extensive bibliography to underscore the point. From the perspective of this paper it is especially such works as Yehoshua Arieli,

Individualism and Nationalism in American Ideology (Baltimore: Penguin, 1966), Richard Hofstadter, *The American Political Tradition* (New York: Knopf, 1948), Christopher Lasch, *The Agony of the American Left* (New York: Random, 1969), and Harold Cruse, *The Crisis of the Negro Intellectual* (New York: Morrow, 1967) that become crucial for the peculiarity involved, specifically in regard to liberation theology, in "Liberation Theology Begins at Home," *Christianity and Crisis*, 34:8 (May 13, 1974), pp. 94–98.

33. Robert Jewett, *The Captain America Complex* (Philadelphia: Westminster, 1973), pp. 165f. The obfuscation of selfhood in the U.S. has not at all been carefully examined in theology in recent times. There are self-contradictory elements even in the most progressive theological definitions of selfhood. See, for example, Arieli, *Individualism and Nationalism*, p. 336.

34. Wade Green, "Triage," *The New York Times Magazine*, January 5, 1975, p. 51.

35. It is unfortunate that in U.S. Protestantism we do not have elaborate church statements such as those in Latin America stemming from the Medellín Conference (1968). But we are not completely left in the cold. *The Bishops' Call for Peace and the Self-Development of Peoples*, adopted by the General Conference of the United Methodist Church in Atlanta, Georgia, April 1972, is for many of us a platform offering leverage similar to that of the Medellín documents. See also my article, "Commentary on the Bishops' Call," *Perkins Journal*, 27:4 (Summer 1974), pp. 5–12. Related reflections are found in my article, "United Methodism in Agony," *Perkins Journal*, 28:1 (Fall 1974), pp. 1–10. I find the work of Robert McAfee Brown especially supportive in this context. See Robert McAfee Brown, *Religion and Violence* (Philadelphia: Westminster, 1973), pp. 73–88.

36. Cf. Samuel S. Hill, Jr., ed., *Religion and the Solid South* (Nashville and New York: Abingdon, 1972). This is just one example of how we are trying to work through the acculturation issue in the South. I should stress that what has developed as liberation theology in the South can bank on highly technical work in a goodly number of fields. I am especially indebted to my colleagues in biblical studies. See, for example, William A. Beardslee, "New Testament Perspectives on Revolution as a Theological Problem," *The Journal of Religion*, 51:1 (January 1971), pp. 15–33, and Leander Keck, "The Son Who Creates Freedom," *Concilium*, 3:10 (March 1974), pp. 71–82. It ought to be more widely understood that these discussions have a solid history among us in the South. One of the first steps toward southern liberation theology was Robert T. Osborn, *Freedom in Modern Theology* (Philadelphia: Westminster, 1967). While we seem to have moved a long way since then it is still instructive to read his call for "A Theology of Freedom," pp. 235–73.

37. My first fledgling attempts in this direction are found in "Liberation Theology or Culture Religion?" *Union Seminary Quarterly Review*, 29:3, 4 (Spring and Summer 1974), pp. 94–98.

38. Reinhold Niebuhr, *Moral Man and Immoral Society* (New York: Scribner's, 1932), p. 71.

39. Robert N. Bellah, "American Civil Religion in the 1970s," in Russell E. Richey and Donald G. Jones, eds., *American Civil Religion* (New York: Harper & Row, 1974), p. 257.

40. Ibid.

41. Martin E. Marty, "Two Kinds of Civil Religion," in ibid., p. 141.

42. Robert N. Bellah, *The Broken Covenant* (New York: Seabury, 1975), p. viii.

43. Ibid., p. 109.

44. Ibid., p. 141.

45. Ibid., p. 144.

46. Ibid., p. xv.

47. Ibid., p. 109.

48. Ibid., pp. 18ff. Bellah provides enough data for us to understand how the covenant was broken time and again. But it appears helpful to call attention to verbatim reports on what occurred. See Martin E. Marty, *The Righteous Empire* (New York: Dial, 1970). In 1782 the Pennsylvania jurist Hugh Henry Brackenridge called for "extermination" of "the animals vulgarly called Indians" (p. 12). Benjamin Franklin linked the extermination to divine Providence. He observed that it might be "the design of Providence to extirpate these Savages in order to make room for cultivators of the Earth" (Benjamin Franklin, *Autobiography* [New Haven: Yale University Press, 1964], p. 199). A Massachusetts missionary and novelist, Timothy Flint, said very much the same: "In the unchangeable order of things, two such races cannot exist together" (Marty, *Righteous Empire*, p. 12). So it is understandable that U.S. President Theodore Roosevelt later could claim: "I don't go so far as to think that the only good Indians are the dead Indians, but I believe nine out of ten are, and I shouldn't inquire too closely into the case of the tenth" (Ibid.).

49. Robert N. Bellah, "American Civil Religion," p. 270. I have conflated Bellah's phrase, "merciless criticism," with his stress on applying it to ourselves. The radical self-critique in regard to civil religion is strongly supported by one of the keenest churchmen: see James Armstrong, *The Nation Yet to Be* (New York: Friendship Press, 1975), pp. 54–84.

50. Ernst Troeltsch, *Christian Thought* (New York: Meridian, 1957), p. 44.

51. *Durham Morning Herald*, July 21, 1974.

52. One needs to understand the tradition of indoctrination that lies behind this statement. Cf. Arieli, *Individualism and Nationalism*, "The observation of the English economist Cliffe Leslie, that theology was the backbone of American economic science, was literally true" (p. 246).

53. Bellah, *Broken Covenant*, p. 62.

54. Ibid., pp. 112ff.

55. Arieli, *Individualism and Nationalism*, p. 336.

56. Niebuhr, *Moral Man*, pp. 83ff.

57. Ibid.

58. Ibid., p. 85.

59. See Green, "Triage."

60. Gibson Winter, *Being Free: The Possibilities of Freedom in an Overorganized World* (New York: Macmillan, 1970), pp. 17ff.

61. Ibid., pp. 36f.

62. *Liberty and Justice For All* (Washington, D.C.: National Conference of Catholic Bishops, 1974), p. 23.

63. Andrew Greeley, "Catholic Activism—Real or Rad/Chic?" *National Catholic Reporter*, February 7, 1975, pp. 7–11.

64. Ibid., p. 7.

65. Greeley points to an article by Peter L. Berger, "Consciousness Raising: To Whom—By Whom?" *Social Policy*, September/October 1974, pp. 38–42. Berger's article is helpful by indirection, since it shows how terms not indigenous to our own culture get lost in the smokescreen of rhetoric. There is dire need to converse about the uniquely Christian terms. As long as we do not zero in on them, we will be tempted to deal with more or less peripheral matters. That exactly is indicated in the title of the

response to Greeley by David O'Brien, "Greeley's Scenario Features Straw Men," *National Catholic Reporter*, March 7, 1975, pp. 10–11.

66. Greeley, "Catholic Activism," p. 11.

67. Livingston, *Modern Christian Thought*, p. 443.

68. Harvey Cox's early work is here a great exception. We need also to recall that in his foreword to Rubem A. Alves, *A Theology of Human Hope* (Washington/Cleveland: Corpus, 1969), he wrote: "It is the whole inherited paradigm of Western theological thinking that must undergo a death and rebirth" (p. x). This is as good a place as any to call the attention especially of the Latin American participants to the callousness to liberation theology in this country. Not many see what Cox saw already years ago. In the *Christian Century* series, "New Turns in Religious Thought," the latest article is by Stanley Hauerwas, "The Ethicist as Theologian." About liberation theology the ethicist has this to say: "The rhetoric of 'liberation theology' often makes it appear that the goal of the Christian life is to free us of all limits. That theology's proponents fail to discern that the gospel does not free us of all limits, but rather provides us with the skills to embody our limits in nondestructive ways. 'Liberation theology' tends to become a theology without the cross"(April 23, 1975). I do not know of any liberation theology that advocates freedom from all limits. To use my book on *Liberation Theology* (New York: Seabury, 1972) as an example, the premise was that the nails that go through the hands of the Son on the cross also go through the hands of the Father in the back. I do not know how much more one could stress the cross. But theologians and ethicists continue putting up smokescreens as to liberation theology in North America.

69. We are touching here on the nerve center of liberation theology. Cf. Gustavo Gutiérrez, *A Theology of Liberation* (Maryknoll, New York: Orbis Books, 1973): "The Latin American Church is sharply *divided* with regard to the process of liberation" (p. 137). The North American churches have a long tradition of covering up conflict. But perhaps in the distortions of liberation theology's goals (see above, footnote 68) smoldering conflict is reflected. I have held for some time that we are living in a deeply conflictual situation. See my introduction, "A New Church Conflict?" to *Theology of the Liberating Word* (Nashville and New York: Abingdon, 1971), pp. 11–24.

70. The realization of what is *theologically* involved is the major point of Gutiérrez's book. Besides *The Cruel Choice* (New York: Atheneum, 1971), we should take note of Goulet's *A New Moral Order* (Maryknoll, New York: Orbis Books, 1974). Again, significant bibliographies are available. There is no point in this context of expanding the footnote with further references.

71. Goulet, *Cruel Choice*, p. 327.

72. Ibid., p. 328.

73. The title of a book by Gordon D. Kaufman, *God the Problem* (Cambridge: Harvard University Press, 1972).

74. Peter L. Berger and Thomas Luckmann, *The Social Construction of Reality* (Garden City, New York: Doubleday, 1967), p. 6.

75. Major J. Jones, *Christian Ethics for Black Theology* (Nashville and New York: Abingdon, 1974). Merely the idea that in the black/white confrontation in theology we should be dealing with the "ex-master-ex-slave relationship" (p. 19) is something that still remains largely concealed in U.S. systematic theology discussions. J. Deotis Roberts, *Black Political Theology*, brings a vast array of ideological concealments to light. But U.S. systematic theology hardly knows as yet how to cope with the fact that "society lures all toward the American Dream" (p. 126)—as a theological datum. With the publication of James H. Cone's first work, the challenge was to relate the black unconcealment efforts to white theology. See my essay, "God: Black or White?" *Review and Expositor*, 67:3 (Summer 1970), pp. 299–313.

76. Vine Deloria, Jr., *God Is Red* (New York: Grosset and Dunlap, 1973). In some sense, Deloria's analysis digs even deeper to the roots of our ideological malaise: "Americans in some manner will cling to the traditional idea that they suddenly came upon a vacant land on which they created the world's most affluent society. Not only is such an idea false, it is absurd. Yet without it both Western man and his religion stand naked before the world. . . . Where, if not from Christianity, did Western man get his ideas of divine right to conquest, of manifest destiny, of himself as the vanguard of true civilization, if not from Christianity?" (p. 127).

77. For the context of this turning see my *Liberation Theology*, p. 176.

78. Friedrich Schleiermacher, *The Christian Faith* (Edinburgh: Clark, 1928), p. 450.

79. Notice how Sheila D. Collins, *A Different Heaven and Earth*, struggles even with Paul Tillich's theology in this regard (p. 43). The explanation is not difficult. Tillich stood squarely in the tradition of Schleiermacher.

80. The crux of the issue here in Protestantism is the history of the *legitimation of power* in theology. See my contribution to "Whatever Happened to Theology?" *Christianity and Crisis*, 35:8 (May 12, 1975), pp. 115–17. In view of the awesomeness of our disease, radical surgery is called for. Robert N. Bellah, *The Broken Covenant*, speaks of "a failure of our central vision" (p. 157). From the Protestant perspective, the response is not first of all to create a new vision of American identity, but to identify radically with God in Christ. In the kind of world into which we have been catapulted of late we might as well quit worrying about our American identity. Protestantism has sinned too much in legitimating dual loyalty. Bellah suggests: "Probably more of the old biblical culture needs to be included in a new pattern for America than the counterculture would allow" (p. 160). One cannot state the issue sharply enough. Liberation theology in the U.S. requires identification with the selfhood of Christ. To what extent this results in a new pattern for America is a later worry (*cura posterior*). We cannot do everything at the same time. But as theologians we can concentrate on the reeducation of the church. It belongs to priority No. 1. As far as our American identity is concerned, we first of all need a radically secular view of our history.

81. It requires getting back to the issue at the very roots of theology. A reexamination of ideology in biblical studies is very much part of our Southern discussion. Cf. L.E. Keck, "On the Ethos of Early Christians," *Journal of the American Academy of Religion*, 42:3 (September 1974), pp. 435–52, and my essay, "Liberation Hermeneutic as Ideology Critique?" *Interpretation*, 28:4 (October 1974), pp. 387–403.

82. I have called attention to the socialism option in several contexts. See "The Burden of Southern Theology: A Response," *The Duke Divinity School Review*, 38:3 (Fall 1973), p. 161; "Theologie am Scheideweg," *Evangelische Theologie*, 34:1 (January/February 1974), p. 80; "Liberation Theology Begins at Home," *Christianity and Crisis*, 34:8 (May 13, 1974), p. 97; "Commentary on the Bishops' Call," *Perkins Journal*, 27:4 (Summer 1974), p. 11.

83. Juan Luis Segundo, "Capitalism-Socialism: A Theological Crux," in Claude Geffré and Gustavo Gutiérrez, eds., *The Mystical and Political Dimension of the Christian Faith*, Concilium 96 (New York: Seabury, 1974), p. 106.

84. Michael Harrington, *Socialism* (New York: Saturday Review Press, 1972).

85. Bellah, *Broken Covenant*, p. 137.

86. Paul H. Sherry, "A New Conversation," *Journal of Current Social Issues*, 11:7 (Summer 1974), p. 3. The paper "The American Journey," prepared by Joe Holland in collaboration with Mary Burke and William Ryan at the Center of Concern (May 6, 1975), dovetails well with the major thrust of my argument. The lack of a fundamental or comprehensive social theory is acknowledged. It also expects a "socialist

coalition." And yet in the end it keeps separate social analysis, theology, and strategy for action. I can only applaud the final point: "Of course, any analysis has implications for the construction of a theology and of a strategy, and vice versa. But at the explicit level, social analysis remains only social analysis. The explicit tasks of theologizing and of strategizing are distinct." By the same token, I can say: At the explicit level, theology remains only theology.

87. William A. Simpson, "Socialism: For Saints and Other Sinners," *Journal of Current Social Issues*, 11:7 (Summer 1974), p. 17.

88. *The Role of Transnational Business in Mass Economic Development*, a working group report prepared at the request of United Church Board for Homeland Ministries, United Church Board for World Ministries, United Church of Christ Center for Social Action, United Church Foundation, Pension Boards-United Church of Christ (February 1, 1975). In this same context one should study *The Social Impact of United Church of Christ Invested Funds 1971–73*, Report of the Four National Instrumentalities with Invested Funds (May 9, 1973). I should also call attention to the important studies under the direction of Jorge Lara-Braud in the Faith and Order Commission of the National Council of Churches. A paper by Jorge Lara-Braud and Harold Schlachtenhaufen, "Theological Position Paper For Church World Service," *Occasional Bulletin from the Missionary Research Library*, 25:1 (January/February 1975), lists some of the significant steps taken by the National Council of Churches in regard to national and global justice (p. 10).

89. Paul Abrecht, "Technology: New Direction in Ecumenical Social Ethics," *Christianity and Crisis*, 35:7 (April 28, 1975), p. 96.

90. *Time*, February 10, 1975.

91. Reading social scientists on this score can have a sobering effect. See, for example, Victor Ferkiss, *The Future of Technological Civilization* (New York: Braziller, 1974), p. 97.

92. Friedrich Schleiermacher in *The Christian Faith* has offered definitions that have influenced Protestantism for a long time: "The antithesis between Protestantism and Catholicism may provisionally be conceived thus: the former makes the individual's relation to the Church dependent on his relation to Christ, while the latter contrariwise makes the individual's relation to Christ dependent on his relation to the Church" (p. 103; cf. p. 57). It would be sheer folly if we were to act as though there were only social science problems to deal with in U.S. Protestant theology. We have to take a long mental journey back into our origins to understand how we got to where we are. This makes for the complexity of our situation. Gutiérrez, in *A Theology of Liberation*, can say: "In Latin America those who have opted to participate in the process of liberation. . . comprise, in a manner of speaking, a first Christian generation. In many areas of their life they are without a theological and spiritual tradition. They are creating their own" (p. 136). I wish it could be that simple for us in the United States. We not only have the Teutonic tradition to contend with, but also the Anglo-Saxon (besides numerous others). As to the Anglo-Saxon dimension, see Thomas A. Langford, *In Search of Foundations* (Nashville and New York: Abingdon, 1969), pp. 88–142. This work and essays by Thomas A. Langford have been a constant reminder to us in the South that there is unfinished business for theology across the board. Liberation theology would soon be truncated if it would not pay attention to the holistic challenge remaining with us also today.

93. See my essay "Political Theology in the American Context," *Theological Markings*, 1:1 (Spring 1971), pp. 28–42; also "Political Theology as New Hermeneutical Focus," *Theological Markings*, 3:1 (Spring 1973), pp. 27–34. The whole area of political

theology has not been dealt with in any thorough way with our North American reality as hermeneutical focus. It appears that only now in J. Deotis Roberts, *A Black Political Theology*, we are getting a serious dialogue possibility for our North American situation. Francis P. Fiorenza, "Latin American Liberation Theology," *Interpretation*, 28:4 (October 1974), p. 443, has stressed the unique dimension of our North American situation in regard to political theology. Gerald A. Butler, "Karl Barth and Political Theology," *Scottish Journal of Theology*, 27:4 (November 1974), has underscored the point in regard to my own work: "There is then a significant difference between Herzog and Metz and Moltmann concerning the nature of political theology. It is fundamentally a disagreement over the extent to which political theology should influence the theological task as a whole. Metz and Moltmann seek to give political theology a more important role in the theological task than does Herzog. This is clearly seen by the fact that Metz and Moltmann want political theology to function as the hermeneutical norm while Herzog wants it to function as the hermeneutical focus" (p. 456). What has challenged me to a special emphasis is, for example, indicated by the title of the book by David Wise, *The Politics of Lying: Government Deception, Secrecy, and Power* (New York: Random, 1973). I am not trying to be programmatic with political theology. It is a matter of dealing with an emergency situation, the concealments, etc., of the American empire. The difficulty is that the dilemma we're up against is not as simple as often outlined. One can learn this by carefully pondering the black/white issue. Sydney E. Ahlstrom, *A Religious History of the American People* (New Haven and London: Yale University Press, 1972), claims: "Without depriving the gospel of its comfort, Cone would animate the black churches—and the white churches, too, if they would listen—with grounds for faithful social action" (p. 1078). Much more is at stake than some more social action. The very nature of the gospel itself is at issue. It seems that this is not something that only whites don't allow. Here a core issue is shaping up for debate in regard to political theology. See Julius Hester, "Review: The Black Experience in Religion," *Christianity and Crisis*, 35:5 (March 31, 1975), pp. 73–75. Part of the rub lies in Hester's claim that only political liberation is hoped for by black theologians: "If blacks are defined as victims, then it is easy to conclude that freedom is synonymous with political liberation. If anyone should know better, a theologian should." (p. 74) This is a significant issue for clarification at the Detroit conference.

94. Míguez Bonino, *Doing Theology*, p. 87.

95. Alves, *Theology of Human Hope*, p. 69.

96. Míguez Bonino, *Doing Theology*, pp. 86–90.

97. Gutiérrez, *Theology of Liberation*, pp. 146–217.

98. Juan Luis Segundo, *Our Idea of God* (Maryknoll, New York: Orbis Books, 1974), p. 44.

99. H. Richard Niebuhr's work should be especially kept in mind in this regard. Yehoshua Arieli (*Individualism and Nationalism*, p. 336) makes a significant point about the ideological bondage of even the best attempt to realize Christianity on earth.

100. The whole struggle toward the discovery of Christian identity breaks through once more. It is not American national identity that primarily challenges the reflection of the theologian. This was one of the points I tried to make in *Liberation Theology*, in emphasizing "Liberation in the Light of the Fourth Gospel."

101. John Coleman Bennett, *Foreign Policy in Christian Perspective* (New York: Scribner's 1966), p. 159. I wanted to close with a word from John Bennett, since we need to be reminded of work done before us. Much of the liberation compact between Catholics and Protestants is due to Vatican II. See Walter M. Abbott, ed., *The Documents of Vatican II* (New York: America Press, 1966). Insights that will also draw

the perimeter for the Detroit conference were already expressed then. John C. Bennett spoke of "the need to allow the secular to be itself" (p. 653). Robert McAfee Brown called attention to the "many opportunities for ecumenical social involvement" (p. 316). Avery Dulles voiced "the need of setting forth a radically different vision of the Church, more biblical, more historical, more vital and dynamic" (pp. 10f.). It is within the "tradition" of such reflections that we are putting our shoulder to the wheel today. One of the things that keeps haunting me in liberation theology in the South is the curse of "triumphalism on the fringe"—being "out" so far that one is never anything but "in," "in" with the rhetoric that never makes a difference in the first place. Christian triumphalism on the fringe is especially painful as regards the Jew. Speaking of God's involvement in history after Auschwitz is a matter of radical questioning for the Jew. How do we "Christians" relate to it? See Emil E. Fackenheim, *God's Presence in History: Jewish Affirmations and Philosophical Reflections* (New York: Harper & Row, 1970), pp. 67–104. What is more, there is also the datum of the liberation of the Jew. See Albert Memmi, *The Liberation of the Jew* (New York: Grossman, 1966). We are especially indebted to Rosemary Ruether for battling against Christian parochialism in this context.

SECTION THREE

Theological Reflection on the Liberation Struggle in America

This section includes various documents prepared by representatives of minority groups at the request of the organizing committee. The committe hoped to obtain an up-to-date presentation of the history, culture, and theological reflection of the various minorities. The documents were to be distributed to the participants to stimulate dialogue and contribute to the enrichment of all involved.

This ambitious project was only partially achieved. The organizers did not have the time, the money, or the contacts necessary to find the most representative and capable spokespersons of each minority. Moreover, with the exception of the paper on black theology, the documents were working papers completed in haste under the pressure of a deadline.

"Black Theology and Liberation Theology" reflects the maturity and the suffering of the black community and the depth of the religious interpretation of the black theologians. It includes a brief but profound description of black oppression and sketches the bases of black theology. This paper was also read at

the conference itself, where there was some criticism of its position on the relationships between black theology, feminist theology, and Latin American liberation theology.

*As background for the women's liberation movement, the organizers recommended two articles by women theologians involved in the conference process: "Sexism and the Theology of Liberation" by Rosemary Radford Ruether (*The Christian Century, *December 12, 1973) and "Toward a Feminist Theology" by Sheila D. Collins (*The Christian Century, *August 2, 1972). These articles, together with "The Structure of Women's Oppression" (prepared by Mary Burke with the collaboration of Joseph Holland and William F. Ryan), included below, represent the introduction to this theme offered by the organizers for the participants' reflection.*

The other papers reflect the struggles of the native Americans and the Chicanos to achieve a better life and to interpret their frustrations and their hopes in religious terms.

Once again, in spite of good intentions, minorities were given a second place in the planning of the conference. This deficiency points up the task ahead if we are to have a theology that is truly rooted in the experience of the poor.

12

Black Theology
and Liberation Theology

by Herbert O. Edwards

Historical and structural analysis are essential to understanding where we are and what is required of us if our vision of where we ought to go is to be radically different from where we are. We have to realize the interdependent character of the unfolding events of history and the formation of societal structures.

Unless we are willing to be honest about our history, we will be hampered in our attempts to understand the structures which stand over against us and are in us at the same time.

The historical experiences of different groups tend to create within them different perspectives, both on their history and the history of other groups, and in regard to the structural arrangements of the political and socio-economic orders. The black experience in America differs from the white experience; the black experience in America differs from the Latin American experience. We must address some of these differences momentarily. Suffice it to say at the moment that some of the issues as well as the options facing black theology differ in many ways from those facing liberation theology in Latin America.

Rising Expectations in the Third World

Levels of expectation are informed by a fusion of one's perception of the present circumstances, including the power and will of the enemy, the resources available to alter those circumstances, the will to use these resources, and one's view of the world, including one's understanding of the "politics of God."

When slavery in the South became identified and synonymous with blackness; when state after state altered their laws, making manumission of any slave for whatever reason more difficult; when one's black body was not one's own; when family joys and possibilities were destroyed by law, religion, and custom; when memory of the ancient homeland—Africa—was no longer strong enough to evoke even the remotest hope of returning: what could one really expect, at best, but flight to the North or to Canada, where one might at least have something to say about one's own individual destiny.

When the awareness of the reality of the limited freedom and dignity afforded blackness in the North dawned upon the escaped or freed slave; when he realized that there was not, in actuality, any Red Sea in America for blackness; when he realized that the spirit that informed slavery in the South also informed and shaped the ethos of the North in its response to his blackness: what could one really hope in except the remote possibility that North and South might go to war and occasion the destruction of the institution, if not the spirit, of slavery?

When war finally came and required such a tremendous expenditure of treasure and blood for the North to emerge physically victorious, with the elimination of slavery as a penalty imposed upon the South for its failure on the battlefield, the hopes and expectations of blackness seemed justly to soar and know no bound. The Day of Jubilee is just around the corner! Patient trust in God and struggle for freedom will be rewarded, not only with forty acres and a mule, but also with the right to freely participate in the decision-making processes of the country, to become, at last, a participant in history.

At last a historical congruence has been effected between one's perceptions of the former "unreality of the then objectionable present," one's fondest dreams and hopes, the resources of oneself and allies, and the view of the world as being indeed in the hands of a just God. The historical nightmare is over. The Four Horsemen of the Apocalypse rode, in succeeding order, from 1861 to 1865. The blindfold has been snatched from the eyes of justice; now she can see to set things right. Did not Lincoln himself, that paragon of racist ideology, proclaim that he saw the hand of God in it all?

The Almighty has His own purposes. Woe unto the world because of offences for it must needs be that offences come; but woe to that man by whom the offence cometh. If we shall suppose that American slavery is one of those offences which, in the providence of God, must needs come, but which, having continued through His appointed time, He now wills to remove, and that He gives to both North and South, this terrible war, as the woe due to those by whom the offence came, shall we discern therein any departure from those divine attributes which the believers in a Living God always ascribe to Him? Fondly do we hope—fervently do we pray—that this mighty scourge of war may speedily pass away. Yet, if God wills that it continue, until all the wealth piled by the bond-man's two hundred and fifty years of unrequited toil shall be sunk, and until every drop of blood drawn with the lash, shall be paid by another drawn with the sword, as was said three thousand years ago, so still it must be said "the judgments of the Lord, are true and righteous altogether.[1]

Lincoln was not alone in seeing the hand of God in the crisis-filled events of the Civil War. Some saw the hand of God threatening before the terrible events began to unfold; some stood within the eye of the hurricane and loudly proclaimed it; some, with the benefit of hindsight, interpreted it all as the work of God in some measure.

Gayrand Wilmore quotes a letter from Theodore Weld to Angelina Weld, dated February 6, 1842, which read:

The slaveholders of the present generation, if cloven down by God's judgment, cannot plead that they were unwarned. . . . Well may the God of the oppressed cry out against them, "because I have called and ye have refused. . . . Therefore will I laugh at your calamity and mock when your fear cometh. When your fear cometh like desolation and destruction like a whirlwind, then shall ye call but I will not answer."[2]

In 1827, the Reverend Nathaniel Paul, pastor of the First African Baptist Society in Albany, New York, declared at the celebration of the abolition of slavery in that state:

The progress of emancipation, though slow, is nevertheless certain. It is certain because that God who has made of one blood all nations of men. . . has so decreed. . . . Slavery. . . is so contrary to the laws which the God of nature has laid down as the rule of action by which the conduct of man is to be regulated towards his fellow man, which binds him to love his neighbor as himself, that it ever has, and ever will meet the decided disapprobation of heaven.[3]

During the later afternoon and early evening of January 1, 1863, Negroes throughout the country held meetings to celebrate the promised signing of the Emancipation Proclamation. Frederick Douglass spoke at such a meeting in Boston at Premont Temple. In his autobiography, Douglass described the meeting:

Every moment of waiting chilled our hopes, and strengthened our fears. . . . A visible shadow seemed falling on the expecting throng. . . . At last, . . . "It is coming. It is on the wires." The effect of this announcement was startling beyond description, and the scene was wild and grand. Joy and gladness exhausted all forms of expression, from shouts of praise to sobs and tears. My old friend Rue, a colored preacher, . . . expressed the heartfelt emotion of the hour, when he led all voices in the anthem, "Sound the loud timbrel o'er Egypt's dark sea, Jehovah hath triumphed, his people are free."[4]

But the joy and exultation were short-lived. With the cessation of hostilities came the passing of stringent black codes in the South to "regulate" the relationships between white society and the newly-freed slaves. However, the North reacted vigorously at first, seemingly determined not to lose in peace what had been purchased so dearly on the field of battle.

So for a brief period of time the nation again, as once before at its beginning, toyed with the idea of trying to shore up the defenses around every inalienable right to life, liberty, and the pursuit of happiness/property. The Reconstruction period was even more propitious than the revolutionary one, because in the latter no one any longer had legal title to another person's being as property. Nonetheless, after a short, dizzying period of flirting with justice and equality of opportunity, the North and the South "came to its senses" and returned to their father's house, a house of oppressive and racist bondage.

As the Cotton Curtain had fallen in 1789, so now in 1877, the wall of racism, supported by fledgling science, an apostate religion, and political expediency, was raised to shut out the light of hope and to place impenetrable ceilings on the aspirations and expectations of five millions. Violence and injustice had kissed each other; the union resulted in an unforgettable harvest of slaughter.

For fully two generations, black religious and social institutions scaled down the level of hope and expectation in the black community to fit the limited possibilities occasioned by the oppressive power of the white community to destroy blackness coupled with an almost sadistic will to use that power.

World War I caused hope to soar again. Surely if the world is made "safe for democracy," black people can expect better things. But it was not to be. Wilson, like the Founding Fathers before him, knew how to use universal language with particularistic application.

When World War II came, accompanied as it was with the openly declared racist ideology of Nazi Germany, the country had to be a bit more subtle and ingenious in proclaiming its hatred of a system which was simply carrying to its logical conclusion the philosophy which both lived by.

By this time the social scientists and theologians had "come of age" and proved more than equal to the task. The *soul* of white America was really different from that of Nazi Germany. Whereas Nazi

Germany's problem lay in being consistent, America's problem really was occasioned by an "uneasy conscience" which was caused by the awareness of the gap between creed and deed. However, the dilemma could and would be resolved because America's commitment to justice and equality of opportunity was real. Also, the victims of injustice were growing in numbers, ability, and determination.

The theologians, sometimes following the lead of the social scientists, sometimes not, set out to show how "different" America really was from Nazi Germany, and how this country had been placed by God in a peculiar position in history for a special, if limited, destiny.

In *Christian Realism* (1941), Professor John C. Bennett confesses: "No one can say that in America we live according to a high standard of *interracial justice*, but we know in our hearts that every institution that perpetuates racial discrimination is wrong. We are on the defensive when we consent to such a wrong."[5]

We are better than Nazi Germany, however, for Dr. Bennett continues: ". . . Contrast that situation with what happens when discrimination is taught as a good, when anti-Semitism is an officially recognized policy, supported by the agencies that mould public opinion as a higher form of morality than interracial justice."[6]

Could one possibly say, in 1941, that racist policies were not officially supported by the opinion-moulding institutions in the United States? Was not racial discrimination taught as a higher form of morality than interracial justice?

Federal aid to housing was officially based on a philosophy of white racism. All branches of the Armed Forces were completely segregated along racial lines. The New Deal programs were operating in a manner respectful of racist principles. The Supreme Court was continuing to interpret the exercise of citizenship rights along racial lines.

The stepped-up defense industries excluded black employees. Almost all educational institutions, from nursery schools to universities, including especially theological seminaries and Bible colleges, operated so as to give aid and comfort to white racism. White political primaries were the order of the day in our southern states. Hospitals, prisons, churches, cemeteries—all were guided by racist policies in their practices.

Restrictive covenants were respectable and legal methods for keeping undesirable racial and other groups out of certain areas and neighborhoods; lynching was not an uncommon occurrence; and more than a third of the states had laws on their books which denied to clergymen the right to join persons together in holy matrimony without using race as the most determinative factor.

In Professor Bennett's American society of 1941, there was not nearly as much of a difference as he would have us believe, if there was any, between America's commitment to racism as a "positive good," and the racist beliefs of Nazi Germany. At least in Germany, according to Paul Tillich, the "Nordic blood theory" was artificially imposed upon and reluctantly accepted by the German people. Racism has had no such difficult time in America. It has been a part of the moral ethos from the very beginning of the country's national existence.

In an article in the October 4, 1943, issue of *Christianity and Crisis*, entitled "Anglo-Saxon Destiny and Responsibility," Reinhold Niebuhr responded to the critical situation in which the Western world found itself by reminding the Anglo-Saxon peoples that the crucial and strategic point at which they found themselves in the building of world community was of such significance as to require that it be apprehended in religious terms. "Without a religious sense of the meaning of destiny, such a position as Britain and America now hold is inevitably corrupted by pride and the lust of power."

Although Niebuhr felt that it would serve no good purpose to try to compare the special destiny of the Anglo-Saxon peoples with that of Israel in olden times, "nevertheless," he said, "only those who have no sense of the profundities of history would deny that various social groups and races are at various times placed in such a position that a special measure of the divine mission in history falls upon them." In that sense God has chosen us in this fateful period of world history.

World War II created the possibility—even as it was proclaimed by our spokesmen to be the occasion—for extending freedom throughout the world. However, God was apparently not choosing the Anglo-Saxon peoples to help remove the yoke of bondage from those who suffered under their oppression. As Winston Churchill made clear, he was not prime minister to preside over the dismemberment of "Her Majesty's Empire."

The problem for the theologians during this period was how to justify fighting for the "Four Freedoms" against Hitler, and denying the extension of those freedoms to non-Anglo-Saxon peoples. However, as in times past in their responses to the black presence in America they proved equal to the task.

Albert C. Knudson believed that one of the conditioning factors in the application of the law of love is that due to the "orders of creation"; the "orders of creation" are all but synonymous with the various divisions that exist in the world. People are divided into different families, different economic and cultural groups, different nations, and different *races*.

Professor Knudson makes a great deal of freedom, and of the free relations of men to each other, as does Christian ethics generally. But this freedom is not and cannot be absolute. There are two important limitations upon the exercise of freedom.

One is in the case of children, and the other limitation is in the case of *undeveloped* peoples or races. "Children require restraint and discipline for their proper training. They need to have their wills to some degree subjected to the wills of their superiors. . . . In a similar way, *undeveloped* tribes and races may to their own advantage and that of the world be kept in tutelage by more highly civilized peoples."[7]

It is clear that the Third World, including black Americans, could find very little in the writings of Christian theologians during the period of World War II to give them any reason for hope. White theology, drawing upon psychology and a biased cultural anthropology, could justify the West's hegemony over the rest of the world.

So the rising expectations in the Third World generally, and among black Americans particularly, were once again proved to be unfounded. Nonetheless, following World War II, neither the United Nations nor the Western plea for realism and patience was sufficient to still the voices calling for freedom in Asia, Africa, and the Americas.

The Cold War between East and West led the United States to pridefully assume the role of "leader of the Free World." Translated into geo-political terms that meant that this country would support every regime, however oppressive, in every country, so long as it was willing to mouth the ideological rantings of the West.

The war-torn and economically weakened countries of Western Europe turned to America to gain support and assistance to enable them to hold on to their colonies which were "undeveloped" and "not ready for independence." Much to the dismay of revolutionaries in Asia, Africa, and Latin America—many of whom thought, like Ho Chi Minh, that the adoption of the American Revolution as a model would be a clear signal to America and the rest of the world that they were not enemies of the "Free World," but oppressed people longing for and determined to gain freedom—the United States generally entered the struggles against them.

So we attempted to bail out France in Indochina, and only after sacrificing thousands of our own youth, visiting unprecedented devastation on the Indochinese, killing thousands and thousands, wasting as much of the area as we could, and spending billions of dollars, were we forced to give up the struggle.

In Africa, for the most part we have settled for neocolonialism, since we could not preserve the colonial situation intact for most of the European countries. And in Latin America we have alternated between "dollar diplomacy," "gunboat and marine diplomacy," "CIA diplomacy," and "plans for progress."

There is little question that economics has played a significant role in shaping this country's responses to the aspirations of Third World peoples. However, it would be shortsighted indeed to ignore the social, political, and racial factors that have played and continue to play an important role in this area.

There is little question that the racial factor has been the most important single determinant in the responses of the religious, educational, political, economic and social forces in this country to the black American's demand for justice.

The civil rights movement served to raise the hopes of black Americans. For a time, during the early sixties, it appeared that white theology was changing its stance toward the oppression of blacks and entering the lists, at long last, on the side of an interpretation of the gospel that saw freedom as being at least not incompatible with the gospel.

However, the Black Power movement, the Black Manifesto, the rise of black caucuses in the white denominations, and the early attempts at black theological formulations resulted in theologico-ethical appeals for order as necessarily prior to justice. It did not seem to matter that the "order" which was being given theological support was really "ordered injustice."

How was it that the inspiring and encouraging fifties gave way to the rising expectations of the sixties, only to eventuate into the despairing seventies? In all probability, Martin L. King, Jr., analyzed it correctly in 1967:

Throughout our history, laws affirming Negro rights have consistently been circumvented by ingenious evasions which render them void in practice. Laws that affect the whole population—draft laws, income-tax laws, traffic laws—manage to work even though they may be unpopular; but laws passed for the Negro's benefit are so widely unenforced that it is a mockery to call them laws.[8]

Black Theology: View from the Bottom

White theological interpretations of American history often remind one of the drunken man who was stumbling around under a lamppost. When asked what he was doing, he replied that he was looking for some money that he had lost. When asked if he thought that he had lost it near or under the lamppost, he replied, "No, I lost it over there but it is dark and I can't see over there. I am looking where the light is."

The historical truth about America, a truth which includes what America has done to Indians, blacks, and women, in the name of God, has been and remains covered by a self-imposed blanket of preferred darkness and silence. And so as we approach the bicentennial observances, an increasing number of historical and analytical, moral, and theological treatises and monographs are being produced, calling us once again to remember, to appeal to, to transmit the values of the Founding Fathers in order to revitalize America and recall it to its original noble foundational purposes.[9]

One sometimes gets the feeling that many Americans have convinced themselves that Vietnam, Watergate, and all its attendant White House horrors did something to our national heritage. But the view from the bottom is that these were all consistent with our national heritage.[10]

Some want to elevate Watergate to the status of a Fall. Why? Because for the first time in the history of the country, the White House consciously tried to subvert our ideals (?), destroy our tradition of fair elections (?), used agencies and departments of government to violate the constitutional privileges and guarantees of our citizens (?).

Therefore, some spokesmen for black and women's liberation have been very proudly pointing to the fact that neither group was represented among those who were at the center of the Watergate disaster.[11]

The view from the bottom, as articulated by black theology, does not see Watergate as a Fall in any sense of the word. Black theology must remain conscious of the vast gap that has always existed between the religion and religious interpretations of the white, Western world, and the religion and religious interpretations in the historical black community.

At the center of the religious life of the black community has been the application of the promises of God to those who are not only among the dispossessed and the disinherited, but also to those who have not been considered human and worthy of participation in the Western processes of history.

James Cone's claim: "We were not created for humiliation!" does not and has not led to its obverse in the black community: "We were created to humiliate!" But it is this latter claim that white religion has supported even when it has not proclaimed it as such.

Consequently, we have had a religiously divergent history in this country. The black churches have been the churches of the oppressed; the white churches have been the churches of the oppressor. These differences can be spelled out in much greater detail. However, for our purposes in this context, we are concerned about the implications of these differences for our understanding of some of the differing concerns and options between white North American theology, women's liberation theology, Latin American liberation theology, and black theology.

Let it be clearly understood that I believe that women's liberation theology has a very real and a very long list of grievances against white theology (and perhaps no less so against Latin American theology).

It is also true that Latin American theology, concerned with all of the problems facing their countries, must inevitably challenge the patriotic stance of North American theology, which has too long been too supportive of the expansive, imperialistic policies of this country. Some would also say that black theology's very reason for being is related to the failures of white theology.

So, at first glance, it may appear that women's, Latin American, and black theology, having a mutual enemy, are, therefore, very much alike and are operating on the same theologico-liberation wavelength. There are, however, some very compelling reasons why this may not be so.

More is required than the fact that we may have a mutual enemy to make us allies. If we can discover a way for our varying experiences and perspectives, viewed through the prism of every person's relationship to God, to lead us through our theological wrestling to a shared vision of a different future, under God, then we may be able to move from being nonenemies, perhaps to shared membership in a liberated community.

Women's liberation theology and Latin American theology are presently both more acceptable to the enemy than is black theology. Both are primarily white and whatever their concern for liberation and justice—and it is real—they speak out of a context of shared power with the enemy in a way that black theology never has and cannot.

Both the women's liberation movement and the Latin American movement are spearheaded by those who are *concerned about* the suffering of the powerless and the poor; but all of black theology's spokesmen are *among* the powerless and the oppressed. They do not have to *assume* identification with the struggle, for their blackness makes them one with the despised whether they will it or no.

Neither the history of the base of the Latin American spokesmen's church, nor that of white middle-class women, forces them to identify with those who are "outside the camp." Granted, there may be some instances of individual awareness of powerlessness in both groups; it is not the same as the history and, therefore, the perspective of the black theologian.

It should be remembered, for example, that when Frederick Douglass, Sojourner Truth, and other black men and women joined in and supported the struggle for women's suffrage, the struggle was successfully concluded at a time when black men were being systematically and "legally" denied the right to vote. I have yet to uncover any significant protest being made by the women suffragettes for the enfranchisement of black women, or for the "re-enfranchisement" of black men.

The willingness to listen to, to learn from, Latin American theology by U.S. theologians must not blind the former to the past history of the United States in its totality of effects on Latin American life and thought, theory and praxis. Latin American liberation theology, in its dialogic encounter with North American theology, must not be unaware of the ease with which one can speak universal language with the understanding that it is not really inclusive of all in the society.

How much racism, Western, North American style, has entered the veins of Latin American thought is difficult to say; that it is not absent from it is almost a certainty. For my part, I have discovered all too little attention being given to it in the literature that I have read. There is no question that the U.S. ethos of racism has followed its dollar and military power wherever it has gone.

In this context, the statement by Gustavo Gutiérrez gives us both pause and hope. "Although until recently the Church was closely linked to the established order, it is beginning to take a different attitude regarding the exploitation, oppression, and alienation which prevails in Latin America."[12]

What is Liberation?

Black theology is committed to the prosecution of a theological task which must hold in creative tension the need of the oppressed for dual liberation—from sin and guilt and from physical oppression in all its varied forms in a racist society. Black religious experience has always been conscious of and sensitive to the eschatological and the historical.

During the days of slavery, liberation was conceived of as the antithesis of human bondage. It was not difficult to provide content to the term "liberation." To be free meant no more auction block, no more being owned and used by another, no more denial of one's right to go and come, to hope and dream. It meant being able to project marriage and family life, to be paid for one's labor, to be able to defend oneself and family when attacked, and to worship God without humiliation.

Following the wholesale, explicit institutional capitulation to discriminatory practices based on racism, liberation seems clearly less complex than now. The removal of all discriminatory legislation, the passage of laws guaranteeing equal access to the institutional resources of the community, and the judicial invalidation of those laws which denied equality of treatment and opportunity represented liberation.

The Civil Rights movement did succeed in large measure, in the legislative and judicial arenas, in effecting the passage of laws and of having other laws declared illegal. But liberation did not follow; Black Power did.

Black Power was the needed corrective to the major thrusts of the Civil Rights movement because the movement raised primarily the question about the access to resources, but did not raise the issue of power redistribution.

Throughout the historical struggles involved in the black experience in America, black theology, whether articulated in sermon, song, testimony, or essay, has always been cognizant of the celebrative aspect of life. Black religion talked about the caring and the acting God who was working to set the captives free. Consequently, in the midst of historical oppression, degradation, and exploitation, participation in the earnest expectation of their liberation led to what has been ineptly defined as "otherworldliness."

However, when the slave experienced the liberating power of the gospel, he was also made free to acknowledge the "unreality of the present" and to project a new and different future. Some may call it "escapism," but who could have foreseen, in 1793, except through the "eyes of faith," that seventy years later black slaves would be standing on the threshold of "freedom?" So one works and prays, wearing loosely the mantle of loyalty to any oppressive system and structures, knowing that God is not captive to American history, but is working through and in it to set the oppressed free.

Further, who could have foreseen, in 1972, considering the massive landslide won by Mr. Nixon for his platform and program of "keeping blacks in their places," that less than two years later a chagrined, though not chastened, country would conclude that they were indeed paying too large a price for the ceilings placed on black aspirations?

Liberation is not yet, to be sure, but God is still at work in the affairs of this world, and it may not be quite as incredible as some think to project the liberation of the oppressed and the destruction of white racism.

Marxism

The attractiveness of Marxism, whether appealed to for critical analysis of capitalist society, or for its vision of a new society void of the evils attendant upon capitalism, may very well be due to its distance from the Christianity which the churches preached and practiced in Latin America. When people are caught up in an apparently hopeless situation and their hopelessness seems informed and occasioned by their powerlessness, only a different analysis and a different vision seem to hold any promise of real and meaningful change.

The black theologian, whether North or South, however, knows that ideological changes have not made any significant difference in the black situation in America. This country has evidenced a tremendous capacity and versatility in shifting ideological stances while holding on to the basic fundament in ethos—creating, namely, racism. Consequently, whether Adam Smith or Karl Marx, whether Herbert Hoover or Franklin D. Roosevelt, whether Richard M. Nixon or Lyndon B. Johnson prevails, racism continues to be the one overarching and informing principle of action.

When it is suggested that a "peculiar American" brand of socialism is what is needed or desired, we are too consciously aware that what has in the past made almost any economic, political, or social policy or practice peculiarly "American" is the same racist spirit that informed and supported its "Peculiar Institution" for two and one half centuries.

Civil Religion

Black theology, viewing the historical development of civil religion in America, views the content of the "covenant concept" that informed it differently from some interpreters.[13]

The faith that bound together Protestant, Catholic, Jew, rich and poor, educated and illiterate, liberal and conservative, laissez-faire capitalist and New Dealer, high churchmen and low, pious and irreverent, Republican and Democrat, was white racism. Racism has been the only ecumenical faith that America has consistently subscribed to.

Civil religion began to unravel and to come apart at the mythic seams not because the myths were no longer possessed of symbolic value, but because the victims of the mythic and symbolic interpretations of America's history were raised to a new level of consciousness and action.

Black theology, then, does not envision that a future in the restoration of civil religion holds any hope; neither does it place much confidence in an American brand of socialism. We are too conscious of British socialism and its racism. Rather we envision a future which is brought about by the liberating activities of God and the struggles of the oppressed, toward which we must move without a blueprint or a utopian scenario spelled out in detail.

However, those policies and practices which prevail today must give way to the new. The task at this time involves the destruction of the myths that have supported the old way and a calling to all who can will the destruction of the old, and who under the aegis of the Holy Spirit can go forth to a land which God will show us.

NOTES

1. Second Inaugural Address, March 4, 1865, in Don E. Fehrenbacher, ed., *Abraham Lincoln: A Documentary Portrait Through His Speeches and Writings* (New York: New American Library, 1964), p. 278.

2. Gayrand S. Wilmore, *Black Religion and Black Radicalism* (New York: Doubleday & Company, Inc., 1972), p. 40.

3. Quoted in Benjamin E. Mays, *The Negro's God* (New York: Atheneum, 1968 [1938]), p. 42.

4. Frederick Douglass, *Life and Times of Frederick Douglass* (New York: Collier Books, 1962 [reprint rev. ed. 1892]), p. 353.

5. John C. Bennett, *Christian Realism* (New York: Scribner's, 1941).

6. Ibid.

7. Albert C. Knudson, *The Principles of Christian Ethics* (New York: Abingdon Press, 1943), p. 190; italics added.

8. Martin L. King, Jr., *Where Do We Go From Here: Chaos or Community?* (Boston: Beacon Press, 1967), p. 82.

9. Cf. special 1776 issue *Time* magazine; Harry Jewell, *The Bicentennial—A New Look* (Detroit: Stress American League, 1973).

10. Cf. Charles H. Long, "The Ambiguities of Innocence": ". . . innocence of the American is not a natural innocence, that innocence which is prior to experience: rather, this innocence is gained only through an intense suppression of the deeper and more subtle dimensions of American experience. Americans never had or took the time to contemplate the depths of their deeds. America's. . . future lies in its ability to live with, support, and understand the new world of Asia and Africa" (in William A.

Beardslee, ed., *America and the Future of Theology* [Philadelphia: Westminster Press, 1967], p. 50).

11. I am not sure how the women view Rose Mary Woods and her role in Watergate.

12. Gustavo Gutiérrez, *A Theology of Liberation*, trans. Sister Caridad Inda and John Eagleson (Maryknoll, New York: Orbis Books, 1973), p. 133.

13. Robert Bellah, *The Broken Covenant: American Civil Religion in Time of Trial* (New York: Seabury Press, 1974).

13

The Structure of
Women's Oppression
in the United States

by Mary Burke

Although the vision called forth by the idea of liberation has appealed to many within our society, it has had particularly powerful impact on those in our society who have come to recognize their second-class status. Blacks, Chicanos, Asians, and native Americans are beginning to define what liberation might mean in terms of their own history and culture. Women, who in our society as elsewhere have always been exploited, are also drawing upon the concept of liberation to construct the elements of what they see as a just society.

In this paper I have examined some of the structural burdens carried by women in the United States. At this stage of our consciousness we do not, cannot, know the full weight of these burdens, but we do know enough about them to support some of the changes that must take place. In the discussion of the economic inequities faced by women, the burdens of the present structuring of marriage and family, and the role of the institutional church, the directions for change are noted. Attention is also given to the need for new models.

Introduction

This is a time of challenge and contradictions for women in the United States. It is a time marked by both hope and fear—hope that women will be able to build a movement that will contribute to the liberation of all women and men, fear that faced by overwhelming pressures women will settle for token changes that will further alienate them from each other and from other oppressed people and, in the long run, increase the restrictions and limitations all face.

An overview of the condition of women in the United States leads to two general statements: (1) No matter what their status or position, women are oppressed. (2) Women, in addition, share in the privilege or oppression of the class and/or race to which they belong.

Oppression is a harsh, hard generality to ascribe to all women. The fact remains, however, that with few exceptions, most achieved at great cost, women are relatively more powerless than the men who share their status and position in our society. Women are excluded from decision-making processes that have real and substantial impact on their lives. Women are conditioned from early childhood to believe that they are less than their brothers and other males in their lives, that their happiness lies in dependency and subservience to men. A part of this conditioning, especially in the white community, imprints deeply in women's attitudes an idea of the inferiority of other women as well as themselves. Thus, men are the focus of authority and expertise, as well as of social life. These characteristics of the lives of women are found in both public and private life.

Economics and Class

All women share in conditions of subjugation, dependency, and isolation. In addition, women are members of socio-economic classes and take part in the situation of their class. Many women carry a double burden; they are women and they are poor. In 1973, for example, 45 percent of all women sixteen years of age and over were a part of the labor force.[1] (If this percentage has decreased since then the decrease is due to unemployment.) Most of these women (about 60 percent) work outside the home because they must. Either they are single, widowed, or divorced and often must provide financial support for children and/or other dependents, or their husbands' incomes are less than $7,000 per year, insufficient for even a modest standard of living if there are any dependents to be supported. The statistics for "minority" women show that the economic needs of these women are even greater. Only 25 percent of "minority" women workers are wives whose husbands have incomes of $7,000 per year or more.

Incomes for women who are in the labor force are low. In 1972, the average income for a white male was $10,786, and $7,548 for a "minority" male, while for a woman, it was $6,131 if she was white, and $5,320 if she was a "minority" woman. More than one-third of these labor force women are employed as clerical workers, where even skilled stenographers receive salaries that approximate those of unskilled laborers (average of $141.50 and $129.20 per week, respectively, in 1973). Fifteen percent of the women in the labor force are classified as professional or technical workers, including about 2 million teachers and about 1 million nurses. An additional six million women work in service positions, including about 1.3 million who work in private households and 2.4 million who work in food service jobs. All of these positions rank as the lowest paying in their category.

There are 54.5 million families in the United States. Women are responsible for the total support of about 12 percent (6.6 million) of them. Over half (3.5 million) of the women in this situation are in the labor force. About two-thirds of these working women are the sole money-earners of their families—receiving no money from former husbands, welfare, or children. Almost half of the 1.9 million "minority" women who have sole responsibility for households work outside the home. Almost one-third of all families for which women alone have financial as well as nurturing responsibilities fall below the poverty level. In 1972, for "minority" families this number was higher, almost one-half. Only 9 percent of all families fall below that inadequate income level.

These statistics have importance in their own right. They point to the economic discriminations against women. Some of these statistics are good illustrations, as well, of the fact that sexism is not the sole basis of discrimination against women. Racism and economic deprivation are burdens that women share with men.

The statistics cited reflect society's perceptions of these realities. For example, within the categories of male and female workers, only one further breakdown occurs in much of the government data—white and minority. This breakdown is, however, misleading. The minority category includes blacks (89 percent), Asians (8 percent), and native Americans (3 percent). It does not include Hispanic people. These people, Puerto Ricans, Chicanos, Latinos, and other Spanish-speaking people—often with Indian or African ancestry, as well as European—are categorized as white. They are lumped with New York bankers and the rural poor, with industrialists and Appalachian miners. The conditions of life for Hispanic people are vastly different from those of the majority community, and include language and cultural oppression. The extent of oppression is indicated by the fact that key governmental departments do not, at this time of increased awareness, see Hispanic people as distinct. The above statistics, and others prepared by government departments, obscure the real spread of poverty among women. They also point out some of the discrepancy between popular myths and present condition.

Our popular image of the mother-housewife caring for her family and home with a sense of security is more myth than reality, since many women must work outside the home. In 1972, 61 percent of the "minority" women and 52 percent of the white women who worked had children between six and seventeen, while 49 percent of the "minority" women and 32 percent of the white women with children under six worked. The facilities needed for these working women and their children are missing; day care facilities, despite their importance to working families, rate very low in the national priorities. Adequate health care is beyond the reach of many.

Women are faced with other social exploitations. Advertising preys on many frustrations of women, telling them constantly that they must buy. They must have things, new things, for their homes and themselves. Their value and worth, they are told in many ways, are tied to how they, their families, and their homes look. Women are told at the same time that their reckless consumption depletes our reserves; that their "labor-saving" devices are wasting our energy; that they buy junk and convenience food that improperly nourishes their families, while wasting grain and other food reserves. The list continues, and the contradictions are compounded when women find that the clothes, appliances, and other goods they purchase do not stand up, despite their care, that a lot of the food available has been processed in such a way as to destroy its nutritional value, and the Secretary of Agriculture keeps urging them to buy more beef.

Many women, increasingly conscious of the contradictions they live with, are trying to appropriate to themselves all responsibilities and rights that are properly theirs as adults. This is what the women's movement is all about. If this effort is to be more than an exercise of the comfortable to increase their well-being, the movement is going to have to work for fundamental structural changes. Some segments of the movement are already dealing with this necessity.

Marriage and Family

The questioning and challenging about family, an example of this searching for new structures, is a source of both strength and weakness for the women's movement. The family itself and women's place as defined in relation to it are being attacked from many sides. Some women say much of what they think about marriage simply by choosing to postpone or bypass marriage in favor of a satisfying job. Others marry, with the understanding that their career is as important a facet of their lives as marriage. Still others, after some years of marriage and child-rearing, have separated themselves from that world and are pursuing independent lives.[2] Even those women who assume the responsibility of a job when married, not so much by choice as by necessity, see many benefits to holding a job.

The feelings of dissatisfaction with marriage and mothering are not, however, shared by all women. For some women, the attack on marriage represents a threat that much that is precious to them will be lost. For this reason women, satisfied in their role as wife and mother, are neutral, if not antagonistic, to change. They present a two-fold challenge to the women's movement. The movement, in justice, must recognize and respect the interests and the rights of these women and at the same time enlist their support for restructuring that will change the position of women in our society. The importance of this challenge cannot be overstated: in all probability the majority of women identify themselves, with reservations, primarily as satisfied homemakers and mothers.

Nevertheless, recent psychological surveys show that many women are dissatisfied with marriage. Single women have less emotional problems than married women, while married men have less problems than single men. Clearly, in too many cases marriage is supportive of men, but a burden to women. The *Washington Post* of April 20, 1975, reports on the findings of the special task force of the American Psychological Association on the attitude of psychologists and psychiatrists (mostly men) toward women. In addition to pointing to the discriminatory attitudes held by men, the findings reinforce the judgment that the social conditions of women are a source of widespread emotional difficulties for them. All of these indicators show that women are responding consciously or unconsciously to a social reality.[3]

It is interesting and important to note, in this context, that the dissatisfactions and problems of women in marriage and in other phases of societal life have been and usually still are attributed to personal inadequacies, rather than to structural oppressions. Attempts to deal with the problems still usually focus on adjusting women to the status quo rather than on modifying the social conditions in which women live. Even an analysis of the present reality is unavailable to most women, especially if it involves a class and/or radical analysis. This is not to say that there have been no studies identifying and examining the structures that restrict women. There are many, but most have been pushed to the fringes, if not simply ignored.

Even with these limitations, however, social science research is providing us with important insights. People, women no less than men, need the social affirmation and status that comes to them as productive members of society. In our society, a part of this affirmation is marked by a pay check. Even with that pay check, women have to struggle for equality of responsibilities and rights. Without it, the struggle is gigantic. Despite the many popular myths of the importance of homemakers and mothers to society, women's experience proves that society does not value these essential roles. No society, at the present time, includes women's domestic labor as part of the nation's Gross National Product. Women must fight for a say even in those areas where society says they are authorities.

Oppression of women can be traced back to the beginning of history. With the coming of the industrial revolution and the market society, Western women's status fell even further. The work place was moved from the home. No longer did women work along with men to produce the textiles, clothing, and other tools and material needed by the community. Wives, who once shared with their husbands in the social productivity necessary for family and society's well-being and thus had some public standing, found themselves relegated to the home with a loss of public role and public standing. The poor were the exceptions. The working conditions of these latter women were life-destroying.

The separation of the work place from the home has had two consequences. As mobility of the labor market created the nuclear family, the care and upbringing of children, at one time a shared responsibility of the extended family, community, and parents, became increasingly the responsibility of one person—the mother. Even when the schools took on some of the task of educating and socializing children, this only placed additional demands on the mother as she was held responsible for the motivation and self-discipline required of all "good" students.

A second, impossible responsibility also devolved upon the family, and especially the marriage relationship. Work increasingly isolated individuals, placed them in competition against one another, and subjected them to the demands of machines. Relationships within the community followed the same pattern of competition, defining human value in terms of material holdings. Society, in response, turned to the family to supply all the human needs of friendship, affection, spiritual nourishment, etc., absent outside the home.

Women were told that their job was to create a warm, tension-free, conflictless home for their husbands, where men could relax and be renewed. Wives were supposed to meet all the unfilled needs of husbands. The wives, in turn, were expected to receive all the satisfactions and stimulations—intellectual, spiritual, psychological, and social—they required to grow as persons from serving in the home, isolated from other adults, performing mostly menial tasks. This pair of expectations was humanly impossible, yet wives were told they failed if they did not realize them.

The major ideal for women today reflects the dual responsibility for child and husband placed on wives—the women who devote their energy, talents, and time to the well-being of their husbands and children, who sacrifice themselves for their families. If these women work outside the home, they still keep up with their household and family responsibilities and usually feel guilty for depriving those they love of the nurturing they feel is needed.

Other models are surfacing—painfully, with great effort. Women are struggling to be free, complete persons. Whether working at home or outside the home, women are appropriating responsibility for their lives, with all the consequences this implies. Women are working with their husbands to bring into being marriages that better respect and encourage each other's strengths and support each other's weaknesses. Single life, for women and men, is becoming a respected option. The small but growing number of women who are involved in creating and testing alternatives are increasingly dialoguing with women in conventional situations. Some women, married and single, are beginning to build the network of information sharing and support essential if meaningful changes are to take place. Women everywhere are demanding equal treatment for themselves and their sisters on the job and in other areas of public life.

The process is not an easy one. At best, it involves tensions and reaching into the unknown. Often it involves confusion, disruption, and pain. The difficulties are compounded because the process involves many persons—some unwilling participants. As women take responsibility for their own lives, they take this responsibility and all it implies in terms of power from others—others who do not see the oppressions they are responsible for and who do not wish to give up the power they hold over the lives of women, even if this power is oppressive to them as well. Women do this with little support since the institutions which should be helping them either do not see the injustices involved, or, seeing them, turn away.

Religious Institutions

Traditionally, women have been closely linked to religious institutions.[4] Rather than being an active participant in women's struggle for justice, however, many churches have played an ambivalent role. As a whole, they are not yet coming to grips with the many questions women and the women's movement are raising.

To begin with, churches must come to grips with the traditional teachings about the nature and place of women. Jesus, in his life, opposed almost all restrictions his culture placed on women in his time. He treated the women he met as he treated the men—with respect and sensitivity to them as persons. The churches succumbed to the pressures of culture and have misplaced this vision. The current efforts of women to retrieve it are met with indifference, if not outright hostility. The role of women in church governance and ministry, ethical questions on family, the rights of women over their bodies, the place of the feminine in worship are just a few of the topics that are not receiving the serious and sensitive attention they need.

The ordination of women to sacramental ministry has become the symbol of the Christian churches' treatment of women. Some traditions—the Catholic, the Episcopalian, some Baptist, the Missouri Synod Lutheran traditions—deny women the right to be ministers. Others ordain women, but have been unable to overcome the barriers that will effectively open the full range of ministry to women. Thus, women are found in the bureaucracy, in special parishes, and in nonparish ministries, but are rarely found as ministers, pastors, in parishes, especially the larger parishes. This pattern does not seem as prevalent in black churches, where women ministers have often been accepted as leaders and ministers.

The reluctance of religious leaders to take seriously the questions raised by women has created unnecessary obstacles to the liberation of women. The divisions among women, for example, stem in part from the responses of church leaders. Many women interpret the actions and statements of these leaders as condemnation of the women's movement, and oppose it. Others, encouraged by their own experiences to accept the status quo, are not open to dialogue because those they look to for leadership have declared women's rights a nonissue.

Women involved in the struggle for liberation find not only obstacles but pain in the church's stand. There has been much conflict—both within individual women and between women and their church communities. Many women have found themselves with feelings of frustration, ruptured loyalties, and a deep sense of betrayal. Some have given up the struggle and left the church. Others have left but see their separation from the institutional church as an important part of the struggle itself, their leaving as a positive, political statement. Whatever the motivation, a break with the established church is increasingly the only option some women seeking liberation see open to them.

There are, however, other women who, despite all indications to the contrary, still hope for justice within the church. These women have remained within the structures to challenge them, to push them to be true to the message of Christ, to be just. They have been joined by men who recognize that true liberation for all can come only when women are liberated. Their beginning breakthroughs are bearing fruit, but much remains to be done.

There is one task which the women's movement shares with other movements—the creation of a just society. Its contribution lies in assuring the end of oppression for women without shifting oppression onto others. In this task, women must cooperate with other liberation movements while refusing to be co-opted or manipulated by them. Within this broad goal, there are many specific tasks to be done. One, particularly important, is the discovery and creation of new models. The women traditionally held before us have been presented in a distorted manner. They have been robbed of realness; they have been used to domesticate women. The task of discovering who these women really were has begun; it must continue. In addition, new models, reflecting the needs and struggle of our times, must be developed. These models must incorporate the best of our traditions and the insights women are gaining as they struggle for liberation. There are other, equally important, tasks before women. Some have surfaced as women have reflected on their situations; others will be identified as this reflection continues.

NOTES

1. Statistical information on women in the work force may be obtained from the Women's Bureau, Employment Standards Administration, U.S. Department of Labor, Washington, DC 20210.

2. About one in four marriages ends in divorce. Many factors contribute to this rate: immaturity, especially in teenage marriages; increased longevity; pressures that force people to grow apart; and the increased acceptability of divorce are among those acknowledged. The willingness of women to strike out on their own is not yet a major contributor, but the increasing number of middle-aged women seeking divorces is one more indication of the dissatisfaction with marriage as it is presently structured.

3. A summary of some recent psychological studies of married and single women and married and single men can be found in Jessie Bernard's *The Future of Marriage* (New York: Bantam Books, 1973), especially chapters 2, 3, and 4.

4. No attempt is being made in this essay to deal with the experiences of women who profess faiths other than Christian.

14

Liberation and the Native American

by Sister Jeanne Rollins, O.S.F.

We are afflicted in every way possible but we are not crushed; full of doubts, we never despair. We are persecuted but never abandoned, we are struck down but never destroyed. Continually we carry about in our bodies the dying of Jesus, so that in our bodies the life of Jesus may also be revealed. While we live we are constantly being delivered to death for Jesus' sake, so that the life of Jesus may be revealed in our mortal flesh. Death is at work in us, but life in you. We have that Spirit of faith of which the Scripture says, "Because I believed, I spoke out." We believe and so we speak, knowing that He who raised up the Lord Jesus will raise us up along with Jesus and place both us and you in His presence. Indeed everything is ordered to your benefit, so that the grace bestowed in abundance may bring greater glory to God because they who gave thanks are many.

We do not lose heart, because our inner being is renewed each day even though our body is being destroyed at the same time. The present burden of our trial is light enough, and earns for us an eternal weight of glory beyond all comparison. We do not fix our gaze on what is seen but on what is unseen. What is seen is transitory; what is unseen lasts forever [2 Cor. 4:8–18].

From these words we can perhaps come to grips with what it means to be born into society today as a native American. We are born into a community native to this land and yet displaced because of historical and sociological events by which the white man usurped our land using it in a way very much different from our way.

We did not think of the great open plains, the beautiful rolling hills and winding streams with tangled growth, as "wild." Only to the white man was nature a "wilderness," and only to him was the land "infested" with "wild" animals and "savage" people. To us it was tame. Earth was bountiful and we were surrounded with the blessings of the Great Mystery. Not until the hairy man from the East came and with brutal frenzy heaped injustices upon us and the families we loved, was it "wild" for us. When the very animals of the forest began fleeing from his approach, then it was that for us the "Wild West" began.[1]

Today many of our people live on reservations where land has been set aside for us. There are as many reactions to reservation life as there are a variety of economic situations due to the climate, location, and natural resources of each particular reservation. Some feel the reservation system must be abolished and Indian people integrated into the mainstream of white society. This would follow the original intention of setting up reservations: that they be a temporary place for us until we could mix into society in five or ten years. Instead the system has been in progress for over a century now. Many don't mind this however, because they see the reservation as the last sign of self-pride and more than likely we would have been completely eradicated had this system followed its original course. Oppression in its many forms—social, economic, educational, and physical—would be total without the reservation. As Chief Seattle stated:

Every part of this soil is sacred to my people. Every hillside, every valley, every plain and grove has been hallowed by some sad or happy event in days long vanished. The very dust upon which you now stand responds more lovingly to our footsteps than to yours, because it is rich with the blood of our ancestors, and our bare feet are conscious of the sympathetic touch. Even the little children who lived here and rejoiced here for a brief season will love these somber solitudes and at eventide they greet shadowy returning spirits.

And when the last red man shall have perished, and the memory of my tribe shall have become a myth among white men, these shores will swarm with the invisible dead of my tribe, and when your children's children think themselves alone in the field, the store, the shop, upon the highway, or in the silence of the pathless woods, they will not be alone. At night when the streets of your cities and villages are silent and you think them deserted, they will throng with the returning hosts that once filled and still love this beautiful land. The white man will never be alone. Let him be just and deal kindly with my people, for the dead are not powerless. Dead, did I say? There is no death, only a change of worlds.[2]

In this change of worlds, we do not say that the reservation is best or actually what it should be. Many of our urban brothers reap greater fruit and are more easily enabled to endure life's hardships. Much has to be done to improve the health, education, and living conditions of our people. The alcohol problem has had serious consequences among us. We would like to see it and other social problems eliminated from our people, but this is most difficult. Attention must be given to these areas in order to lift our people up out of the oppressive weight bearing upon them.

We are a people who live in community closely to one another. Our way of life centers around a brotherhood that is permanent—deeply observed and deeply offended. The laws, values, and customs of our people are taught to our youth by the elders who have the wisdom and spiritual insight of age and experience. The Indian way is to live with nature, not against it. It is important to maintain a compatible and working relationship with all living things. Whatever one holds sacred is to be respected. We do not bother about little things nor do we force our way upon each other. "Who you are and what you are reflects as in a mirror and hopefully people emulate the good that is done and not the person doing that good."[3]

A sense of group responsibility is evident especially in our upbringing and discipline. For instance, a household without a father image is given one by another member of the community who may or may not be related. As the fruits of the womb are shared within the community so too are the fruits of our Mother, the Earth. Each and all must be cared for. In the past we were taught our responsibility for this, and today we must continue on if we are to survive and be liberated as a people. Naturally we are a reticent people—too often confused by others with insecurity, fear, and hesitancy. Any insecurity, fear, or hesitancy that can be evidenced in our people is due to the oppression, injustice, and crimes that we are made to endure. We must work together therefore as brothers and sisters to encourage one another and to stand up for that good in which we believe.

Although the organized culture and tradition of our ancestors has largely been lost, we still retain certain parts of it. Much of it is still in our attitudes such as respect for the spirit, family ties, and community gatherings: where time is used to accomplish these things and they are not put aside because there isn't enough time. There is a spiritual strength still with us today. An Indian has said, "This is the place where my ancestors communed with the spiritual world. I have a relationship with it even though I DO NOT LIVE THERE. We must combine the good things of the past and present with the future."[4]

To do this we must continue to live closely with the Great Spirit in the way He is familiar to us: Wakan Takan, Nabi, Jesus, Whoever. . . . It is our responsibility to provide for the good of all the community and also to have respect and reverence for all of creation. We must be ready to carry on the role of the Spirit and not allow or wait for the black robes and/or their followers to lead us. We must recognize and work with the young of our community. They are the prize of today and the hope of our tomorrow. And if growth is to continue we must educate our people. To provide this educational setting, communication is of the utmost importance. Most of our communication is the heart, in the remembered spoken word rather than the easily forgotten ideas that lose their meaning in abstractions. We have an "eye" for what is there and miss much of what is on the printed page. We are also unfamiliar with the spirit of competition as it is manifested in the white man's world; therefore there is much cause for "burning" and being put down.

Where do we look? What do we do? "We have already learned that waiting for someone else to take positive action on Indian issues is a lesson in frustration. If things are to change in line with our expectations, then the answers must ultimately come from ourselves."[5] And so we pray:

O Great Spirit,
Whose voice I hear in the winds,
And whose breath gives life to all the world,
Hear me! I am small and weak,
I need your strength and wisdom.

LET ME WALK IN BEAUTY,
and make my eyes ever behold the red and purple sunset.

LET MY HANDS respect the things you have made
and my ears sharp to hear your voice.

MAKE ME WISE so that I may understand
the things you have taught my people.

LET ME LEARN the lessons you have hidden
in every leaf and rock.

I SEEK STRENGTH, not to be greater than my brother,
but to fight my greatest enemy—myself.

MAKE ME ALWAYS READY to come to you
with clean hands and straight eyes.

SO WHEN LIFE FADES, as the fading sunset,
my spirit may come to you without shame.[6]

NOTES

1. Chief Luther Standing Bear of the Oglala Sioux, as found in *Touch the Earth, A Self-Portrait of Indian Existence*, ed. T. C. McLuhan (New York: Outerbridge & Lazard, 1971).

2. Chief Seattle, in 1855 when he surrendered the land of his people to Governor Isaac Stevens; also found in *Touch the Earth*.

3. Herb Barnes, Chairman of the National Association of Blackfeet Indians, 1975.

4. Tandy Wilbur, Sr., in a speech delivered in 1970 and printed in *Kee-Yoks*, the Swinomish Tribal Newsletter, March 1975.

5. David Grant, Director of the Pacific Institute of Native American Programs, taken from his brochure, *Indian Is*.

6. Words of a Sioux Indian prayer.

15

The Chicano Struggle

by a Chicano Reflection Group

Our effort in this presentation is to consider if our Chicano struggle finds significance in the theology of liberation of Latin America. Our struggle for liberation resulted when some concerned Chicanos reflected on the concrete reality of our existence in our U.S.A.—a country whose political system is democratic, whose economic system is capitalistic, and whose dominant culture is white Anglo-Saxon. Within this political freedom, economic wealth, and dominant culture, we discovered that we were (and still are) among the poorest of the poor; this can be proven statistically. The Chicano came face to face with his/her *barrio* and *colonia* conditions: minimum education, poor housing conditions, economically poor and politically weak. The Chicano/a further discovered his/her own Catholic church had failed to address itself to our plight (academic, economic, and political). We are a large minority in the church with practically no hierarchical representation. Through this reflection, the Chicano/a started a *movimiento* that addressed itself to our oppression within this land.

In the sixties and seventies, various leaders and groups in the Southwest brought a certain militancy to the *movimiento*: César Chávez in farm labor; José Angel Gutiérrez in politics and education; Reyes Tijerina in land reform; Corky González in education; and PADRES, Las Hermanas, and Católicos por la Raza in community involvement and church matters.

In 1848 with the Treaty of Guadalupe Hidalgo, our lands, language, and religion came under the control of U.S.A. Although the treaty gave guarantee that we could keep our land, language, and religion, the manifest destiny of our country soon became the reigning power that made us a people exiled in *nuestra tierra*. We are mostly *mestizos, indios, e hispanos*, a rural people that for the most part still belongs to the poor rural-urban class, although the majority of Chicanos live in urban areas. The political, economic, social, religious strength of the dominant culture, WASP, enslaved us to serve with cheap labor. We were those citizens who had been conquered militarily and then became second-rated citizens until you heard *el grito "ya basta."* After World War II, our returning GIs experienced a certain freedom. We had fought for our *Patria*, we had seen some of the benefits of how the dominant culture lived, and our GI benefits gave us a chance to further our education, which ultimately prepared us for the service of our communities. But we were still subservient to the economic, political, and cultural needs of the ruling class that has control of the system that provides for these needs.

Our efforts to provide for the basic needs of survival caused us to take low-paying jobs in *el campo y pueblo*. Our people migrated as fieldworkers primarily, and eventually some of our people stayed in the Midwest, West, and East Coast; some of us graduated from janitors to become *técnicos* and *algunos cuantos profesionales*. This need to migrate from our land and culture and the strong influence of the dominant culture made us want to become good citizens and added another flavor to the melting pot *atole*. However, *con el tiempo* and with the collective efforts of the minorities—blacks, Indians, Chicanos, *Puertorriqueños*—and *la mujer*, we began to consider our cultural identity. Big migrations from Mexico brought our poor brother and sister to this land that promised them *trabajo*. Many of them worked below ordinary salaries because *la familia tenía hambre*. Still, we are faced with the human struggle that exists with the situation of green card workers and our *compadres* and *comadres* without documents. In the 1970s there was a national moratorium in Los Angeles, California. This moratorium was in protest that our *hermanos* were the "*carnada*" for the Vietnam War, and the percentage of our boys being drafted and killed was high compared to the percentage of our people in this country. Once again, the obvious: the Raza, el Chicano, was "*el fregado*" and the dominant culture, the ruling class was exempt from serving because of their political and social pull; as for enrollment in colleges and universities, *dicen que tenemos algunos con grado de maestría y doctorado*, but these are a token few. One still has to beg to join the ranks that eventually are recognized as qualified for academic, professional, and technical fields.

Part of our religious history is greatly influenced by the dominant culture of our country, which is White Anglo-Saxon Protestant, and our cultural heritage from Mexico, which is Indo-Hispanic with emphasis on Spanish. Even our Catholic church is dominated by the WASP mentality, and the Spanish Catholic influence neglected the vision of encouraging a native clergy—Mexican-American or Chicano.

The Catholicism that we received from Mexico is one that stems from the Spanish Catholic church, highly governmentally controlled. The Spanish power is historically viewed as geo-politically aggressive and economically exploitative of the land of our forefathers. These two religious factors, the American Catholic church and Hispanic Catholicism, are influential in our religious heritage. The Indo-Hispanic influence is evident by our devotion to Our Lady of Guadalupe, whose image-banner is carried at times in our public protests against injustices. The Spanish-speaking Catholic population, which composes one-fourth of the church, is still a minority in hierarchical representation; only one Chicano has an archdiocese.

The racial, economic, and political discriminatory oppression that was practiced upon our black brothers and sisters was felt by us too. However, ours was not considered a discrimination. After all, this was our land; we were considered Caucasian, not completely black but not completely white either, only brown, and we did have a history, a culture. This *abrazo* was only a gentle one, never seriously wanting us to share as first-class citizens in the political structure, much less in the economic empire. Although there has been a serious concern for the Chicano to become politically involved, there is evidence of low political registration. The two dominant political parties, Democrats and Republicans, still have the majority of the Mexican-American voters. The Latino, Hispanic, Mexican-American, or Chicano congresspersons do not form a public bloc or caucus as the blacks do when legislation comes up that seriously affects the lot of our poor people. An expression of political independence from the major parties arose with the formation of La Raza Unida Party. In small town politics, especially in Texas, there has been some strength shown for La Raza Unida Party. The La Raza Unida Party candidate for governor in Texas, Ramsey Muniz, challenged the strength of the Democratic Party. However, La Raza Unida Party nationwide still has to make a serious effort to unite La Raza so as to be effective politically in the cause for Chicano justice.

Religion plays a very important role in our lives. Our Indian forefathers were a people very close to nature, and nature's unknown elements were our gods. Living in harmony with nature meant that the gods were pleased, and it meant *la madre tierra* needed *el dios de la lluvia y del sol* so as to give us *la cosecha* which was necessary for living. A religious, cultural difference between the Chicano and the North American is evident in relation to nature. Our heritage has taught us to live in harmony with nature, whereas the Anglo-Saxon has conquered nature and has abused it to become a powerful nation. It is only recently that ecology became a national concern.

Our religious acculturation has been heavily influenced by both the American Catholic/Protestant ethics and the Indo-Hispanic cultural ethic of our Mexican ancestors. For the Chicano, God has always been a personal God, never dying, because to us God is *Diosito,* who personally intervenes in our life. The dogmatic God given to us by the American Catholic/Protestant and Hispanic Catholic religious is not primarily for us a Sunday occasion or a sacramental presence, but a God whose divinity did not hinder him from being humanly present with us. God enters into the total celebration of our lives. Christ, *nuestro hermano,* in his passion and death is very close to us; oppressed Christian people easily find identification with Christ. We make our suffering Christ's suffering, as is evident in *El Cristo de la Agonía.* Christ, *nuestro redentor,* has been for Chicanos *una persona muy buena.* He is for us a person who was more concerned with our repentence than our sinfulness. For the poor Chicano, Christ is very human, concerned more with curing the sick, feeding the hungry, and being for and *con el pobre.* Christ who died for us wants us in *el cielo* (Christ *es tan bueno que me salvará!*). The closeness of Christ to *el carnal* is often experienced through the tatoo of a cross on the hand, and the blessing of ourselves ends most of the time in the kissing of our fingers that form the cross.

Our faith is not one only of belief, but one that has to be expressed externally: *nuestras medallas, altares, curaciones,* and *días de los santos, vivos y difuntos* still exist despite the strong Hispanic and Anglo-Saxon religious influences that would interpret these religious events as superstitious. For the Chicano, the sins that are committed because of the weakness of the flesh are easier to understand than the sins that put us against *nuestro hermano/a.*

It is just recently that we have begun to relate the Sacred Scriptures to our Chicano struggle. With the *movimiento familiar, cursillo, retiros, encuentros matrimoniales* and the teaching of adults, the *palabra de Dios* became more meaningful in our lives.

La Iglesia for the Chicano is still *madre*, but one who was confronted out of love, especially at the beginning of our struggle for liberation. Lately, however, an attitude of indifference has occurred among a significant number of Chicanos, because they do not see the institutional church as one that is relevant to them or they do not see *el padre*, *la monjita* being present with them *en la lucha*. Other Chicanos see the church as contradictory in its expression of poverty or its alliance with the powerful upper and middle class. There are however, among the Chicanos, some that do recognize the church as being involved, as in the farmworker struggle for justice and the latest concern with *nuestros hermanos* without documents.

We would like to compare the Chicano religious experience to the period of the Babylonian Exile. Chicanos have a memory of a time when their ancestors possessed the land and the political power. Many Chicano activists stem from the *Californianos*, *Tejanos*, or *Nuevo Mejicanos* who had unique lifestyles, communal forms of ownership, an identity of their own, and were not recent immigrants. Later, there was a massive wave of immigrants from Mexico, mostly poor people as well as a few middle-class people who entered into real exile. But the more powerful experience, the one recounted over and over again in the Chicano mythology of Aztlán, is that of the people who became Exiles-in-Their-Own-Land by the treaty of Guadalupe Hidalgo in 1848.

The Israelites of the Exile were not slaves when they were carried off into exile, but were carried off into exile because they had a powerful influence on their home turf. During the years of exile, they did not forget the religion of their fathers but purified it, interiorized it, and personalized it. Their God was one very close to them, though they were away from the Temple in Jerusalem. He took notice of what each person did and looked out, not just for the whole nation, but for the individuals. It is with this phase of the Israelites' Exile that the Chicano seems to find more identification.

In the *lucha* for liberation, we have our Aztlán, a place, *una tierra*, that is *aquí, prometida*, and *más allá: aquí*—in the concrete world of reality that oppresses us; *prometida*—in the hope that we will arrive to it and return by fighting for the cause; and *más allá* (eschatological) in the belief that *el Reino de Dios debe de ser formado entre nosotros y no solamente un cielo después de nuestra vida aquí en la tierra*.

We Chicanos, or Mexican-Americans, have to seriously address ourselves to the question of our brothers/sisters of Latin America, and we hope that, in our efforts to become a prophetic voice of liberation in our country, we do not become the oppressors or ignore the fact that our country continues its oppression upon Third and Fourth World people.

We hope that through this paper we have shown that Latin America's theology of liberation is significant in our struggle.

Sister Mario Barron
Rev. Lonnie Reyes
Rev. Edmundo Rodríguez, S.J.

Rev. Juan Romero
Rev. Luciano Hendren
Rev. Roberto Peña, OMI

SECTION FOUR

Methodology of U.S. Liberation Theology

Included here are two preparatory documents dealing with theological methodology.

Some professional theologians may be disappointed with this chapter–and perhaps with the whole book–for they will not find here their traditional theological categories.

Nevertheless these documents reflect an original aspect of the conference process: the joint effort of professional theologians and grassroots people. The documents synthesize the preparatory work of the reflection groups.

"Exploring the Meaning of Liberation" represents the work of a Chicago reflection group, in which theology students collaborated with well-known U.S. theologians. An original synthesis of social analysis and theological reflection, it describes the meaning of liberation from oppressive structures; it treats of the goals of liberation (liberation to) and relates them to the means of liberation (liberation through) in the U.S. context.

The second document, "A Theological Quest," summarizes the contributions of those reflection groups that submitted written reports. The first section contains critical comments on the development of the process itself: its organizations, the activities of the groups, the planning of the conference. The second part synthesizes the comments on the preparatory documents, and the third contains suggestions and criteria for theological reflection submitted by the participants. Excerpts of "A Theological Quest" are presented here.

New dimensions of the process are apparent in this document, particularly the reaction of many to the idea of the United States as the head of an empire. There also arose the question of the methodology for theological reflection in the United States. Two tendencies emerged: The first held that theology should be based on the concrete experience of Christians who are attempting to deepen their understanding of their faith; the second held for biblical and religious tradition as the starting point.

A third document, not included here, also dealt with theological methodology. "How Do We Do Liberation Theology?" by Lee Cormie, Diego Irarrazaval, and Robert Stark, has been published in Radical Religion *2, no. 4 (1976), pp. 25–31.*

Together these documents represent an attempt to explore the methodology for a theological reflection that corresponds to the aspirations and needs of ordinary Christians.

16

Exploring the Meaning
of Liberation

by a Chicago Reflection Group

*(Walter Cason, Lee Cormie, Diego Irarrazaval,
Alvin Pitcher, Robert Stark, Richard Tholin, Gibson Winter)*

As a group we came together from various backgrounds to participate in the process called Theology in the Americas. This paper represents our attempts to share experiences, information, and perspectives on the meaning of liberation. We feel that its value lies in its reflection of this shared process and of the necessity we felt for understanding our present economic and political situation as the context for doing theology, as much as it does in the tentative interpretations it conveys. We are aware that there are limitations on any reflective process which does not include members of poor and oppressed groups, especially racial groups and women, in an integral way. And we have as a goal the formation of such a broad-based group as the context for our future analyses and reflections.

In the last few years we have become increasingly aware that there are powerful and pervasive forces in the U.S. that function without the knowledge of the great majority of its citizens. The truth seeps through the programmed superficiality of the media news and gradually sinks in: Vietnam, Watergate, the so-called oil shortage, CIA disclosures, FBI harrassment of Martin Luther King and left groups all point to an industrial-military-government complex which functions clandestinely and autonomously. More and more clearly we see that, as a people, we are not informed about important issues and decisions. What is worse, we see that we are in fact deliberately misinformed and that political groups are deliberately manipulated so that we may not participate in the formation of policy or in the evaluation of operations. Realizing the extent to which we live in a political illusion, we believe that fundamental changes in our society are necessary if, in solidarity with poor and oppressed people throughout the world, we are to escape the collective grave which is being dug by current policies regarding the national and international distribution of food, scarce natural resources, opportunities for development, and energy use, especially in relation to environmental pollution. Indeed, fundamental change appears inevitable. The questions we all face are: change by and for whom, and in the name of what values?

Of course, we recognize that within the U.S. there is a long tradition of democratic participation of the people in the governing of the country, of concerned criticism and action for justice and a better way of life. Undeniably many positive advances have been the result of these efforts throughout our history; the emergence of the labor unions is a major example. We are also aware that new elements of social criticism are emerging which cover the whole range of crucial issues today. But we are also aware that democratic participation in the governing of our country is severely limited by the exclusion of economic decision-making and fundamental social criticism from the democratic process; and it seems to us that these issues are at the heart of the basic problems confronting the world. It also seems to us that these elements of social criticism are often not sufficiently elaborated and interrelated, or widely communicated.

Thus, in our reflections together we found ourselves continually returning to the question of the relationships among economics, politics, and the ideology that legitimates them, out of a sense that these structures and ideology form the inescapable framework within which we all live—a framework which theological reflection on the meaning of God's presence in history also cannot escape.

Against this background our group has taken as its tasks the exploration of some issues, and their interrelations, concerning liberation as a fundamental religious and political theme among poor and oppressed people throughout the world. We are convinced that in our historical situation, liberation involves, in part, unmasking the demonic structures of autonomous power and the ideology which obscures and legitimates them. In this paper we offer our reflections on these issues.

We have approached the meaning of liberation through two case studies: (1) recent events in Chile, and (2) the power and influence of the multinational corporations (MNCs). Our reflections have centered on the oppressive structures and ideology *from* which poor and oppressed people seek liberation, but we have also referred to the process *through* which liberation proceeds, and to the goal *to* which the process of liberation points. We feel that our discussions have been tentative, and that this paper is to be understood essentially as pointing to elements for a more systematic analysis which must inform a liberating theology.

We are especially aware of certain limitations of this study. In particular, we acknowledge that this kind of analysis can be vital only when linked concretely to the struggles of particular oppressed groups, for this link provides the ground for assessing the value of the analysis in clarifying the historical reality, and for assessing its value as a response to the demands arising from dehumanizing experiences. Throughout our exploration we focus only on global and national economic structures and forms of ideology. We see the need of relating our analysis more directly to specific instances of exploitation. Otherwise, analysis and theological reflection on the meaning of our situation become excessively abstract and purely theoretical, and often in these forms actually function in support of the dominant ideology. We feel that social scientific analysis and theological reflection, if they are to be meaningful to more than an elite few with privileged places in the system, must reflect the conditions of life of the great majority within capitalism; and if they are to be liberating, they must be rooted in the struggle of the poor and the oppressed who suffer most from the injustices of the system.

LIBERATION FROM

The Case of Chile

The internal and foreign opposition to the social transformation carried out in Chile during the Allende period reveals many features of the MNCs' economic interests, of class structures, and of the dominant ideology within the worldwide capitalist system. Between

1970 and 1973 the Chilean government was involved in two major programs. First, there was a program of nationalization of foreign corporate interests so that these companies could be managed in the interests of the Chilean people instead of in the interests of foreign investors. And, second, there was a program for the creation of new social relationships within Chile, so that the great majority of people, and not only a tiny class at the top, could actively and equally share in the profits of their labor and in the decision-making concerning their future, including the direction of future economic and social development in Chile.

Conflict between corporate interests and the Chilean people focussed especially around the copper mines. But the copper industry was only one instance; many MNCs had interests in Chile. In fact, over 50 percent of Chile's larger industries were controlled by foreign interests, especially U.S.-based interests. Thus, the Chilean government's programs of nationalization and redistribution of profits, within the project of a socialist economy linked to democratic political structures, threatened both Chilean and U.S. elites and their program of corporate expansion and ideological legitimation.

In particular, U.S. government and corporate leaders were threatened by the Chilean project for two reasons. First, there was the threat of Third World control of its resources which would cause drastic changes in U.S. foreign policy and undermine its dominance in world economics. This is similar to the threat currently being confronted in connection with the OPEC nations. Second, but unlike the OPEC nations, the Chilean people were proposing a radically different type of economic and political system—a socialist system in which the gap between the tiny minority of rich people and the great majority of poor and oppressed people would be eliminated, a system where all would share equally in the results of their labor and in economic and political decision-making.

If Chile had succeeded in building a genuinely democratic socialist society, it would have become a model for other Third World countries, and it would have struck a mortal blow to the cold war mythology which equates democracy with capitalism and totalitarianism with socialism. It is true that capitalist democracy promotes certain freedoms. But these freedoms are strictly limited. In particular they do not include involvement of the majority of people in the processes of economic decision-making which so profoundly shape the lives of all people. By struggling to involve all the people in decision-making in these areas, while preserving, within an atmosphere of deep respect for the constitutional processes, traditional democratic rights such as the right of free speech, the Chilean revolutionaries were promising to unfold a deeper meaning of freedom, a freedom which called into question inequalities not only within Chile, but within the U.S. and other advanced capitalist countries.

U.S. government and corporate policy toward the democratically elected government of Allende and its programs reveals profound contradictions: In the name of "freedom and democracy" U.S. policy actively supported the overthrow of the democratically elected government by a military coup and its replacement by a brutal military dictatorship—a policy which most of us in the U.S. knew nothing about and could do nothing to change when we did. These are not isolated events. For example, Nelson Rockefeller's report to President Nixon after his "fact-finding" tour of Latin America maintains that the U.S. may have to support strong military governments in order to keep Latin America "free" for democracy and progress. These events call into question the democratic rights the people in the U.S. supposedly possess to participate in government decision-making which affects the lives of millions throughout the world. And they call into question the very meaning of "freedom and democracy" when this phrase is used to legitimate such inhuman policies.

The criteria broadly used by government spokespeople and reporters in the media to justify this intervention, when it finally became public knowledge, reveal the ideological nature of phrases like "freedom and democracy" when they are used in this way. Generally this propaganda focussed around the claim that socialism means the end of political order and freedom, the destruction of economic order and the "free market," the institutionalization of inefficiency, and the inadequate production of consumption items. In fact, these slogans function to support and extend the power, "efficiency," and "freedom" of the MNCs, especially in the Third World. In the name of so-called "freedom" and "efficiency" the opposition to socialism in Chile took many well documented forms: the ITT plan, the blockade of international economic credit by the U.S. Export-Import Bank and the U.S. dominated World Bank, the influx of CIA personnel and funds, reduction of U.S. aid to Chile (except that to the military, which was doubled in order to keep it antileftist), internal strikes in Chile carried out by truck owners, small business and professional groups, internal boycotts by middle- and upper-class groups which contributed to the disruption of the economy and the development of a black market.

According to the dominant ideology, Allende's program was disrupting the economic and political order. And, indeed, an *unjust* economic and political order was being disrupted with the goal of transforming it and creating a new society. The opposition led by corporate interests, the Chilean elite, and their supporters in the U.S. government won this time, but only at an incredible cost: Allende was murdered, along with thousands of others; thousands have been brutally tortured; thousands more have been forced to flee the country. A strong military government, the type recommended by Rockefeller presumably, has been installed. "Free market" policies, an inflation rate of 600 percent per year, and a 25 percent unemployment rate plague the people—and this in a country without an elaborate welfare system; in other words, many people are literally starving to death.[1] "Order" and "efficiency" are insured by the new government: by fascist repression and the complete elimination of all democratic rights and freedoms.

The cold war mentality, which has long been so prominent within the U.S., was operative again. Foreign intervention and the fascist coup were justified on the grounds of the so-called "Marxist" threat to freedom. In this perspective, world politics is understood in terms of two simple alternatives: the absolute good of capitalism against the absolute evil of socialism. This ideological view of our nation as the guardian of capitalism and democratic rights was the rationale for U.S. government and corporate intervention in Chile, for the destruction of its democracy. The Chilean case reveals very clearly that this ideology functions largely as a defense of the interests of the MNCs and of the international elites, interests which were being nationalized in the Chilean project for a democratic socialism.[2]

The Chilean people were struggling to create a new order, free from exploitation and oppression. We have found that an analysis of their struggles and their defeat at the hands of their own elite and U.S. corporate interests unmasks the nature of the economic and ideological structures within which we all live. The Chilean case shows forms of slavery and alienation generated by the capitalist system and the extent to which those who enjoy the fruits of this system will go to preserve it.

The United States and the Multinational Corporations

In reviewing recent developments in Chile we learned much about the economic structures and the dominant ideology within which we all live. But we feel a need to understand more clearly the impact of these structures and this ideology on our own lives, for in terms of internal U.S. policies too we hear so much about economic order and efficiency and about the free market.

Studies of the MNCs and their policies here as well as in countries like Chile reveal the ideological nature of these values and the ways they mask structures of domination and dependence. These huge corporations operate largely in terms of their own profits and notions of efficiency in terms of these profits. They attempt to locate factories where wages are lowest, unions are weakest, antipollution laws are nonexistent. These policies often involve sudden moves from one location to another, regardless of the welfare of the communities involved, a process which is accelerating as the MNCs become more internationalized.

Here it is important to unmask the value of "efficiency." For corporate interests, efficiency is related primarily to their profits and to their power to control. The relations of profit, power, and control are complex, since some corporate policies are better understood in relation to future control of markets than in relation to actual money profits in the present. (This is clearly not the popular understanding of profit, the type of profit with which the person in a small business or on a small farm is concerned.) In this perspective Allende's programs were judged inefficient. Indeed they were inefficient in the narrow terms of the profits and future economic power of the Chilean and international corporate elites. However, in terms of greater equality and a more human life for all Chileans, these programs promised much more efficiency than previous capitalist policies or the policies instituted under the military junta.

The military-industrial complex provides a clear example of the way the dominant ideology, with its narrow definition of efficiency and profit, is manipulated to the advantage of the corporate elite within the U.S. (In this short space we will not even begin to consider the many ways in which the products of this complex, the instruments of war, are used to force uncooperative classes and nations to support policies favorable to the U.S. government and U.S. based MNCs and which by their proliferation throughout the world increase the likelihood of war.) The military accounts for 70 percent of our shipbuilding and 50 percent of our electronics work. The military establishment demands the services of 53 percent of our technical researchers and 32 percent of all engineers and scientists. While the military spends about 10 percent of our GNP ($104 billion in fiscal year 1974–1975), the social and long-range economic cost must be calculated in terms of the resources directly used up plus the productive use-value foregone, since no military product is in turn useable for further economic production or positive social value. Thus, the $1,000 billion military outlay by the U.S. from 1945 till 1970 ($1,550 billion to 1975) actually cost the nation $2,200 billion—the value of the total reproductive wealth of the nation excluding only the land.

Since only about 5 percent of military research and development is directly applicable for civilian use, we are technologically far behind in such important areas as mass transportation, urban housing, health delivery, education, and full employment.[3] Huge defense budgets result in the employment of many in the U.S., especially in times of economic crisis. But, ultimately, the greatest beneficiaries of U.S. militarization are the MNCs themselves. For the huge federal defense budget promotes the growth and development of the MNCs, and U.S. military aid to foreign governments, as in the case of Chile, maintains policies favorable to the MNCs and assures additional markets for their products.

It is clear that the military-industrial complex is not efficient in most senses of the word. The government will bail out a failing defense contractor rather than let it suffer the consequences of its inefficiency and waste; huge cost overruns are the rule, not the exception, and, for example, when even these payments could not save Lockheed, the government stepped in with guaranteed loans. Thus, there is no incentive to minimize costs—weapons systems average 3.2 times the first estimates of production costs. Moreover, the government will not allow foreign interests to compete with or to buy out U.S. defense corporations, insuring their survival regardless of their efficiency and profitability; Lockheed again presents an example of the government's blocking an attempt by foreign interests to buy into a defense corporation. Accordingly, even in the terms of the dominant ideology itself, the military-industrial complex fails. This case reveals how the values of efficiency and profit are manipulated in the interests of the dominant groups, for the military-industrial complex is efficient only in maintaining itself in power for profit.

It is important to note that in the post-Vietnam War era there has been a lot of propaganda about the necessity for a large military budget in the U.S. in order to support the economy. This propaganda is false, unless the frame of reference is narrowed to include only the interests of the military-industrial complex as it is presently constituted. For example, the economic argument for maintaining a wartime economy is false if our accounting includes the total dollar costs of these expenditures, as distinct from the costs to special industries and areas. Moreover, there is not even a valid argument for the costs to special industries and areas if the accounting period is five years or more. And, finally, the costs of conversion to new products and services would clearly be less than that of maintaining research and development for a changing weapons market.

Thus, the corporations of the military-industrial complex are not even efficient in terms of the dominant ideology, and analysis of them reveals the ideological use of values like "efficiency," the "free market," and in this case especially the "national good." Moreover, the close relationship between the government and large corporations, which is so evident in the case of the military-industrial complex, reveals the historic movement of corporate capitalism toward state capitalism, toward the increasing manipulation of politics and government in the service of economic interests. There is no better indication, then, of the nature of our past prosperity and of the depths of our current troubles than the military-industrial complex.

This analysis reveals that values like efficiency are ideological in two senses of the word. In the first place, as we have seen, these corporations are not even efficient in terms of costs and profits; indeed they are very inefficient. And beyond this the very meaning of efficiency itself requires closer examination. The increasing rationalization of work by the introduction of assembly lines, by the vertical integration of worldwide corporations, by refined cost accounting, by time studies of the minute details of different types of jobs—all these developments promise greater efficiency, and yet contribute to the increased alienation and dehumanization of workers[4] and to the increased deterioration of the environment, while they provide justification for manipulation of foreign governments and of political decision-making processes within the U.S. In other words, what is at stake is the very meaning of human life and work. It seems to us on the basis of our study of events in Chile and of the military-industrial complex within the U.S. that values like "efficiency" and the increased "rationalization" of the means of production to promote such efficiency are fundamentally dehumanizing and destructive of human communities and of nature.

The giant agribusinesses are another example of the way the dominant ideology, with its narrow definitions of efficiency and profit, is manipulated to the advantage of the corporate elite. For instance, today the giant agribusinesses are reshaping agriculture throughout the world. These MNCs are the leading proponents of high energy, fully technological agriculture as the most efficient way to feed the world. And it is true that one person operating huge farm machines and using large amounts of fertilizers can do a lot of farm work. But if the notion of efficiency is broadened to include the total energy input, agribusiness becomes the least efficient form of farming. And there is growing evidence that an agriculture based upon human input and a cooperative, just social order is much more productive in the long run when measured by output per unit of land than the version sold by the MNCs.[5]

What becomes clear in such studies is that high-energy, fully technologized agriculture is extraordinarily efficient, not in producing food, but in producing profits for the MNCs. These examples force us to ask fundamental questions when confronted with ideological justifications of economic and political policies in terms of efficiency and increased rationalization: Efficient in producing what end using what means? Efficient in terms of whose interests?

The power of the MNCs in shaping the U.S. policy in Chile is, then, no occasional aberration. It is much more the rule. The rise of the MNCs has developed a massive concentration of power in the hands of the corporate managers—power to define values, to shape industry and agriculture, and to control U.S. foreign and domestic policy. This power works primarily for the good of private interests; it promises, not more efficiency in meeting human needs, but greater alienation and greater concentrations of power and wealth, and a correspondingly greater ability to extract profits for the few who own and control the MNCs. Richard Barnet and Ronald Müller point to the danger of this power:

In short, the managers of the huge corporations are not elected by the people, nor are they subject to popular scrutiny or popular pressure, even though in the course of their daily business they make decisions with more impact on the lives of ordinary people than most generals and politicians ["Global Reach, II," *The New Yorker,* December 9, 1974, p. 100].

It is crucial to any project for justice and liberation to recognize that the evils confronting us are not simply occasional aberrations, the results of a few flaws in an otherwise just system, or the results of a few wicked political and corporate leaders. Rather, they are the normal and unavoidable consequences of the basic principles of capitalist production as they work themselves out in our global, technological time.

For example, apologists for advanced capitalism point to the degree of material affluence enjoyed by many within these countries as evidence for the "superiority" of capitalism over other political and economic systems; and they often claim that it is just a matter of time until the "underdeveloped" countries of the Third World catch up to the "developed" countries. But these apologists conveniently overlook the fact that this affluence in the "developed" countries has been achieved through the exploitation of the people and resources of the "underdeveloped" world. In other words, "development" and "underdevelopment" are not two independent realities. The Third World's underdevelopment is the other side of the coin of the First World's development. More precisely, development in the First World produces underdevelopment in the Third World. Accordingly, it is not simply a question of time until the "underdeveloped" Third World catches up to the affluence of the advanced capitalist countries.

The search for higher profits, efforts to avoid higher costs by exploiting cheap labor, the increasing concentration of economic power—all are essential characteristics of worldwide capitalist structures. And they are resulting in an increasing gap between the rich nations and the poor nations and between the rich classes and poor classes within nations; in their fundamental irrationality they are also contributing to the increasing deterioration of our natural environment. We discover, then, that the terms "development" and "underdevelopment" are ideological masks which obscure oppressive patterns of domination by a few and dehumanizing dependence for the great majority.

Apologists for capitalism also overlook the systematic exploitation and oppression of certain sectors within the U.S. itself. It is a fundamental tenet of the dominant ideology that capitalism promotes equality of opportunity and affluence for all within the U.S. It is widely proclaimed that anyone who tries can make it up the ladder of success and be happy. Those who fail do so primarily because they haven't tried, so it is said, and evidence of women and men from all racial, ethnic, and economic groups who have succeeded is eagerly offered. Yet despite these "rags to riches" success stories of isolated individuals and small groups, there are profound inequalities within the U.S. It is essential to unmask the structures of these divisions if we are effectively to criticize the consequences of capitalist economic relations and values, and if we are to understand the historical possibilities for justice and liberation before us.[6]

If a simple layer-cake image of society is somewhat appropriate for many Third World countries today, with their relatively clear-cut class divisions between the tiny minority of rich and powerful corporate owners at the top and the great majority of the powerless poor and oppressed who actually do the labor, and if it is appropriate for the early laissez-faire capitalism Marx himself analyzed, it is less appropriate for advanced capitalistic societies like the U.S. Social classes in culturally and socially complex societies cannot simply be identified with levels of income and consumption, or with other similar indices of stratification; in addition, the issue of the ownership of the means of production is complicated by the emergence of managers who virtually run many corporations and by the apparent dispersal of actual ownership of many corporations through individual and institutional ownership of stock.

We cannot present a complete class analysis of U.S. society here; indeed there are many unresolved problems concerning class analyses of advanced societies. But we feel that attempts to analyze such divisions within the U.S. must include reference to the emergence of a tendency toward a total social process under the control of technological organization; we have already referred to some examples of this tendency. We can call this process the cybernetic process of contemporary society which tends to organize industrial relations, social processes, political instruments, and even nature in a total organization of domination.

Examples of this process include time studies of the most minute fractions of activity involved in work on industrial assembly lines; they also include attempts to structure primary and secondary education along business lines, even to paying corporations to run schools according to "objectively verifiable criteria" of how much students learn in relation to money spent. These cybernetic processes also involve political leadership and campaigns for office by opinion polls, where so-called leaders "leak" statements to the media and wait for measured public reaction to them before deciding publicly to support or repudiate various positions. And these processes are present in attempts to measure the environmental impact of various technological projects in terms of dollars and cents, attempts which are often evident in the decision-making of the MNCs concerning the location of factories. While these cybernetic tendencies toward a total societal process—under the control of technological organization which organizes different aspects of life for thousands of people in widely disparate jobs and life situations into an apparently automatically self-regulating process of domination—are most evident in countries like the U.S., they are being extended throughout the world through the impact of the MNCs. Within the context of these tendencies toward a total organization of domination, the crucial issue becomes control over and participation in the network of functions that are rewarded in the system.

This perspective points to three social clusters within a high technology society like the U.S. The first cluster is the very small group of owners and managers of large corporations, surrounded by a larger group of programmers and controllers. The core of this cluster is the top 1 percent of the U.S. population, which receives 10.5 percent of all the income in the U.S. and holds 28 percent of all wealth (bank deposits, real estate, stocks, etc.). From their perspective, politics is largely a corporate affair of management in the interests of economic order, profits, and efficiency. This cluster also includes congresspeople and high government officials who play the game of musical chairs as they move from corporate boards to government posts and back again. Scientific, educational, and other elites also strive to participate on this high level of manipulation, as science and technology become more and more important to economic development, giving rise to the phenomena of "the best and the brightest," to borrow the title of a well-known book.

A second cluster in this system is the highly differentiated and complex network of functionaries. This cluster is comprised of those who are rewarded for their participation in the process, even though they do not own corporations or exert corresponding power. There is enormous diversity within this cluster and in the ways different groups within it are rewarded. It includes most university faculty, technologists, other professional people, blue- and white-collar workers, lower functionaries in offices and plants, and many housewives. While individuals within this cluster are rewarded in different ways in terms of money and prestige for their support of the system, they are also essentially dependent on it. Their lives are fragmented, they have not contributed to defining whatever autonomy and rewards they enjoy, and they have no power to change them. This fragmentation and dependency is the core of their alienation.

The third cluster is the increasing mass of marginalized and unrewarded sectors. These are the nonparticipants. This cluster includes especially nonwhite minority groups and poor whites in places like Appalachia. This is the sector of alienated and deprived groups which are growing larger and larger in the midst of increasing unemployment and rising inflation, the other side of the coin of the increasing concentration of power and wealth in the hands of a few.

The crucial point in this analysis is that, except for the dominant class, there are no homogeneous strata in a high technology society; every other social group is fractured and reconstituted in terms of participation and rewards on the one hand and marginalization, on the other. Thus, some blacks and some women, for example, will make it up the ladder of success, although the great majority will be only minimally rewarded or will remain marginalized. Nevertheless, this process, which promotes success for a few, fosters the ideology of the glories of our economic system where, it is claimed, everyone is free to make it on his or her own.

These examples point to racism and sexism which, in addition to marginalization and poverty, also divide U.S. society. It is clear that racism and sexism precede the emergence of capitalist society and its class divisions. Yet it is also clear that the capitalist system provides the context and the structures within which these forms of oppression continue to exist in the U.S. While it may be true that the tendencies toward a total social process under the control of technological organization and values do not intrinsically require racism and sexism, and the willingness to promote a few select blacks and women who support the system supports this contention, the fact remains that capitalist development is inherently uneven. It promotes wage differentials within industries, between national minorities, and between men and women. In other words, the same uneven development which is produced internationally in the relationships between the dominant and the dependent nations is produced also within the advanced capitalist countries like the U.S. Since, inevitably, not all groups can make it within the capitalist system, some groups are always marginalized.

In this atmosphere of competition for scarce jobs, security, status, and other rewards, skin color and sex are easy identifying marks of those who are to be excluded. (Language becomes an identifying factor for other oppressed groups like the Hispanics, and, historically, the Italians, the Poles, etc.) Violence, discriminatory attitudes, and policies of segregation are vehicles for the outlet of frustration and insecurity experienced within the capitalist system. Capitalism promotes the mass psychology of racism and sexism. These attitudes are so pervasive that many nonwhites and women actually internalize attitudes of inferiority, thereby reinforcing racist and sexist tendencies within society and deeply splitting social groups which otherwise share the same oppressive conditions in capitalist society. And, of course, racist attitudes within the U.S. facilitate imperialism abroad; U.S. policies in Southeast Asia clearly depended in part on the assumption that Asians were inferior beings who could not long resist superior U.S. strength and wisdom.

Yet beyond this fact of uneven development we believe that the tendencies toward a total social process under the control of technological values are themselves dehumanizing—even for the few who enjoy the affluence they promote. It is the nature of these dehumanizing values which we especially want to stress. In other words, we find that we are confronted not only with the problem of distribution of resources and opportunities for personal and social development, but also with the problem of the values legitimating technological developments.

We believe, then, that the social class phenomena in our society are as different from their predecessors as the high technology society and its multinational agencies are different from mid-nineteenth-century capitalist industry. Oppression in a highly complex society like the U.S. involves a tendency toward a total way of life, embodied in institutional processes and legitimated by a dominant set of values, which oppresses different sectors in different ways; but these different ways are all part of the same system. We have seen how this process is global, a process in which whole peoples participate in worldwide structures of imperialist domination and dependence. Our case study of Chile revealed this process in stark form: The concentration of power and interests that came together in the Committee of 40 under Kissinger deliberately set out to destroy the Allende regime with the new society and values that it sought to implement. Like Chile, any sector within this system, domestic or global, which fails to function obediently is quickly marginalized, or destroyed. However, it would be erroneous to assume that the system can always destroy its enemies so easily. The case of Vietnam is here of the first importance.

Exploitation of foreign peoples and resources has resulted in affluence for many within the U.S. Still, this affluence for some people within the U.S. has also depended on a systematic exploitation of blacks, native Americans, women, and poor whites. There have never been enough jobs for all, even in times of prosperity. In addition, many are obliged to remain within unsteady, dehumanized, and underpaid jobs. Rising unemployment, coupled with high rates of inflation, have long been painfully familiar to developing nations dominated by economic forces they cannot control politically; they are becoming more familiar in the U.S. And, if the MNCs continue toward greater and greater internationalization, which certainly seems to be the trend, we in the U.S. can look forward to fewer jobs, more unemployment and poverty, and even less public influence in economic decision-making. The irony of this new pattern of power mediated by the MNCs is that it is beginning to have the same impact on its base country, the U.S., as it has had for decades on developing nations like Chile. Barnett and Müller describe this trend as the "Latin-Americanization of the United States."

These trends suggest that the U.S. is beginning to face a reduction of the standard of living of the middle class and the increase of those, particularly among racial and ethnic minorities and among women, who will never gain access to the education and jobs that can lead to middle-class status. True, the MNCs spread wealth across national boundaries, but they do it by strengthening economic elites who participate as managers and investors at the expense of workers and the unskilled. This has long been clear in developing countries, and it is now emerging as a major factor in creating a more obviously dual economy in the developed countries also. There seem to be two alternatives before us. As a people we will become more and more willing to put up with less and less in order to hang on to jobs, to keep factories in our communities, to maintain the prosperity and "order" of our "democratic way of life." Or we may opt for the struggle for justice and liberation and a new life in a new society.

We recognize that further refinement of this type of analysis of national and international structures of oppression and the dominant ideology which legitimates them is necessary. In particular, we feel that the most important problem for such analysis concerns the relationships between the economic and the other dimensions of social class and the dominant ideology, including the values of efficiency which legitimate dehumanizing technological developments. But whatever directions this analysis takes, we believe that theology and social ethics must come to terms with these realities, for they form the context within which we interpret the meaning of God's action in history. Such analysis offers our only hope for understanding the ways different forms of oppression are linked and for unmasking the ways in which different beliefs and values, including many so-called Christian beliefs and values, have come to function ideologically in support of an unjust social system. And this kind of critical understanding, in turn, offers our only hope for constructive action with the poor and oppressed for justice and liberation.

In particular, as Christians we are deeply interested in the contribution of the churches to the perpetuation of the status quo. In Chile the dominant forces in the Catholic church attempted to play the role of reconciler between opposing political groups, while maintaining the traditional Catholic anti-Marxist posture. The Catholic church did not officially support the military coup, but religiously promoted anticommunism clearly functioned in support of the military. Of course, this ideological posture of anticommunism was vigorously resisted by minority voices from within the various churches, including the Catholic church, such as the Christians for Socialism movement and one or two denominational leaders. But the dominant official voices, supported by the middle-class membership of the churches, directly or indirectly legitimated the repressive economic and political forces that overthrew Allende. These events reveal the inevitable political implications of religious stands, especially those concerning broad questions of social ethics. In other words, we are convinced that we cannot escape the political ramifications of our beliefs, and that, if we are to be faithful to the deepest meaning of these beliefs, we must critically examine them in the light of analyses of social structures and the dominant ideology.

This type of analysis of the U.S. churches has seldom been developed in detail. It is our impression, however, that in the U.S. the prevailing church leadership, backed by the broad middle-class membership of the denominations, also assumes an antisocialist stance and sees itself as a reconciler between contesting economic and political forces. This perspective denies class conflict and urges reconciliation. But it is a reconciliation without repentence by those who benefit from an exploitive system and without justice for the oppressed. Representatives of this perspective talk of unity in a way that would draw some marginal, oppressed people just far enough into the circle of benefits of our social system to co-opt or mute the voices calling for revolutionary change. They speak in individualistic and personalist ways, exalting the person as more important than social systems in a way that enervates efforts to create a new society built on greater human fulfillment for all persons. A church which takes this view, no matter what its pretensions to Christian piety, finally supports the status quo against radical change for a more just social order. Of course, in the process of defending these values, the churches also protect their own place in the system and their value to it.

In the light (or darkness) of these reflections on our reality, several questions confront us: Can we afford to channel so much of our resources, research and development efforts into the dead end of endless technological development for its own sake? Will more millions of people starve to death because of unequal distribution of food and uneven development of local resources throughout the world? Will countries go to war, nuclear war, over dwindling natural resources? Will we pollute ourselves to death with technology supplied by the MNCs? What is the cost of continuing "prosperity" within the U.S.? Will we continue to exploit the poor within our country? Will we continue to support oppressive governments in other countries which have policies favorable to U.S. based MNCs, countries to whom the MNCs can sell increasing supplies of military hardware? Will we increase oppression within the U.S. in order to control growing numbers of unemployed and rising discontent in the face of the increasing deterioration of the environment and the cities? Will the churches, educational, and other institutions continue to support the status quo and to avoid the fundamental issues of the social system and of the dominant ideology which have contributed to the problems confronting the world?

The two aspects of our reflections, the case of Chile and the issues of the MNCs and the dominant ideology, reveal the basic problem of the economic and political context within which questions about justice and liberation are shaped. Our reflections point to two crucial and interrelated questions among all the others: Whose interests and what values rule in our present economic and political context? It seems to us that the problem is one of a multinational upper class and its control, of its political, economic, and military power, and of all those who support such a system in the name of values like efficiency, consumption, the free market, the autonomous individual, technological and economic development. We have begun to see how the policies of the MNCs and the U.S. government, in terms of both foreign intervention and internal manipulation, represent the interests of this upper class, and how the churches function in support of these interests.

Since these interests and values are not assumed in the same way by all social groups, as the analysis of social sectors suggests, the crucial issue for social ethics concerns how the struggles of various oppressed groups can overcome the interests and ideology of the controlling upper class. More precisely, we see the issue before us in these terms: How can coalitions be formed on behalf of justice and liberation which will overcome the interests of the multinational upper class and its service to such alienating values?

We wish to stress again that the basic issues involve the structures of capitalism and the values incarnated in these structures; our problem is not just that of a few wicked corporate and political leaders who can be replaced, or of a minor flaw in an otherwise good system. Therefore, the resolution of these problems requires radical structural change in the economic and political spheres on the basis of a new vision of humanity.

LIBERATION TO

Any critique of social structures and ideology is made in the light of at least implicit assumptions concerning the goal of liberation. In our group we have tried to be conscious of our view of this goal of liberation, while recognizing that specification of it can only come through the process of actual struggle against oppressive structures, as people reflect on the alienation of present structures and as they envision a better future on the basis of solidarity in the struggle. If the goal of liberation in its proximate stage is something like the democratic socialism of the Chilean project, then it is rooted in a universal vision. For the multinational character of the economic system and of the dominant ideology means that the project for overcoming the injustices involved in class structures, racism, sexism, and imperialism, for establishing more human communities and social structures, for finding a more balanced relationship with the environment can only be undertaken in terms of both the Third World and the "developed" part of the world. A vision of a new reality cannot be imagined in terms of nation states. The "to" of liberation is thus a new society and a new world.

We are convinced that liberation is a total process involving everything that is at stake in the kind of life we are creating (or, as some would say, given the present structures and values, the kind of grave we are digging). A vision, like that which inspired the Chilean socialist project, points to liberation from the domination of economic growth, from the endless production of new things, from the endless elaboration of technologically sophisticated but dehumanizing services (like those in our present medical system), from the forces creating physical and psychological obsolescence, and from the pressures for greater and greater consumption.

Liberation is liberation from the domination of the new, a domination which is so prominent in the mass media, especially in advertising. It is liberation from the inescapable press toward new things, new knowledge, new ways of doing things, new relationships, new morals, and new religions—for the sake of the new or because of newness. Liberation involves the space and time for individuals and groups, the physical, psychological, and spiritual space and time to resist the dominant directions, to experiment, to reflect, to weigh alternatives, to consider consequences, to consult with people at home and abroad, to revisit the past. In other words, liberation points to a society where all participate in decision-making and genuinely share in the goods produced, where the cultural, religious, and other differences between individuals and groups are respected and promoted, in their institutional as well as personal forms.

This liberation involves liberation for participation in mythic, cultic, and ritualistic realities that involve more communal, worldly, global, and aesthetic dimensions than do our present cultural institutions. Liberation is, then, a liberation to participate in and to embody a different ethos, a different conception of "the way we like to see things done"—a way beyond the sexism, racism, class conflict, and imperialism which now control our way of life.

Specifically with respect to the economic dimension, it seems to us that economic growth and development in a new, more human society must be subordinated to human development. This principle points to the type of education and mass communications that promote the capacities of all to contribute to a more human way of life, to innovation, decision-making and development on local, national, and international levels. It also points to the type of technological development which promotes meaningful work for the maximum number of people with a minimum of capital investment and use of energy. Most important, it points to a planned development so that all sectors of the economy—agriculture, industry, services—are shaped to insure the best quality of life for all people in harmony with nature.

The vision of the goal of liberation involves a total vision of personhood and history. Liberation means overcoming racism, sexism, imperialism, and class conflict; it means unfolding new values and promoting new kinds of social and cultural institutions. For many the struggle today is for immediate physical survival, as well as for personal and cultural meaning. But ultimately, given the threats to ecological balance and social freedom which all experience within the cybernetic processes of a total society, it is a matter of survival and meaning for all.

Obviously much more could be said about this issue. Indeed many are prone to want to fill in all the details about the new society before doing anything to change the present one. But we feel that it is important to stress that the operative core of this vision is necessarily related to political breakthroughs, and not simply to idealistic discussions about humanity. In other words, the vision is universal, but it must also be realistic and recognize the mediation of political breakthroughs—breakthroughs which can only take place one at a time and require endurance in a long struggle. There is no place for apocalypticism or naive utopianism; radical changes will not occur suddenly or all at once. Accordingly, there is a need to develop basic political organizations within nations, for the process of socialization of the economy and creation of a new culture imply that those who carry out the vision be a history-bearing coalition that seizes power through many concrete struggles. Only in this way, it seems to us, can there be a creative process of discovery of new ways of being human both collectively and individually, leading to a real transforming of the foundations of an alienating social reality, not simply to a replacing of the old ruling class with a new one.

The struggles for a new earth, then, imply a practical vision which grounds every concrete step, as well as the holistic vision that gives meaning to these steps. We feel that it is important to stress again that the operative core of this vision is fundamentally related to political breakthroughs, and not just to idealistic discussions about humanity. Thus, the specification of this vision can only be worked out as different groups live together in the struggle for a better way of life for all.

In this context we see a role for a genuinely liberating theology, a theology which articulates the Christian dimension of subversion. These concerns lead to a new way of doing theology which involves the social appropriation of the Christian tradition by those who suffer, struggle, and risk their lives for justice and liberation; it implies a positive link between the goal of liberation and the gift of God's presence. The goal of liberation is, thus, both a demand and a gift, both a task and a responsibility. Gift and task make it possible for the vision of liberation not to become a new idol.

LIBERATION THROUGH

In our discussions we continually confronted the inseparability of the questions of liberation *to* what and liberation *through* what. Here we acknowledge our debt to our Latin American sisters and brothers who insist on the interdependence of these two moments of liberation. Separation of the critique of present structures and ideology and the vision of a new society, on the one hand, from the experience of strategy and action for radical change, on the other, promotes the co-optation of efforts toward liberation. The so-called cultural revolution of the 1960s offers examples of the incredible power in the ideology and structures of capitalism to absorb social criticism without fundamental change when the criticism and vision are not rooted in concrete political activity.

Another example of the danger of co-optation concerns social criticism which is done only in the name of "democratic principles" such as "self-determination" and "equality of opportunity." We are convinced that this approach can lead only to liberal reforms, since they do not even begin to address the issues at the level of social structures and basic values. At best, reforms based on such principles will make it possible for only a few more individuals to make it into the present system of rewards. However, the class structures and dominant ideology will remain, and, with them, the dehumanization and the grossly unequal distribution of resources, power, and opportunities which separate the controlling elite from the marginalized poor.

The middle class in the U.S. (people in the dependent yet rewarded sector) enjoys greater access to resources and opportunities than the poor, but these advantages are in no way comparable to those enjoyed by the ruling class. Thus, there is a major split in U.S. society between, on the one hand, the controlling class, the only class with real decision-making power, and, on the other hand, the rest of the people. (Of course, as pointed out above, within this great majority there are significant groupings which reflect, within the context of the class system, important differences in life experiences, cultural backgrounds, and religious traditions; racial and ethnic groups and women are major examples.) Thus, rather than reforms based on the principles of self-determination and equality of opportunity, we see the need for radical cultural and structural change rooted in a new vision of the person and society, a transformation which was being attempted in the Chilean project.

But the crucial point of our reflections on social sectors, which was sketched above, is that there are no homogeneous social strata which can be organized in any direct way to constitute self-conscious class entities which would be vehicles of this radical social change. For the dynamics of participation/marginalization cut across all social groups. In other words, it is the nature of the cybernetic process to fracture any social grouping or network and to reconstitute it in terms of participation and marginalization. Thus, the black community, like other minority groups, is divided by promises of various modes of participation and reward, which a few achieve in the above-board exploitation of functioning within the system, and a few others achieve through success in the underworld. Similarly, ethnic and youth sectors are fragmented, their ethnicity and life styles accentuated and exploited for profit. In such a context, critical consciousness of the oppressiveness of the system is not a simple function of the social determination of the modes of labor within class society, as some traditional class analyses maintain. This new situation of social class in a high technology society accounts for the ambiguous role played by labor in the U.S., and the difficulties which different radical groups have experienced in finding other sectors in the society with which they can collaborate.

Revolutionary change, then, calls for the development of networks of communication and organization in which the character and limits of the cybernetic process are unfolded in terms of each cluster within the system. Clearly, however, the oppressiveness of this system is most evident among those who most deeply experience the contradictions between the illusory promise of well-being within capitalism and the harsh realities of violence and manipulation in the name of profits, efficiency, order, and the free market.

This observation points to the issue of the social standpoint for the critique of capitalism. Some people claim that there is a standpoint beyond social classes and beyond the actual groups struggling against oppression. But it seems to us that the critique of capitalism, like the content of liberation, can only be articulated through the struggles of oppressed groups, especially the struggles of the most marginalized, for here the contradictions of capitalist structures and ideology are most obvious—and they cannot be overlooked as they usually are in other, better rewarded sectors.

This observation recalls the issue of the relation between the vision of a better world and the organization with power necessary to carry out the vision. If there is not both vision and organization, any critique is eventually co-opted and made functional to the established order; again, many aspects of the so-called cultural revolution of the 1960s offer examples of such co-optation. This makes us re-emphasize that an adequate alternative vision must always be rooted in the concrete struggles of oppressed groups and in the building up of political organizations which will be the vehicles for structural change. Only such involvement, it seems to us, can promote the emergence of a vision and a social practice which is faithful to the diverse experiences of exploitation and oppression lived by blacks, poor whites, native Americans, women, Hispanics, Asian-Americans and by all those in the so-called middle class whose dependence cn the rewards of the system leaves them fragmented, isolated, and powerless. This experience, rooted in solidarity with the poor and oppressed, is analyzed and reflected on in an ongoing way as groups learn to struggle better together for a new society.

So far the Christian churches have not contributed much systematic social criticism or offered much of a vision for a better future. On the contrary, the churches have essentially supported the status quo. However, there have been Christians who have struggled with the poor and oppressed. One example is the movement of Christians for Socialism (CfS) which emerged in Chile in 1972 and which has since spread to other Latin American countries, to Italy, Spain, France, England, Quebec, and the U.S. Comprised of a growing number of

Christians who are making an option for the struggles of the world's oppressed people, CfS promotes a new practice of the faith and new forms of church life. Members are convinced that the revolutionary task is the place where the faith acquires its true dimensions and its subversive force; in the demands of Jesus' practice they recognize the foundation of a new humanity. For CfS, being Christian means opening up to the burning questions arising from the situations of the oppressed; living and reflecting on the faith means faithfulness to the appropriation and announcement of the gospel by the poor and oppressed in word and deed. It means rejecting a society which exploits and oppresses. It means building a just society.

These Christians also confront the institutionalized church realities which contradict the political affirmation of their faith. They insist that the churches cannot be apolitical, and that attempts to be so ultimately result only in support for an oppressive status quo. Instead, they affirm the call of the gospel to share in the life and struggles of the poor. They are convinced that the churches will be an effective sign of God's love and of the liberating Christ only when they become in themselves a sign of love and prophecy for a different future, not only beyond history, but in the heart of history.

Such unofficial witness within the church has precedents in the North American situation. Between World Wars I and II most major denominations had unofficial activist groups on the political left. Two of the most active were the Methodist Federation for Social Action and the Church League for Industrial Democracy (Episcopal). These groups supported the struggle to organize labor, with their bodies and their money as well as with their words, raised the consciousness of the larger church to the injustices of the dominant economic system, and fought against fascist developments in the U.S. and abroad. The Methodist Federation was the most radical of these, supporting the International Workers of the World (the Wobblies) as well as more middle-ground unions, carrying on the masthead of its publication its opposition to the profit motive as the basis of a just economic order and participating in united fronts against fascism that included socialist and communist organizations.[7]

In the U.S. today there are also many elements of a liberation theology within the different traditions; there are many Christians on the side of the poor and manipulated. From these Christians, we hear a challenge to all Christians in the U.S. in simple terms: how can Christians, in response to God's action in history, struggle in solidarity with the oppressed for justice and liberation?

Conclusion

In conclusion, we feel that it is important to re-emphasize that genuine liberation demands participation in the international struggle against class exploitation, racism, sexism, and imperialism. The universality and solidarity of this struggle is the first and final reference point for critique of the present system and for the vision of a new earth. Anything less can only reflect an alienating theorizing so characteristic of our present society, which provides for circumscribed and often alienating individual liberties within a radically discriminatory system.

At the heart of these political struggles is the question of the very meaning of human life. Accordingly, not only economic and political order is at stake in these struggles, but also the deepest meanings of our religious and cultural traditions. It seems to us that our religious and cultural institutions, which are major supporters of values and definitions of what it means to be human, too often stand mute in the face of fundamentally alienating and exploitative social structures, when they are not actually twisting traditional values in support of the status quo. Yet we believe that the unfolding of new values and of a new understanding of what it means to be human, if it is to be genuinely liberating, can only take place in the process of creative reappropriation of the meaning and values within our traditions in the midst of concrete struggles for a new future; these values and this vision, in turn, inspire these struggles and are informed by them. Ultimately, then, we believe that the project of a new earth is a political and a religious struggle.

In this spirit we want to affirm the surfacing of a network of reflection groups relating to the Theology in the Americas conference in Detroit, August 1975. The promise of this network is its grounding in the struggles of various groups working for radical social change and in the opportunity for shared analysis and reflection the network offers. We feel that both these dimensions, solidarity in the struggles of the oppressed and a communal or shared process of reflection, are vital elements for liberation theology.

We hope this exploration has contributed to a deeper understanding of our present situation (liberation *from*), provided some sketches of goals envisioned (liberation *to*), and drawn us further on our way to struggling together for those ends (liberation *through*). We present this paper as one reflection group's shared exploration of the meaning of liberation. We recognize some of its limitations and we welcome critical and constructive response from other groups to help further the process of liberation for all.

NOTES

1. With the elimination of most price controls and a tight regulation of wages and salaries, the purchasing power of those on minimum wages has gone down drastically. From September 1973 to September 1974, the construction workers had lost 42 percent of their purchasing power and public functionaries on the minimum scale had lost nearly 50 percent on the basis of the most basic requirements for life. (The Consumer Price Index makes the situation look better but is based on some three hundred articles or services, many of which are out of the reach of the worker.) From September 1974 to March 1975 the worker lost another 13.6 percent in purchasing power (José Aldunate L., S.J., *Mensaje*, May 1975, and *Latinamerica Press*, June 12, 1975). Unemployment is listed as 16 percent of the work force (Ramón Marsano, *Latinamerica Press*, September 18, 1975) and getting worse. In some areas Caritas-Chile reports it is 40–60 percent and those who are employed often work only part-time or for short terms. Those who supported the Unidad Popular government of President Allende are unemployable (*Latinamerica Press*, May 8, 1975). With foreign investors unwilling to come in, the government's effort to divest itself of 519 state-owned companies leaves the bidding to about fifty Chilean financiers and industrialists, known as "piranas" locally. The reversal of agricultural reforms for fifty thousand campesino families is a return "to the regime of the latifundium," according to Msgr. Rene Vio Valdivieso (*Latinamerica Press*, July 10, 1975. See Michel Chossudovsky, *Trimestre Económico*, no. 166 (1975): "Hacia el nuevo modelo económico chileno—Inflación y redistribución del ingreso, 1973–1974"; Chossudovsky, "The Neo-Liberal Model and the Mechanisms of Economic Repression, the Chilean Case," *Co-Existence* (1975); Chossudovsky, "Chicago Economics, Chilean Style," *Monthly Review*, April 1975.

2. For further information concerning the MNCs and Chile see Armando Uribe, *The Black Book of American Intervention in Chile* (Boston: Beacon Press, 1975); Richard J. Barnet & Ronald E. Müller, *Global Reach* (New York: Simon & Schuster, 1974); Harry Magdoff, *The Age of Imperialism* (New York: Modern Reader, 1969); Kenneth E. Boulding and Tapan Mukerjee, eds., *Economic Imperialism* (Ann Arbor: University of Michigan, 1972); Samir Amin, *Accumulation on a World Scale* (New York: Monthly Review, 1974); Louis Turner, *Multinational Companies and the Third World* (New York: Hill & Wang, 1973); articles by Louis Turner, Richard Eells, Ronald E. Müller, and Michael P. Sloan in *Business & Society Review*, no. 11, Autumn 1974; Harry Strharsky and Mary Riesch, *Transnational Corporations and the Third World*, bibliography (Washington: CODOC, 1975).

3. For further information concerning the military-industrial complex, see Seymour Melman, *Permanent War Economy* (New York: Simon & Schuster, 1974); Derek Scherer, "Swords into Ploughshares," *Working Papers*, AFSC & CALC; Emma Rothschild, "The Weapons Market Goes Wild," *New York Review of Books*, October 2, 1975; Donald Bletz, *Role of the Military Professional in U.S. Foreign Policy* (New York: Praeger, 1972); Mark J. Green, James M. Fallows, David R. Zwick, *Who Runs Congress?* (New York: Bantam, 1972); Morton Mintz, Jerry S. Cohen, *America, Inc.* (New York: Dell, 1971).

4. For an example of this process of increasing rationalization in the service of profits, see "Clerical Workers Face Automation," *Dollars and Sense*, October 1975.

5. For further information on agribusiness see URPE, "Concentration of Power in the Food Business," *Science for the People*, March 1975; Susan Demarco and Susan Sechler, "Agribusiness Goes Abroad: Corporate Myths in a Hungry World" in *The Fields Have Turned Brown* (Washington: Agribusiness Accountability Project, 1975); Cliff Conner, "Hunger: U.S. Agribusiness and World Famine," *International Socialist Review*, vol. 35, no. 8 (September 1974); articles by Joel Solkoff, Daniel Zwerdling, and Thomas Redburn in "Can We Afford to Eat?" *Skeptic*, no. 10 (November-December 1975); Jim Hightower, *Eat Your Heart Out* (New York: Crown, 1975); William Robbins, *The American Food Scandal* (New York: Morrow, 1974).

6. The prospects of a multinational oligopoly exercising self-control or self-policing, as currently proposed by baby-food manufacturers in their Third World advertising, seem highly unlikely. To use a Chilean idiom, this is like asking a cat to guard the butcher shop. Most of our U.S. regulatory agencies seem to be more guardians of those whom they are to regulate rather than champions of the public interest, with exchange of personnel and a common outlook. (For instance, see Mark J. Green, Beverly C. Moore, Jr., and Bruce Wasserstein, *The Closed Enterprise System* [New York: Grossman, 1972]; Ralph Nader, Peter J. Petkas, Kate Blackwell, eds., *Whistle Blowing* [New York: Grossman, 1972].) "Governments, for all their ideological skirmishes with business, have always been the silent partners of business . . . " (Robert L. Heilbroner, "None of Your Business," *New York Review of Books*, March 20, 1975). At the international level even a General Agreement on Multinational Corporations patterned after GATT seems too ambitious at this stage (United Nations, *Multinational Corporations in World Development*, New York, 1973, pp. 92–93; cf. United Nations, *Impact of Multinational Corporations on Development and on International Relations*, New York, 1974). Cf. Walter L. Owensby, "Multinational Corporations in Less Developed Countries: Impact and Accountability," in *The Social Accountability of the Corporation* (Chicago: Institute on the Church in Urban-Industrial Society, 1975). Most nations do not fund, staff, or empower their regulatory agencies in any way comparable to that of a major transnational corporation. At one step further removed, and seeking to coordinate disparate national regulatory agencies and policies, it would seem unrealistic to put our hopes in a small, minimally empowered U.N. office to regulate the new giants of the earth.

7. See Ralph Lord Roy, *Communism and the Churches* (New York: Harcourt, Brace, 1960) for a critical history of these groups; Walter Muelder, *Methodism and Society in the Twentieth Century* (New York: Abingdon, 1961) on the MFSA; and Richard Tholin, "Prophetic Witness and Denominational Unity: Unofficial Social Action Groups in the Methodist and Episcopal Churches since 1900," doctoral dissertation, Union Theological Seminary, New York, 1967.

17

A Theological Quest: Synthesis of the First Stage of Theology in the Americas: 1975

by Anne Marie Harnett, S.N.J.M., and Diego Irarrazaval
in collaboration with Mary Burke and Joe Holland

APPRAISAL OF THE PROCESS

A significant section of the group reports and correspondence dealt with process: its difficulties, mistakes, and achievements. Does this mean that priority was given to methodological issues? It does not seem so. Rather, the concern reflects both an inadequate organization of the process and the experimental character of doing theology of liberation.

General Procedure

Negatively, several groups complained that the emphasis was on discussion of documents, rather than reflection on situations, experiences, and actions—as seems to be the case in Latin American theology. There was also concern that the participants in the process are mostly middle-class, theologically trained persons, and Catholics. Some remarked that there should be more participants from the grassroots, minority and ethnic groups, the poor, the working class, and women. Regarding the interaction between the participants and those coordinating the process, there were several comments on the lack of real dialogue, of provision for grassroots input, of adequate procedures for communication, and of adequate materials for reflection.

On the positive side, it was pointed out that this was indeed a process, with some grassroots participation, with interaction between different groups and persons, and with a genuine search for a way of doing theology. In most of the correspondence there were expressions of gratitude for the efforts of others in the process and an enthusiastic affirmation of the need of such a process in the North American context. Some remarked that the process itself demonstrated a new faith experience by Christians detached from the status quo and provided incentive for deeper commitments.

Responding to these reactions through its research reports, the Center of Concern emphasized several points: Readings and documents are catalysts to stimulate original work from the reflection groups. The process has a praxis framework—an organic unity of action and theory—"trying critically to articulate and to change our experience, both social and religious." There is a need for a holistic framework linking up the complex and distinct experiences portrayed in the work of the reflection groups.

In the overall process two issues appear to need further discussion. The first refers to the types of participants in a process of liberation theology. It has been difficult to achieve an interaction between grassroots and professional theologians, and to have more oppressed persons and grassroots workers in the process of reflection. As an inner city group put it,

The people in the street seem to be into a praxis of liberation, but one that is not given to much reflection, . . .[while] for ourselves as well as for others, the *praxis* of liberation is more oriented to a critical and holistic kind of reflection.

Does this imply that grassroots workers have insights only on problems of human survival and immediate solutions and that only others can accomplish a radical questioning? Isn't it possible and necessary to find a way to go from survival questions to global questions? Are not both grassroots people and theoreticians needed for this qualitatively new kind of theological reflection?

A second issue concerns the difficulty of doing structural and historical reflection. Is liberation theology possible if things are seen and examined in "bits and pieces"? In such an approach any kind of systemic analysis is rejected as irrelevant to immediate experience. Perhaps the objections to "theoretical" discussions of imperialism and of a systemic alternative to it arise from a lack of experience in social analysis. What we are suggesting is that underlying these two issues—more participants from the grassroots and less abstract reflection—is a demand to discover a way of reflection based on the lives of the oppressed and reaching a historical understanding of the structures that explain everyday experience.

A summary evaluation of group responses to the process leads to a formulation of three general requirements for further stages in the process: (1) a clear initial accord on the nature and means of the process, by mutually examined proposals of the coordinators of the process and of groups involved in it; (2) a careful programming of the different and complementary contributions of grassroots participants and professional theologians and social scientists, in such a way that a praxis framework of practice and theory may be effectively carried out; and (3) a permanent effort to engage in a theological reflection that brings together communication of experiences, systemic analysis, and an understanding of God's presence in history.

There were also concrete proposals regarding procedure. A first proposal refers to doing theology, not for or about the oppressed, but among and with the oppressed. As one group formulated this procedure,

the lifestyle of ourselves as participants [should] be in process, so that we can listen to the voice and the authentic reflections of workers and poor. Some programs and structures are going to be needed to rescue those reflections from the inundation of mass media, . . . to create forums for their voices that somehow are in their control.

We may further suggest that this kind of reflection among the oppressed is not just a preliminary stage; it is also a permanent characteristic in a process of liberation theology.

A second proposal is related to the former. One reflection group suggested that there is a need

to reflect on our commitment to poverty as a way of liberation according to the gospel and to think through what new action this reflection might lead to. Some theology of liberation has been a felt need for us and we are anxious to pursue it as a means of unifying our lives of action and contemplation as Christians.

This proposal raises the question of reflecting on the basis of lived experience and the dialectic of action and theory. But such reflection is done in terms of the experiences of oppressed persons and groups of society and their efforts towards liberation. To reflect on our action and contemplation as Christians is no abstract proposal if it is carried out among and with the more oppressed groups of our society.

The procedure suggested to the groups by the Center of Concern was (1) a description of the situation, (2) a religious meditation, (3) a return to experience. Few groups followed this whole sequence. The majority spent most of their time on the first stage of social analysis, adding reflections on the mission of Christians within practical situations. The groups emphasized an understanding of personal and communal experiences informed by their reading and discussion of documents. Some groups emphasized action, exploring ways of practicing the insights achieved through discussion of global issues.

Two patterns of reflection seemed to be carried out by these twenty-three reporting reflection groups. One pattern was to deal with global issues through discussion of articles and documents. The discussion was followed by an analysis of aspects of the participants' experience in relation to those documents. As one group explains this procedure, it was to

understand the reality we live and work in, . . . reflect on our own experiences, . . .understand the liberation/oppression realities in our work and lives, and to see better faith and gospel values in relation to these.

In this way there was a movement from global issues to particular instances, from social analysis to shared experiences and religious meditation.

Another pattern of reflection was to begin with a sharing of experiences and proceed to a systemic understanding of reality and to theological reflection. As one group explains this process:

We shared, by means of a two-page summary, the kinds of liberating activities we are involved in, following this schema: (1) describing our situation, (2) religious meditation on the situation—looking to Scripture for themes, and (3) returning to the situation—recommending further actions and asking deeper theological questions.

In this way there was a movement from particular events to global issues, from concrete experiences to systemic issues and theological questions.

In contrast to the considerable amount of criticism of the overall process, the group reports for the most part lack self-criticism. There is not much evaluation of the procedures and problems in each group. Such an evaluation could raise three types of questions: (1) Does the group achieve a systemic understanding of the participants' experience and of the lives of the oppressed? Is there a disclosure of the economic and political implications of social concerns? (2) Does the group consider a strategy of structural change? Does reflection lead to a discussion of a systemic alternative—called socialism or whatever—and a practical strategy? (3) Does the group achieve theological insights in the praxis framework of action and theory? Is religious meditation a legitimation or a challenge to revolutionary faithfulness to God's commissioning?

The Detroit Conference

Both in reports from reflection groups and in numerous letters, there are suggestions for the success of the conference. Several groups and persons focused on the problem of the goal of the conference. It was suggested that this event both discuss issues of praxis and reflect on theological problems, focusing on

a theology which is on the verge of emerging within the North American situation, . . . drawing together Christians from different oppressed groups who, while recognizing their differences, nonetheless struggle together for liberation.

One problem is how to deal with the theology developed in Latin America. One proposal is that in the conference there be either an exposition and critique of Latin American theology or an exploration into an autochthonous liberation theology. Another proposal is to have Latin Americans challenge North Americans, so that international structures of oppression might be examined. This examination would be followed by an analysis of oppressive structures in the U.S. and the formulation of a theology that would grow out of the struggle for liberation.

Emphasizing the need to spell out a direction for the conference and follow-up, a group from Durham, North Carolina, suggested several goals: An action objective could be ecumenical social action at a local level; a consciousness-raising objective could be to face an end to affluence and the danger of right-wing reactions; a theological goal could be to witness to the liberating power of the gospel and the value of asceticism now in the U.S.

Another set of suggestions refers to the participants in the conference. There is consensus in favor of an interaction between professional theologians, the grassroots, and church officials; only one proposal suggests a meeting of a small number of theologians, thus avoiding chaos and disappointment. Concerning the distribution of participants, one strong statement demands 50 percent women and the presence of Third World women. Other suggestions are that there be more practitioners than theoreticians, in a proportion of 60–40. There is also an insistent demand for participation of representatives of oppressed groups: poor, white working class, women, blacks, Chicanos. Some remarks point out that underlying the problem of numbers is the issue of structuring the conference in such a way that grassroots people and reflection groups have real participation.

In regard to social analysis there are some brief suggestions. Some show concern for the relationship between the personal and the structural dimensions of both oppression and liberation. Others suggest that attention be paid to the whole North American reality without neglecting its positive aspects when systemic evils are examined. There is also concern that social analysis include sexism and racism. Considering the present economic crisis, downward mobility, and social tensions (in which right-wing totalitarians gain strength), some suggest analyzing new values which are required and a Christian response. Finally, regarding the method of reflection, some persons argue for a sample case or issue-oriented approach, since from good case studies it is possible to develop social analysis.

Many groups and persons offer suggestions about theological reflection during the conference. The emphasis must be on the Christian faith in any effort to relate particular experiences and broader issues, action and theory. As some formulate this point, "The truth has to do with Christ for all men and women." Some remark on the characteristics of liberation theology in the U.S. According to one group, what distinguishes our reflection from the Latin American is that the North American movements of liberation are part of the context for doing theology here; another group emphasizes that while liberation is not nationalistic, in the U.S. we have to see the relations and differences between liberation of different groups and diverse dimensions of the human experience. Several groups suggest themes that relate faith, the church, and global social issues. What are the scriptural challenges and the ethical implications in a socialist decision? How is the gospel ideologically distorted? How can the church not be an instrument of oppression and become a church of the people? If evangelization is a priority, how can it be done in a liberating way?

Finally, there are some remarks about the postconference period. A group suggested that in Detroit there should be a decision about what has to be done in the future. It is important both to continue the reflection process and to be in communication with the Christian people. For some, the great task after Detroit is the manner in which the participants address themselves to small situations and relate them to larger struggles. The main value of the whole experience, according to many group reports and letters, is the process itself of creating a liberation theology among the struggles of the people.

THE AMERICAN EXPERIENCE

Ten groups reported specifically on their discussion of Preparation Document No. 1, "The American Empire" (see above document 1). The consensus of these groups was that the style and tone of the document is offensive, inflammatory, and judgmental. It was suggested that its slant led to the feeling that being a citizen of a country in which the capitalist system flourishes involves culpability. It was also suggested that the approach seemed contrary to the "conscientization" process—the gradual discovery of the shape of a problem through a process of common searching based on common experience.

The commentary on the content of the document was varied. While there seems to be some agreement that the basic information in the document is correct, or at least that it is a view held by most Third World thinkers and by many people in the U.S. and so must be dealt with, still there were criticisms of its content and its bias. Generally the criticism can be divided into two categories: first, the content of the document is too "Third Worldish"; it does not deal sufficiently with values at the heart of American life and heritage and so is lacking a true historical view of the U.S. scene today. Second, the word "empire" created problems. Some felt that the impression given was that the U.S. has a monopoly on oppressive power structures, whereas this is not completely true.

As one group asked, "Who is the enemy—the U.S., the capitalist system as such, the exploitation (beginning with an exploitation of people in the U.S.) by unscrupulous capitalists?"

The Center of Concern research committee has already clarified their intent in writing the document: It was intended simply as a brief sharing of the perception of the U.S. by leftist Latin American Christians. Perhaps if some sort of preamble and statement of assumptions had preceded the text, much of the consternation could have been avoided. The Center also sees the criticism not as "a judgment of the accuracy of the external analysis," but rather as a "desire to proceed first from our own experience."

From all parts of the U.S., wherever women have spoken to the issue of liberation theology and the American empire, the cry has been the same: The intentions and goals of such a gathering would be undermined by a failure to include the realities of sexism and the women's liberation movement. These realities are not addressed by Latin American theology of liberation, which raises the question of class struggle and of capitalism/imperialism but does not deal with racial and sexual oppression, which are not simply reducible to the question of class.

Likewise the call of black Americans is a strong and urgent plea to look honestly at their oppression, to listen to their theology, and to reflect on their constant striving for liberation. As one group composed of blacks said, "Is white theology still more willing to look beyond its borders to find out the truth about itself rather than listening to the voices from within?"

It has been evident that all involved in the process see the necessity of relying on the American experience. Would not then the struggles of native Americans, of women, of blacks, of Hispanics, of Asian-Americans, and of white ethnics provide at least part of the framework for a new theology?

As the Research Coordination Team stated in its Research Report No. 2:

Each element—race (and cultural ethnicity), sex, class—is both interwoven with the others, yet unique. None can be reduced to another, yet none can be left to itself. Working out, both in theory and practice, a creative coalition of the three is probably the most important task for people concerned with social change in this country. We would be both naive and arrogant if we thought we could accomplish that in this small process. Yet our efforts, based on honesty and seriousness, could be an important contribution.

The question of the frame of reference and the language of criticism of structural evils and injustices in the U.S. today has often been posed. Groups referred to efforts of the U.S. to deal more justly with its neighbors, to the fact and language of liberation movements within the U.S., to the appeal to American idealism by such leaders as Martin Luther King, to the current awakening of the U.S. public to political, social, and economic oppression, to a hope for bicentennial repentance. A letter from Rosemary Ruether to Sergio Torres sums up quite well the thought of several individuals and groups on the subject of national liberation language and religious resources from which Americans could be expected to respond and criticize (see above document 4).

Another point raised in the responses to "The American Empire" is the connection between the oppressed people of the Third World and the working people of North America.

Several groups developed a social analysis out of their experience. Most of their insights refer to oppressive conditions; there was not much reflection on liberating experiences. A Detroit group decided to examine oppressions known and felt by its members—taxes, education, pollution, drugs, property, and mass media. But since the group faced more immediately problems of racism in housing and education and the task of consciousness-raising, their analysis dealt with actions taken in those areas. They concluded that systemic change is achieved through gradual steps and that the task is to become aware of our own power and ability to cause change. Another group reflected on injustices encountered in the welfare system and antipoverty campaigns; its members gave different emphasis to liberation—personal, social, and consciousness-raising in the church.

One group in Chicago carried out a case-study approach on the oppression experience of black women, children, and men. Each case was described and then examined in its systemic implications. The group emphasized an unjust welfare system, unfair housing policies, inequities in the judicial system, racism in education, the myth of white superiority, and economic oppression. The actions recommended were mainly consciousness-raising, organization of blacks, and pressure on social institutions. In the context of each case, scriptural materials were meditated upon as imperatives for justice and action. The Word of God, in this group's experience, is a judgment on concrete injustices and a demand for action.

Two unique reflections came from a prisoner and from a native American. A person serving a life sentence in California examined the conflict between an ethical conscience and conformity to a prostituted judicial and social system. He portrayed his experience in the following way:

My personal struggle for spiritual liberation equates with the struggles of minorities against the oppression from a centralized government and the octopus of business tyranny. . . . I went through the torment of rebirth in the cold seclusion of a prison cell, wrestling silently, hour upon hour in the darkness.

A native American, reflecting on the bondage of his people exploited by government agencies and by whites who have usurped their land, acknowledges that "oppression is felt most of all at an economic level, as the people suffer want." For this leader of the Blackfeet, liberation is not to be considered an "Indian," a name given by others, but to be treated as a human being, able to live out real values—values of brotherhood and sisterhood, justice, solidarity in faith and trust, and closeness to the Spirit.

In all these reflections, there is an attempt to understand immediate experiences in the context of social structures. Although there are many good insights, what seems lacking is a method of reflection on the basis of experience that will lead to an appraisal of the whole social system and to the discovery of paths to systemic change.

THEOLOGICAL REFLECTIONS

The following statement from the Research Coordinating Team's Research Report No. 2 states quite plainly the team's position regarding the purpose of the process and the starting point for doing liberation theology:

The dominant task of this process, from the preconference through the postconference period, in a modest and experimental way, is to raise the question of a fresh theology from our U.S. experience. Latin American theology of liberation cannot simply be imported as is into the United States and mechanistically applied here. That would be a betrayal of the very theology itself, which insists that a people's historical experience must be the point of departure in theologizing. Other reasons why it is not directly transferable are:

1. This is an advanced industrial nation and a global superpower.

2. Racial, ethnic, and sexual struggles overshadow class struggles, at least in popular consciousness.

3. The early separation of church and state has created a religious superstructure which does not have the direct power of legitimation found in heavily Roman Catholic countries. Civil religion is important here.

4. The U.S. produced a populist Protestant religion among the nation's poor, black and white, qualitatively distinct from the feudal Catholic tradition or the bourgeois urban Protestant tradition. Religious language in this tradition tends to be heavily biblical, as opposed to the more philosophical language of Roman Catholicism.

5. There were also strong utopian forces in the U.S. religious tradition.

There is general agreement among the groups that Latin American theology cannot simply be imported. However, there is divergence of opinion on methodology. In Latin America, religious meditation follows and is rooted in actual experience and social analysis. What seems to be the feeling among some groups is that religious experience, including biblical symbols and magisterial documents, should be the existential point of departure. This feeling seems to be under-lying this statement of one group: "While genuine theology must be done in connection with praxis, it helps to have *enlightened* praxis."

Members of other groups expressed the need to find in Scripture a source of courage, forward thrust, and action. Another group stated, "There is a power for critical analysis and correction behind the biblical language. The power for doing liberation theology will finally spring from this source, not from 'critical social theory.' " And another: "The philosophy of Christianity has the potential means to accomplish justice and fraternity in society."

Other groups who addressed themselves directly to the question of methodology indicated strongly that the starting point should be lived experience and analysis. For example, it was noted that the mandate has always been there; we know why to be involved, but not how. Maybe we have been looking to the wrong sources, or to the right sources, but in the wrong order. Some are now finding the *how* of involvement clearly spoken by efforts of the social sciences (especially those based on critical theory) and of ordinary people in efforts they are making.

There are cogent historical reasons for not starting with religious language and symbols in Latin America. Yet it has been suggested that the same reasons exist in the U.S., at least in some areas, for such symbols and expressions of religious truths have been used and manipulated to support a power structure. Does the whole discussion relate to the problem of integrating theology and the social sciences? "This is a complex question of theoretical foundations, interdisciplin-ary relations, and value orientations. We will not answer these ques-tions in our short effort. Our experience, however, of interaction between the two may make some contributions" (Center of Concern, "Research Report No. 2").

Redefinition of the Goals of the Conference

The reactions—favorable and unfavorable—were incorporated into the process. The dialogue established between the secretariat and the reflection groups led to further clarifications and several important changes.

First, it was agreed to give special emphasis to the milestones of justice and struggles for freedom in the civil and religious history of the U.S.

Second, it was decided that ordinary Christians should participate more fully. A sign of the change was the criterion for the invitations to the conference. It was agreed to invite 60 percent grassroots people and 40 percent academicians, theologians, and social scientists.

Third, there was a change in tone of the documents sent out by the organizing committee. The earliest documents, it was found, tended to impose models for reflection and detract from the freedom and spontaneity of the reflection groups.

Three important documents circulated during this stage. The Center of Concern of Washington, D.C., coordinators of the preconference research, sent two newsletters that clarified the dialectical and democratic nature of the process and the role of the central committees in relation to the grassroots groups.

The third document, which we include here, was the result of the contributions provided by other participants. It reformulated the goals of the conference in light of these contributions just prior to the conference itself.

18

Goals of the
Detroit Conference

by Sergio Torres

The overall purpose and goal of the conference will be to explore theologically the significance of liberation theology for Christians in the United States. This means:

1. The conference will be part of a process; the objectives are long-term. At the Detroit meeting we will plan for the follow-up.

2. Latin American liberation theology is not a package for import. However, we can point toward the possibility of a similarly critical and constructive theological understanding in the United States.

3. The emphasis of the conference will not be action or consciousness-raising, nor does it intend to be abstract dialogue about the methodology of liberation theology. The emphasis will be theological reflection on the United States experience in an atmosphere of prayer and mutual respect.

CHARACTERISTICS OF LIBERATION THEOLOGY

*Historical experience is the starting point
of theological reflection.*

Theology is a historical interpretation of the revelation of God in Jesus Christ.

As the experiences of each region or country are different, so there will be differences between Latin American theology and North American theology.

It will be helpful for U.S. Christians to hear how brothers and sisters from Latin America see the foreign policy and the international image of the United States. International relations constitute a key element in both societies.

On the domestic scene it is essential to uncover the various movements of liberation in United States history and their contemporary expressions. In Detroit we will have a significant presence of the minority groups in the U.S.

Liberation theology is a theology of concrete reality and of the "praxis" of liberation.

The historical praxis of Christians in Latin America is the place in which they acquire a new understanding of man's situation and of the social and ecclesial reality of their continent. In the praxis they come to a new living knowledge of their faith in Jesus Christ, especially in the concrete demands of their fidelity to the Lord.

Liberation theology is created out of praxis. It intends to clarify the relationships between this praxis and the Christian faith. In Detroit, "practitioners" and "theoreticians" will meet; both are assumed to be committed to the praxis of liberation.

This praxis is not only commitment for justice and change. For Christians, praxis is an exigence of the love of Jesus. It is the manner of being Christians, followers of the gospel. This love has to be efficacious; it must help to resolve the injustices. It is not enough to be a witness of the love of Jesus. This praxis is a process of action and reflection, which starts from critical social theory. Social scientists will help to spell out a social theory.

In Detroit we want to make an effort to discover both the deepest causes of oppression in the United States and the many seeds of liberation which are present in its history. We seek new ways to better integrate the liberation movements which are struggling against sexist, racist, and class oppression.

The language of liberation theology is not primarily philosophical, but is derived from the social sciences.

Theology always uses a certain rationale, even if it does not consciously identify with it. Liberation theology uses three levels of knowledge. The first is the level of social science which explains the economic, the social, and the political realities. The second is the level of anthropology and the philosophy of history which illuminates the meaning of man and of history. And the third is the level of theology which describes the historical future in the light of Christ's salvific work and orients it toward the eschatological consummation.

In the United States, we have to consider the country's own history, its unique traditions, and its present experience. Some aspects that we have to consider are:

1. The meaning of the religious language
2. The relationship among history, democracy, freedom, social structure, economic system, and religion
3. Historic relationships between church and state
4. The centrality of religious consciousness
5. The notion of civil religion

Liberation theology is authentic theology.

Sometimes people who study liberation theology emphasize its starting point, the praxis, or its relation with political liberation movements, and do not realize its theological relevance.

Latin American theologians have developed certain theological themes more than others. But they are still in the process of praxis, reflection, prayer, and conceptualization.

Methodology:

In the unique process of liberation it is necessary to understand the relationship between the three levels of knowledge (social science, philosophy, and theology) and the three processes taking place in Latin America. These processes are social and political change of structures, humanistic plans to create a new society, and the process of salvation in and through Jesus Christ.

Liberation theology attempts to integrate the three processes in coherent and dialectic discourse as these levels express realities which are united existentially in the single process of liberation and in the liberating praxis of Christians.

We have to deal with hermeneutics, the tool for approaching the Bible. It is necessary to clarify some themes such as faith and ideology, hermeneutics and culture, hermeneutics and social conditioning, ideological theology, as well as the use of certain biblical symbols.

Liberation theology reminds us that there are three functions of theology. First, it is a "wisdom" which nourishes the spirituality of Christians. Secondly, it is a rational effort to clarify, conceptualize, and justify our faith. Finally, it is a critical reflection on Christian praxis in the light of the Word of God. This third function, closely linked to the other two, is essential in liberation theology.

Theological disciplines and theological themes:
   1. Faith and Utopia. Theology of liberation is a theology of salvation. Salvation in Christ is also an intrahistorical reality, the fulfillment of all dimensions of existence in a Christ-finalized history moving towards its complete fulfillment.
   Liberation theology tries to clarify the relation between Christian faith and political action. It proposes the concept of "utopia." Even if this concept is controversial, it should be understood here as a historical project to establish a new society with new relationships among people. It necessarily implies a denunciation of the established order and, at the same time, it announces a new society.
   The relations between faith and "utopia" are governed by the fact that liberation only exists in the praxis which concretizes "utopia."
   2. Soteriology. Today in the faith experience of many Christians in Latin America, Jesus is seen and loved as the Liberator. The process of liberation affords a hermeneutical context for the elaboration of a new image of Jesus Christ. Even if this image exists among the people, it has not yet been well elaborated by the theologians.
   3. Ecclesiology. Ecclesiology is the theological discipline developed in greatest detail in liberation theology. The church, as a sacramental community, should signify the salvation by Jesus in its internal structure and in its presence in society.
   The church is called to place itself at the service of the advent of liberation in history.
   The model for the church in liberation theology is clear. It points out the need for the church to be a community of Christians in active solidarity with the interests and struggles of the exploited. From this position, the church can announce the gospel.
   In the understanding of Catholic theologians, the Eucharist has a central role in building the Christian community. But Eucharist is linked with the advent of human solidarity. We cannot celebrate the cross and the resurrection of Christ without entering into his paschal mystery by accepting the demands of a liberating praxis.

Liberation Theology and Evangelization:
   1. A new way of evangelization. Insertion into the process of liberation is a spiritual experience. Because of that insertion, Latin American Christians read the gospel message in a new light. Within their own cultural context, they strive to reformulate the message.

But the faith has to be communicated, preached, shared. Theological discourse operates here as a mediator between a new manner of living the faith and its communication.

2. A new style of life. Participation in the liberating process, with its political implications, is a new spiritual experience. It is a true conversion, a metanoia.

The tension of living the faith in solidarity with the oppressed and at the same time belonging to the church in which the oppressors are also members is a difficult experience.

The Christian praxis of liberation is the matrix of a new understanding of poverty, prayer, and spiritual experience.

Sergio Torres, M.Th.
New York, May 1975

II

The Conference in Detroit

The Opening of the Conference

On the afternoon of Sunday, August 17, 1975, participants gathered from all over the Americas at the Sacred Heart Seminary in downtown Detroit. The meeting opened with an ecumenical service of praise and prayer.

In his opening address, Sergio Torres, executive secretary of the organizing committee, summarized the preparation period of the conference and invited the participants to explore together the meaning of liberation theology for North America.

19

Opening Address
of the Conference

by Sergio Torres

I still have a dream today that one day men and women will rise up and come to see that they are made to live together as brothers and sisters.

The echo of these words expressed by the late Dr. Martin Luther King still resound loudly in our ears. Moreover, they provide us with an appropriate starting point tonight. They remind us of our Christian commitment and they stir us in our efforts to carry out the radical demands of the gospel we all profess. May this total process we call "Theology in the Americas: 1975" be characterized by the immortal spirit of Martin Luther King's words and actions.

Since the beginning of this undertaking we have repeatedly referred to "Theology in the Americas" as a *process*. We have tried to remain faithful to this original objective, namely, that this endeavor be a process. And we have planned this conference and the postconference stage with this concept of a total process first and foremost in our minds and hearts.

The first stage comes to an end with the opening of this conference in Detroit. More than fifty reflection groups throughout the country have participated in the process. Documents and working papers have been produced by several persons and groups and by the Center of Concern. We hope that this conference will provide the impetus to propel us to a second stage of the process. We hope to continue and improve the network of reflection groups, have local and regional conferences, and foster experiences and publications which show the creative witness of Christians who respond to the Lord of history.

There is a profound relationship between the period of preparation and the conference itself. For that reason I will refer frequently to the document entitled "A Theological Quest," which is a synthesis of the work accomplished by the participants during the first stage of the process [see above document 17].

I will try to convey to you a feeling of the process thus far, underlining some important issues that may be dealt with during the conference. I invite each of you to personally assess your own participation in the process. Let us review our personal and communal journeys and be ready to share them this week, so as to grow together in our commitments and reflection. Also, I will present and share with you some insights that I have gained during my participation in the process.

Issues That Emerged during the Preparation Stage of the Process

In the beginning we defined our goal as follows:

The dominant task of this process, from the preconference through the postconference period, in a modest and experimental way, is to raise the question of a fresh theology from our U.S. experience. Latin American theology of liberation cannot simply be imported as is into the United States and mechanistically be applied here. That would be a betrayal of the very theology itself which insists that a people's historical experience must be the point of departure in theologizing.

The conviction underlying the whole process, briefly stated, is that our own historical experience is the starting point for a theological reflection. Consequently, we suggested a network of reflection groups who out of their own experience portray the different aspects of the North American reality. We initiated our work with an analysis of the history of the American experience and its present situation. A major theme was the problem of *imperialism* ["Preparation Document no. 1"; see above document 1]. We emphasized imperialism since it can reveal the major contradictions in our world. For most Latin Americans, to speak of oppression is to speak of imperialism. This has been a starting point for liberation theology in dependent societies like Latin America, which is quite different from starting out with oppression experienced by minority groups in the U.S. But since there was significant resistance to that approach, we then examined in a historical way the American struggles against racism, sexism, class exploitation, and imperialism [see "The American Journey"].

I believe we have to examine this latter issue again and again, in terms of the growing gap between the rich and the poor countries. This is the main contradiction in our world. The relationship between domination and dependency focuses the issue for theology. Therefore, the task of theology in the affluent countries will differ from the task in the poor countries.

Many of the participants experienced some difficulty in dealing with a holistic reflection. This is why we see the need of discovering a way of doing theology that starts out from practical experiences and goes into a holistic analysis.

Since the beginning we have tried to remain faithful to the way of doing theology in Latin America and similar experiences carried out in North America. This method of liberation theology has what is called a "praxis framework." The Center of Concern suggested a "praxis framework" containing three moments: (1) a description of the situation, (2) a religious meditation, and (3) a return to experience.

Although most of the participants sought to do theological reflection in a "praxis framework," it seems that few have been able to do it consistently. Why is this so? Is it too academic? Is it too political? Rather, the problem seems to be that we are all starting out in a new way of doing theology. It is a matter of sharing particular experiences of oppression and liberation in order to understand the global system and design adequate strategies. It is a new way of reflecting on God's demands through our historical commitments. So, it is most important for us to honestly acknowledge that we have started out on a new road. We need each other's help and inspiration so as to continue on this communal journey and do our theological reflection in a "praxis framework."

From the beginning we grappled with the situation of women in American society and the role of sexism as a key factor in our theological reflection. Some felt that "the realities of sexism and the women's liberation movement are not addressed by Latin American theology of liberation." Therefore, the authors of the reflection group synthesis report concluded that a "U.S. theology of liberation would necessarily rely heavily on the experience of women, an important part of the U.S. experience." "The Structure of Women's Oppression," written for the conference by Mary Burke, is thus one of the central working papers for our deliberation [see above document 13].

Equally if not more insistent as an absolutely central issue of the American experience is the question of race, of racial oppression and especially of the reality of black people in this country. Most of the persons who initiated this present process are white and most of them had particular experiences in Latin America. It was inevitable that some would find the process too inattentive to the role of race. It only follows that they would be too little aware of the theological advances of the black community. One black reflection group asked pointedly: "Is white theology still more willing to look beyond its borders to find out the truth about itself rather than listening to the voices from within?" Just as the black man in this society used to be called "the invisible man" (the title of Ralph Ellison's famous but we hope dated book), black theology is still an "invisible theology" as far as white Christians are concerned. Professor Herbert Edwards's paper, "Black Theology and Liberation Theology," is one of several responses made to that question in the course of our process [see above document 12].

In the same manner, "would not then the struggles of native Americans, of women, of blacks, of Hispanics, of Asian-Americans and of white ethnics provide at least part of the framework for a new theology." The question is clearly before us. Initial probes made by some native Americans and Chicanos have been circulated among you [see above documents 14 and 15]. Several longer papers submitted by an Asian-American theologian have also been received. We have as yet to hear a theological reflection from the white ethnic community, but we have no doubts that it, too, will soon arrive on the scene.

One of our main concerns has been the examination of the class structure in the U.S. "The American Journey" takes up this particular examination. We also submitted for discussion an article by Andrew Levison entitled, "The Working Class Majority" (*New Yorker*, September 2, 1974). All of this awakened us to the need of inviting more workers to the reflection process. However, we regret to have to mention the fact that one of our main failures is the absence of a paper written by a member of the working class. At the same time there is an inadequate representation of workers here at our conference.

The Starting Point for This Conference

During the reflection group part of the process one of the expectations that surfaced many times was that this encounter in Detroit produce a challenge from the Latin Americans to the North Americans "so that international structures of oppression might be examined." At the same time, "this examination would be followed by an analysis of oppressive structures in the U.S. and a formulation of a theology that would grow out of the struggle for liberation." In order to respond to this expectation, which seems to us more than appropriate, the design of the conference will follow this sequence of events:

1. *The Latin American Challenge:* On Monday the Latin Americans will share the experiences of the people of their countries who suffer

the consequences of U.S. foreign policy, coupled with a theological reflection on that situation.

2. *Analysis of Oppressive Structures in the U.S.:* Tuesday we will devote the whole day to an analysis of the North American reality. The social scientists will try to present "at least the rudiments for an understanding of imperialism, class structure, racism, and sexual oppression, and, to the extent that it is possible, relate them to each other in the broader matrix of contemporary U.S. capitalism." The authors of "A Theological Quest" expressed a similar idea:

Each element—race (and cultural ethnicity), sex, class—is both interwoven with the others, yet unique. None can be reduced to another, yet none can be left to itself. Working out, both in theory and practice, a creative coalition of the three is probably the most important task for people concerned with social change in this country.

Theological Reflection

"Whatever happened to theology?" A recent issue of *Christianity and Crisis* (May 1975) was totally devoted to this question. Not surprisingly, it has also been one of our chief concerns. Although we are possessed of a markedly different orientation, we are asking the same questions that the eighteen theologians asked at Hartford, Connecticut, when they signed the "Appeal for Theological Affirmation," better known as "The Hartford Statement." But we ask it in the midst of our participation in the struggles of oppressed peoples here and in other nations. Moreover, the quality of the process so far has been marked by a variety of efforts and achievements in the task of doing liberation theology. Our question, then, is better formulated to read: How do we do liberation theology?

Some have expressed doubts as to whether we are really doing a theological reflection. It is interesting to note how few groups in the process dealt extensively with what the Center of Concern called the second moment of a religious meditation on the situation. According to the synthesis report, "the majority spent most of their time on the first stage of social analysis, adding reflections on the mission of Christians within practical situations." Herein lies a challenge for all of us. Social analysis and reflection on communal commitments is an integral part of liberation theology, but it must give birth to new specifically theological insights. Our religious heritage and the spiritual experience of the oppressed must challenge our analysis.

Some groups feel that "religious experience, including biblical symbols and the teaching of the Church, would be the existential point of departure." According to Frederick Herzog, "situation analysis is not always a good starting point for theology. What we need to learn today is to live more dangerously, which for Christians means to live biblically." The synthesis report concludes that these kinds of statements "would lead to an option in favor of starting with biblical reflection and then proceeding to action."

Others involved in the process feel that liberation theology starts out from lived experience and social analysis, since many religious truths have been used to support an unjust system. Thus, only through a reflection in the struggle for a new reality can there be a liberating appropriation of Christian symbols and truths. All of this certainly requires careful examination. What seems most important is that there be a creative interaction between practical experiences, social analysis, and theological resources. Only through a consistently creative interaction between these elements can we hope to advance in our theological journey.

The relationship between faith and ideology emerges as another major concern. One reflection group groped with this complex relationship, and finally based their reflection on the question: "What is wrong with the American dream?" Another group suggests that "the problem facing Christians is to dissociate religious stories from secular myth, and reappropriate Christian symbols in relationship with a newly formed critical consciousness." Undoubtedly, this relationship between faith and ideology will have to be explored during the conference. We dare to predict that it will become an ongoing topic of discussion in the postconference stage.

Throughout the process we have also become more acutely aware of the continuity and discontinuity between traditional theologies and liberation theology. We hold that liberation theology is a task of the whole people of God, to all who are called to conversion and faith in Christ, son of the living God. In this task we consider ourselves a part of the multitude of witnesses to the gospel who have preceded us and who now walk together with us. But we are also convinced that this task of liberation theology belongs in a special way to those who are most oppressed and to those who courageously struggle for a new life. In this context we examine the sources and norm for theology and discuss the interpretation of God's revelation. In a "praxis framework" we find deeper and newer meanings of God, Jesus, church, and eschatology.

Liberation theology breaks away from the methodology of traditional Western theology. Unfortunately, many European and North American theologians still believe that theirs is the only valid and universal methodology for the whole world and the whole church. In our experience, however, we have seen how the Western theological pattern is most functional to oppressive structures and ideologies. Liberation theologies, both in Latin America and North America, are rooted in a historical praxis and reflect on the commitment of all those who seek a new earth and a new heaven. As it was so vividly expressed during the process, "We look for a theology which is on the verge of emerging within the North American situation, . . . drawing together Christians from different oppressed groups who, while recognizing their differences, nonetheless struggle together for liberation." This is our methodology for this conference and for the process ahead of us.

Perhaps the most striking characteristic of our process has been the participation of so many different types of persons and groups, representing the whole gamut of experiences we find in the Americas. This stands in sharp contrast with the usual notion that theology is done only by professional and academic experts. Our experience has been completely different. In this process we have forged a new interaction between people involved in grassroots commitments, in church institutions, and in professional theology. We all feel part of a common endeavor. Undoubtedly, there have been tensions and difficulties in this new interaction, but we are learning to work through these difficulties and overcome many of them. Faith in the Lord of history and a shared experience of oppression plus the demands of liberation are able to keep us together allowing us to discover the paths of the Spirit.

Our theological path is not only scientific. It is also a path of wisdom and celebration. Wisdom comes from our commitments, our reflections, and our obedience to the Spirit. Celebration of God's graceful salvation is certainly the climax of our theological journey. We come together both in praxis and in worship. As several reflection groups have emphasized, our process responds to a call to a communal conversion. This implies a faithful obedience to the Word of God as it becomes flesh in history. Consequently, our theological reflection responds to the call to conversion from sin and all forms of oppression and conversion to the living God, who is present among the poor and those who struggle for a new earth.

Conclusion

Many may wonder why we are meeting in Detroit when we might have chosen other sites. Why would anyone want to come to Detroit in the sweltering heat of the August "dog days?" The answer to that question can be found right here on our doorstep. Step into the street outside Sacred Heart Seminary. There you will encounter the glaring contradictions of the domination-dependency relationship, the oppression, the racism, sexism, and exploitation of the working classes. We need look no further for more fertile ground for theological reflection. In Detroit—symbol of the automobile, the idol at whose feet we worship—all of the forces of oppression converge to form an unholy alliance. If we isolate our week-long reflections from what is going on in Detroit, we are forfeiting a great opportunity to do liberation theology.

I would like to invite you to the work ahead of us this week. May the spirit of ecumenism that has characterized our process thus far manifest itself this week. This is your conference and, hopefully, God's conference. We can't predict what will happen. The path awaits us. We only hope that this conference marks the opening of a new stage. I could more accurately say that the work will begin after Saturday. During this week we seek no new formulas, but directions, no statements or appeals, but commitments, not a creed, but a strategy for the future.

The Latin American Theologians

The program of the first day of the conference, Monday, August 18, called for presentations by Latin American theologians. Many of the conference participants were familiar with the works of the theologians, some of which have appeared in English translation.

The high expectations for the day were more than satisfied, as the group, working as a close-knit, proficient team, provided a day-long introduction to the Latin American theology of liberation.

The morning and the afternoon presentations each included four panelists. José Míguez Bonino began the session. An Argentinian theologian, he is one of the outstanding Protestant contributors to the theology of liberation. He sketched the milestones of Latin American theology in recent years, pointing out that his task was difficult since the major figures of the movement are not only still alive but were present at the conference.

Jesuit Juan Luis Segundo, educated in the strict tradition of his congregation, has exemplified an evolution toward commitment to the liberation movement in Latin America. His presentation delineated three discoveries of liberation theology: reinterpretation of the concepts of salvation, of the gospel, and of theology.

Third to speak was Javier Iguíñiz, a young sociologist from the University of San Marcos in Lima. He had been encharged by his colleagues with describing the theory of dependence, which provides the sociological analysis underlying the theology of liberation.

Enrique Dussel, historian and theologian from Argentina, grounded his reflections on history and geopolitics. His historical perspective illuminated the relationship between present-day Latin American oppression and the North Atlantic centers of power.

In the afternoon José Porfirio Miranda, Mexican theologian and exegete, offered a brief but deeply human statement on Christ the Liberator.

Brazilian theologian Leonardo Boff, a new name for many at the conference, synthesized what might be called a Latin American Christology.

Hugo Assmann, one of the best-known theologians of the group, referred to several crucial issues in the methodology of liberation theology: the context of the word of God in history, the role of the poor in understanding revelation, and the relationship between Christian faith and revolution.

Argentinian Beatriz Couch, the only woman of the group, provided an exposition on criteria of biblical interpretation.

Here we include edited excerpts from the presentations.

Gustavo Gutiérrez, the doyen of the liberation theologians, was not able to speak with his colleagues. Detained by political events in Peru, he arrived only at the end of the conference, at which time he addressed a general session. His address is included here.

20

Statement by José Míguez Bonino

The task that was assigned to me was to present a sort of historical introduction to the theology of liberation in Latin America, an assignment about which I have two main problems. One is that usually the historian has the advantage that the people about whom he speaks are dead; but the protagonists of this history are very much alive and many of them sitting in this room—which makes things a bit difficult. On the other hand, I imagine that most of you already know much about the origins of the theology of liberation, having read the works of Gustavo Gutiérrez, Juan Luis Segundo, Enrique Dussel, etc., and therefore I run the risk of repeating what you already know. What I will try to do very briefly is to set the stage, so to say, in which the theology of liberation began, trying to recount a little bit the outward history of this process, which then from a more internal point of view will be discussed by the other people on the panel.

How do you go about tracing the history of a theology? Usually, you find the originators and the influences that played upon them, the precedents and the evolution of their thought. And you must somehow find a way of saying that there is a first and a second Gustavo Gutiérrez and a younger and an older Juan Luis Segundo and so on. You could do this with the theology of liberation; I'm quite convinced there must be at least a dozen dissertations in European and American libraries dealing in this way with the history of the theology of liberation; but I think that one would entirely miss the center of the process that way. What is the corpus which you have to use? Books, articles, etc. But what lies behind them is more important. In order to get at the real sources you have to move outside the field of proper or classical theology to the Christian communities, and beyond that to Latin American secular history. What I offer is a very simple interpretation of the dynamics in which a theology of liberation arose. I think that it is this history which makes it possible for us to speak of *a* theology of liberation. Otherwise, you would have to speak of many

275

theologies of liberation. There is not a homogeneous doctrinal school of theology, but there is a common historical matrix of this theology.

I begin with a very superficial observation: Throughout the second quarter of the present century a movement was visible in Latin American life. The most obvious way to see what was happening is to look at the displacement of masses of population from one area to another: people who moved from country to city, immigrants who came from outside, those who went from one place to another place within the same country. This movement has sometimes been described as the birth of a society of masses in Latin America.

Now, on the surface, several aspects immediately drew attention. There was the fact of the political weight of these masses. Whether in the form of organized labor movements or of populist attempts, they were a new factor in Latin American history. There was a new cultural, religious situation. Segundo speaks of the disruption of closed spaces in this displacement of the population and a loss of religious practice. I'm not going to speak of secularization because that's already an interpretation which one would like to discuss; but the loss of religious practice was clear.

New religious movements arose; particularly, there was the great growth of Pentecostalism all over Latin America and especially in some countries like Chile and Brazil. The churches became aware of this situation at this superficial level of what was observable, what was happening. I think it is justified to say that the Roman Catholic church took a defensive attitude. It was so interwoven with the tradition of society that it was natural for it to take a defensive attitude. When you read the letters of the bishops up to the Second Vatican Council, you find the search for some way of combatting the enemy, of raising dikes against the new trends; and the enemies were communism, Masons, and Protestants. (I don't say in that order: This depends on the circumstances.) In order to do that, it was necessary to reorganize the life of the church, to reorder it, to unify it, to purify it from certain abuses, so to say, to put it in working shape. There was also a more positive angle: the attempt to organize the laity as the extended arm of the hierarchy in the secular world. There was the whole important movement of Catholic Action and the creation of a number of other movements: Catholic youth, Catholic workers, JAC, JEC, JIC, JOC, JUC (for those who know the names). A number of priests began to work as advisors, chaplains, directors; and there was the development of a strategy and a thinking which could give strength to this movement. This is very important because through this movement of the laity, a number of priests began to enter into the life of Latin American society at another point—not merely as priests performing in a religious situation but as collaborators in a movement which penetrated or had within it the problematics of the student world or the worker world or the peasants in the rural area.

Protestantism had a more aggressive action. Protestants felt that they belonged to the new world that was beginning to develop in Latin America. I have tried to document that elsewhere. They tried their best to make their presence strong and clear through institutions like schools and hospitals because they were the pioneers of a new way of life, a modern way of life over against the traditional society. They worked in the wavelength of the future in Latin America, which was a modern liberal society. Congregations were created which followed the traditional Protestant social mobility; they moved up to lower, then higher middle class in a couple of generations. Social thinking in the Protestant church was inspired in the liberal Social Gospel theology.

I think that the rest of the story is very simple. People involved in these situations were forced to a deeper and more coherent understanding of the situation and to a more radical praxis by the logic of the situation itself. I use the word "radical" not in any enthusiastic sense, but in the sense that they were forced to move toward the roots of the situation in which they were placed. Now, in order to document this statement, one would have to trace this history of movements and people. Obviously, I cannot do that here. It has been done in several places. For the Catholics, Dussel's history of the church of Latin America offers a detailed history of this process. There are also a number of essays on the Protestant side. I would only suggest some places to trace this history. For example, you could trace the history of Catholic Action in the university groups of several countries, for instance, in Argentina; or of the Catholic workers' groups in several places; or the Catholic labor movements; or Catholic agrarian or peasant groups. They have radicalized their understanding, and usually either split or moved toward more revolutionary positions.

There is a very interesting history which I will not attempt to trace here because there are some experts present: the Christian parties in Chile. Catholic political life in Chile has moved in successive splits from Catholic solidarity with the conservative party through corporatist ideology to Christian democratic, to left-wing parties to a militancy in Marxist parties. I don't say that everyone moved in that direction, but there is a movement in the history in which a number of groups took this route. For another example, one can look at the best-known Protestant movement in Latin America, ISAL (Church and Society in Latin America). From the organizing conference in a reformist frame of reference, idealistic, inspired in the Social Gospel, in 1961, it moves through theological and ideological change to participation in popular liberation movements.

You could even trace the process in people, in persons. I would say an archetypal case is that of Camilo Torres: his itinerary as university chaplain, through sociological analysis, theological reflection, and active participation up to his final decision. If you read some of his most elaborate essays, those on the Christian obligation to participate in the revolution, you find a rigorous, at times almost scholastic argument which reflects this experience appropriated through theological and social analytical reflection. Several years ago, Gustavo Gutiérrez gave a very precise expression to this process when he spoke autobiographically. (Unfortunately, the published version of his speech to be found in *Fe cristiana y cambio social in América Latina* [Salamanca: Sígueme, 1973] has lost the autobiographical expression.) He spoke about his own experience as he began to work, to serve the poor in a very traditional frame of reference. And he said (in summary): I discovered three things. I discovered that poverty was a destructive thing, something to be fought against and destroyed, not merely something which was the object of our charity. Secondly, I discovered that poverty was not accidental. The fact that these people are poor and not rich is not just a matter of chance, but the result of a structure. It was a structural question. Thirdly, I discovered that poor people were a social class. When I discovered that poverty was something to be fought against, that poverty was structural, that poor people were a class, it became crystal clear that in order to serve the poor, one had to move into political action. Then, he says, "I discovered the nature of political action, its rationality, radicality, and all-encompassing character."

Now this is a stylized way of describing the process through which many of the groups and people I have mentioned have gone. The situation I tried to describe is one which initially impressed Christians only in its cultural and religious consequences—trying to stop the trend towards secularism or trying to impose a modern way of life. This situation which was understood only in its cultural, religious dimensions took on now clear and rationally understandable features. This was not developed by theologians. It is most important to understand that the theology of liberation is not in the first place a work of theologians. They came to this situation as theologians to a certain extent at a second moment. The basic fact is the constant, although at times contradictory, struggle of the people themselves

—workers, students, peasants, the poor themselves, if you want to use that expression—for their own liberation in this situation. And the social analytical work which took up the study of this process was at first based on the model of the sociology of development, and then later on the understanding of dependence and the refinement of the tools of analysis. It is in the arena of the struggle of the people where the praxis of liberation was born. We are not dealing, therefore, with just an idea—or any sort of idea—of liberation, but with one linked to and defined by this praxis. Only against this background can we see what the theology of liberation means in Latin America. It is the result of and a response to a process in which certain Christian people and groups have arrived at a historical action and an analytical and ideological stand. This is—in general terms—the outward history of the theology, the contents and dynamics of which we shall try to deepen and analyze during the rest of the morning.

21

Statement by Juan Luis Segundo

In this first step of our working together, it is, I believe, of primary importance to let emerge what is or can be common to all of us. What is common in all theology of liberation? This question can be answered theoretically; I prefer to answer practically.

We began our theology of liberation simply by being sensitive to *our own* oppression. This precise source of our process of theologizing may be different from yours in the sense that one kind of oppression can differ from another, even if it is my deepest conviction that there are no unrelated oppressions. We will later discuss these differences in this meeting. If all kinds of oppression are intimately related and interdependent with others, we must establish *priorities* for liberation to be effective.

Let us assume now that all oppression calls for a liberation. We, then, in Latin America began to think about liberation before thinking about a *theology* of liberation. I can say that this human (not precisely Christian) sensitivity to the fact that our people are oppressed was the basis for a praxis of liberation. And the liberation theology or, if you prefer, theologizing about liberation was only *one part* of a much wider task. Our own particular kind of oppression led us in this specific field of theology to three discoveries—discoveries, at least, for us. The beginning of the Latin American theology of liberation consists in these three discoveries and subsequent commitments.

1. The first discovery was that we, in the Christian churches, were unconsciously summing up the message of Christ by the word "salvation." But in modern languages, at least in Latin languages, "to be saved" is to escape, as an individual and in a passive manner, from a common disaster. We began to suspect that this was not the true sense of the word "salvation" in the Bible. We were challenged by a new understanding and a new translation of this key word in the Bible and, particularly, in the gospel. Jesus, explaining a prophecy and apply-

ing it to himself in the fourth chapter of Luke, gives himself explicitly the task of *liberating* the oppressed. Moreover, he defines this task in social (poor-rich) and structural terms, speaking of that special year in Israel when, after forty-nine years of the exercise of demand and supply, all property should be redistributed.

Liberation is not, then, a new focus in theology to insist upon instead of salvation. It is the true meaning of a biblical salvation for both the old and new covenant. That is why the name "theology of liberation" is neither a name for a part of the whole of theology (like the theology of sin or the theology of death) nor a theme specially important for a definite epoch or social system (like the theology of work or the theology of captivity). Theology of liberation is the name for a theology totally understood and totally engaged toward liberation in a historical praxis much wider than the task of theological reflection.

The first discovery, then, led us toward a first commitment: to join, in a *theological way*, that wider liberating praxis common to all human beings, Christians or not, that is to say, human liberation. I say "in a theological way." By this I mean that our theology, although respecting and recognizing other ways of joining this fundamental human task, wants to remain strictly theological, based on a serious biblical and ecclesiastical basis. Our service for liberation is not one of a vague humanistic thought (even with a Christian starting point), nor a philosophical or occidental anthropology, nor a political manipulation of some Christian ideas. We intend to serve liberation with a Christian theology.

2. The second discovery was the realization that the Christian gospel is aimed at liberating human beings in a very real manner, that is to say, in the process of history, even if the total liberation from the last bondages will be the result of the eschatological intervention of God. In other words, God him/herself through Christ assumes and participates with us in the historical process of humanization and liberation, for this is the plan of God for humankind.

This second discovery introduces a new criterion for theology and puts it paradoxically *outside* theology itself. As the criterion for the Sabbath lies outside the Sabbath in its function for human good, so also the criterion of a true theology consists not in an orthodoxy elaborated by the theology itself, but in a real, and even material, success in a historical liberation. This same criterion can be found in the gospel too.

In my opinion, this difference in criteria sharply divides theology of liberation from academic theology. To make such a change presupposes a real conversion in methods and, what is much more difficult, in life. I call your attention to this crucial point: If you don't keep in mind, *at the same time*, that theology of liberation has radically changed in its final criterion, but remains a theology, and a serious and strict one, you will be confused by the criticism of an academic theology which tries to show that, in putting orthopraxis as a criterion, liberation theology loses its seriousness and becomes a romantic and vague rhetoric.

A second commitment came from the second discovery: The truth that God revealed, the church that God built up, the signs that God established—all these must be viewed in functional terms. All this is a function and must work as a function of a praxis of liberation in history. Human beings are not made for dogmas, sacraments, church, but the contrary. The commitment I was alluding to is to rediscover the true sense, the human sense, of all these and to reconstruct them as a function of a historical task. That is why theology is no longer a matter for theologians only, but for Christians as well.

3. The third discovery followed the second one. When we took care of this recreative task of making theology a function for liberation, we were confronted *in two manners* with socio-political structures.

First of all, we discovered that no significant and real liberation is made possible by theology (nor by any other means of education and criticism) without a simultaneous change of structures in society. For these structures condition, from possibilities of time for reflection to the cultural ideals, passing through possibilities and means of understanding theological statements.

On the other hand, when theology of liberation, in a naive manner, tries to *speak about* liberation, to convey the message of God about liberation, it discovers very soon that its own concepts and images of God, grace, sin, sacraments, come not directly from the word of God, but from a culture created by ruling groups and internalized by oppressed groups. In other words, we actually discovered that theology and social structures (both national and international) are politically and mentally interdependent; that without a holistic view and praxis in a process of liberation, theology cannot be a real interpretation of the word of God, but only an escape, a toy for intellectuals, a learned profession among others within the establishment. We discovered, therefore, a *hermeneutic circle*, essential for a theology of liberation. The more we are conscious of the oppressive forces and structures of society over our minds, the more we become able to understand the word of God concealed by these forces. And the more we understand the liberating word of God in human history, the more we are confronted with inhuman and unjust structures in our societies.

This is the basis for a third commitment: the commitment to praxis. Praxis, however, is not merely action. Praxis is action plus theory for action. Therefore, doing theology leads us to ally ourselves with the real, though profound and even concealed sources of suspicions working in the hearts of oppressed people. That is to say, the so-called objective sciences are not completely objective when applied to social realities. These sciences can become "partisan," even if that stance is the result of perhaps unconscious manipulation.

Our commitment as theologians is, then, to dialogue with human and social sciences conscious of this bias. Theology can no longer be isolated in its own methods, problems, and means. But be careful, please. This statement does not mean a tendency towards a secularized theology, as it is often understood by sociologists or theologians like those of the so-called "Hartford Statement." On the contrary, it is a hermeneutic condition, that is to say, the only way to reach in its extreme force the liberating word of God.

This is, I believe, our experience of doing theology in Latin America, that is to say, in an oppressed context. My only question here is this: Is this also your experience, your commitment? Can we follow together this path? Or is there something different, requiring a further and basic discussion, from your experience, about what it means to do theology of liberation?

22

Statement by Javier Iguíñiz

Liberation presupposes not only oppression, but also consciousness of the oppressive situation. There are many oppressions we are not aware of because they are not expressed as such. There are others that are more manifest in certain situations than in others. In any case, oppression is not always apparent to the eyes of the oppressed. It can be concealed by bourgeois conceptions of society and their organic interpretations. Such theories do not deal with oppression.

Bourgeois social science separates poverty and wealth; it makes them independent of each other. The situation of the poor is not related to that of the rich. Latin American poverty and North American wealth are not linked. Economic theory undertakes to "demonstrate" how the wealth of the capitalists is the result of their "effort" or their "contribution" and therefore is "their" product. The distribution of income depends on the different productivities of the factors of production and is therefore a technical problem—unconnected with class relationships. Marx demonstrates, on the contrary, that the wealth of some depends on the poverty of others. This is his fundamental and most subversive point.

When bourgeois social science deals with oppressions, when the facts cry out so loudly that oppressions cannot be masked by the ideology of universal harmonies, then the oppressions are presented as independent of each other, as isolated realities. They are disconnected from the basic source of contemporary oppressions, which is capitalism. The most important motive, open or hidden, behind the many varied oppressions is the anxious need to extract surplus-value. Capitalism oppresses in order to exploit.

Capitalism is not the origin of all the relationships of social domination, nor will the end of capitalism necessarily mean the end of all domination. But no oppression is independent of the social system in which it exists; to consider it so would be to abstract from the conditioning factors which make it, historically speaking, specific.

The primary social phenomenon of our age is capitalism, and the capitalistic process reorients pre-existent relationships of domination, stimulates old forms of oppression, and cancels out other kinds of oppression. What capitalists fear is that all those who suffer every kind of oppression might come to share the same viewpoint. They fear that those who have suffered the accumulated burden of a thousand different forms of oppression together might come to see that the capitalists are, if not the cause, then the hidden final benefactors of oppression.

On the other hand, oppression is dynamic; it changes in form and content. It changes with the character of the oppressor, but also with the form of resistance engaged in by those who are subjugated. At the most general level, oppression varies with the kind of societal organization (slavery, feudalism, etc.) and with the stages of development of each of these. Oppression also varies according to the place within the international division of labor and according to the conditions antecedent to the present situation.

But equally important is the fact that the character of oppression depends on the character of the defeat of the oppressed. And we say this because all dominion has been conquered; it is never natural. The oppressed do not disappear when they are defeated; the oppressors have to defeat them again and again. And in one form or another the vanquished resist again and again. Suffering is never natural; it always hurts. Mothers never get used to the deaths of their babies.

Likewise the resistance of the moribund social system conditions the particular character adopted by the new social organization. The image of the inert system vis-à-vis the new means of social production or of the passive individual vis-à-vis the oppressor is false. When we begin to look at things from the bottom, the world appears different: Within an overall imposed framework those who have been defeated impose on the oppressors the particular conditions that domination assumes. This is immediately discovered when energies are released that have been hidden from the exploiters for centuries. What the exploiters have been able to extract under the whip is given twofold by a people liberated for the construction of their own society.

But it is not sufficient to have a theory of demystification or to be with the people to discover and understand the true character of oppression in its multiple forms. The discovery of how oppressed we really are occurs when there are already buds of liberation. We do not know the conditions we are in, in a certain sense, until we have left those conditions, until we have begun to live the alternative. In the construction of a new society we discover the depth of the marks left by the previous society. In the struggle for liberation we discover how difficult the task is, how oppressed we are.

The discovery of the authentic dimensions of oppression and liberation, therefore, does not suppose simply theory, but also revolutionary practice. It is not enough to be with the people, to live with them; we must struggle shoulder to shoulder with them.

A hotly debated question is "What is the greatest oppression?" Some express the fear that by insisting on one we might overlook others. I believe that there is no little oppression and that there is no useless liberation. But any liberation that does not include the elimination of capitalism will be nothing more than a lovely achievement erected upon the hunger and misery of many races, of both sexes, of all ages, and—in our day—upon contempt for richly endowed cultures and nationalities.

23

Statement by Enrique Dussel

I want to make a short theological reflection, departing from geopolitics and history. If we look at a map from the year 1492 we see that there were several imperialist centers in the world: Europe, the Turkish-Arabic world, India, China, and the Mayan-Incan worlds. Europe tried to conquer the whole world. The first attempt was the Crusades, under the aegis of St. Bernard. Later, in the sixteenth century, Russia conquered Siberia, while Spain crossed the Atlantic to conquer the Americas. At that moment the geopolitical reality of the world changed, because Europe was transforming itself into the center of world history. For example, an Englishman went out from the port of London to Africa; he bought a black—with Indian money. With the purchase of the black with Indian gold, primitive capital was acquired from the English empire. The origin of capitalism was based on the accumulation of capital that came from the periphery to the center.

By the twentieth century, the world centers had become the U.S., Europe, Russia, Japan. The periphery is Latin America, the Arab world, black Africa, southeast Asia, and China. Of all these peripheral worlds, only China has been liberated.

The history of America began in the Caribbean when Columbus and the conquistadors arrived from Spain. It continued through Mexico. On the Pacific side it centered in Peru. The Portuguese conquered Brazil. And when the whole conquest was terminated in about 1620 another history began. At about that time the pilgrims arrived from England, and soon the two histories would meet. At the moment the U.S. won its independence from England, Latin America was still a Spanish colony. And then there began the conquest of the West: first of all, Louisiana, then California, New Mexico, and the other areas that were the northern province of Mexico. The U.S. won a million kilometers from Mexico. In 1850 a priest from Santa Fe named Martínez published a newspaper called *The*

Dawn of Liberty. The name seems paradoxical for those who remained within the conquered Mexican territory, for it was really the beginning of their oppression.

Little by little the Far West was won. Then began the conquest of the Caribbean. The Caribbean too came under the influence of North America. Latin America has remained under the sole disposition of the big brother to the north.

The geopolitical system that we have today is a totality, one system. The Bible refers to the "flesh." The flesh is the totality of the system. This flesh, this system, subjugates the poor one, who can be a nation, a social class, a race, women, children, youth. The poor one is not respected as the other, but is considered as a thing within the system, as something to be used—as the Indian was used in the colonial epoch of Spain, as the black was used in the slave system in the South in the U.S., as Latin America today is being used, as the proletariat class today is being used.

The using of another as a thing is the *only* sin; there is no other. When the woman is used as a sexual object, when the child or youth is used as the recipient of ideology, this is sin, just as when Cain killed Abel, the other.

What did God do? He sent his Son into the system of sin; although of divine origin, Jesus took on the form of a slave. He became in a certain way the son of a despised race, a despised class, and a despised nation. Jesus, then, became oppressed; but he gave a consciousness, an awareness of liberation. He revealed this to the people and was condemned for having revealed it. When the people start to mobilize for their liberation, domination becomes repression. The passage from domination to repression is occasioned by the love of the poor for their liberation.

Love is not everywhere. I should hate the prince of this world, Satan. Love should not direct itself to Satan. And people are the angels of the prince of this world. The empire was represented by Pilate; Jesus died under Pontius Pilate. Herod represented the dependent national government. The gospel says that Herod and Pilate became friends on the day Jesus was condemned. In the gospel there is the empire, there are dependent nations, there are dependent races, there are dependent classes. Jesus was a man of the people, of Galilee, a dependent region within the Roman Empire.

The church in the Roman Empire made itself poor with the poor. The Christians were sent to the arena for being atheists; they would not worship the emperor. The Christians did not worship the god of the empire. The Christians were the atheists of the empire. I see on the dollar bill a theological phrase: In God we trust. In which God? In the god of the empire or in the God who is different from every possible system? The God of Israel is the other of any possible system. The Christian is an atheist of every historical system. In 1551 a bishop in Bolivia said, "We lost this land in a very short time because the Spaniards offered to their god a great quantity of Indians and this god is the silver mines of Potosi." In the sixteenth century the fetish of money reigned. To be an atheist of that god is today, both here and in Latin America, to be in danger of death. And I am not speaking metaphorically.

What is called liberation might be nothing more than integration into an unjust system. What is called liberation of the woman might mean that a woman becomes equal to a dominating male—with the poor still on the periphery. "Liberation" might mean the liberation of the Chicano to participate on an equal footing in a system that oppresses. It might mean the liberation of blacks to participate in a system that oppresses other nations.

Tactically, Christians in Latin America are experiencing the capitivity and the exile. We are in Babylon or Babel, where the blood of martyrs, as the Apocalypse says, the blood of all the saints, the blood of all those who are immolated on the earth is found.

In Latin America the theology of liberation has arisen slowly. I will mention several stages.

First, from the Vatican Council to Medellín (1962–68). This is still the time of imitation of Europeans. This is the time of "development." We used to believe that a developed nation could be a model for an underdeveloped nation, and the question was to imitate the model of a developed nation.

From 1968 to 1972 is the time of the formulation of the theology of liberation. Gustavo Gutiérrez wrote his first work. (If he is not here now it is because he is committed to the process of liberation; I believe his absence is the best lecture he could have given.) But during this time repression also intensified. Christians have been more and more persecuted.

There are saints in the new church. For example, in 1969, the martyr of Brazil, Antonio Pereira Neto, was taken, tortured, assassinated, stripped, and hung by his feet from a tree. He is a Christ figure. There is Father Gallegos in Panama. He lived like the peasants of Panama and for this he was assassinated. It is still not known where his body lies. In 1974 in Argentina there was a demonstration of students in which one was killed. Carlos Mugica, a priest from a poor barrio, prayed over the body. The following day he was killed with a machine gun as he left church in Buenos Aires. This past month in Honduras, Father Ivan Betancourt was assassinated in Olancho, together with a North American priest. I believe that the bodies of two priest-martyrs in a hole form the basic foundation for our discussion.

When the church involves itself in liberation it suffers repression. This is the basis for our theology. We don't ponder things that are heard, but things that are suffered. Theologians who are here can recount what they have suffered. Yesterday I heard someone say that the Latin American theologians are a little old, but many of us have grey hairs when we are still young. One of those present has been expelled from Brazil, Uruguay, Bolivia, and Chile.

We cannot be good Christians unless we are good atheists of the fetish. Let it not be said that we Christians are atheists of the true God, atheists because we have not criticized the system, because we have lived within it with the spirit that gives us powers to function better within it. That spirit is not of God; it is of the devil. And the only criterion of discernment that our spirit is the spirit of God is if we struggle unto death for the poor. That is an objective, concrete Christological criterion: "I was hungry; you gave me to eat."

24

Statement by
José Porfirio Miranda

I am very glad to meet you, very glad to talk to you, Americans. It would be easy to read in your presence a draft redacted by me and translated by an American friend, but I am not accustomed to speak reading; I need to see your faces, I want to talk to you; so I prefer to speak without reading, notwithstanding the fact that my English is very deficient.

But now that I am facing you, I am afraid I will not be able to express without tears how much I love you Americans.

And do you know why? Do you know why I love so much, all you who have come to this meeting? I read in the first chapter of the fourth gospel:

Philip found Nathanael and said to him: "We have found the man spoken of by Moses in the Law, and by the prophets: Jesus, son of Joseph, of Nazareth." And Nathanael said to him: "Can anything good come out of Nazareth?"

Well, you all who have come to this meeting did not say to yourselves, "Can anything good come out of Latin America?" That is why I love you.

But there is a further question to this point. Why did you not ask yourselves that skeptical question? Why did you not say to yourselves, "Can anything good come out of Latin America?" Because you have hope. That means: because you believe that the world can change. This is the real meaning of having hope.

This is my whole point this afternoon. If you do not believe that the world can change, you cannot believe in Jesus Christ. Everybody can say with his lips, "I believe in Jesus Christ." But if he does not believe that our world can be changed, he really does not believe in Jesus Christ; he is only pronouncing a formula void of any meaning, void of any contents.

"Christ" is the Greek translation of the Hebrew word *Messiah*. And to believe in Jesus Christ is to believe that Jesus is the Christ, that Jesus is the Messiah. Morever, the Messiah is the bringer of the kingdom of God to our earth. This is historically the only meaning of the word "Messiah." So, if you do not believe that the kingdom of God can be realized in our world, you cannot believe in Jesus Christ.

That is precisely what happened with the Pharisees, and later on with the churches. They could not believe that our world can change and become the kingdom of God.

That a Messiah had to come the Pharisees knew perfectly well; it was a dogma for them. That the kingdom of God had to come, in which no injustice and no oppression and no lack of love could exist, the Pharisees knew perfectly well; it was a dogma for them. But when those truths, when those dogmas try to become reality, the Pharisees (and the churches) have only scandal and rejection as an answer. They believe those truths so far as they remain abstractions, so far as they are only thoughts, not reality. Theirs is no real faith, only a cogitation faith, a notional creed. They take care that "Christ" remains a title, a *diploma honoris causa*, a thought, a pure and simple idea. They cannot stand any person nor any movement which sustains that Jesus is *really* the Messiah; they discard that as a heresy. They have projected all those things for another world (or for an always adjournable, always procrastinable future; it is the same), so that our real world cannot change.

For theology, for faith, for history, there is no question more serious than this one.

You have heard this morning a geopolitical and an economical exposition about the only recently reached unification of the world. For the first time in history we can speak realistically of *a* world. In the time before capitalism there were on earth truly many worlds: the Mediterranean world as a real unity, the Chinese world as a real unity, the Arabic world, the Indian world, etc. In our century, on the contrary, everything on this planet is interconnected, interdependent, unified: There is one world. We are all on the same ship. And, as Marx demonstrated, the future of this world depends upon what happens in the most developed countries; today that means in the United States. My American friends, I believe that. And I ask myself somehow doubtfully if Jesus perhaps came too early to our earth; his world was, in reality, the Mediterranean world. We can now speak about the salvation of *the* world in the complete sense of the term. So you can see that we Latin Americans are not struggling for the liberation of Latin America; we are fighting for the liberation of the world. But this liberation depends more upon you than upon us.

We do not intend that our liberation theology is the only possible liberation theology; we do not intend to impose anything at all. I can only express my wish and my hope that out of this meeting comes a fuller and richer interpretation of the gospel, a fuller and richer Christian faith and Christian action.

But there is certainly a condition *sine qua non:* that we believe that Jesus is *really* the Messiah (in spite of churches and Pharisees), that we all believe that the world can change.

25

Statement by Leonardo Boff

It has already been said many times that the theology of liberation constitutes a new way of doing theology, beginning from the praxis of faith and bringing a new, more efficient and liberating praxis. In this sense, theology of liberation represents a new lens through which the whole content of Christianity may be considered. But it cannot remain only a new and different perspective, that is to say, a fundamental theology. There is a need for theology of liberation to specify itself and fill itself with a liberating content. What do God, grace, sin, church, Jesus Christ mean from the viewpoint of commitment to liberation? How does the liberation of Christ appear from within a praxis of faith?

Witnessing the impoverished majority on our Latin American continent, Christians had a profound spiritual experience. Love brought them to commit themselves in a revolutionary and liberating way. Praxis, accompanied by reflection and a more detailed knowledge of the mechanisms which generate poverty, led to the postulation of a new society in which fraternity and equality are less difficult. A global strategy of liberation was elaborated: the utopia of a free and liberated society. But such a fundamental project is not enough. The tactics and the mediations which make the liberating project historically viable are also necessary. It is exactly at this point that there enters the liberating commitment against economic poverty and in favor of a qualitative social change.

Within this dynamic, Christians began to reread the gospels and to discover a new face of Christ. Of course, Christ is always the same, yesterday, today, and always. Nevertheless, the images of him change according to the times and the historical demands of faith. Only in this way does he make himself real and alive. It was in the womb of the liberating praxis where there exist a global strategy and concrete steps that Jesus Christ the Liberator was discovered.

He also announced a global project: the kingdom of God. This category—kingdom of God—was in the tradition of a theology emptied of its liberating and critical content, emptied of its ability to generate hope for the oppressed. The term had come to mean the other world or the institutional church. For Jesus, the kingdom of God possesses two meanings, one negative, the other positive.

The negative meaning: It implies rejection of this world in its historical concretization; it is against poverty, hunger, hatred, the exploitation of one's brothers, legalism, pharisaism, false religion, sin, and death.

The positive meaning: It is in favor of love, justice, reconciliation as the result of conversion, the fullness of life, and the total transformation of this world according to the plan of God.

The "no" to the present world gives birth to a radical "yes" to a better and utopian world. We must remember that Jesus' project is a utopia. But "utopia," according to modern sociology, psychology, and anthropology, does not have the negative meaning of illusion or flight from the conflictive reality of the world. It possesses a highly positive depth and signifies the capacity to transcend, a creative fantasy, the dialectical reason of man. Man can rise above his own historical constructions and project a not-yet-experienced but still possible reality. From this moment on, historical expressions are relativized, criticized, and placed in a process of liberating conquest. The utopia of the kingdom of God does not mean the consecration of a certain type of world and a certain kind of future. Rather, it surpasses the totality of the concrete forms of this world in function of another, more human and more open to the coming of God. Jesus, with the announcement of the kingdom of God, did not postulate another world, but rather a new world; this old and broken world would be totally transfigured.

On the other hand, Jesus did not preach only a utopian future. He did not remain on the level of a global strategy. He provided mediations, gestures, actions, and attitudes which anticipated the kingdom in history and made it present in our midst. The liberating praxis of Jesus challenged his world, which was socially and religiously oppressed. He entered into conflict with the law, with the religion of his time, with the imperial cult, with the Judaic traditions, and with their dogmatic and moral prescriptions. This constitutes only one aspect of liberation: liberation *from*. More important is liberation *for*: for a new type of relationship, a new sense of goods, of liberty, of equality with the little and the weak, and a new relationship with God.

In Christ there is maintained the dialectical tension that we also encounter in our liberating praxis: openness to a project of global liberation on the one hand and mediating actions that translated it within a historical and conflictive process. If Christ announces the utopia of a reconciled world without providing some anticipatory signs in history, he would nourish fantasies without any credibility; if he introduces partial liberations without a perspective of the totality and the future, he would frustrate the hopes placed in him and would fall into a form of immediatism without consistency. Jesus maintains this difficult dialectical tension: On the one hand, the kingdom is in our midst; it is the object of the joint construction of God (a gratuitous gift) and of man (conversion and liberating praxis); on the other hand, the kingdom continues to be in the future, the object of hope.

From the strategy and tactics of Jesus—it is impossible here to enter into details—we learn how we should work out our own action. And our action leads us to discover the essence of the action of Jesus.

The concrete steps of historical liberation are always conflictive and burdensome. All true liberation rests upon a convenant of blood and death. All the prophets, both of yesterday and today, know this; the prophet cannot be worried about his own neck. No prophet ever died in his bed. It is the same with Jesus, the Liberator par excellence. I would like to underscore the political-liberating aspect of the death of Christ.

We are accustomed to understand the death of Jesus according to the way it is told in the Passion narratives. In these it appears clearly that his death was because of our sins and in fulfillment of the Old Testament prophecies. It was part of the plan of the Father. These affirmations are true only in the sense that they bring out the transcendent and salvific meaning of the historical fact of the condemnation of Jesus to death. They presuppose the historical fact, with all its religious, social, and political implications. The theological interpretations of the Gospels constitute the result of the whole process of reflection made by the early church on these facts, that is to say, on the historical acts of Jesus, his arrest, his torture, and his crucifixion—in the light of the greatest act, the resurrection.

Nevertheless, the drama of the Passion is not outside history. The actors—Jesus, Judas, Pilate, and the Jews—were not puppets at the service of a previously traced plan. They were not free of responsibility. The death and the passion cannot be separated from the life and the activity of the historical Jesus. Jesus did not die just any death. He was condemned for his attitudes, his ideas, and his praxis, which was considered to be dangerous and subversive for the religious and political situation. His death was human, that is to say, it is situated within the context of his life and the conflict which he provoked. Death was imposed upon him by concrete men who were committed to a certain interpretation of religion and a certain type of political power. It was not by an implacable divine decree to which men could do nothing but submit. Rather, it was the result of the historical freedom of concrete men. Once it was imposed, Jesus and God gave a salvific meaning to it.

Jesus died for the same reason as all prophets, for the same reason that many in Latin America have died: He placed the values of justice, fraternity, and the sovereignty of God above his own life. He preferred to die freely rather than renounce justice and commitment to his brothers and to religious truth. His prophetic death is a condemnation of this world with its established interests and values; it is the presence of a love and a courage that anticipate a new world more worthy of God and men.

We should not imagine that the Jews, the Pharisees, and the guardians of order were evil or vindictive. On the contrary, they were pious observers of the Law of God. The accusations that they make against Jesus are born of a drama of conscience arising because Jesus questioned the status quo. They wanted to bring Jesus back to the established order. But when they didn't succeed, they condemned him. Historically, the death of Jesus resulted from this conflict.

The crass ideology of national security within the Empire could kill, but it could not define the meaning that the one who died gave to his death. Jesus defined the meaning of his imposed death as free sacrifice, as love, as a gift to others.

To die in this way is dignified and it is liberating; it is the perfect work of liberation because it is to free one totally from oneself for God and for all men. Jesus liberated death from being without meaning. Death can no longer be absurd because it signifies the opportunity for a great gift. In this sense, it is truly liberating.

The resurrection revealed this profoundly liberating aspect of the life and death of the Son of Man. It brought to fruition the project of total liberation: the kingdom of God concretized in the reality of Jesus. Through the resurrection we have the certainty that the Christian utopia can be both "topia" and concrete reality. Because of this, it fills our praxis with a hope that reaches beyond the historical achievements and frustrations. It encourages us even in the moment of repression because it was the Oppressed One who revealed the ultimate meaning of the whole process of liberation.

What meaning does the liberation of Jesus have for us in Latin

America? Universal discourses and proclamations are not enough: He has liberated us from sin and from death. How is this shown? We can speak meaningfully of redemption and liberation only if we begin from the experience of oppression.

What is our greatest oppression? It is in the struggle against the greatest oppression that the liberation of Jesus Christ is anticipated and revealed concretely. Our greatest oppression consists in the poverty of the millions. This is not born by spontaneous generation. Rather, it is generated by a type of society that provides for the private ownership of goods and the means of production. This society is sustained by a system whose center of decision-making is found outside our countries, maintaining them in dependence and impoverishment. This system in itself is the result of a mode of living which people—motivated by money, power, domination of the world and of their brothers—have established. To struggle against such a civilization with its pseudo-values for a different society means to anticipate concretely the salvation of Jesus Christ within our historical situation; it is to move toward the kingdom.

Jesus appears, then, as the Liberator. He encourages us in our struggles, comforting us in our weakness and nourishing our hope that it is worthwhile to struggle for the creation of a new heaven and a new earth. The Liberator is the expression of our anxiety, it is the title of our love, it is the sign of our hope.

26

Statement by Hugo Assmann

I'm not going to apologize for not speaking better English. I'm always reading a great amount in English, and I find it dangerous; if I knew English better the danger would be even greater. First, I want to speak about text and context of the word of God in history, the role of praxis in our ability to hear the summons of God's word. Second, I want to consider the epistemological privilege of the poor. My third remark has to do with the possibility of revolution as a precondition of Christian faith. And finally, and most important, I want to talk about the strange fact that the Christian churches have so many absolutes, so many certitudes, and yet, when it comes to the basic contradictions in the world they have only humble opinions. How can we relate this fact to the minimal but basic certitudes we have in Latin American theology?

First, the word of God is no longer a fixed absolute, an eternal proposition we receive before analyzing social conflicts and before committing ourselves to the transformation of historical reality. God's summons to us, God's word today, grows from the collective process of historical awareness, analysis, and involvement, that is, from praxis. The Bible and the whole Christian tradition do not speak directly to us in our situation. But they remain as a basic reference about how God spoke in quite a different context, which must illuminate his speaking in our context.

It is true that this kind of historical hermeneutics may destroy the false security of the word of God given once for all, the absolute of the word of God in itself. The word doesn't exist for us in that sense. We deny the possibility of any direct summons. Before the summons can occur, we must first analyze the multiple blockages behind which the word has been transmitted for two thousand years, and we must be engaged in real praxis in a dialectic relationship with analysis.

There is a basic blockage of the word of God because it is now being held in an in-system captivity. Think about "manifest destiny" and its religious implications. There have been many falsifying mediations in the past, especially the intrasystematic inclusion of biblical interpretation within the bourgeois mentality of the capitalist system. This must be broken up. The word of God is not directly accessible. The primary references of traditional theology—Bible, tradition, in whatever sense tradition may be understood—are not sufficient for doing theology because their accessibility is not direct. Our access to the basic references of our Christian faith are conditioned, both by the blockages of the past and by our decision to take into account both in analysis and praxis our own specific context, which is our basic text.

Second, what about the epistemological privilege of the poor? It is not necessary here to give demonstrations of the biblical notion of privilege. In what sense is it true that the poor are more open to the word of God? With regard to our Latin American history, it is important to be a little critical of Christian voluntarism, Christian spontaneity, false Christian faith in the poor. The poor are not, in a spontaneous way, privileged as hearers of the summons of God. The poor are also in captivity, not only in the sense of material oppression; they have within themselves ideological oppressions, and, in Latin America, Christian oppression in particular. Christianity in our history in Latin America means, first of all, the internalization of oppression. In what sense can we say that these poor and oppressed people who have the internalized oppressor within themselves are privileged to hear the word of God better than the rich ones? Not in every context, not under every oppression, can the word of God be heard. In order to be in such a privileged position, it is absolutely necessary to be a *struggling* poor person, to be a poor person struggling in an efficient way, not just moving around. So many people move around, discussing their little problems. A struggling poor person means a poor person with at least a beginning of class consciousness, class awareness, and this implies a lot of things on a socio-analytic level. Struggling means loving in an effective way, with a revolutionary horizon, with strategic goals and practical praxis steps. I can't accept a general privilege of the poor. Many Christians do, but they forget that the poor are oppressed and have the oppressor within themselves. The privileged poor of the gospel are the struggling poor, struggling within a holistic perspective of revolution.

So I come to my third point. I am deeply convinced that it is impossible to be a Christian without a holistic revolutionary perspective. What possibilities remain for Christian faith if Christians have no possibilities of changing their history? In a world that moves on the level of necessities and not of real historical possibilities there is no possibility for Christian faith. Faith becomes virtually impossible when the horizon of transformation by revolution as a historical possibility disappears. Then the Christian message is deprived of its indispensable precondition and content. It has to be said once and for all and very clearly that for those who have understood the historical character of the Christian faith, the loss of revolutionary vision implies simultaneously the emptying of the biblical theme of salvation and faith. Nowadays, the major part of the churches believe in a different kind of faith and a different kind of salvation.

It is really very strange—and I come now to my main point—that the churches have so many certitudes about so many dogmatic truths and yet have only opinions about the basic issues of history. One of the greatest successes of bourgeois ideology has been the reduction of the world's hardest problems to the level of opinion. The presumed impossibility of understanding the significant aspects of historical reality—in a scientific fashion with dialectical connections to action—is, in fact, one of the most fearsome ideological weapons to be found within the system of domination. The mechanisms of this ideological domination can't be reviewed here, but it is not so difficult to analyze them. The churches' lack of concern with history and their failure to understand the causal laws of historical process ought to be one of today's most important theological themes, in my opinion. We must avoid both the scientific myth of neutral certainties as well as any new kind of dogmatism regarding the objective laws of historical dialectic. The opinion gaps among Christians must be bridged by scientific instruments, by the tools of analysis that will at least enable Christians to have minimal common certainties vis-à-vis the world's problems. To what extent is doctrinal dogmatism on the religious plane the exact counterpart of distance from the comprehension and transformation of the world?

Now, a few final words about our minimal certitudes in Latin America. And perhaps here I must change from "our" to "my." We maintain that there is only one history. It is impossible to make a real historical distinction between the history of salvation and world history.

We hold that praxis, struggle, is the basic reference for social analysis, and this means that all socio-analytical tools can never be free, liberated from ideological implications.

There are some other basic convictions. Christian love doesn't contain within itself the criteria for its historical realization, its historical identity. In the same sense the church doesn't contain within itself the criteria for its realization in history. Only from history and its transformation, from effective love in history can we have the criteria to see where love really exists. The socio-analytical tools provide us with the criteria to see where and how love is being effective.

There are some other certitudes. Measuring ourselves according to the theory of dependence remains valid. This morning you heard a lot about that. There are new issues, but the methodology is still valid. The intimate connection between a certain type of social analysis—I say a certain type of social analysis—and the theology of liberation generated in Latin America is a new process of interdisciplinary interrelations among theologians, social science, and social scientists. Many Latin American theologians like myself (I'm a sociologist and a theologian) have had this experience of intimate contact between the use of socio-analytical tools and theological reflection. The result of this process is that we have not only won acceptance; there is a deep respect between social scientists and theologians in Latin Americas. I didn't see this in France, in Germany. I think it's important.

The difference that being a Christian represents becomes prophetically real for nonbelievers only if this difference improves the Christian's qualifications both in the practical struggle for a more human world and in the intellectual struggle to interpret social realities. Confessional fidelities don't have in themselves a prophetic significance. All professional and ecclesiological internal criteria for an improvement, a historical improvement of Christian charity in the world are not sufficient for prophecy.

Class struggle and political strategies are factors of division but also are factors for new possibilities of community. The class struggle running through the churches must also be brought into the liturgical act. The indecision of the churches and many Christians to take a clear position toward the major social problems of humanity—they have instead taken refuge in a purely spiritual mission, presumedly apolitical—is a form of resistance to the Spirit and often means criminal participation in oppression and death-bringing violence.

I come to another point. Leftist Christians of Latin America have learned a lot during these last few years. We have learned that Christians involved in revolutionary praxis are often victims of irrationality and emotion derived perhaps from their previous religious experience. We have learned that it is very difficult to give Christians an awareness of holistic perspectives. Christians have very few realistic experiences in revolutionary strategy and tactics.

When they become revolutionary, Christians are generally anti-Communists from the left. That for me is a very important point. It is clear that old-fashioned ecumenism, namely, interconfessional ecumenism, has a certain relevance for internal issues of the churches; but Christians involved in political praxis need a new notion of ecumenism that deals with the ideological polarizations in Latin America and many other situations.

I guess we have many questions in common. But it may be a little difficult for us to come to the same holistic perspective. We from Latin America believe that you must come to see clearly—not as opinion but as a minimal certitude—that there is only one history, that Christian love has no criteria in itself, but only political, historical criteria for its justification. We believe you must come to see the basic contradiction of the rich countries' oppression of the poor countries; you must see the main point of holistic analysis, that is, the contradiction between a rich world and a dependent, dominated poor world. If you don't see these things then our dialogue here may be very friendly, but we really do not have the same basic reference for our hope, for our possibility of revolution. We do not have the same reference for our hearing of the word of God. And we do not have the same faith.

27

Statement by
Beatriz Melano Couch

I was asked to deal briefly with the question of hermeneutics. What kind of hermeneutics does the theology of liberation use? How do we deal with the whole issue of interpretation? I believe that this point is what greatly divides contemporary theologies, cutting across confessional boundaries.

Let me point out some issues that we have to keep in mind which are essential to any kind of theology. In the first place, Christianity is not a collection of ideas but the continual interpretation of facts, of fundamental events. These events are told and already interpreted in the Bible. Therefore, Christianity is a biblical religion. These events record the dealings between God and his people. Even though God may speak through individuals, he is always pointing toward a more global action which has to do with humanity as a whole. From the very beginning the Old Testament, as well as the New, is the interpretation of these basic events. Therefore, the hermeneutical task is not something which we have initiated, but rather it is already present in the Bible itself, describing reality as it has been seen and lived by the prophets, by the people of Israel, by Christ himself, by the early church.

Secondly, let us keep in mind another basic point. It has been presupposed that we can approach the Bible in a state of what I would call an "original naiveté," disengaging ourselves from culture, from our own ideals, from our own internalized images, from our own philosophical and ethical presuppositions, and then apply Scripture to the reality of the world. Theology has been thought of as an endeavor that one can do as if one were working in a laboratory with 100 percent pure containers. This is false. As an example that has nothing to do with the theology of liberation: When Bultmann tried to approach the task of hermeneutics, he looked for what he called "the right philosophy" to approach the Bible, and found it in Hiedeggerian existentialism. Bultmann recurs to philosophy because, as he himself explains, each interpreter is conditioned by a certain cultural tradition and all tradition depends upon a certain philosophy. Thus the exegesis of the nineteenth century was conditioned by idealist philosophy. He seeks a just philosophy which will provide him with just presuppositions. By a just philosophy he does not mean a perfect or a final philosophy, but rather the most adequate in this moment for understanding human existence and approaching biblical interpretation. He finds it in existentialism because this type of philosophy does not give us models of existence; it describes existence as a particular phenomenon of concrete life; it does not offer us self-understanding nor does it describe the relation between God and man.

We have to be aware when we approach the Scriptures that we are already conditioned by some kind of philosophical, ethical, political, and social background. The hermeneutics of the theology of liberation starts with what we may call the *hermeneutics of suspicion*. Paul Ricoeur initiates a kind of hermeneutics of suspicion and Juan Luis Segundo also uses this expression, but this type of thinking is already present in Marx, Nietzsche, and Freud. Ricoeur points out the need to expose the *false conscience* which poses itself as the foundation of meaning. But he does not go beyond this point, as the theology of liberation does, that is to say, to the consideration of the political, social, and economic situation. We have to suspect our own ideas with which we approach the Bible and be aware that they are already the product of the kind of political and social background in which we are immersed.

As I see it, we should begin with two considerations. The first one is the suspicion about our own ideas as we approach the Scriptures, the second is suspicion about our methods. There are no innocent methods; every method presupposes a theory with its own limitations and within its own purposes.

The theology of liberation turns to the modern social sciences as necessary tools for describing in a more scientific and objective way the reality in which we are immersed, not only to unmask our own false conscience but to unmask the distortion and oppression under which the peoples of the Third World live today. It hopes to avoid (and this word "hope" is important because I believe that this is not only a hermeneutics of suspicion but also a *hermeneutics of hope*, which I will call later the *hermeneutics of engagement* or the hermeneutics of commitment) the danger of reading into the text only our own conditioning, with the aim of freeing the text, letting the text speak with all its urgency, depth, and power. And then it hopes to let the text itself rephrase our own questions and rephrase our own conceptions about life and death, our own epistemology, our own knowledge of society, our ethics, politics, etc. A more accurate knowledge of society will also rephrase our own questions and conceptions. Summing up, the hermeneutics of the theology of liberation is done in a dialectic relationship between reality as it is described by the modern social sciences and then reflection on the Scriptures, going back and forth from the "reading" of reality to the "reading" of the Scriptures and vice versa.

Let me point out something important about the kind of reflection that we try to do on the Bible. It is a reflection which is being born of the way we experience reality in Latin America; this reflection points out the contradictions of our own society, the contradictions within our own selves, between the church and the gospel, between the Bible and academic theology. I would insist that these reflections have to spring from suffering; by this I mean from the immersion in conflict and in struggle to survive as free human beings. Only if the reflection emerges from that kind of situation can we move on from just condemning what is wrong. Usually to condemn is very easy; we just point out, we get out our hate and our anger. But when we are immersed in the situation—when a little boy comes to look for left-over food in the garbage at my doorstep; when a friend is assassinated in the streets, or when an ex-student of ours is taken to jail—then it is not a matter of merely pointing out what is wrong. That very situation leads us to commitment, a commitment to change what is wrong and not just to condemn it, to change it not by our own authority but by entering into God's purpose and dealing with what the theology of liberation calls "efficacious love."

In summary, the hermeneutics of liberation theology is a hermeneutics of suspicion and a hermeneutics of hope born of engagement.

I would call it then a hermeneutics of engagement or a hermeneutics of commitment, of political commitment.

I will now draw some theological implications from this type of hermeneutics in the very few minutes I have left. I am not going to elaborate upon these ideas; I will simply mention them. I think we have to get away from some mortal (fatal) alternatives into which it is easy to fall. These alternatives are:

1. Existential engagement vs. theoretical engagement (which we

can call a state of neutrality!). To think that one can be neutral in today's world is to believe that one can fail to be present, that we can afford the luxury of being simply absent, taking no sides, no options. We are all present one way or another in this historical moment and we either contribute to the liberation of the oppressed of the world or we contribute to exploitation and injustice.

2. Love of God vs. love of neighbor. "For he who does not love his brother whom he has seen cannot love God whom he has not seen" (1 John 4:20).

3. Violence vs. non-violence. Love is always violent, love breaks, love erupts, love brings forth, love creates. If it only destroys it is not love, but if it is only an idea, a feeling, or a resignation, it is not biblical love.

4. Theology of liberation of a people vs. theology of liberation of individual groups. In the first should be included the liberation of all groups. I cannot be free while my neighbor is under oppression. Is there such a thing as individual liberation?

5. Ideology vs. faith. Faith is expressed in praxis, not only in ideas but in action. Ideology is a coherent nexus of values, ideas, beliefs, customs, attitudes. Both faith and ideology are expressed in ideas and in ways of life. Even though, for the Christian, faith is communion with Christ, it is very difficult to make a clear-cut distinction to determine where one begins and the other ends.

6. History vs. eschatology. We have to interpret eschatology in terms of the kingdom that is already here and now—the kingdom that is present and the kingdom that is to come. Therefore, we shall move away from the dichotomy between the future of man and the future of God. God's future is our present, our present should reflect God's future.

7. Theology of the elite vs. theology of a people on the march which is seeking to be faithful. Being immersed in the situation means being one with others, becoming one flesh with the "other," especially those who are the oppressed of the world. The future of theology is not going to be the task of prima donnas; it is not going to be the responsibility of a few, but our common reflection *as a people* as we search to interpret God's word and his purposes for our time. The New Testament shows us that the events of Christ were interpreted within a community. The New Testament writers were not isolated people; they belonged to a community of proclamation, worship, and service. The theology of liberation is a theology on the march. It is an open theology in the sense that it is not a finished product; it is open in the sense that it is not a closed system of abstract dogmatic truths. If

theology is disengaged from the particular situation, we would say as Latin Americans, it is irrelevant. It cannot be separated from the common church experience, from the common sharing of the struggles and hopes of the people who search for a more human and just society. It assumes suffering; it assumes praxis; it assumes the challenge of faith today.

There is an additional dichotomy which I have not yet mentioned. We have to get away from the alternative between one truth and many interpretations. That is a mortal alternative too. The truth is not something we invent, of which we have an intuition, it is not something we create; it is not an ideal we produce. It is an incarnate reality that we discover, that judges our action and confirms it, and that throws light on the road ahead.

Just one final word. What does this mean to us women in the church? I think that, precisely because of the rediscovery of the evangelical truth in the situation and in the Scripture, we dare not fail as women to assume the challenge with which we are faced in the task of doing theology today. We must assume together with men the task of the theology of liberation. And probably some light will be thrown on a theology that was done by only one-half of the population of the world for two thousand years.

28

Statement by Gustavo Gutiérrez

It is difficult to come and interject myself at this point in the meeting. I would have liked to have been much more aware of the dynamics of these days, and I'm sorry that I couldn't be present here with you. However, I don't want to take any more time in apologies. I'll say something about what people have told me and what I know has been the general orientation of these days. Before making three observations, I would like to give a few introductory remarks.

This week we are discussing theology, and all of us are aware that doing theology is important; but it's a secondary thing in the Christian life. The difficulties which we find in the first act, which is the act of liberation and of faith, are reflected when we start to do theology. I believe that there is progress in theology when the difficulties of the first act are reflected in the second act. In the past the difficulties in theology were strictly theological. Perhaps this was because the theologians were not actively committed to the social process, to the struggle against oppression and for a just society. And so the discussions were more theological than Christian. I'm happy to see the contradictions that are present in this assembly because they express a new way of living our faith and therefore of doing theology.

My observations consist in some reflections on this theology that we call the theology of liberation. First, we all know that Christianity has been very linked to a culture, to a race, and to a mode of production. By Christianity here, I understand something which is doctrinal, institutional, as well as cultic. That stage of Western history which we call Christendom is the largest and the longest experience that we have of Christianity. It dated from this time that Christianity expanded and extended itself to the rest of the world. At the same time in various ways the Western world began to dominate the rest of the world. These historical reflections always disturb us, and yet they're the backdrop against which we must do our present reflection. The extension of Christianity in the Western world has been linked with the expansion of the Western world itself. And we know that this Christianity as it expanded is marked by a Western culture and by the white race of the West. At the same time that religion, Christianity, and the West expanded there arose simultaneously a different mode of production which we, of course, call capitalism. This connection of Christianity, culture, race, and bourgeois class (the dominant class in the present mode of production) still marks the social and cultural world in which we find ourselves today.

The second observation: I believe that our job today is to reread history in terms of the poor, the humiliated, and the rejected of society. History, as some of our friends have said, has been written by a "white hand." I believe our first homework is to reread this history, to reread the struggles and the fights that have taken place in the last century. We all know the efforts that have been made to have those who have been beaten, the losers, forget their past. Today, we would like to return, to understand our own and each particular history. This is what has happened, for instance, with the history of Latin America. There are numerous attempts to turn history around and to reread it from the perspective of the poor. We must regain the memory of the "beaten Christs of the Indies," as Bartolomé de las Casas called the Indians of the American continent.

Nevertheless, a term like "rereading" may appear to be very intellectual. We are not capable today of rereading history if we are not present in the struggle for liberation. To reread history means to remake history. The rereading of the history of the humiliated is not a job for intellectuals on the left; rather, it is the result of a commitment and the struggle of the social classes that takes place today. And we enter into this class struggle by entering into what we call the historical praxis of liberation. What we understand by "praxis" is "transforming action," not simply any kind of action, but rather a historical transformation. *Historical* praxis means a transforming change, a transforming action of history. History, in this sense, must be understood as nature and society. It must be understood not simply as the history of groups but also as the transformation of nature. When we speak of a historical praxis we are speaking of the transforming action of history understood as transformation of nature, as the relationship of the person to nature, and as the relationship of the persons among themselves. By transforming praxis we mean a transforming action by the poor and the humiliated, by the despised races and marginated cultures themselves. It is a transforming action of history by all those whom the established order today does not recognize as persons: exploited classes, marginalized races, and the feminine sex. We are talking, then, about an action and a praxis which is subversive in the double meaning that subversive might have here. In the first place, we are talking about changing history, turning it on its head (*vertir*), and secondly, we are talking about a transforming historical praxis which comes from below (*sub: subvertir*-subversive). The established order has taught us that we are to think in a pejorative way of the term "subversive." But what we would rather reject is a "superversive" (coming down from the top) way of making history. The history which we have today is one which has been written by those who are conquerors and dominators. This subversive history is the place for a new experience of the faith, a new "spirituality," a new proclamation of the gospel. The poor are not only the hearers of the gospel; they are also, and especially, its bearers. The poor, the oppressed, must bring about a social appropriation of the gospel, and to do so they must seize it from the hands of the powerful of this world.

The third observation: We want to do theology from the "other," from a point outside of ourselves, that is to say, to recognize that until now Christianity has been linked with a culture, a race, and a certain way of production and, therefore, in great measure with a particular class. In the second place, it is to do this rereading from the point of view of the people who even now are seemingly outside of history. If this element is not present, the theology of liberation will be assimilated and co-opted by the system; it will be converted into just a new toy of theologians. The traditional theology has begun to be bored with itself; the theology of liberation might offer it some diversion and enable it to write something new—as with a toy. That would be to lose the locus, the place where the Christian faith is lived and pondered: among the people who are absent from history. As Peruvian writer José María Arguedas said, "The god of the *señores* is not the same," not the same as the God of the poor. The dominator is always an atheist, an atheist of the God of the Bible.

We all know that in recent years theology has entered into what we call a crisis of rationality. For some time there has been employed a way of thinking that is coherent but hasn't had much impact on contemporary thinking. To this must be added a great eclecticism in the manner of thinking theology. There are always some people who have a great nostalgia for the old system (scholastic and traditional theology), but the great majority have really understood that there is no real way of returning and doing theology as it used to be done. In this crisis of rationality it seems there are some things that began to bud and to appear which show the difficulty of rationality, and it appears on the part of those we call the nonpersons. It's clear I'm not using "nonperson" in a metaphysical sense but rather as a social reality and as a political argument. The marginated nonpersons have a way of understanding history and their social situation (social sciences, Marxist analysis, socialist path) that begins to be illuminative for thinking through faith in our day. In this whole new way of thinking, there is something very fundamental, that is, the rediscovery in some ways of God as love or, in the image which the New Testament uses, of God as Father.

To create this new history is to receive and grasp the gratuitous gift of God. That's why for many of us the great *pastoral* question—I don't like to use this old, rural term, but it says what I want to say at this moment—our great pastoral question from this situation of the oppressed and marginated of history is not in the first place how to talk about God in an adult world, as Bonhoeffer suggested. This is also an authentic pastoral question, and that's why the question of Bonhoeffer entered into a dialogue which gave new theological perspectives. (Theological questions give rise to new theological books; pastoral questions give rise to new theologies.) *Our* question is rather how can we say to the poor, to the exploited classes, to the marginated races, to the despised cultures, to all the minorities, to the nonpersons—how can we say that God is love and say that all of us are, and ought to be in history, sisters and brothers. How do we say this? This is our great question. How do we announce the free and gratuitous gift of God and his love for these "nonpersons"? If theology has any meaning, it is as an attempt to respond to this question, and consequently to offer something new, some suggestions in this social struggle to form this new society as sisters and brothers. And we know this is also a conviction. It is impossible to situate ourselves in the situation of the nonperson and not carry forward a conflictive struggle, a conflictive theology that will allow us to understand in a true way that we must love our enemies. Maybe in order to practice this part of the gospel it is necessary to have enemies. We must recognize our enemies in history; we must live our faith in this difficult commitment. It will lead us to understand the ways of the Lord on the road that we are walking today.

"How do you sing to God in a strange land?" the psalmist asked in exile. But how do you sing to God in a land alien to God's love, on a continent, in a country of oppression and repression? This is a serious questioning of the faith that leads us to something like a "new covenant," "with us who are here today all alive" (Deut. 5:3), breaking the historical alliance with the classes, culture, races that up until now have dominated. This leads Christianity to an alliance with the world's poor, toward a new type of universality. In some this creates real dread, and in others uneasiness, the loss of old securities. It is a path where, to use again Arguedas's words, "What we know is much less than the great hope that we feel."

SECTION EIGHT

A Sociological Interpretation of American Reality

By the second day of the conference the participants had been assigned to small working groups, which were to complement the general sessions.

In the morning a panel of social scientists presented papers to help provide the sociological basis for theological reflection. One of those invited to speak, Ronald Mueller, was unable to participate because of illness. His topic of multinational corporations was therefore not adequately dealt with in the presentations. The other three panelists, whose papers are included here, were Joseph Holland of the Center of Concern, Manuel Febres of the New School for Social Research in New York, and Michele Russell, black scholar and activist from Detroit.

North American Christians, and theologians in particular, find it strange and difficult to analyze their situation with the tools of social science. Many participants were hoping to find at Detroit a sociological analysis that provided an alternative to that of the established schools. The expectation was fulfilled only partially, but the panelists did provide an introduction that helped the participants to continue their social anlaysis throughout the week.

There was a consensus that to explore the meaning of the liberating message of Christ for North America we must understand the forms and mechanisms of

315

oppression that now exist. Identifying them will facilitate an understanding of the spiritual and social dimensions of Christian action and the theological task.

Russell, whose presentation had a profound impact on the participants, spoke on sexism as one of the most generalized forms of oppression, but also stressed that it cannot be considered as an isolated phenomenon.

Holland pointed out that, appearances notwithstanding, social classes do indeed exist in the United States today. The classical analysis of social stratification cannot be applied, however, because of the relative affluence and the ideological mystifications of the dominant sectors. But these should not be allowed to conceal the great difference in access to the means of social production.

Addressing himself to racism, Febres said that we must include in our analysis of this oppression the fact that the ruling classes used racism to prevent the multiracial coalition of liberation forces.

Several general themes emerged from the discussion around the social sciences: First, there is an important tradition of liberation struggles in the United States, especially the permanent resistance of blacks, workers, women, native Americans, and others to accepting the social world imposed by a small minority.

Second, one way of analyzing oppression in this country is to point out four of its forms: imperialism, sexism, classism, and racism. None of these can be reduced to another. Each has its own identity and its own historical, cultural, economic, and psychological roots. Nevertheless there is a relationship among them that must be discovered.

29

Marxian Class Analysis
in American Society Today

by Joseph Holland

Introduction

About ten to fifteen years ago, most people here today, including myself, would have thought only strange people would take the time and energy to discuss the question of Marx once again. It was presumed that question, which loomed large in the 1930s, was settled for American society in the post-World War II years. The extended postwar boom, which produced a dynamic sense of upward mobility as well as increased consumption for the domestic working classes, seemed to rule out the claims of Marx and socialism. During those years one could probably do even doctoral work in the social sciences, including economics, without dealing with Marx. Of course, he was always there as the enemy, but so presumed was his defeat that he no longer needed to be studied.

This was what certain sociologists referred to as the era of the "end of ideology." America had produced a "postindustrial society" whose dramatic growth, if it had not eliminated all poverty, soon would. Even in the sixties, when social pressures were brought to make the system keep its promises to the still large percentage of poor in the nation, people talked of expanding the system still further, not of changing its basic nature. The names given to government programs typified this consciousness, for example, "Upward Bound," "Manpower Development," "Office of Economic Opportunity," "Alliance for Progress," etc. The view was that the system simply had to be opened up more, its capacity for opportunity expanded, and social problems could be solved.

About midway through the sixties, a new consciousness began to emerge among many groups. Cut off from the old American left by the McCarthy purges on the domestic side of the Cold War, the new left (as it came to be called) sensed that the operating analysis was not adequate. People began to speak vaguely of the "system," although neither its nature nor the instrument of its change were clear. We stand today, perhaps, near a point of maturity within the new left, when it is retrieving the earlier tradition of the American left and when also it is developing sophistication and creativity about the social contradictions and resources of American society. I only say "near" because the contemporary American left is still small and weak, and not in good communication with the broad range of ordinary American people. Yet I say "near" too because there is a new seriousness, both in the depth of analysis and in its long-range commitment to processes of fundamental change in American society. Different from instant demands for overthrowing a vague system, the present American left is attempting to lay the theoretical, analytical, and organizational foundation for a historical project which may well reach beyond our own lifetimes.

But the American left is not the only group which has raised again the question of ideology and capitalism as fundamental social questions. Despite the many people in our society who maintain these still are not serious questions, there is one group outside the political left who disagrees, namely, American capitalists.

It seems we are witnessing a period of fresh offensive by the domestic capitalist class, at the economic, political, and cultural levels, against the fertilizing of socialist imagination and organization among the American people. At the cultural level, this is indicated by such "pop" phenomena as the cover article of the July 14, 1975, issue of *Time*, entitled, "Can Capitalism Survive?" Ten full pages are devoted to this discussion, concluding with a section on "The Virtues of Profits." It insists,

The freedom of capitalist society at its best must be prized above all. Capitalism demands by definition that the individual be free within broad limits to spend and invest his money any way he pleases, to own private property and to enter any business or profession that attracts him.

Obviously, for too many Americans, this freedom is not a practical freedom of everyday life. Also, it was recently announced that the Advertising Council of America will begin a massive publicity campaign on the "free enterprise system" and that Exxon is joining hands with Disney Productions to design a multimedia series on energy and free enterprise for high school seniors. Politically, the new offensive is signified in the strong rightist trend in American politics. This covers a wide range of phenomena, including the Nixon and Ford administrations, realignment of coalitions within the two dominant political parties, the Moynihan appointment to the United Nations, the growth of military presence within the executive branch (e.g., General Haig under Nixon, and Calloway, Ford's campaign manager), the increase of spying and of repression in general (e.g., the attempt to pass the S. 1 Bill), and the shift away from New Deal social policies. Economically, the offensive is clear in the strong attacks against the labor movement, the destruction of purchasing power by inflation, the willingness to tolerate as normal high levels of unemployment, and the sacrifice of domestic consumption for massive exports of food and arms in order to maintain a favorable national balance of payment within the international capitalist system. In sum, the outlook seems to point toward a stronger ideologizing of American life.

Presuming now that the question of Marx and capitalism or socialism are important within contemporary America, I would like to share some personal reflections on the substance of those questions. These reflections center in three areas: (1) the issue of Marxism and Christianity, (2) a Marxist retrieval of our past heritage, and (3) an analysis of the contemporary class structure of American society.

Marxism and Christianity

At the conscious level, the first question which arises among Christians is the atheism of Marx. Generally Marxist movements and religious movements have been bitter enemies across the world. This is in part due to the fact that Marx developed his thought within the climate of the secular and even antireligious currents of the Enlightenment. Like most scientists of his time, whether natural or historical scientists, Marx shared this climate. Also, the dominant religious elements of nineteenth-century Europe—Catholicism, Judaism, and Protestantism—were tied in their leadership to either reactionary feudal classes or to the new exploitative bourgeoisie.

While the question still remains a major one, and there is no space even to do justice to it here, we might simply observe that it is no longer so simple an antagonism as it first appeared. The churches have learned much from the physical sciences, despite the atheism of pioneers in this area. Thus, Darwin is assimilated creatively in the religious thought of Teilhard de Chardin. So also, it seems theoretically possible to assimilate the social thought and practical stance in the social world of Marx without rejecting the living God. Of course, this means in both cases a dramatic reinterpretation of the meaning of God, in the first case in relation to the processes of nature and biology, and in the second to the processes of history and societies.

Furthermore, we have the contemporary fact that there actually are many Marxists in the world who keep their religious faith, as well as many Christians who for some time now have turned to Marxian analytical tools in order to live more scientifically their struggle for justice. In turn, the two traditions are being affected by this encounter, both theoretically and practically. While it is premature to spell this out in any detail, it might be said that on the Marxian side there may well be an opening to transcendence as a critical source for continued social struggle, and on the Christian side there seems to be a return to history and social conflict as a locus of disclosure for the religious mystery.

Finally, the issue of Marxian class analysis is important for religious people simply in order to formulate adequate religious institutional policy within broader society. Because Western European Catholicism of the late nineteenth century did not understand the new socio-economic forces emerging in industrial capitalism, it was not able to design creative pastoral strategies for its own people. The result was the loss to the church of much of the Western European working classes. Pius X later called this the greatest religious tragedy of the nineteenth century. It may be today that religious institutions in the United States are experiencing a similar crisis. This might perhaps be said of American Catholicism, as both the immigration experience and the hope of upward mobility vanish from the horizon of the majority of Catholics, especially younger ones, who still remain working-class. The church is no longer the cultural or political center for their social life, as was the case until recently. So too, perhaps the black church, in its shift from the rural South to the urban North, may find the cultural consciousness of its working-class youth shifting in a way that no longer fits the old religious models.

It may be, then, that Marxian thought, despite its atheism, would be helpful in contemporary pastoral reflection.

Marxist Retrieval of the American Past

Unfortunately little work has been done in this area. A great deal of the Marxian tradition in the United States was built up and shaped by immigrant peoples whose perceptions were shaped by social struggles elsewhere. These Marxists came especially from Germany, but also from Italy, Poland, Hungary, Russia, and even the Caribbean. Most recently among many Christians the interest in Marxism is coming out of international struggles, either from the anti-imperialist movement against the Vietnam War or from people with experience in Latin America. These contributions are all helpful and important, but they do not give us direct access to our own past or present experience.

Part of the Theology in the Americas process has been to take some steps in precisely this area. I would, therefore, like to report to you the barest outline of some reflections shared more fully in my working paper, "The American Journey," done in collaboration with Mary Burke and William Ryan (sub-titled, "Toward a Critical and Constructive Analysis of the American Struggle against Class Exploitation, Imperialism, Racism, and Sexism"). The paper has three sections, the first dealing with independence and democracy in the American foundation; the second with the period of American expansion, both outwardly in geography and internally in productivity and in the size of the labor force (a period which covers most of American history); the third, the present period of limits and crises, with some projection of possible scenarios out of the crises.

The paper begins by pointing out what great hopes the American experiment raised across the world. It then asks how could America in two centuries come to be viewed by so many people in the world community as the enemy of freedom. It is certainly not because the struggle for freedom has been absent from American history; America contains perhaps one of the world's richest and bloodiest stories of that struggle. It could be that the structural context of the struggle, namely the economic, political, and cultural institutions of capitalism, either neutralized or retarded it.

The foundation of the United States was a period more complex than our school books tell us. Already there were strong class and racial antagonisms in the society. The American elite—merchants and traders in the northern and central Atlantic coast and planters in the South—decided on independence because the British empire, itself shifting to industrial capitalism, began to turn harsh economic screws against the formerly comfortable colonies. Since these screws were felt by the poor, the workers, and small farmers as well as by the elites, the controlling classes were able to gather national solidarity around the independence struggle.

Structurally, however, the bid for independence had to be also a bid for a separate American empire, since the colonies were already well integrated within the world trading system of the British.

Gradually in American history, the imperial side of the American experience took on racist tones and its control of new territories, markets, and labor forces was justified along ethnic lines.

But if the independence movement produced great national solidarity against the British, that solidarity was only a fragile coalition. Immediately in the postwar period there were great struggles between workers and small farmers on one side and the controlling elites on the other. Shays Rebellion in Massachusetts is the best known example. This, of course, says nothing of the still deeper conflict between the native Americans or black slaves and the rest of the society. In reaction against populist pressures, the political structuring of the society took a conservative course along the lines of a system of checks and balances which, while preventing the tyranny of a single person, also made it difficult for popular will to take institutionalized expression.

Really there were two interpretations of democracy in play, undifferentiated in the Declaration of Independence: the freedom of people and the freedom of property; but in the early Constitution the power of property gained the upper hand.

The period of expansion which followed the foundation is also rich and complex. In the course of two centuries the United States grew from a cluster of tiny colonies snuggled along the Atlantic coast to a giant nation dominating the world both militarily and economically. Territories, peoples, and markets came under the sway of the U.S.A., either explicitly or implicitly, both by subtlety and by brute force, across the continent and throughout the world. Similarly, the industrial productivity of the nation grew dramatically, especially after the Civil War. America moved into the maturity of an industrial capitalist society by crushing semifeudal patterns in its South, by amassing a giant labor force from the displaced European peasantry and from its own southern and western peasantries, by attracting capital both for venture and for security from the world over, and by spurring productive capacity in a long series of wars.

At the same time, the majority of the people were exploited in a complex process which affected distinct groups differently. Native Americans were driven from their lands in near-genocidal patterns. Slaves were converted first into a rural peasantry of tenant farmers and sharecroppers, and then into a secondary labor market for the industries and service sectors of the North. Chicanos were converted into a migrant and stationary agricultural proletariat as well, and partially drawn into the secondary urban labor market with other peoples of color. European and Asian immigrants were lured with the promise of riches to staff the mines and factories and build the railroads of the new industrial base. In turn women of these groups were sought as cheap labor, especially in textiles, where men demanded higher wages. All these peoples and groups of people were whirled together in an exploding and expanding nation. Each was often pitted against the other, not only by conspiracy (although that too), but mainly by the complexity and dynamism of the new social experience organized around chaotic markets of capital, commodities, and labor.

The story of the nation throughout this period is paradoxically marked by the combination of a single and shallow official history and a pluralism of forgotten and repressed particular histories. On the official side was the myth of the melting pot and the WASP ideal (never real even for most WASPs); on the other were the separate stories of the many racial/ethnic groups whose unique tales—both in their separateness and in their commonality—carry a rich stream of dreams and hopes, as well as of tragedies and bitter struggles.

These separate forces simply could not come together so long as the nation was young, still filling its spaces and expanding outwards. People were structurally running from one another and from themselves, rather than discovering at the same time both the self and the other again in uniqueness and commonality. Finally, their separate and common sufferings were consoled and even hidden by the dream of upward mobility and "making it"—a real fact for a significant minority of the working classes, at least so long as expansion continued.

American expansion, however, was not a consistent process; it was marked by severe crises, such as the depression of the 1930s. As a result of periodic crises beginning after the Civil War, a socialist American left began to emerge. Counting among its ranks such great names as Gene Debs, the American left attempted in varying degrees to challenge the negative elements of American society, while affirming the best promises of the nation's dream. The American left remained weak in contrast to its European counterparts, and under the Palmer Raids of the twenties and the McCarthy purge of the fifties was subjected to massive repression.

There were many reasons, however, other than repression, for the weakness of the American left. America was a young and unstable nation. Its working class was racially, culturally, linguistically, regionally, and sexually divided. Finally, at critical points, the system was able to "deliver the goods" for a significant number of workers, in addition to promising generous opportunity for upward mobility in a distinct American climate of egalitarianism.

The third period begins with American defeat in Vietnam and the end of the Cold War, with the recent crisis of both supply and price around raw materials and energy sources like oil, and with the structural inability of the social system to support its population. This is the limit of the American experience, the closeout of the frontier which even President Kennedy could not expand. In one sense it marks the end of all that America has been so far, but in another sense it marks the beginning of a search for an authentically common, but pluralist identity and purpose. In this latter sense, it is perhaps the true beginning of the history of the *American* people. (The philosopher Hegel argued that American history would not truly begin until this point was reached.) In this latter sense too, it is a period of great creativity, but also a period of great danger.

We might speak now of two separate scenarios projected out of this crisis. There is no absolute compulsion that history go either of these two ways, and indeed history is always more cunning than human imagination, but let us project two polar opposites.

The first scenario, and the more probable based on the present course, is for "friendly fascism" in the land. For many reasons too numerous and complex to describe here, the nation is not able to make good on the promises which nourished the personal struggles of so many of America's working-class people. We might foresee a tendency of downward social mobility across all sectors of the population, coupled by higher visibility for the social elite. High rates of unemployment will be taken as normal, as well as decreasing purchasing power for workers. Consumption will go down among the lower and middle classes. In turn, competition over scarce economic resources could intensify, causing bitter tensions along racial and ethnic lines, as well as geographic division. This in turn would generate great social unrest, requiring strong repression of the labor movement and of leftist political forces. Force could begin to replace persuasion in the system and government in general could take on a repressive character. There might still be elections, but the realm of choice would be limited. In addition, American capital might be drawn more into lucrative foreign investments, while the domestic economy might be structured around financial and technical management of a global system, and the defense production required for it. The American dream would at worst turn into a nightmare, or at best into a sad disappointment.

The second scenario would be some form of "socialist challenge" to the present structures of American society. Given the weak and divided state of the present American left, it would be difficult to say at this point what shape that might take. The point, however, remains that it would be theoretically possible to undertake a fundamental restructuring of the nation in all its relationships—a restructuring which could improve the quality of life for all, while simultaneously eliminating the structural exploitations of contemporary capitalism.

Given the still weak stage of the American left and the acceleration of the present structural crisis, the odds for triumph of this second alternative in the short run are very weak. Those interested in fundamental restructuring of American society, therefore, should probably be thinking in long-range terms, although the potential radicalization of American populism should not be ruled out. One factor which may make a difference in which way America goes is how people concerned with social change deal with the question of class.

Class Structure of American Society

Since the United States is a complex society, its internal class structure and the dynamic of that structure are both also complex. The conflict between capital and labor at once tells us everything and nothing. Therefore, there is need for a complex and concrete analysis of class in contemporary American society. I will not try to do that here, since I do not believe it has been well done by anyone so far, but will simply outline some elements for such a project.

The issue of class is not well defined in Marx's theoretical work. The one point where he did attempt to deal with this issue systematically—the last volume of *Capital*—breaks off before he finished. We do know, however, that classes are rooted in the relations of production, not consumption. Thus social classes are determined not by how much money you make or don't make, but by your relationship to the society's process of economic production.

The first fundamental division is between those who control the means of production and those who do not. Now because the production system of the United States is complex, this is not a clear-cut area. Still, in any analysis those who control the main productive facilities of the United States would be very few—including their families probably much less than 1 percent of the population.

At the other extreme, we have the very poor who in many cases are excluded from production, or who interact with production in the precarious secondary labor market.

What falls between these two is extremely complex and I won't even approach it here. For some initial efforts in this regard, one might examine Judah Hill's *Class Analysis in the United States in the*

1970's (available for $1.75 from Class Analysis, P.O. Box 8494, Emeryville, CA 94662).

In analyzing class, there are perhaps four ingredients which are important for a holistic class analysis.

1. *The relation between structure and process.* It is important to develop a sophisticated and concrete analysis of the class location of all sectors of the American population, but it is also important to understand those sectors as expressions of a dynamic process, changing within themselves and in their relation with other classes. One important question which arises out of the process is what political alliances or coalitions are evolving, either actually or potentially, and what is their relation to fundamental social change.

2. *The relation between objective and subjective factors.* While most people have not thought of American society in class terms (the subjective side), it in fact has a class structure (the objective side). Marxists generally devote their energy to the objective side, which is very important and even fundamental. But in American society, where the myth of classlessness is strong, or where class is often disregarded in popular movements of social protest, it is very important to investigate the subjective side. What myths and rituals inform the consciousness of the many sectors of the American people? How do these interact with the objective side? In this regard, Marxists could learn much from non-Marxist social scientists who have studied more the processes of consciousness. The names of Freud, Jung, Weber, and Durkheim come to mind here. It may be that the forces of reaction understand much better than leftists the importance of subjective processes of consciousness like myth and ritual. Recall the use of fire by the KKK or the Nazis. Marxism, coming directly out of the Enlightenment tradition, may not understand well the metarational elements of the human psyche. This may be especially true of Marxism in advanced industrial societies, which cannot automatically draw on the old poetic or mystical traditions, in the manner of say the Chilean Marxist poet, Pablo Neruda. Marxism may be successful in the Third World precisely because the rationalism of the West has not been strong enough to divorce intellectuals (even leftist intellectuals) from the metarational in human culture. Here, of course, religious peoples with leftist orientations could be very creative.

3. *The relation between class and other social factors.* There is a danger for Marxists to reduce everything to class. It is ironic that while Marxism was born of a strongly antinationalist sentiment, Marxism has been most successful precisely where it has understood and integrated itself with national identity. It has historically been the

weakness of American Marxism that it was not really able to deal with the issues of patriotism, race, ethnicity, or sexuality in American society, despite some important political and theoretical contributions. So too the matters of functional differentiation within social class, or the matter of regional differentiation within the nation, remain to be probed. Again, the tendency for Marxists, when examining religious phenomena, to reduce all to class may actually impede them from tapping powerful resources in support of movements of social change.

The issue of class, I suspect, will become an ever more powerful factor in social analysis and social movements in contemporary American society. Yet there will be differing interpretations of class, even by those who accept its importance. For example, in the present busing controversies, most people from the black community are saying it is a racial, not a class issue. Many in the "white ethnic" community are saying it is a class issue, not a race issue, and that white liberals and their establishment allies are manipulating class groups. Yet the Communist party, probably the greatest advocate of class analysis in American society, is strongly probusing, while many of the Third World-oriented Marxists in American society view community control as more important than bused integration. I say all this not to favor one side or the other, but to point out that it is hardly enough to raise the issue of class. That brings me to my fourth and final point about class analysis.

4. *Who does the analysis?* In the busing issue, we have seen that one can accept class analysis and still come out on either side of the issue. The same could be said about any number of issues from détente with the Soviet Union to the strategies of the women's movement. Therefore, it seems that the process of class analysis must involve as seriously as possible the two following factors:

a. Grounding in critical *theoretical* resources of the Marxist tradition itself: This would mean that Marxism not be accepted as an established canon of dogmas, but as an organic and on-going intellectual tradition constantly in need of criticism and creativity.

b. As broad an action/reflection *network* as possible: This would mean that the participation of people from all sectors and groups of American society, within a broad proletarian framework, must be built up and constantly improved.

The coordination of these two factors could probably occur only within the framework of a political party or political movement. It would have to be, however, a party which takes seriously both the intellectual ground and the perceptions and needs of ordinary people.

The structure and nature of such a party in turn raises other issues which go beyond the task of this paper.

Conclusion

To end, I would like to recall something from the beginning. We are, it seems, entering a new period in which American capitalism will undertake a fresh offensive out of deep crisis. It may well win this offensive despite our resistance, but it will certainly win if we do not understand well the economic, political, and cultural class strategies it undertakes. For that reason alone, I suggest, the question of Marxian class analysis will become increasingly important for all people concerned with the real welfare and the common good of the people of America and of the whole world.

30

Racism in the U.S.A.

by *Manuel Febres*

The discussion on racism in America revolves primarily around the history of slavery, types of race relations, and the racial attitudes of citizens. We do not deny the importance of these factors in analyzing contemporary racism. Neither do we limit the boundaries of our study to a mere evaluation of how cruel or liberal slavery was, or how humane interracial relations are today. Psycho-cultural approaches, better represented by Frank Tannenbaum,[1] are partially responsible for an idealistic view which in turn has distracted both the antiracist struggle and debate. Such a bourgeois outlook can induce us into psychologistic positions and possibly into purely moralistic strategies.

To avoid those erroneous and dilatory consequences racism must be seen in connection with and within its class context. In this work we argue in support of these points: (1) Racism, as an ideology of control, emerges after discrimination; (2) United States capitalism sustains and strengthens racism as a means to protect the ruling classes and to prevent the formation of a broad multiracial revolutionary coalition. These two points can be amply confirmed by U.S. history from the colonial times to the present. Considering space and time limitations, the author chose to provide a broad historico-theoretical framework for the study of racism in the U.S. rather than an account of the many struggles against racism. For this reason, and with reluctance, subjects like the Civil Rights vs. the Black Power approaches were not analyzed in this paper. A "face-save" mentioning of these important issues would not do justice to them.

We are not concerned about the Europeans' early reactions after their first contact with black Africans. This reaction could have been prejudicial and still would not discard our contention. These individual reactions did not constitute the basis for discrimination; neither did they provide sufficient grounds for the development of a modern racist ideology. Racism may be defined as a set of social institutions and ideas geared toward the "systematic oppression of one racial group by another."[2] This compact definition includes, but is not limited to, individual expressions of racism. In other words we are referring to an entire social machinery whose objectives include the segregation, exploitation, and degradation of a supposedly inferior racial group.

Defined in this fashion racism does not have to be linked, by necessity, to slavery. As an expression of discrimination, slavery has existed without racism on almost every continent. When involuntary servitude provided a socio-economic basis for the ancient Greek democracy, slave status was determined by circumstantial rather than racial factors. Being member of a defeated army or conviction by an authorized court were among the means by which an individual became a slave. There was no generalized theory in which a particular racial group was inseparably identified with slavery or a condition of natural inferiority. A second example can be seen in the subordination and exploitation of American Indians during the Spanish conquest. Countless sixteenth century chronicles tell us about the Indians' great technological and organizational achievements in Central and South America. Spain, with its greed and inclination toward plunder, did not hide its admiration for those achievements. Once Spain realized the economic potential involved, rationalizations to keep the Indians dominated emerged. Very seldom were these justifications made on the principle of the Indians' intrinsic racial inferiority.

The institution of the indentured servants during the seventeenth and eighteenth centuries makes our point even clearer. Inasmuch as servant and master belonged to the same white race, this institution left only a class difference between slaves and masters. Even this class difference could be at least theoretically avoidable in the future, if the ex-servant turned into a successful planter. These and other factors made virtually impossible a racist justification of white slavery. Our examples show that racist slavery as such has not been the typical much less the only form of slavery throughout history. This kind of servitude was to a great extent the last and most efficient expression of this mode of human exploitation.

How then did racist slavery come about in North America? What were the material conditions that gave impulse to racist slavery? To answer these questions we must look at the problems faced by English imperialism during the seventeenth century. By mid-century England already had a general idea of the vast economic potential of a plantation empire in the New World. This realization developed into the important "triangular trade," prime source of capital accumulation for the first industrial capitalist nation.[3] But before this accumulation could develop, an efficient mode of production and a politically stable colonial system had yet to be established. This was not precisely what the British planters were experiencing at the moment. On the contrary, contemporary documents show a very uneasy and fearful propertied class. Far from being a remote possibility, joint actions and conspiracies by the oppressed occurred on more than several occasions. These actions, ignored by pseudohistorians, frequently involved indentured servants, black slaves, free blacks, and even small farmers.[4] The importance of those plots or actual rebellions was the subordination of the fact of racial differences to the larger question of class condition. Living through a similar oppressive situation, multiethnic groups carried out a united action in a way that many would consider impossible today.

Bacon's Rebellion is one of the best examples of those anti-ruling class coalitions. Originally a dispute with Indian rebels during the winter of 1676, it took only a few months for the people to reorient their forces against their real class enemies: the plantocracy. Hundreds of black and white guerrillas, free and slave, addressed their weapons against the propertied and their government representatives in Virginia. Their demands were freedom from servitude and a fair chance to develop a decent livelihood. Once part of the main city was burned and Governor Berkeley forced out of its borders, these rebellious workers still demanded their liberation. After a government-promoted truce the rebels were betrayed and disarmed by one of Berkeley's representatives. The promises of freedom and amnesty for the rebels were never met. On the contrary they were returned to their masters and punished for their "crimes."

Developments like this and other slave rebellions in the Caribbean forced a change in British colonial and slave policies. This new policy had to yield better social control. It is precisely at this historical juncture where great impetus is given to racial divisions as a means to protect imperialist and class interests. Deliberate promotion of racism will constitute an instrument of division and manipulation of the working classes for the benefit and security of those in power. Through various means and forms of institutionalization, racism reached the strength of many other important components of the

American way of life. Racism, in different degrees and styles, will be applied to other non-black immigrant groups, but always with the same class fragmentation effects.[5] The aim does not change: the prevention of another Bacon's Rebellion.

Significant changes were observed with the implementation of the new policy. The composition and ways in which labor was organized changed. Aside from small farmers much of the agricultural work would be done by African slaves. This was accompanied by the gradual elimination of indentured servants, who formed a group larger than the African workforce before the eighteenth century. Substituting one group for another and thereby increasing the profits from an ever-growing slave trade was not enough to appease the colonies. It was necessary to involve poor whites, at least symbolically, in the ideology and structure of racist domination. Therefore they were recruited as enforcers (policemen and soldiers) of the established order.[6] Other whites were encouraged to keep guard and "protect their own interests against the niggers." Negrophobia, cultivated and assimilated, became a norm in Virginia, the pacesetter in these matters. Identification of slavery with being black not only cast shadows over class contradictions among whites but also strengthened the control over black people. As T. W. Allen puts it in his excellent article, "The non-slavery of white labor was the indispensable condition for the slavery of black labor."[7]

The eighteenth century marks the development and consolidation of racist slavery and its distorting effects over class consciousness and class struggle. At the moment of independence racism was already established in North America.[8] The "Founding Fathers" and the Constitution reflected this fact by disregarding abolition of slavery and ignoring black people's rights in general. Property rights were considered above everything else. It was particularly important not to disturb the ruling classes' coalition or balance between the industry-inclined North and the slavery-based plantation economy in the South.

Although Northern states also used slavery to some extent and benefited from Southern slavery for some time, this state of affairs did not last long. By the 1820s British anti-slave trade policy already threatened this commerce. Later, high costs of slave-produced raw commodities imposed even worse conditions on Northern industrialists. These and other developments deteriorated the original conditions upon which collaboration and support of slavery were founded. Further acceleration of North-South contradictions provoked what many have called "the inevitable conflict." Resolution of these contradictions was a *sine qua non* requirement if a unified and progressive capitalist economy was ever to emerge. For Marx and other contemporary observers it was "certain that the North [would] win in the end."[9] By mid-century the South was economically dependent on the industrial North at the same time that the North refused any significant accommodation.[10]

What was the situation among the oppressed classes? Generally speaking they remained effectively divided. However, there were several instances in which abolitionists—blacks and whites—joined efforts to push emancipation as a decisive issue before the nation. Both slave runaways and free blacks on the one hand and militant white abolitionists on the other helped and succeeded in popularizing the antislavery issue. It can be claimed that without those men and women, emancipation would have been disregarded as an unimportant consideration. Among the blacks, each in his or her own historical context, we can mention David Walker, Nat Turner, Sojourner Truth, Harriet Tubman, Frederick Douglass, and other true militants. But these heroes and heroines should not be confined within the narrow view of the Western idea of a hero. They were reflections as well as integral components of the black masses' struggles and aspirations. White abolitionists such as Wendel Phillips, W. L. Garrison, John Brown, Charles Sumner, and Thaddeus Stevens also helped shape the final form of the "irrepressible conflict."

Although most abolitionists' actions were not executed by interracial coalitions, many antislavery activists were conscious of the broader class implications of their own conditions and actions. Despite the blurring effects institutionalized racism has over class contradictions, militants like Frederick Douglass, an ex-slave, saw the similarities in the exploitation of both blacks and poor whites. Douglass clearly saw racism as an instrument of the ruling classes. As he said just before the Civil War:

The slaveholders, with a craftiness peculiar to themselves, by encouraging the enmity of the poor, laboring white man against the blacks, succeeded in making the said white man almost as much a slave as the black man himself. The difference between the white slave and the black slave is this: the latter belongs to one slaveholder, and the former belongs to all slaveholders collectively.[11]

On the question of manipulation of oppressed whites to distract them from their objective class condition, Douglass continued:

They [the plantocracy] appeal to their pride, often denounce emancipation, as tending to place the white workingman on an equality with negroes, and by this means, they succeed in drawing off the minds of the poor whites from the real fact, that, by the rich slave master, they are already regarded as but a single remove from equality with the slave.[12]

Unfortunately this progressive view of racial and class oppression in the U.S. was never adopted by the large masses. The agitation and propaganda displayed by the ideologically advanced was not enough to outweigh a long history of racial divisions. This situation became more tragic when the government finally succumbed to reactionary forces.

Immediately after the Civil War the policies in Washington appeared to be solidly behind the formal political rights of blacks. Congressional legislation and White House commissions and representatives demonstrated some initial support to meet the most elementary constitutional rights of all freed men. However, before 1875 the old Southern reactionary power structure was regaining its strength. To this the presidents, the Congress, and the Judiciary responded with traitorous complicity as they retreated even from their lip-service "progressive" positions.[13]

This retreat in Washington only reflected a new accommodation of the ruling classes. It is true that during reconstruction there was a new emergence of interracial workers' alliances. But the rise of populism and other democratic movements warned the developing financial oligarchy and the "new" Southern plantocracy. Fearful of a "Negro invasion" and encouraged by government irresponsibility, Northern racism, differing only in form from the Southern variety, was strongly sustained as a means of socio-political control. The Supreme Court decision upholding the doctrine of "separate but equal" in 1896 symbolized official approval of the triumphs scored by Southern racist politicians during that decade.

It is generally agreed that the 1890s marked the definite recovery of plantation power throughout the South and consequently a worsening of socio-economic conditions for blacks. In this circumstance *Plessy* v. *Ferguson*, with its "separate but equal" stand, added an air of constitutional validity to the conditions of neoslavery which lasted over fifty years. Between 1910 and 1920 racial oppression came into full expression throughout the nation; dozens of race riots and lynchings resulted in the death and injury of hundreds of black people.

Organizations like Garvey's Universal Negro Improvement Association (UNIA) and the National Association for the Advancement of Colored People (NAACP) attempted to provide some direction earlier in the century. Unfortunately, a good deal of their potential was consumed by internal fights caused by personal, ideological, and class differences among groups and leaders.[14] As far as the creation of a massive movement is concerned, the situation remained largely unchanged until the 1950s, when several liberal court decisions apparently turned on a light at the end of the tunnel. In 1954 the *Brown v. Board of Education* case overturned the 1896 racist decision, thereby reviving the hopes of "equality through legal changes." After the enacting of a number of relatively significant civil rights laws, the once vigorous movement began to dwindle after 1965. Despite the general sympathy evoked by Rev. Martin Luther King, Jr., the movement's maximum leader, this weakening trend showed no reversal. Instead, Black Power emerged as an alternative movement, promoted by the speeches and actions of the radical youth who felt dissatisfied with civil rights organizations. Presently, the emphasis on black communities' self-determination seems to be the central point for most Black Power advocates. Nevertheless, in my opinion, the movement is still in the process of developing an improved ideology as well as a realistic strategy.[15]

Returning to the evolution of racism as such, a word must be said about the relationship between the late nineteenth-century "manifest destiny" and North American racial oppression. The new expansionist myth further intensified the old racist contempt toward non-white and racially mixed people. The Cuban-Spanish-American War furnished an opportunity for the expression of economic and racist imperialism beyond U.S. geographical limits. Cuba, Puerto Rico, and the Philippines would be first in line. Later the entire Western hemisphere would feel the impact of this ever-expanding force. All of us experience this force in at least two of its manifestations: that of monopoly-capital imperialism and that of racism under the guise of a "God-given mission" as the "white man's burden."[16] This process of expansion also received consistent approval by the Supreme Court in subsequent decisions.[17]

Racism, class oppression, imperialism, and official sanction, all in one set, comprised more than enough forces to postpone indefinitely a multiracial working class movement. We are not saying that all forms of class struggle were kept in a prolonged abeyance. Capital and labor have never been in complete harmony. However, for the most part of the twentieth century, workers' movements have been influenced by racism and other dividing factors very much like in the past century. The relatively few cases of significant multiracial labor unions deserve a separate paper. Cases such as the early Council of Industrial Organizations and the United Mine Workers could be considered as initial examples. But the experience of union leaders like A. Philip

Randolph indicates that racism still rules within organized labor.

Even some of the better multiracial unions did not go far enough beyond attacking certain internal racist policies and individual attitudes. If we go back to our definition we realize that North American racism is not just a moral—or rather immoral—stand. It needs racist structures, racist socio-political institutions, racist behavior patterns, and an internalized racist frame of mind. Finally, it needs an army of alienated people, mainly white workers and bureaucrats, who, being disoriented enough, believe that by defending the status quo they are advancing their own precarious position. Let us not be naive: The white working class has enjoyed some benefits from the existing racist structures. However, these workers and their pro-establishment leaders are denying to themselves the alternative of a more secure system for all. Any labor union that considers itself seriously opposed to institutionalized racism must then attack the capitalist system which promotes this specific type of racism. In other words, there is no complete freedom from racism within American capitalism unless this system is radically changed.

The last two great wars and their demand for workers and soldiers were events frequently associated with the transformation of the old blatant racism. World War I brought a tremendous stimulus to Southern migration towards the Northern cities. Industrial labor was in great demand and many firms went as far as sending recruiters to the South. Despite the resistance of Southern landholders, migration continued, reaching a high point in 1917. By 1920 New York and Philadelphia had increased its black population 35 and 40 percent respectively. Other industrial centers, originally with small black contingents, had increments of 120 percent (Chicago) or even 700 percent (Detroit).[18]

These newcomers expected a significantly different experience than they had in the South, that is, exclusion from Southern industrial expansion between 1880 and 1915. In fact they did experience something more positive during the first years. The majority of male migrants were absorbed either by industrial firms or the Armed Forces. Although heavy migration was still observable during the early 1920s, things no longer looked as good as they appeared during the early war years. Military and industrial demobilization and increased black migration was met by a new wave of racist industrial practices. Both capitalists and privileged white workers engaged in the old game of blaming "black surplus labor" for the job insecurity of an emerging proletarian aristocracy.[19] The gradual hardening of attitudes and policies geared toward the subjugation of black workers became more obvious. Concentrating blacks into the least desirable, worst paid, and most dangerous jobs was one of the trends that best linked white capitalists and privileged white workers. Popularization of Southern expressions such as "Negro jobs" were clear monuments to the emergent patterns of systematic racial oppression. A growing labor movement, which in some cases allowed black contingents, was not seriously concerned about the black workers' fate. Moreover, in many instances collaborationist unions helped in the active shaping and enforcing of racist policies.

As if this situation were not sufficiently bad, the approaching of 1930 brought even worse conditions for blacks and other oppressed groups. The Great Depression reduced opportunities for both urban and rural jobs. This was supplemented by police and Ku Klux Klan terror in the South. F. D. Roosevelt's New Deal programs heightened black people's expectations beyond reasonable levels. Presidential ambiguity about the special exploitation suffered by black people is well known. Roosevelt's initial refusal to openly support the anti-lynching bill indicated an unwillingness to risk "Southern votes in Congress on other matters." Even L. I. Fishel's mild criticism states that "like Lincoln's, Roosevelt's actual commitments to the American Negro were slim. He was more a symbol than activist in his own right."[20]

Nevertheless, the New Deal and its agencies were largely popular. They assisted in alleviating some of the worst aspects of the depression as it affected the exploited masses. By introducing more social legislation, improving security for the bank system, providing greater government spending, and other Keynesian measures, F.D.R. was able to significantly extend the life of capitalism. As far as black people are concerned, the New Deal programs, at best, ran with insufficient determination to affect racist structures. In many cases local authorities were let free to implement relief programs with obvious discriminatory results. A case in point was Jacksonville, Florida, where "Negro families on relief outnumbered white families three to one, but the money was divided according to proportions of the total city population. Thus, 15,000 Negro families received 45 per cent of the funds and 5,000 white families got 55 per cent."[21] Similar examples were seen at the Tennessee Valley Authority (TVA), the Federal Employment Relief Administration (FERA) and the Agricultural Adjustment Administration (AAA).

World War II brought a number of ambiguous results for black workers. On the one hand it gave a much needed impulse to a depressed economy. This in turn strengthened capitalism and Roosevelt's position. Also it provided more industrial jobs and a postwar improvement of the standard of living. But as in the 1920s, progress was unevenly distributed (see Table I). Unlike the previous wartime, blacks showed more political experience. They became conscious of the contradictions inherent in their cooperation with a racist army which defended a racist U.S.A. against another Western racist regime. Those blacks who remained as civilians confirmed again the dual nature of their oppression as black workers.

Table I is only a partial view of the serious obstacles posed by institutionalized racism. The conformist or the racist would tend to overemphasize the significance of column 2, where nonwhites are shown with a median income increment of nearly 800 percent in thirty years. For us it is more significant that many lives, movements, and aspirations have been dedicated to the cause of black liberation, and yet, after centuries of struggle, black males still earn only 54 to 57 percent of the white median income (see average of column 4). The figures in Table I can be used in a variety of ways; nevertheless they clearly illustrate a persistent pattern of exclusion that for too long has kept nonwhites in the lowest socio-economic stratum. Such a statement may sound too obvious, but the important question here is the critical historical context in which racial oppression persists today. The grim reality shown in the above table would not have created as great a resentment among black people in 1900 as it does today. Racial resentment never coexisted with such catalytic factors as the Third World anti-imperialist and socialist revolutions. Also new is the very fact that blacks have used almost every legal means conceivable in their liberation struggle, only to end with symbolic or piecemeal improvements. Those two factors, that is, the analogous international struggles and the growing historical frustration, are speedily becoming integral parts of the Afro-American consciousness. There is a need to formulate a revolutionary theory that would lead the black movement and translate the new resentment into liberating actions.

As we have suggested, the new scope would have to include a class perspective if some of the past misjudgments are to be avoided. A class approach to racism not only would strengthen the new anti-racist struggle and its ideology but, in addition, it would enable this particular struggle to eventually join and make its own contribution to the liberation forces in general. The new formulation will have to be made by the praxis—combined theoretical and practical political work—of both leaders and all concerned communities. It seems to us that that formulation is slowly but surely taking place today. However, the discussion of this process should be the subject of another paper.

TABLE I:
Median Annual Income of White and Nonwhite Males
(1939–1969)

	1	2	3	4
				Percent of
	White	Nonwhite	White/Nonwhite	Nonwhite
Year	Males	Males*	Difference	to White+
1939	$1112	$ 460	$ 652	41
1945	2176	1158	1018	53
1946	2223	1367	856	61
1947	2357	1279	1078	54
1948	2510	1363	1147	54
1949	2471	1196	1275	48
1950	2982	1828	1154	61
1951	3101	1708	1393	51
1952	3255	1784	1471	55
1953	3396	1870	1526	55
1954	3359	1678	1681	50
1955	3542	1868	1674	53
1956	3827	2000	1827	52
1957	3910	2075	1835	53
1958	3976	1981	1995	50
1959	4208	1977	2231	47
1960	4297	2258	2039	53
1961	4432	2292	2140	52
1962	4460	2291	2369	49
1963	4816	2507	2209	52
1964	4936	2797	2139	57
1965	5290	2848	2443	54
1966	5592	3097	2495	55
1967	5862	3448	2414	59
1968	6267	3827	2440	61
1969	6765	3935	2830	55

*95 percent of this group are black.

+100 percent indicates perfect income equality; 0 percent indicates perfect inequality.

SOURCE: U.S. Bureau of the Census, Current Population Reports—Consumer Income, Series P-60, "Income of Families and Persons in the United States," annual issues, shown as it appears in R.S. Franklin and S. Resnik, *The Political Economy of Racism* (New York: Holt, Rinehart and Winston, 1973), p. 38.

NOTES

1. Frank Tannenbaum, *Slave and Citizen* (New York: Vintage Books, 1946).

2. C. V. Hamilton and S. Carmichael, "Institutional Racism and the Colonial Status of Blacks," in Richard Edwards et al., *The Capitalist System* (Englewood Cliffs, N.J.: Prentice-Hall, 1972).

3. Eric Williams, *Capitalism and Slavery* (New York: Putnam, 1966), ch. 5.

4. T. W. Allen, *Class Struggle and the Origin of Racial Slavery* (booklet reprinted from *Radical America*, May-June 1975).

5. Ibid., p. 9.

6. Ibid., p. 4.

7. Ibid., p. 5.

8. Eugene D. Genovese, *The Political Economy of Slavery* (New York: Vintage Books, 1967), pp. 15–18.

9. Karl Marx and Friedrich Engels, *Selected Correspondence* (New York: International Publishers, 1942), p. 136.

10. Genovese, *Political Economy*, pp. 159–67.

11. Marvin Harris, *Patterns of Race in the Americas* (New York: Norton, 1974), p. 91.

12. Ibid., p. 92.

13. Paul Lewinson, *Race, Class and Party* (New York: Grosset and Dunlap, 1965), pp. 58–60.

14. See E.U. Essien-Udon, "Garvey and Garveyism," in *America's Black Past*, ed. Eric Foner (New York: Harper and Row, 1970), pp. 352–70.

15. This process is seen through the writings and speeches of Stokely Carmichael, H. Rap Brown, Malcolm X, Angela Davis, the *Black Scholar* magazine, and other black publications.

16. Richard Hofstadter, *The Paranoid Style in American Politics and Other Essays* (New York: Knopf, 1965), p. 176.

17. L. Gould, *La Ley Foraker: Raices de la política colonial de Estados Unidos* (Rio Piedras, Puerto Rico: Editorial Universidad de Puerto Rico, 1965), pp. 145–67.

18. H. Baron, *The Demand for Black Labor* (Radical America, 1971), p. 20.

19. Ibid., pp. 22–23.

20. L.H. Fishel, "The Negro in the New Deal Era" in Foner, *America's Black Past*, p. 393.

21. Ibid., p. 395.

31

Women, Work, and Politics in the U.S.

by Michele Russell

In taking this opportunity to reflect on sexism in American society, I would like to raise issues in four areas:

1. the economic context in which women exist in the present-day world;

2. patterns of women's incorporation into the social division of labor, both internationally and domestically;

3. problems of consciousness among women in this country deriving from the conditions of our work lives;

4. some reflections on the relationship of the U.S. women's movement as we now know it to all of these things.

The Economic Context

Yesterday morning, Javier Iguíñez outlined the rise of imperialism in a very useful way and pinpointed one of the most significant aspects of capitalist social relations: uneven and combined development. He indicated both that capitalist development produces underdevelopment, and that the basic characteristic of underdevelopment is the maintenance of historically previous forms of oppression under new social systems. We currently exist in a world where approximately four centuries of production relations coexist. Often they come into direct conflict with one another, as do the people whose lives are conditioned by them. It is also in this context that sexism must be analyzed: as a set of social relations which predate the hegemony of commodity exchange, but which are tied in their origins directly to private property and today are fundamentally conditioned by capitalist social relations.

Taking our analysis of underdevelopment one step further, I would like to emphasize that in addition to creating an affluent national center based on the private appropriation of socially produced wealth, and consequently, a poor and pillaged periphery internationally, international monopoly capital reproduces conditions of underdevelopment even at the national center. What are Appalachia and Twelfth Street in Detroit if not the periphery here at home?

It is common these days for those of us who understand the operation of global corporations to writhe with indignation at development patterns in places like Brazil where, for example, cane harvesters were earning sixty cents a day. With mechanization on one plantation, we learn from the *Wall Street Journal*, seven thousand people lost those jobs at one sweep. We are sensitive to the structural displacement of a sixty-year-old woman, who after working twenty years on such a plantation, was reduced to earning $6.50 a month washing clothes. But we don't need to look that far. Go five miles south of Greenville, Mississippi. Black women there are paid $3.00 a day to clear the fields. When interviewed, one woman worker in such a situation said: "Now the man pays $3.00 a day; I don't know how much the children will get, but he says something, maybe sixty cents a day, maybe more. We need the work and he pays more than most people. Across there," and she pointed to a plantation on the far side of the highway, "the man pays $2.00 a day." And she goes on: ". . . There used to be a whole lot more people on the plantations than there are now when the machines started back in '53, '54, then every year they begin to get more and more and that cut people down out of the pickin'." Poison sprays and crop-dusting machines have ended the demand for cotton choppers. Mechanical cotton pickers have replaced hand pickers except at the end of the rows where the picker makes its turn and cannot reap cleanly for a stretch of about fifteen feet deep. Here, the women and children still get a few sacks.

At the same time that such levelling of economic condition is happening to women in Brazil and women in the U.S. who are being structurally replaced by agricultural mechanization, a process of vertical integration of labor is also occurring: across job categories, industries, and national boundaries. A fourteen-year-old girl assembling transistors in a Hong Kong factory, a German waitress in a hotel, a typing instructor in Mexico, and a senior accountant commuting from Westport, Connecticut: All are women, all also work for the same company. One thing that this illustrates is the existence of new and higher levels of economic coordination and interdependency, controlled and defined by the global corporation. Another thing it represents is an economic range in the market value of women's labor from 30 cents an hour for fourteen hours of work a day to over $30,000 a year plus fringe benefits and no time clock: all legitimated within the confines of one corporate entity. Interdependency does not mean equality. It does not necessarily result in solidarity. *Ms.* Magazine notwithstanding, sisterhood is an ideology that just isn't powerful enough to bridge that distance.

In terms of annual sales vis-à-vis gross national product, General Motors has become bigger than Switzerland, Pakistan, and South Africa combined; Royal Dutch Shell is bigger than Saudi Arabia. General Instruments Corp. is perfectly capable of closing down its New England operations and idling three thousand workers there while creating five thousand jobs in Taiwan at one-fifth the wages. The availability of cheap female and child labor is a central factor in these considerations.

The ability of these and other conglomerates to organize production and a division of labor on a worldwide scale without regard to the political sovereignty of nation-states has created tremendous ferment. In addition to greater possibilities for capital accumulation and profits, it has led to conditions producing workers' struggles in France, West Germany, Italy, Portugal, Puerto Rico, Argentina, Chile, Alaska, parts of Africa, as well as in parts of the U.S. such as Montana, West Virginia, Washington, California, and New York.

As the need for investment outlets grows, the insanity of the capitalist solution becomes more apparent. All the issues involving the increased immiserization of the proletariat that Marx hypothesized now receive clear expression internationally through the dynamics of runaway shops, rising structural unemployment and displacement even in the most advanced sections of the world capitalist system, environmental destruction, so-called overpopulation, and wage differentials within industries, across national boundaries, and between national minorities. Even among the most traditionally stable sections of the U.S. economy, industrial manufacturing for instance, the working class in the last five years experienced declines in real wages, rising unemployment, and increased state intervention in the economy to produce service sector jobs and to sustain capitalist equilibrium. And now even that remedy is in question as thousands upon thousands of city employees across the country are laid off in major metropolitan areas because private industry refuses to bail urban centers out of fiscal crisis.

Javier spoke of the increased marginalization of Third World countries. The same situation is developing domestically in terms of the work force, though it is hidden through disaccumulative investment. In using the phrase "disaccumulative investment," I mean the nonproductive investment of capital. I'm speaking here not only of the warfare state that several people made reference to yesterday, but all those sectors of the economy which are partially or wholly subsidized by the state and which are non-commodity producing. We must talk about public services such as transportation, hospitals, schools, the postal service. We have to talk about the advertising and marketing industry, about media jobs whose only purpose in the economy is to mirror the dominant ideology and rationalize commodity consumption at ever greater levels both domestically and internationally. Disaccumulative investment is capitalism's way of dealing with the social surplus short of wars or socialist planning. I concentrate on these areas in the U.S. economy because that is where employment is growing and also where women wage earners are concentrated. I'll return to that in a moment.

The Social Division of Labor

In the international social division of labor produced by the global corporations, women are often a majority of the workforce in traditional industries such as textiles and food processing. We are also the semiskilled white-collar workforce underpinning the new computerized management systems and financial bureaucracies. Our economic desperation continues to make us those employed at the lowest pay rates in rapidly expanding labor intensive industries in the Third World, such as electronics. Biologically, women are the ultimate source of human regeneration. We are the direct recipients of the global corporations' population control schemes as well as genetic experiments and consumer marketing strategies in the U.S. and the Third World. In rural areas, capitalism's introduction of monoculture as the solution to food shortages has radically altered patterns of women's agricultural labor. Every aspect of our lives as women has been penetrated and conditioned by the organization of these corporations. They have given us jobs, a society of relationships outside the home, and an environment of social disruption so profound that our consciousness as a group is only at the first stages of formation. We have learned that through our labor we hold up half the sky and our history has taught us the eloquence of speaking bitterness. But the complicated texture of our lives remains hidden from history.

In the U.S., we find ourselves concentrated in the sectors of the economy that on the one hand are the public, institutionalized extensions of long-standing domestic roles: waitresses, laundresses, nurses, cooks, sales clerks, seamstresses, teachers, maids, producers of non-durable consumer goods. You know the list. It's lengthy and no matter how much you multiply and mystify the titles, all we're seeing is the workforce mirroring those jobs we've always done in the home anyway. On the other side are the new communications: data-processing, marketing, and management systems that almost by re-mote control keep the financial and industrial empire humming —keypunch operators, computer analysts, clerk typists in lower echelons, administrative assistants in higher echelons, file clerks, telephone operators, market researchers, copy readers, even com-mercial artists and fashion designers. Unequal pay, high turnover, and a low degree of unionization compound our vulnerability in all these jobs.

Problems of Consciousness

Often, when women involved in feminist concerns struggle for equal rights, celebrate "new careers," even raise the demand of "pay for housework," feminist vision focuses on money. In the absence of any ideology other than economism, tremendous energy is expended on compiling masses of empirical data which only measure progress in a bourgeois context: the accumulation of individual advantages. Even in the arena of parliamentary rights, you begin to count congress-women and public appointees as if that guaranteed representation and were an adequate substitute for a mass program. While money and body counts are important, I think that one of the things Vietnam taught us is that they may divert our attention from the real motion of people, may act as a smoke screen blinding us to deeper political and economic and social realities. Statistics can be manipulated. How-ever, an understanding of the specific structural profile of women's participation in the economy can shed some light on patterns of family life and the institutionalization of patriarchal values within a capitalist work context. It can also enrich our appreciation of the particular mentality with which many women in America struggle for self-determination, for liberation from psychological oppression, and for the alleviation of a whole range of injustices that are part of a much greater reality.

Whether we women are engaged in all the jobs I've just described in the home or outside of it, our legitimate social function in our "down time" is to be professional consumers: protecting the equilibrium of capitalist commodity production and enhancing the social prestige of our families through our purchases. Keep consuming. This is what it means for women to be good Americans, North and South. As Isabel Larguia reminds us in an article in *Obrero en Marcha:*

The working-class woman who cannot afford the latest consumer goods is no less a prisoner of the mass media than the middle-class woman. . . . Glorifying the role of the housewife through the mass media, consumer society pushes her to buy TVs, refrigerators, mixers and so on. Capitalizing on both roles, advertising has joined the two ideas: the beautiful, fashionable woman (be lovely, retain your husband), and the good housewife firmly anchored in the kitchen. This media woman suffers from a contradiction which can be resolved only through the acquisition of costly household appliances, since she must provide her family with a high level of consumption without ever having the appearance of a worker.

Ready cash is not the issue. That's why credit was invented. Layaway. Time payments. The names themselves tell the story. One way or another, indebtedness to the system gets built into survival. Couple this with the additional institutions capitalist ideology has supported (such as sororities) in order to mystify women's position as part of the working class, and it is easy to understand some of the problems our movement is having developing a mass political consciousness with revolutionary potential.

In trying to analyze the full implications of the underdevelopment of political ideology in the U.S. women's movement, however, we must turn to women's work lives outside the home, where we are told our "future" lies. Look at the ideological structure of work in the social services. What are social workers? What are nurses? What are teachers? Even at their most benign they are big sisters, cleaner-uppers, looking after others, friendly helpers, domestics. What consciousness does that ideology produce if not simply a reinforcement of all those patriarchal values which family life trains us to justify?

In the religious communities women enter to find associations and opportunities beyond the home, whether they be Roman Catholic, Greek Orthodox, of the various Protestant denominations, or Jewish, my contention is that we will only find more ideological support for the mentality of the friendly helper or the domestic. Volunteer labor. Consider, for instance, the way in which the female religious communities in the Roman Catholic church are used as escape valves by working-class women. On the positive side, they are sanctuary from the very brutal economic and psychological realities of Catholic blue-collar marriage. They choose being sisters rather than mothers. They may even be trying to create a utopian community of women, bound together in spiritual unity and collective work, safe from the more gross forms of exploitation rampant in the secular world. But it is a medieval accommodation. The women in these communities have renounced commodity culture only to become commodities themselves. We understand that the church as an institution would not find it useful for these communities to exist even for propaganda's sake if the women in them were not a captive cheap labor force. Any pursuit of theology from the feminist viewpoint which doesn't deal with that feature of the exploitation of women in religious communities is not getting at the heart of the problem.

Now let's take a step further and talk about the mentality encouraged in white-collar, administrative positions, whether they're the flunky positions of the army of typists and clerks in operations like Blue Cross-Blue Shield, or the chic appointment secretaries of executives. Is there any difference between them? Is their work being proletarianized? Is their outlook the same?

On the lower levels, plush office furnishings are used to soften the realization that women are in dead-end jobs. No matter how many clothes they buy, no matter how many elevated shoes they wear to work, every minute of their day is monitored with military precision. They are sitting in rows which are regimented. Their bathroom breaks are clocked. They do segments of tasks that are miniscule beyond the point of rationality. They are as interchangeable as the parts in their machines. As in high school, they are most easily organized around issues of dress codes and lunch breaks. At the same time, stratification is intensifying, not decreasing. There may be as many as ten grade steps between an executive secretary and a woman in a typing pool or a receptionist, even though their skills may be functionally interchangeable. This stratification is ideological in character—ideological and political. Its function is social control, not economic efficiency. Its result is to totally individualize promotion and work-evaluation criteria.

Most of these women are not unionized. The structure of ever-expanding job ladders fosters the illusion of mobility and replaces the incipient proletarian consciousness of the production worker (female and male) who is clear that a line is crossed when someone becomes a foreman. Your supervisor is perceived more as a counselor or teacher encouraging you to "achieve," rather than as a boss forcing you to produce. The product is often "service," not guns or cars. Rebellion hurts "the public," not government or the capitalist. The frictions and antagonisms created by actual production demands and surveillance systems of supervision borrowed from the military in all-female offices intensify distrust between women at the bottom. The male boss, benign, floating like God-the-Father above the "petty" details of bureaucratic work, remains exempt from blame.

Being chained to a typewriter or keypunch produces an entirely different set of mental responses than being chained to the land. And I would say that this happens both to the black and the nonblack women in those situations. The culture of the "all-girl" office, the pursuit of perpetual youth, the actual segregation of female work-groups by age, all have tremendous impact when we're talking about organizing women at these places of work for liberation.

That's a brief review. It's too sketchy; it's too fast; it's incomplete. I hope it suggests some of the dimensions of the problem.

The Women's Movement in the United States

By and large, the women's movement in the U.S. has been mute on these issues. When it has been content to accept capitalist terms of incorporation, its development model has had a quantitative and accumulative character which assumes eventual equality with the oppressor. In its few transcendant moments, it has adopted a moral outrage politics in which individual heroines, like a Joanne Little, who are distinguished only by their victimization, arise and are immediately taken over as "woman of the year" by bourgeois elements of the movment. Or feminists adopt a maximalist rhetoric in which sexism gets elevated to the primary contradiction in the world since time immemorial. They have argued for the colonial status of women as a metaphor rather than a concrete historical condition, and have often confused biology with politics. I don't think we have the luxury to do any of those things anymore. It produces chaos. And it is particularly confusing when we try to define "women's politics" or "women's issues" and then add the variable of race.

In my experience in the movement, I have seen black women courageously attack the right of the government to define their children's socialization in the schools. They demanded community control. They unmasked the racism in the curriculum and the bank-ruptcy of the whole credentialling system by proving their own ability to teach. They actually forced their own access to the educa-tional process through para-professionalism and then wound up, in the words of one sister I know, as "teachers' maids, not teachers' aides"—running errands, cleaning the classrooms, and accomplishing only the further stratification of janitorial service. Reinforced in their children's eyes as domestics, they found themselves still under the tutelage of white women often half their age whose feminist concerns surfaced in striking for higher salaries for less work.

I have seen white women build on the corporate analysis movement of the sixties and develop very sophisticated rationales and organizational strategies to break through the channelling system that feeds women into jobs that are the public extensions of housework. I've watched them demand and achieve access to so-called "non-traditional" careers and in their escape still give scant attention to how work for their sisters trapped in those other jobs could become just as political.

I've seen black and white women come to blows over the issues of birth control and abortion, because for white women such reforms meant increased freedom of choice in the context of family-centered oppression, but for blacks such measures meant all the horrors of involuntary sterilization, the further extension of government control over our lives, and the specter of genocide.

We must ask ourselves some difficult questions at this point in our history. What makes the black registered nurse resist hospital unionization drives that the white Croatian woman orderly welcomes? What perpetuates the tunnel vision with which white career women pressure their corporations to institute child-care facilities so as to maximize their vocational options without regard to the wage scales, welfare legislation, and institutionalized values that will ensure that Third World women will be those taking care of their kids? What prompts black women to say, "Please, Lord, let me have the luxury to stay at home and be a housewife"? Against what historical background should that be judged? By what feminist criteria do white women celebrate token jobs as truck drivers when not only the mob connections but the racism of the trucking industry is legendary and the unemployment rate in the black community as a whole continues to be twice that in the white?

None of these are false issues. They all describe part of the problem. To resolve them we obviously must go beyond change within the system because we all know, I would hope, that it was never meant to stretch that far. Our problem is not just that the dominant patterns of socialization for white women in America have been home-centered, privatized, male-dominated, self-sacrificial—they're all that and more. And white women suffer cruelly and resist these forms of exploitation. It is not just that black women in America (and I'm sorry that my own historical experience and the time limitations combine to restrict my comments today to the situation of black women) have been on the public auction block, meat for sale, from day one. Slavery, tenant farming, and industrial labor left little room for bourgeois role differentiation between the sexes in the black community. It's not just that in the cultural mystification of our society, black women will almost involuntarily associate white women with cloisters and pedestals and being pampered; and white women will flash "sexual promiscuity," "Aid for Dependent Children," and "strength" in characterizing black women as a group. Black women voluntarily take pay cuts in order to have white-collar jobs associated with gentility while white women voluntarily submit themselves to severe psychological and physical hardship, racing into the male preserves of assembly-line labor and the skilled trades, eager to demonstrate their strength under the lash as well as enjoying higher wages.

For those of us who tend to look at things as a monolith, I must say this. In present-day America, the black community is almost as socially and economically stratified as the white community. Black women, I'm here to tell you, have maids and they have Tupperware parties. And white ADC mothers go hungry and know the reality of forced labor. Black women are still used by corporations as double statistics to substantiate the sham of progress and to avoid employing black men. And white women, believing the corporate figures, continue to have faith that the economy will at least be able to provide them with personal and occupational opportunities—never mind that general unemployment keeps rising.

I touch on these things in order to say to you that in contemporary America we experience at least as many varieties of subjective human alienation as there are job categories in the system. Our immediate impulse as individuals fighting for self-respect is to legitimize only our particular form of victimization. But that simply isn't enough. We unfurl the flag of our separate and personal situation and make that our morality. And because we have been trained to survive in the context of capitalistic hierarchical relationships at home and on the job we tend to reproduce those values even as we organize for our rights.

We each have our range of personal needs, granted, which obviously must find expression before we can join with others as full and strong human beings struggling for social revolution—political, economic revolution, if necessary, by military means. That's a long struggle, a difficult struggle. I do not hold out hopes for peaceful transformation; I'm sure the representatives from Chile do not. I think we have a lot to learn from the Latin American experience in that regard and I would like to see some of that discussion incorporated into our consideration of the American reality—but we don't have time now.

The point is that we ought always to measure our struggles in a collective context; we ought always to seek the proletarian standpoint in our individual situations; we ought always to realize that, as Che Guevara said, "to be a revolutionary, one must be guided by feelings of great love"; and we must never settle for less than the entirety.

The Black Theology Panel

On Wednesday the various minority groups at the conference presented religious interpretations of their own historical experience.

Several well-known black theologians together planned and participated in the black panel. They requested that Herbert Edwards, professor of social ethics at Duke University Divinity School, read the paper that he had prepared for the conference (see above document 12).

Many of the participants had already read the paper, but it did serve to introduce the theme and open the dialogue. The black panelists, Protestant and Catholic, then answered questions from the floor.

In the lively dialogue that followed, the Latin Americans, in particular, asked whether the black theological reflection failed to emphasize sufficiently the necessary change in the overall system that produces racial, economic, and cultural exploitation. Their feeling was that the insistence on racial oppression detracted from the global struggle.

The black theologians responded that racial oppression cannot be identified with any other kind of oppression and that the Latin Americans cannot comprehend the historical and sociological roots of black oppression.

Here we include edited excerpts from the discussion, taken from the tape recordings. In some cases the identity of the speaker could not be determined from the tapes.

32

Black Panel:
Excerpts from the Discussion

Basil Matthew: There are substantive reasons for approaching theology in so-called "national" terms: in black or white or Latin American or North American terms. First, we tend to confuse theology with faith and belief. The content of Christian belief ought to be universal and common to everybody. But the content of theology ought not to be common to everybody, because theology is essentially an intellectual assessment of the content of belief. As soon as we talk about an intellectual assessment we are postulating differences. So "black theology" and "Latin American theology" and "North American theology" are far from being scandalous concepts: They are what ought to be. The reason for our Pharisaic scandal at the emergence of these various theologies is maybe that we have been so oppressed for centuries that we feel that there is only one way of looking at and experiencing God. The different theologies are articulations of the different ways of different people of experiencing God.

Secondly, while all people are oppressed, people can be oppressed in significantly different ways. Liberation theology differs in the conceptualization of the different ways in which people are oppressed. Just as significant differences of content and approach make significant differences in sciences and the categorization of sciences, so too significant differences in the methods of oppression of different peoples contribute to the making of specifically different types of theology or approaches to theology.

Hugo Assmann: My question is about this point of particularity in theology today. It's not so particular that more than thirty million people die every year of starvation, hunger, and other oppressive means. It's not so particular that two-thirds of mankind today are oppressed people. Are we not falling into a new ideological control when we speak always from our particular or contextual point of departure? Is it not defensive theology when we speak about a black Christ? Must we remain in a defensive position? We are representatives of two-thirds of mankind today. What kind of particular theologies do we need? Do we not need to come together for a common struggle against the oppressor?

Herbert Edwards: It would be very good if it were possible to find a universal theological formulation. I do not believe that any one theology is unaffected by the historical experiences out of which it has come. Black people, for example, according to your own statement, brother Assmann, are in even greater need of black theological formulations than I thought. That is to say, if I look at Latin American theology, if I look at European theology, North American theology, I do not find anything there for me. I do not find my experiences reflected there; I do not find any awareness of my being as a person. If theology has nothing to say to me about the totality of my being—not simply about the existential context in which I suffer oppression but also about a sense of meaning for my existence—then what does it have to say? To whom does it speak? We then need a particular theological approach so that we will be able to answer the question: What does the gospel of Jesus Christ have to say to the black man whose back is against the wall?

James Cone: I really want to speak to that question. Hugo is a good friend, and so I want to try to see if I can communicate what the problem is as I perceive it. I think it would be possible, Hugo, for us to actually do what you are commanding and calling for if the members of this conference were primarily people whom I regarded as in the struggle of oppression, that is, if I could readily see that the majority of people here came out of actual concrete struggles, people that I wouldn't have to be as suspicious about. Then I would probably concede a little bit of my own particularity in order to hear what others are talking about. But most of the North American participants here are people I suspect. Therefore, I have to be very conscious about my language. If I were in Latin America right now and most of the people present were from other countries, then I would have no reason whatsoever to talk about black as such. I would be ready to concede a lot. But in this setting, in Detroit, U.S.A., I see people I've been fighting against. Here I don't talk about liberation; I've got to talk about black.

———: On this question of the autonomization or the particularization of the black struggle or of black theology, because of the deepness of the oppression here I understand the emphasis on the blacks' own situation and on doing their own thing. But I see the situation only as temporary. There has to be a long-range plan in which once you have your own things together you have to gradually get together with other oppressed people in order to deal with the ever-growing oppressive structure. Without that, I don't think we will have any hope.

———: Being a Puerto Rican I appreciate and sympathize very much with this stress on particularity. We are a Latin American nation with North American citizenship. The question is this: Despite the stress on particularity, I ask, aren't you once more positing a universal category of oppression? First, when you stress so much and so intensely your particular form of suffering, aren't you in danger of forgetting other particular forms of suffering? Second, when you posit racism as a kind of universal ideology, aren't you once more positing a universal category and, therefore, in a sense doing something other than a particular theology?

———: [Edwards's] position is one that I understand, but it is essentially a very hopeless position. He makes it sound like there is no hope for a solution at all because the problem is so big. The only hope, presented in the last few lines of the presentation, is that God will give the strength to be able to deal with the situation. But would an oppressed people relate to a theology or to an institution or to a movement that doesn't offer anything beyond that hope that God will intervene and provide strength? Would people relate to something that offers no more or less foreseeable (I don't want to say "immediate") solution to the problem?

———: It seems like there was a certain skepticism [in Edwards's paper] about the relevance of Marxism as a way of analyzing the reality of the nonwhite world. I'd like to point out one fundamental fact which we ought to realize when dealing with this problem: In the recent past the most creative application of Marxism has been in the nonwhite world. Surely we must take into consideration the liberation movements in Mozambique, Guinea-Bissau, Angola, and Cuba. Surely, we must take into consideration the contributions of the Chinese and the Vietnamese.

Herbert Edwards: I was not concerned with pointing out who has made the best application of Marxism. My skepticism about the utilization of Marxism as a tool of analysis in our context is due simply to this: In our history in this country, whether one was Marxist, non-Marxist, pre-Marxist, or post-Marxist, if he was white, he was also racist; if he was black, he was also oppressed.

————: I think we should keep in mind that Marxism is at least three things: It's a philosophy in general, a methodology, and a praxis. When we reject Marxism we should be clear as to which of these we are rejecting. I think Marxist methodology could be very useful for all oppressed groups.

Martin Garate: Black theologians are suspicious that liberation theology is a white theology; in the same way theologians in Latin America are suspicious that black theology is more American than black.

————: What is the goal of black liberation and black theology? If the goal of black liberation is to become an American citizen equal to all others, I think that perhaps black theology is an American theology. Are free blacks to be part of an imperial nation that is the oppressor of other nations? That is imperialist theology.

————: I'm an American Indian. North America was our land. We've been oppressed, repressed, and, I see today, double-pressed. What I'm wondering is which is the road we can look forward to walking down with other peoples. How do we resolve some of the differences that you speak about?

Herbert Edwards: I see no barriers among oppressed people to paticipation in liberation, whatever the oppression they are struggling against, if, however, they are clear about their loyalty. The problem, it seems to me, very often is that many oppressed persons are concerned not about looking at the system of oppression and altering that, but simply improving their situation in the context of that system.

SECTION TEN

The Other Minorities
in America

Following the black panel, representatives of native Americans, Asian-Americans, and the Spanish-speaking were scheduled for presentations in a session entitled "Emerging Theologies." Unfortunately, time limitations had led the conference organizers to schedule simultaneous panels, with the conference participants having to choose among them.

There was a strong negative reaction to this plan; tensions were high and conversations impassioned; caucuses began to form.

One group representing the minorities asked to read a statement before the entire conference. An important point in the process, this "Statement from the Coalition of U.S. Nonwhite Racial and National Minorities" is included here.

Sergio Torres, executive secretary of the organizing committee, officially apologized to the assembly for the committee's deficiencies in planning.

This session again demonstrated the importance and difficulty of obtaining just representation of the nonwhite minorities.

33

Statement from the Coalition of U.S. Nonwhite Racial and National Minorities

We would like to express our appreciation to Sergio Torres and the planning committee for convening a conference on liberation theology, thereby making it possible for us to be in conversation with our brothers and sisters from Latin America. We know that they are dedicated and committed to the struggle of the oppressed. We have become aware of their persecution and suffering due to their fight for justice.

Because we believe that the struggles of oppressed peoples are interconnected, we are deeply pained that the programming of this conference prevented us from sharing our similar experiences with our Latin American brothers and sisters.

We noted the following:

1. The North American section did not express the conditions, experiences, and theological reflections of the nonwhite racial and national minorities living within the United States.

2. The way the conference was structured perpetuated a tone of divisiveness among us nonwhites. We feel that the section on "Emerging Theology" was a token one. We were forced into a situation which objectively appeared that we were competing with each other.

3. We have noticed that there has been a tendency to look at the Latin American liberation struggles in a way where the real essence of this struggle and the solidarity it should evoke from everyone is not really grasped.

4. This lack of understanding results in insufficient will, sensitivity, and understanding to embrace the oppressed U.S. racial and national minorities and their liberation struggles. But we believe that

liberation theology in the U.S. must be written in the struggle of the oppressed and by the oppressed. Liberation theology written in any other way could be easily interpreted as being elitist, co-optive, and presumptuous.

We express our solidarity and support with all oppressed peoples of the world. We, the people of color in this conference, expect and demand recognition of our existence and contributions in the area of liberation theology. We expect and demand an expression of the concrete reality of what was put forward as the goals of this conference.

In the spirit of solidarity and being able to correct these very shortcomings of the conference, we submit that the following are indispensable:

1. For future planning, representation of North American minority peoples on planning committees.

2. Participation of a significant and substantial representation of minority peoples in the conference, or any process.

3. A serious examination in the process of the conference of oppressive structures and situations of the black people, the Asian people, the Hispanics, and native Americans in North America.

Sister Jamie Phelps, O.P.
Preston N. Williams
Willie J. Dell
Roberto Peña
Nelson Trout
Jun Atienza
Dominga Zapata
Joaquina Carrion
Maria Antonia Esquerra
Dr. J. Deotis Roberts
Gilberto Marrero
Walden Bello
Clarence G. Newsome

Margarita Jiménez
Toinette Eugene
Geline Avila
José Luis Velazco
Rafael Jiménez
Sister Mario Barron
Miriam Cherry
Sister Juana Clare Jose
Violet Masuda
Ricardo Parra
Herb Barnes
James H. Cone
Joseph B. Bethea
Herbert O. Edwards, Sr.

The Feminist
Theology Panel

The panel on feminist theology had been planned to follow the format of the other sessions, that is, there would be substantive presentations by two or three speakers well-known in the field, with a question-and-answer period following.

At the beginning of the week, those who had been asked to make the presentations were called together by the women's coordinator—along with other women who were interested in or who identified with feminist issues—to talk about how the panel was to be arranged. It was clear during that initial meeting that the original plans for the panel would have to be scrapped. Feminism makes a break with the old way of doing theology. It represents a communal process and a healthy disrespect for spokeswomen, experts, and "stars." The women at the meeting made it clear that they wanted the feminist panel to reflect this concern for collectivity and process. Thus began a series of "women's caucus" meetings open to any woman at the conference who wished to be involved in planning the panel on feminist theology. Members of the caucus spent the greater part of the week discussing both the content they wished to have emphasized in the presentation and the process they wished to have demonstrated.

The resulting presentation was in striking contrast to the others. Three women with some background in the field were asked to make brief, five-minute introductory remarks, each touching on an aspect of feminist theology which had been determined by the caucus. These presentations were to be followed by brief responses from two other women. An empty chair was placed on the podium and an invitation extended to any woman from the audience to come up and join the conversation at any point she felt moved. After the major presentations were over, the speakers vacated their own seats so that more places were made available for women to join the discussants. The result was a fluid and shifting body of participants, each adding her own dynamic and perspective to the topic. In this way the process nature of feminist theology and its concern for the experience out of which every woman speaks (whether or not she considers herself an ideological feminist) was made clear.

Because of the contextual nature of most of the discussion, only the prepared introductory statements and two substantive responses are included here.

34

Statement by Sheila Collins

In order to set a framework for our discussion, I would like to say a few words about the history of how women came to be engaged in theologizing from our own experience.

First, I would prefer not to use the term "feminist theology" to describe what we are about, for it connotes a systematized, somewhat static body of knowledge, which is not at all what we are in the process of creating. I would rather use the terms "women's role in theology" or "women's theologizing" to express the fact that we are engaged in a dialectical, open-ended process of action and reflection growing out of our experience of being female in a male-dominated world. Our reflection focuses on the nature of that alienated experience and describes a new vision of human justice and community which utilizes the insights, experiences, and talents of the female half of the race, long denied an active role in shaping the course of human civilizations.

It was about five years ago that women began to take their own experience seriously as the basis for doing theology. At that time a growing women's movement was taking shape in the religious community—a movement which had been given impetus by the changes which were taking place in women's lives and consciousness in the secular arena. Impressed by the militant critique of roles and institutions being made by the secular women's movement, Christian women (and even many women who had "given up" on religion) began to extend this critique to the ideology of religion and to the institution of the church which, they soon found, was the most potent legitimator of women's oppression in every other sphere.

I want to point out that women's engagement in theologizing did not arise five years ago suddenly and without any precedent. There was a nineteenth-century feminist movement which attempted to do the same thing. The nineteenth-century feminist movement arose first among women who were working for the abolition of slavery. When such women got up to·speak and organize against slavery and found themselves ridiculed because of their sex by the "Christian" gentlemen with whom they were working, they soon began to detect an analogy between their own situation as women and that of the Negro slave. It was not long before they saw the connection between their subordination as women and the ideology of the church.

Many women in the nineteenth century made critically incisive analyses of the role religion played in reinforcing patterns of dominance and submission. Perhaps the most ambitious effort was that undertaken by a group of women in the 1890s under the direction of Elizabeth Cady Stanton, which resulted in the publication of *The Woman's Bible*, a critical commentary on certain books of the Bible deemed of especial importance to women. Essentially, *The Woman's Bible* was a critique of Christianity as the ideology of sexism and a plea to return to the essence of all great religions, shorn of their cultural and sexual biases. This was the true beginning of the feminist engagement in liberation theology.

But the nineteenth-century effort never got beyond *The Woman's Bible*. It was soon nipped in the bud because its radical critique of religion was beginning to jeopardize the gains of the larger women's movement of the time. Women learned that religion was the one sacred cow they dare not debunk for fear of bringing the whole pack of cards down around their heads. Because Christianity was such a controlling force in nineteenth-century America, they could not attack it and expect to be supported in their efforts anywhere else.

I want to stress that neither the nineteenth- nor twentieth-century feminist movements started among bourgeois housewives who were seeking to grab a bigger chunk of the economic pie for themselves. Although both the earlier and later feminist movements did become diverted along class lines later on, they both owe their beginnings to women who were activists in the struggle for the liberation of the oppressed. Women who were civil rights and peace workers in the 1950s and 1960s came to feminism, like their nineteenth-century foremothers, out of the realization that, while working for equality and justice for others, they themselves were being treated unequally and unjustly. These women realized that the special gifts which women have to offer the transformation of society would never be utilized unless they worked on their own liberation first.

The feminist movement in theology owes a great debt to activist women who brought to feminism an understanding of the links between various kinds of oppression. I would like to survey briefly some of the lessons we have learned from these women. First, we learned that in spite of our supposed proximity to the centers of power (as white, middle-class women), we had actually been increasingly marginalized as a group during the latter part of the nineteenth century and throughout the twentieth century. We also learned that it was the ideology of sexism—man's age-old fear of women—that industrial capitalism used to keep us from taking any creative initiative in the on-going struggle for social change.

Because we were onlookers to the grand project of Western civilization, we began to see its faults more easily than those men we were associated with either in the home or at the workplace. Increasingly, we saw through the hypocrisy and illusions that those in power maintained in order to keep the machinery going. As the mystique of traditional authorities lost their power over us—whether it was the authority of religious tradition and mythology, the authority of our husbands, bosses, or the state—we began to understand that we had a whole realm of experience and accumulated wisdom which had lain dormant and untapped by the mainstream of Western civilization for centuries. We saw that the experience of our own liberation could be the force out of which new truth and a new social order might emerge.

From the secular women's movement we also learned how to get together in small groups to tell our stories and to hear each other in a way that had not been possible since the rise of industrial capitalism when the extended family was broken up and middle-class women were isolated in their own homes. In these small groups we began to understand the real meaning of community, trust, love. A new word was born among us: "sisterhood." We also learned in these small consciousness-raising groups that what we all had thought were personal, neurotic problems were actually social problems created by the economic and political distortions of advanced industrial capitalism. Though we called these sessions "consciousness raising," what we were actually doing in these communities of women was structural analysis, though in a limited and primitive way.

In 1971 a group of about twenty women theologians were called together at Alverno College in Milwaukee to begin the process of reflecting theologically on the feminist experience. That meeting began and ended with a number of questions—questions which had not been raised in theology before because they arose out of women's experience. It was the Alverno meeting which launched the first communal effort at theologizing as women from our own experience. The year following that about sixty women from the Roman Catholic, Protestant, and Jewish faiths met for a week at the Grailville community in Ohio to continue the process which had begun at Alverno. This was the first time that new forms of worship, new religious concepts, new methods of doing theology—poetry, art, body movement, consciousness raising—were utilized. Since that first Grailville conference there have been all kinds of offshoots. Theology among women is no longer confined to the seminary but is being engaged in by women in many different settings—in local churches and community groups, and among non-academics as well as professionals.

What new insights are we developing in response to new questions? I want to touch on this briefly, for I think it will lead into what some of the others have to say. We are saying that Western Christianity has falsified the "human experience" of God because it has reflected only half of the lived human experience—that of males. Our experience as women has never informed the religious symbology, the holy stories, the development of a Christian response to current events. Because our experience has been outside that which has passed for Christianity, we are able to see its distortions more clearly than those who operate from its center. The realization that we have never been included in the "Christian Story" means that it has lost its authoritative power over us. We are no longer afraid of the boundaries which that tradition set on either our social status or our imaginations. We are now free to explore new sources of meaning, insight, and direction both inside and outside the given tradition. An exploration of the meaning of premonotheistic religious traditions thus becomes possible, as also a new appreciation of Eastern religions and of the religion of the native American.

Freed from the dead weight of tradition, even our reading of the Bible has become more exciting. We see things there that we had been blinded to before. New translations make possible entirely different readings of certain passages. New models of what it means to be a woman jump out at us from the past. Villains in the tradition turn into newly discovered saints, and old saints sometimes become the villains.

But most of all, I think what has happened for us is that woman's experience of herself in her world—the lived, historical existence of women—has become a tremendous source of new themes, images, and methods of doing theology. We become a new lens through which reality is perceived. I believe that this means we are at the end of some old paradigms through which the world has been interpreted, opening the way for new paradigms to take root.

35

Statement by Beverly Harrison

It has been very moving for me to have the opportunity to meet so many of the theologians of liberation from Latin America and to see embodied in them—"incarnated," if you will—what it is that happens to Christian theology and to Marxism when it is expressed in profound human solidarity with the oppressed. I have seen that incarnation of solidarity here in body language and in ways of speaking theologically. I am profoundly grateful for that.

We are, you notice, not doing feminist theology here; we are doing *second-level reflection* on feminist theology. It would take us too long to give you a laboratory by telling our stories, sharing our experiences. To do theology the feminist way here would take too long. All we can do here is to identify certain motifs of feminist theological reflection.

The Latin Americans among us have also had to do second-order theology here—that is to say, they have had to report their *conclusions* out of their struggle, and to report them in shorthand, and we recognize that. We know their writings are *also* second-level reflection, and we remember that those writings have always to be written with one eye on the hierarchy of the Roman Catholic church and another on the "guild" of theologians of the West. We understand that that is part of the reason why we women find ourselves so *invisible* in their writing. But we also must say to the Latin Americans that *whenever* you look *back* at power, whether in ecclesiastical hierarchy or theological "guild," whenever you express what you have to say reactively to that power, women *will be* invisible in the way you speak.

I reflect as a feminist theologian. I am even still willing to call myself a feminist *Christian* theologian, though most feminists (including many of the 1500 or 1700 who met recently at Antioch College at a Feminists for Socialism meeting) would find what I do questionable. The reason they feel as they do is that "feminism" (we can argue about the term, but I do not think that would be useful) is a *radical* commitment to the liberation of *all* women. This "radical" feminism as it began to emerge in the U.S. in the nineteenth century was put down and killed—and it was killed chiefly by the churches! It was pushed out of the churches which then—as a reward for the growing presence and power of women—adopted the bourgeois "cult of true womanhood" as the ideology and "true doctrine" of U.S. Christianity. This must be understood. Nineteenth-century feminism was "domesticated" by Protestantism, such that the doctrine of "the fall through Eve" was replaced by a doctrine of woman as "morally superior" nurturer and childbearer. Mother's Day became the central cultic symbol of Protestant Christianity in the U.S.

Feminists were always accused of being women who had "trouble" with their "femininity." As the suffrage struggle went on and as political pressure increased against it, women tried more and more to prove that they were not defective in "femininity." They "cuddled up" more and more to the dominant and ever-rising ideology of the bourgeois doctrine of women's special virtue. Middle-class women sometimes even argued that they would help (white) men keep blacks and immigrants "in their place." So some women's appeals for suffrage were racist! But the point is that the contradiction between black males and women was created by those in power. There were also many white women in that same period who held their ground, who saw racism for what it was. The story is mixed.

Nevertheless, I stay as *Christian* feminist theologian (and feminism to me *is* inclusive of socialism) because I believe that the Jesus tradition belongs to us *radical* feminists—that Jesus is part of us and is *our* forerunner. I know of *no* theologically developed Christologies which adequately reflect this fact. The Christian canon (and I could document this if time permitted) already reflects the *resubjugation* of women in the Jesus tradition. This is part of the problem we women have of living on the *boundary* of the church, in terms of contradictions it imposes on us.

The enemy that we are trying to expel from *within ourselves* is the idea that we are simply "other"—whatever "the other" happens to be—to man, to male. The subordination of women as "other" to males is in the Christian tradition at a very *profound* level. So our commitment as feminist theologians must be the radical *transformation* of the *Christian gospel* as so far articulated, and the Christian community as so far embodied, in the direction that includes us—*all of us* female persons.

We feminist theologians are grateful that the Latin American theologians of liberation have launched a profound methodological attack upon the dominant paradigms of Western theology. We are not naive. We know that we feminist women would not be here without that profound methodological attack. We know that nobody would pay any attention to us or listen to what we are saying if there were not a great deal of protest from male theologians about the dominant theological paradigms. The problem, the subtle problem for feminist theology, is this: Traditional paradigms of Christian theology have been profoundly "objectivist" in nature. They have been interpretations of problems of human *"otherness"* in relation to God. This objectivism framework of "otherness," which is at the heart of most traditional theology (cut from its roots in deep human solidarity), quickly becomes an objectivist "ism." Latin American liberation theology as it reaches us in written form is still strongly objectivist, and tends toward objectiv*ism*.

Marxism too is oriented to an objective interpretation of the structures of oppression as they are impacted in the political economy of the West. It too is an objective interpretation and readily becomes objectiv*ist*. It too is preoccupied with establishing "the otherness" of oppressed people to those who are oppressors, and to the oppressors in all of us. Marxism often partakes of that positivist, reductionist spirit of objectiv*istic* intellectuality. This is the central problem for women, and for feminist theology. We women, you see, have *lived* always with the paradigm which defines us as being the other. In the English language we say woman is "the opposite" of man.

In most cultures being "other" usually comes out to mean that women are "the opposite" of *fully human*. So our paradigm *begins* with an attack on the body-mind split. The body-mind split is the source of the historical subject's tendency to *either* objectivism or subjectivism. This split is endemic in Western consciousness. How this fits in with a Marxist objective analysis is something we could spend a great deal of time on. Here I can only insist that we feminist theologians begin by rejecting *any* body-mind split. We insist upon a movement toward human *wholeness* and the eradication of that split in *all* its subtle manifestations among us—manifestations still present in *logos* theologies and in Marxist reductionism—toward symbol and ritual.

One further word. I just want to open up the topic. We view the churches, *all* the churches, as so *incarnating* the structure of sexism that we must make this undoing of sexism both a battle line and a boundary line. We see that Christian objectivist theology invariably moves toward an *absolutist dualism*—with a god and a devil, or usually a virgin and a whore. The church is usually seen as "virgin," the "world" as "whore." This is the reason we insist so much on the *demystification* of the *sexual imagery* of theological language. In the Christian community in which "world" is usually seen as "whore" and the church as "virgin," the mediation between God and the human community is carried on by "virgins" who are *not* women. In the churches, women are denied a part in the *fundamental* mediation between God and human beings. We see the subtle ways in which the church continues to reinforce the image that women are less than *full human persons*. We also see the ways in which revolutionary political movements perpetuate reified masculine consciousness and keep women from realizing their wholeness as full historical agents. We see an *intimate* connection between sexist consciousness and the intrinsically imperialist consciousness of the West. Christian theology and Marxism continue to carry the seeds of reified masculine consciousness. We see that, and *we will not be silenced until Christians and Marxists alike see this reality as well.*

36

Response by Rennie Golden

To refer to theology as Christian theology is another form of imperialism. I don't think we can continue to do that, even if we have fallen into the trap; my experience in women's groups is that you can never get away with it. I think it could be said that both within the Judeo-Christian tradition and outside of it there has been a whole aberrant spirituality which includes the consciousness and religious experience of the East. I think the American Indians' understanding of God as Spirit resonates with women's experience in talking about the spirit. We get into a sort of schizophrenia in talking of God the father, God the mother; but trying to talk about spirit pulls us out of that and puts us into a whole new consciousness about spirituality. So that seems important.

Then I wanted to pick up on something that Beverly said about otherness. It seems to me that coming from Latin American theology there is (particularly in Gutiérrez's work) a description of conversion and transformation being a movement toward what is most profoundly *other* in history. That, of course, is the experience of the poor, not meant simply in terms of class position, but in the way in which very poor people experience reality, a way that is so different from our experience, of most people's experience, that a conversion to them is called in Marxist terms "class option." I think, however, that there is another otherness within the class struggle, and that is the otherness between men and women. That is so profound it permeates all of history, and that is a whole other kind of conversion experience. I mention that because there are many men who are not only sympathetic but would join in coalition with women as they talk about liberation, but who do not practice that continual conversion to the other. It's very threatening for men to even *think* of themselves in a feminist context because of this otherness. I think that if there is conversion to any oppressed group or class option, there also has to be conversion to some kind of feminist consciousness and practice.

371

37

Response by Rosemary Ruether

It might be useful to say something about feminist or women's theology or the women's movement vis-à-vis something called human liberation, which includes everyone. I think the women's movement has a commitment to wholeness, and that means wholeness of human beings, starting with ourselves, and a wholeness of analysis that includes race, class, and sex. But I think women in particular have always been encouraged to disappear, to sink themselves in service to others, so that we should always be concerned only with a service to other people's oppression. The women's movement arose, both in the period of abolitionism and also again in the civil rights movement, in the discovery that helping other people with their oppression does not in any way raise the question of women as such. In experiencing the sexism of the abolitionist movement and again of the civil rights movement, women recognized that they had to address their own liberation.

I think the tendency of liberation movements is to reduce the world to a simple dualism of oppressor-oppressed, and I think that's part of patriarchal consciousness. We have to recognize that oppression operates by elaborate interstructuring of many kinds of oppression, and at this conference we have to focus on race, class, and sex, at a very minimum, as distinct and intrastructural forms of oppression. None can be reduced to the other.

Just as the black group was trying to make very clear that race is not reduced to class, that black theology focuses on a very distinct thing that is not reduced to class, by the same token women have to say that sexism is a very old primordial structure of human oppression that must be analyzed in its own right. We only get to human liberation when we are able to really focus in on these specifics—the specific kinds of oppression that happen in particular situations—and then, out of the dialogue of people concerned with these particular situations, begin to paint the larger picture. This larger picture is not the reduction of one oppression to the other, but the very complex intrastructuring of race, class, and sex—and perhaps other oppressions too—whose function is to allow the dominant race, class, and sex to perpetuate oppression by the oppressed killing each other. In other words, you not only intrastructure oppression but you set the oppressed in conflict with each other so that, for example, white workers feel a great stake in racism and therefore they do not feel solidarity with black and brown people, even though they are all workers.

The whole psychology of oppression and the social structure of oppression is to set the oppressed in mutiple relationships of intrastructural tension and therefore to allow most of the control to take place by the way the oppressed control each other.

So I think we really have to recognize the multiplicity of the forms of oppression and the specificity of the analysis of different kinds of oppression. We should not be trying to tell one group that they shouldn't analyze their own problem but be altruistic and serve some other group. Only as these situations are drawn out in their particularities and we relate them to each other do we begin to get a total picture of what oppression is all about.

38

Statement by
Beatriz Melano Couch

I would like to make one observation and try to answer three questions. My observation is that black and feminist theologies have pointed out how important some cultural issues are in the whole matter of liberation. Yet the unjust discrimination based on class, sex, or race was pointed out already a number of centuries ago by someone called Saint Paul. In Galatians 3:28 we read very clearly: "There is neither male nor female, Jew nor Gentile, master nor slave." Yet we Christians have found out how to live comfortably under those divisive categories.

Let me add that as a Latin American I don't see myself as a feminist theologian, but as a liberation theologian. And I'm very glad to find that the women here are speaking about human liberation or theology of liberation, not merely feminist liberation. Or to be more precise, feminist liberation aims at the liberation of all.

My first question is liberation of whom? The liberation of women? The liberation of blacks? The liberation of Indians? The liberation of the poor? My answer is the liberation of *all* oppressed people of the world, whatever form of oppression they experience: economic, political, racial, sexual. And then a corollary is liberation *for what?* I think we have to ask very clearly, for what? We need to be as clear as possible about the *aim.* The aim is the basic transformation of society: a new order, not a new deal—political, social, economic, cultural —what we might call in two words a *new humanity*, the hope and the struggle for the one humanity that God created and expressed in his purposes of creation and redemption. It's not only a matter of equal rights for all—that's a first step. It is a matter of a total liberation and humanization. What does it mean to be able to live as a fully human being? What kind of a "Sunday" do we want? Certainly not the oppressor's Sunday. If that is the case there is only an exchange of roles. The concept of the kingdom of God expresses a new order in human relations and, therefore, a new type of society.

My second question has to do with *methodology*. How do we arrive at a new kind of Sunday? That is why I believe that the basis of our analysis is so important, and that is why we in Latin America stress the importance of the starting point, the praxis, and the use of social science to analyze our political, historical situation. In this I am in full agreement with my male colleagues of the Latin American theology of liberation, with one qualitative difference. I stress the need to give importance to the different cultural forms that express oppression, to the ideology that divides people not only according to class, but to race and sex. Racism and sexism are oppressive ideologies which deserve a specific treatment in the theology of liberation. We have to give due importance to all cultural forms, including the myths, the symbols and the distorted images of the oppressor that we, both men and women, have internalized. Somehow they are present in one way or another in our unconscious. Enrique Dussel speaks of a double oppression: He calls the Latin American women the oppressed of the oppressed. In this sense, *machismo* is an ideology which divides people according to sex. I think it is an oligarchic ideology and by no means the monopoly of the Latin American males. It was brought to Latin America by the *conquistadores*, was reinforced by both Roman Catholic and Protestant missionaries who imported the "Western Christian" culture, and is perpetuated by the mass media which permeate our own culture. James Cone said the other day that we were not created for humiliation; and I would add "of any kind": economic, political, social, racial, sexual. Prejudice, he also said, is not extirpated completely by a new ideology; and I would add "because it doesn't lie in our minds"; it lies in our unconscious and is concretized in our daily attitudes. Women are as guilty of that sin as men are.

As a last question I would ask: How do we unify the *aim* and the *methodology?* I had asked two questions concerning aim and methodology: What kind of a Sunday do we want? How do we arrive at this Sunday? Now how do we unify these two? I see it in this way: We unify aim and method by means of a new vision. I see this vision as a double project, the task of the poet who is the seer, the one who sees ahead, who grasps reality and verbalizes it in a new way, unified with the mission of the prophet who, very much engaged in a historical situation, speaks with a very strong realistic and courageous language to that situation, in order to make people aware of their own particular sins, to awaken consciousness in order to change not only peoples' "minds" but the concrete historical situation of which they are a part.

From where does the vision come? For me it comes from the struggle. In one way or another we all pointed that out in our Latin American exposition. The struggle gives power and strength and hope and concreteness to our vision, and the vision gives direction to the struggle.

Finally, as a woman, how do I see myself doing liberation theology? I say, doing it with men in both dialogue and struggle on the road together.

SECTION TWELVE

Theology and Society

The session titled "Theology and Society" was set aside for reflection on the response of the prevailing theology—that is, the theology of the "Western" white male theologians—to the problems of the poor and oppressed here and abroad.

Frederick Herzog, J. Deotis Roberts, and Aurelia Fule represented the Protestant denominations. John Coleman, Gregory Baum, and Dorothy McCormack spoke in the name of the Catholics. (For an interpretation of what occurred in this stormy session, see document 42, pp. 417–19 below.)

We include here only three of the statements made at this session.

John Coleman commented on the role of language and the preconditions for constructive dialogue.

The statement of black theologian J. Deotis Roberts complements the earlier discussions of the black panel.

Canadian Gregory Baum spoke of where theology is being done today.

39

Statement by John Coleman

I want to reflect this afternoon on what I have learned from my experiences during this week rather than address myself to the paper I wrote for this conference, "Vision and Praxis in American Catholic Theology" [published in *Theological Studies*, March 1976]. There have been three experiences in particular which have spoken to me in a special way.

The first experience—one I had often this week—was a feeling of being a linguistic outsider in terms of the language being used. I am not referring here to the fact that many speakers used Spanish, a language, unfortunately, that I do not speak. Indeed, given the mix of the audience, I wish more Spanish had been spoken. I am using the term "language" in a broader sense. I want to address myself to the question of language and how it enters into the analysis I was trying to make in "Vision and Praxis" and in my earlier paper used by reflection groups in preparation for the conference, "Civil Religion and Liberation Theology." When I listened this week to the language that the women's group used, I realized that it was not totally my own. I would be either co-opting or corrupting it if I claimed that it was. It was and is a language that I have to learn, sometimes painfully. I want to be a careful listener before I try to speak it myself. Similarly, I would be corrupting or co-opting the language of the black theologians if I tried to speak it as my own. I was also a "foreign speaker" as I listened to the language of the Chicanos and the Latin Americans, even when they spoke English. This experience of linguistic marginality has led me to reflect upon the nature of language.

My first point is that language is always particular. There is no way of escaping the fact that *we all* speak limited, finite languages. In the first place, language is always particular because it is material. Any language consists of only a finite number of the almost limitless possibilities for sounds, rhythms, syntax, and grammar open to humans. These possibilities seem infinite in comparison to any language that we actually speak. Moreover, each language includes a rich reservoir of very particular symbols and metaphors. Often it refers to very definite places: a mountain, the sea, a country, a factory, a pueblo in California, a hill hamlet in North Carolina, the mining area in Chile. Language conjures up a particular people and historical events in the life of that people such that a language resonates with that people in a different way than with anyone else. We have all learned this if we have lived for a long time in a foreign country and spoken its language. There is no way of escaping the particularity of language because there is no way of escaping history, which is material and finite. As a Roman Catholic Christian who has been brought up with a vivid sense of sacramentality and the incarnation, I have come to live with the beauty and scandal of the particular. There is no universal that is not embodied in a concrete, particular form. Language's beauty and power lies in the fact that it is finite, limited.

Secondly, language is also always tribal. Language, culture, and religion are tribal because they define a people. Someone in this conference accused black liberation theology of being tribal. To this accusation the proper retort would seem to be "Yes, of course it is, but you mistakenly think that yours is not!" The lesson we all have to learn is the humility to recognize the limited, tribal nature of our own languages, modes of analyses, and traditions.

Every real community needs to have its own language. It needs its own heroes and heroines, its own special places and people and historical events to define itself. If it lacks these, it is not yet a people. The Chicanos have borne witness to the importance they place upon retaining their own language. Through that language, they are finding again their heroes and the events—often hidden and forgotten—in their own history that have forged them together as a people. Only they have a right to find again and rewrite their own history. No one else can do that for them. I have heard the women talking about the need to speak a nonmale language and to recover the "her-story" hidden and forgotten in male dominated history. The language we speak defines the group we belong to. There is a perfectly legitimate tribal interest in renewing or preserving one's own language. This interest is the passion for community and people power. James Cone reminded us of this when he said, "I am afraid that this language of liberation will be misused and co-opted unless I stress the black nature of it." A clear sociological sign that Cone was talking about real community was his insistence on controlling black liberation language and his ability to stake out that control. Real, viable communities have the power to do just that.

If the community is only in the process of forming it will begin to find a new language, as women have been doing here in the United States. In a similar vein, the Latin Americans rightly insist that the liberation language they are speaking includes a reference to a litany of martyrs who have suffered or died for their Christian witness for justice. Without a genuine regard to that litany of martyrs and the community experience that has given rise to Latin American liberation language, no one has the right to speak that language or to turn it into some abstract, speculative ahistorical orthodoxy.

My conclusion from these experiences is that there is no universal language. All pretense to speak *the* universal language stems from either obfuscation or domination. Every language is tribal. No one has had to learn this so painfully as America's white Anglo-Saxon privileged males who thought they could speak for all even though not all had a chance to be part of the dialogue. This is what I mean by obfuscation. It is what the Marxists call ideology. Michael Novak has made the point about the tribal limitations of white Anglo-Saxon male language in a trenchant remark about John Rawls's book, *A Theory of Justice*. Novak claims that Rawls is wrong to think he is speaking the universal language of justice or reason. Rawls's concepts of justice as fairness or his appeal to the disinterested "reasonable" observer in an original position untainted by class bias betrays his British American ethnic origins. Neither blacks nor white immigrant ethnics in America see justice in Rawls's cold, rationalistic, and analytic terms. For them justice is more likely to be found in the sweat and blood of a Martin Luther King, a Cesar Chavez, or the struggles of Appalachian coal miners than in some abstract ideal of the Anglo-American fairness of the "gentlemen's club."

Roman Catholics have recently learned the painful lesson of the high costs in claiming to speak *the* universal language. After centuries of pretension to speak to all in the name of God, humanity, or human nature, Catholics are beginning to learn that particularity, like history, is the human fate. Truth, once again, only comes riding a donkey. Roman Catholic truth will always remain a limited truth but it will be more limited than it has to be until Catholics open up their dialogue to everyone. Catholic theology and the Catholic story in North America will never be a liberation theology until women, the blacks, and especially the Spanish-speaking, who represent such a large portion of that Catholic story, tell their own versions of the American Catholic story. The goal for this kind of Catholic dialogue can be found in James Joyce's remark in *Finnegan's Wake:* "Catholicism means: Here comes everybody."

On the other hand, it is not so easy to learn the lesson that every language is tribal or to forego claims to speak *the* universal language. Several times during this conference I have heard assertions that such or such a position is *the* analysis. Not even science, let alone the social sciences, contains some magic key to the universal language. Every claim to be such a universal language, whether it comes from Marxian or Parsonian sociological schools, needs to be demystified. Every analysis within the social sciences which claims to be *the* universal analysis rests upon either obfuscation or domination. Social sciences work with models, particular, selective perspectives on reality. Models include as well as exclude. Every social science model misses some very important parts of reality or takes them into its analysis only on its own terms. It is only in a multiple dialogue with several models that one achieves the beginnings of truth.

At several points during this conference I heard blacks or women say to those who have used Marxist analysis in a dominative way: "Your category of class which you claim will cover everything does not do justice to sexism or racism. You treat sexism or racism only on your own terms—in a kind of dominative relation. Although racism, sexism, and class are interrelated, we are demanding that you respect the independence of each category and language system."

To my way of thinking, the insistence by some of the participants that scientific analysis—in this instance, Marxist analysis—is sufficient by itself to provide a full analysis of oppression reminds me of what I have been struggling against in university settings for the last couple of years. The ghost of the Enlightenment's claim that analytic scientific reason is the one legitimate language does not die easily. Analytic scientific reason, of which Marxist analysis is only one species, is, like every language, particular and tribal. It is helpful for some kinds of analysis and misleading for others. The insistence that it is not so limited seems to me part of the problem, not part of the solution. Perhaps the vigorous dialogue here between Latin American, black, and women's liberation theologies is a reminder to us all that no one of them taken alone is sufficient to provide a program for liberation from every species of avoidable human oppression. I do not wish here to construe my comments as an attack on Marxist analysis which, in its treatment of systematic economic factors, class bias, and ideology, is a very valuable tool of analysis. It would be as wrong to be blind to the unique and indispensable perspectives for social analysis in Marxism as it would be to forget that it is but one selective and limited perspective. To make it more than that is legitimate only as a faith, not as science. Liberation theology claims to use Marxism only as a scientific tool, not as a faith.

The second experience of the week is an ambiguity I felt about the open nature of the dialogue. I know from listening around to conversations that there is more internal discussion and critique among and within the various caucuses than has been allowed to surface in the open discussions. I know that not all the Latin Americans, blacks, or women fully share the common analysis and public face which is shown in the open forum. Yet, internal differences of analysis emerge only behind the closed doors of each separate caucus. Although we are all aware of this ambiguity, it is difficult to find a way to deal openly with it. The problem of ambiguity is once again related to the nature of language. Behind and embedded in every language is usually a vision of some ideal humanity and community. Languages, like communities, contain ideals. Many languages—Christianity, Buddhism, Enlightenment rationality, Marxism—are potentially liberation languages. The problem is that there is no pure liberation language or movement incapable of corruption. Given enough time all these liberation languages and communities have been corrupted. There is a shadow side to every liberation language.

One way to deal with this ambiguity in every language, community, or movement is to refuse to look at this shadow side or to look only at the best in oneself and compare it to the worst in the other. Another is to take an eschatological turn. Every honest Christian knows the myriad ways in which the gospel imperative of justice and peace has become obfuscated or corrupted. He or she knows the failures of the church. So Christians tend to say that they believe in the church and the Christian vision which has never yet existed. Similarly, an honest Marxist must sometimes feel ambiguous about the way the Marxist liberation language has cloaked totalitarian oppression and the lack of integrity, freedom, and justice in many parts of the Marxist world. What is essentially or, in principle, an open system, degenerates into a doctrinaire belief or institutional rigidity. The world, after all, has already seen its full share of Marxist imperialisms. The Marxist answer is to keep looking for the society that has not yet existed, a society based on the Marxist vision of justice and community. Every liberation language can get corrupted.

In my two papers, I was trying to be both honest to the historical record and open to criticism of the American cultural experience and American Catholicism. My aim in both papers is, indeed, very modest. In the Civil Religion paper [see above document no. 10], I am trying to remind Americans that the American experience contains, in its popular religion, some prophetic strands which could be called upon today to address issues of global justice. I would be greatly misunderstood if anyone thought I was claiming that this prophetic side of America was the only or even the predominant one. Most of our civil religion has been a sham. I would also be misunderstood if I were thought to be staking out some special salvific role for the United States. In our day and knowing what we now know about America's often shameful role in world affairs, great humility is called for by Americans. Nevertheless, because of its inordinate power, the United States will be called upon to play some role in world events in the next decades.

My measured claim for America's cultural civil religion is that, with all its ambiguity and corruption, with all the dominative class uses to which it has been put, with all the jingoism that goes under the name of patriotism, there remains, nevertheless, a liberation potential within it. Whether that potential ever again will be realized depends on what this generation of Americans chooses to do with its initial liberation language. In any event, civil religion will live on in the United States with or without our participation. The responsible thing seems to be to try to retrieve as much of the liberation potential in our national heritage as we can and not to leave the civil heritage to the yahoos. The responsible thing is to break open that heritage to the new questions of a world economic order based on liberty and justice. The irresponsible thing would be to leave the heritage in its best voices to die.

In the second paper, "Vision and Praxis in American Catholic Theology," I locate three historical figures in the American Catholic community: Orestes Brownson, John A. Ryan, and John Courtney Murray. I chose them because they spoke the language of my Catholic community. I chose these three as reminders that at least some of our earlier theologians were interested in questions of justice, peace, liberty, and freedom from oppression. I chose them as forerunners of concern for liberation in America. Brownson has been called a predecessor of Marx and Proudhon. He saw clearly the discrepancies between America's political ideals of democracy and equality and the economic system of social injustice, a discrepancy we still live with today. Ryan was a champion of a living wage and the rights of the oppressed working classes. He also struggled against racism and for a world economic order. Murray worked all his life to extend the sphere of liberty from religious, political, or state tyrannies.

I used these three figures to point out three theoretical weaknesses I see in liberation theology as presently practiced. The first weakness is that there is nothing in this theology to serve as an intermediate between eschatology and politics. In its thought liberation theology tends to move directly from eschatology to politics. This carries dangers that we will identify some concrete political program with the kingdom of God. It also can lead to a sterile impatience with *every* aspect of every status quo. I used Brownson to raise the question about how we can validate claims to know *just how* God is active now in the world, transforming and humanizing structures of oppression. A religious claim to knowledge of what God is doing now in the world and how he is acting demands epistemological warrant. Neither eschatology nor politics can validate a claim to know what God is now doing in the world to transform structures of oppression. I prefer Brownson's term "providence" to "eschatology" because it has built into it a greater tentativeness and humility than eschatology. It keeps us in a position of epistemological humility about claims that our actions here on earth are truly God's.

I use Ryan to make the point that liberation theology at present lacks a developed economic ethics. Liberation theology has a global theology and a global economics. It does not have an ethics which might help us make discriminating ethical judgments about alternative economic and political choices with which we are faced. Neither political praxis, global economics, nor general theology are sufficient to generate such ethical norms or principles. We still need a developed social ethics if we want to make judgments between competing possibilities for action. Otherwise, we must merely trust our intuitions, hunches, or blind stabs at praxis to determine what is just in a social arrangement. I am suggesting that liberation theology must become critical reflection on praxis with the help of ethical norms about the substantively good society and principles of distributive justice. These ethical principles derive from experience to be sure, but they are not reducible to politics or economics as sciences.

The main point I took from Murray was his concern for social pluralism and the civil libertarian tradition. I know from Peru's Ricardo Antoncich that the civil libertarian language is capable of ideological uses to maintain unjust class oppression. I argue, however, that in the United States that language does not seem to be totally corrupt. I agree with Ivan Illich in his book *Tools for Conviviality* that common law, civil rights, and the civil libertarian language

can still be indispensable tools to fight racism, sexism, class discrimination, and imperialism in the United States. We would be fools not
to use this precious, if imperfect and partially corrupted, resource.
We would be likewise fools not to take account of the limits of the state
in our social theology. For unjust totalitarianism, not the limited
state, is the rule throughout the globe. Liberation theology rightly
reminds us of the need to think about the common good, social
structures of injustice, and community. It rightly fights atomistic
individualism in politics and religion. Nevertheless, liberation is at
some point about liberty—freedom from unchecked economic *or*
political power.

My purposes in both papers remain very modest. At any given
point one has to make an empirical judgment about any language and
any community. If we judge that the language is simply corrupt or
bankrupt, we would do better not to try to retrieve the best prophetic
strands within it. It is better to let the language die because the
community has already died with it. If, however, the empirical
judgment is that there is still some kind of viable resource within that
language and within that community, it seems to me irresponsible not
to go about the liberating task of purifying that language, knowing all
the time that it is only one particular, limited national or religious
heritage. My judgment is that neither the American civil heritage nor
American Catholicism is so bankrupt that it is not worth the try to
reclaim its best, most prophetic tradition. My judgment is that
neither the American people nor the American Catholics are so
corrupt that they will not hear that prophetic tradition. Like every
people, Americans are most likely to respond to calls for liberation if
they are couched in their own language and tradition. My two papers
try to show the seeds of liberation theology in the American civil
heritage and in the history of American Catholic theology.

My third and final reflection comes from the rich and exciting
experience this week of hearing many different versions and stories of
oppression and visions of liberation. No one liberation theology is *the*
analysis. Together, they tell of God's mighty justice working to
uncover every oppression. Only if I personally enter into the liberation struggles of Latin Americans, Chicanos, blacks, and women will
I have any right to claim as my own something of their language of
liberation or to criticize it where it seems to me still weak. Only if
American Catholicism expands its present limited store of heroes and
heroines and makes the story of Chicanos, Puerto Ricans, blacks,
women, and oppressed non-Americans part of its story, much as
Israel did when it had to incorporate more than the original people of

the Exodus into Israel, will American Catholics create a liberation theology language in North America. Likewise, only when our civil religion expands its pantheon to include native Americans and other oppressed peoples on whose backs America was built will we have a revival of the now dormant liberation language in North America. My modest claim in my two papers is that there are some faint seeds of hope and some giants in our American and American Catholic pasts. If there were not we would have no reasonable hope that somehow today we will be able to do what *none* of our forebears in any sense did. For all of us, the most honest thing to say is that liberation theology is just beginning among us. For all of us, too, the truth of liberation theology stands as a judgment. History will judge us more by what we do than by what we say, by our orthopraxis rather than by our orthodoxy.

40

Statement by J. Deotis Roberts, Sr.

I have learned a great deal about the nature of oppression this week and also about the overlap of classes of oppression. This has made me more sensitive to oppression throughout the world, and I think this is good. It does not mean that as blacks we have not always been aware of our solidarity with the oppressed, as Professor Herzog would put it. Albert Schweitzer once said: "A fellowship does exist between those who bear the mark of pain."

Lerone Bennett attended the ceremony marking the independence of Kenya some time ago. The British flag was lowered and then the Kenyan flag was elevated. In the darkness there was great fanfare and great excitement. A fellow American, who was white, approached Bennett and expressed his great appreciation for the flag of independence and Kenya's freedom. Bennett, a black American, responded: "I do rejoice with the Kenyan people, but I am an American an I I am not yet free." "White Americans," he said later, "are always excited about the reality of freedom; they will even go to the ends of the earth, as it were, to die and sacrifice for freedom. But why is it that that same freedom is denied fellow citizens at home?"

I recall an incident with a colleague from New Haven, Connecticut. We were travelling from Boston to Philadelphia by car. As we passed through various parts of New England he rejoiced over the participation of his ancestors in the Revolutionary War and how glorious, of course, his past was. And I was thinking that my name was not my own, that my ancestors came to these shores in chains. Ours is a different history; ours is a different perspective on the relationship between religion and history in the American context. I think we have to consider this as a part of the total analysis of the bicentennial. Our concern is "where are we going from here?" What does this mean as far as our future liberation is concerned? Our past in this society has not been one that we can now celebrate.

My experience is that racism is a universal fact. I have experienced it on most continents, especially on the continent of Europe. But I am aware that only in this country and in South Africa is it of such a hearty variety. We have had to battle with it for centuries and have gained some experience with it from this battle.

There are certain psychological ramifications to racism. The pathology in the psyche of black people and white people needs to be brought into theological discussion. I know there is a tendency of "either-or," of talking politically or existentially. But the pastoral aspects of a theology of liberation need to take under consideration not only what Marx has said, but what Freud would have us understand about the unconscious, even the collective unconscious aspects of racism.

Herzog has made the point that U.S. Protestant theology is European-oriented. We do not want to make the mistake of transporting or transplanting from Latin America another form of theology without transforming it so that we can make it useful to ourselves.

There are dimensions of black thought which come not out of the Western orientation, but out of our reassessment of the riches of our African ancestry. In the Fall 1975 issue of the *Journal of Religious Thought* there is a dialogue between black and African theologians on similar concerns in the area of theology. We see this as something that enriches our approach because in the whole context of American Christianity we have not been offered even in integrated church bodies the privilege of input. Interracial fellowships have been one-way streets, and we have not had an opportunity to enter into a kind of mutual sharing of spiritual riches.

And finally, I want to point out that in black religion we can shout on Sunday and march on Monday. We see no contradiction between piety and activism, which seems to be common in both the Latin American and the white American experience. We do have programmers among us as well as theologians. Very few of those people are here, but in our teamwork we see the need to develop very careful programs. We are beyond the period of "rapping" and we are now in the period of "mapping." We do know the mathematics of power.

41

Statement by Gregory Baum

At this point of the conference I feel rather "broken up." We have discovered—in a process that was painful to me—that there are distinct modes of oppression: oppression of class, of race, and of sex. We have heard that these modes are interrelated but that they cannot be reduced to one another. Each stands by itself. What is difficult and sometimes almost impossible is to articulate their interrelationship. And yet we cannot wait until we have resolved this question. We have to act, sometimes even without knowing all the answers. In theology it is our task to bring together these various aspects. As a Catholic theologian I have the tendency to look for a synthesis very quickly: I want to get it all together in a system. But I must resist this temptation, I must try to live with these tensions and make the very tensions the source of action and new reflection. This is where I am at the moment. I have no synthesis. What I try to do as a theologian is to live creatively out of tensions.

In doing theology in this new situation we do not expect much help from the past. Catholic theology in North America was not interested in understanding the historical situation. Yet since I want to move ahead with my Catholic brothers and sisters, and together with them gain a better understanding of where we are and where we ought to be, I do not wish to separate myself from the past. What theologians are looking for is a language that makes sense to the wider community. Theological elitism is no help. To gain this common language and to find words and symbols that unite the community in the struggle for justice, we do want to reread the past and re-examine our history, in the hope of finding in past experiences hints and signs of where the Spirit is leading us. I appreciate this return to our sources. Rereading our history from a new point of view may reveal aspects we have overlooked in the past.

The obvious example of this in Canada is the Quebec experience. It is almost completely overlooked by English-speaking Canadians, even when they are Catholic. Quebec theology is unknown in Anglo-Canada. French Canada is a Catholic culture; it is almost three centuries old; it was for the major part of its history on the defensive, especially after the British conquest. Over the last fifteen years, however, an extraordinary evolution has taken place in Quebec, often called the "quiet revolution," which has affected the self-understanding of French Canadians and, consequently, their religious life and their theology. In the middle sixties, the French Canadian bishops appointed a commission, under the chairmanship of the sociologist Fernand Dumont, to study the crisis of the church and make major recommendations for the future planning of Catholic life. The so-called Dumont Report was eventually published. It presented a careful analysis of the church in the state of crisis and introduced the idea of *l'église comme projet*, the church as project. The church, according to this idea, is still unfinished, it remains to be built, and it must be constructed according to the aspiration of all its members. What the report recommends is the involvement of parishes and other grass-roots organizations in an ongoing discussion on what the church in Quebec should be like. Out of such an involvement the church will take shape. The bishops should understand themselves as planners and enablers of these church-wide discussions and as the responsible leaders in the construction of the contemporary church. This is a new ecclesiology. And yet so great is the indifference in regard to French Canada that English-speaking theologians in Canada (and the U.S.A.) have paid no attention whatever to this development.

What about Catholic theology in the English-speaking part of Canada? English-speaking Catholics in Canada were like the Catholics in the U.S.A., a subculture. The country was owned by Protestants. Catholics did not belong to the mainstream. They struggled to survive, to retain their identity, to be faithful to what they regarded as most precious, and by doing so their religion became to them a wall that separated them from the rest of society. Catholic theology in those days, mainly drawn from Roman sources, was a language that kept the community together and affirmed their difference from the dominant culture. This inherited theology did not mean much to the priests, except as a social symbol; that is why it disappeared so quickly when the changes came in the sixties. These changes were drastic. They were due not only to the teaching of Vatican II and the influx of European theology but also to social success of the Catholics in Canada (and the U.S.A.) and their entry into the mainstream of the culture. It seems to me it would be wrong for Catholics to despise their past and hate themselves for not having produced a perceptive theology. What their religion and their religious culture enabled them to do was to survive as a minority, as a group of late arrrivals, as a despised class. It is important for me to say this; for the Irish are easily given over to masochism and often read their history against themselves. We have to learn to appreciate the Catholic past in North America and its religious and theological expression for the grain of resistance and self-affirmation contained in them.

I wish to make two more remarks in regard to Catholic theology on this continent. When we speak of theology, we usually follow the European model and look for the important theologians and their publications. This was the approach of John Coleman in his paper ["Vision and Praxis in American Theology: Orestes Brownson, John Ryan, and John Courtney Murray"]. He spoke of three significant figures in American Catholicism. But is this a useful model to follow? It is my view that the function and style of theology in North America are different from the European model. In Europe, it seems to me, theology is more specifically academic. It is largely confined to the university. On this continent I have the impression that the outreach of theology is much wider. In the summertime, as we all know well, there are endless numbers of institutes, summer schools, study weeks, workshops, symposia, theology seminars, etc., which involve many people in theological study and reflection in a framework that is task- or action-oriented. It is my view (which I cannot back up by statistical research) that more people are involved in theologizing in North America. When European theologians are invited to speak in America, they are amazed by the large audiences they attract. This does not normally happen to them in Europe. While American Catholic theology, I suppose, suffers from not being sufficiently at home at the university, it also gains very much from being identified with a much wider section of the church.

Now a second remark. If I were asked to comment on Catholic theology in English-speaking Canada, I would not know where to turn unless I took seriously the church's collective documents. The Catholic church as well as the other Christian churches produces teaching documents on a variety of topics, many dealing with practical issues, documents which have been composed by local theologians and churchmen and reflect, possibly more than any other publications, the theology of English Canada. Curiously enough, these ecclesiastical documents often adopt refreshing and innovative theological approaches and defend theological positions rarely found in more academic publications. Catholic and Protestant church documents present a social theology that is remarkable. In the U.S.A. the pastoral letter "Powerlessness in Appalachia," published by thirty bishops of the region, presents a social theology that deserves the closest attention. To find the most important aspect of Catholic theology in North America it may be necessary to turn to ecclesiastical documents of various kinds rather than to the more academic publications.

III

After the Conference

SECTION THIRTEEN

Evaluation

Although the organizing committee made no special effort to publicize the conference in the media, numerous journals commented on the conference. Articles included:

1. Beverly Wildung Harrison, "Challenging the Western Paradigm: The 'Theology in the Americas' Conference," Christianity and Crisis, *October 27, 1975.*

2. Robert McAfee Brown, "Reflections on Detroit," Christianity and Crisis, *October 27, 1975.*

3. Alfred T. Hennelly, "Who Does Theology in the Americas?" America, *September 20, 1975.*

4. Kenneth J. Aman, "Liberation and Theology: The View from Detroit," Commonweal, *September 26, 1975.*

5. "Jesus the Liberator?" Time, *September 1, 1975.*

6. Sheila Collins, "Liberation Theology: A Challenge to American Christians," Grapevine *(Joint Strategy and Action Committee), September 1975.*

7. Gregory Baum, "The Christian Left at Detroit," The Ecumenist *September-October 1975.*

8. Mary Littel, "Theology in the Americas: 1975," Catholic Peace Fellowship Bulletin, *October 1975.*

9. Alice Hageman, "Liberating Theology through Action," The Christian Century, *October 1, 1975.*

10. Thomas C. Fox, "Liberation Theology Tests U.S. Conscience," National Catholic Reporter, *September 5, 1975 (with responses in subsequent issues).*

In this volume we include only Gregory Baum's thorough analysis.

42

The Christian Left at Detroit

by Gregory Baum

A week-long conference, "Theology in the Americas: 1975," was held in Detroit in August 1975. It brought together Christians from South and North America to study theology by taking as their starting point their respective historical experiences. The first idea of the conference, entertained by the Chilean priest Sergio Torres and a group of friends, was to invite the well-known Latin American representatives of liberation theology and bring them into conversation with theologians of the U.S.A. Such a dialogue, Torres hoped, would prompt U.S. theologians to rethink their relationship to the dominant culture of their country and engage in critical reflection on the American experience from the viewpoint of the poor. The conference was to be prepared by study groups all over the country, who would discuss what this new approach to theology meant to them. As soon as this process was set up and the various study groups reacted to the suggestions sent by the organizers, the nature and purpose of the intended conference began to change. The planning and holding of the conference, I should add, remained a process open to feedback and modification.

The first critical remark made by the study groups was that there was no single American experience. A theological reflection on American history cannot be complete unless one invited Christian speakers for the black community, for Mexican-Americans, for Puerto Ricans, for Asian-Americans. And since the experiences of men and women have been so different, Christian women should be invited to reflect on their struggle for emancipation in church and society. The second critical recommendation made to the organizers was that a conference of this kind should not simply be a gathering of

399

scholars. Intellectuals, by their specialized knowledge and, possibly, a certain professional deformation, easily create an elitist climate in which less educated people are condemned to silence. At the conference Christian activists should be invited to speak for their struggling communities. The conference should give voice to the voiceless people. Moreover, should not members of the workers' movement be invited?

Following these suggestions, the nature of the Detroit conference significantly changed. The Latin American theologians were there in good number; the U.S. experience was represented by white academics and social organizers willing to engage in theological reflection, by black Christians and their theologians, and by other Christian representatives of marginalized peoples and groups in the U.S.A. The conference became a more complex undertaking and its purpose was no longer clearly defined. It brought together people and groups that had never talked to one another before. It intended to focus on various forms of oppression—economic, racial, sexual—which are usually considered separately, but which are interrelated in ways that remain largely hidden. The change in the purpose of the conference accounts for the extraordinary richness of the experience, but as we shall see it also produced some of the difficulties that were to emerge.

Since I regard the conference as an important theological event and since it challenged ordinary academic theology in significant ways, I wish here to describe and analyze the Detroit meeting. This is not an easy undertaking. The papers that were sent to the study groups prior to the conference were simply drafts. For this reason, I shall not quote from them. Secondly, the speakers at the conference often spoke as representatives of a community—we shall analyze what this means further on—and hence mentioning their names may not do justice to them nor to the concern they represented. Since the conference was prepared by, and tried to deal with, a wealth of material, a single article must of necessity be a selection. Finally, this account reflects my own interpretation of the conference.

The Common Faith

Since the participants belonged to different groups struggling for freedom in their particular historical situations, and since it was not easy to perceive how these various movements were historically interrelated, it was too soon for the participants to speak of mutual solidarity. In a summary report made at the end of the conference, it clearly said: "At the present time our solidarity is tenuous. It is preferable to suffer for some time with our present consciousness of the difference which we have just begun to explore and not try to contrive solidarity." At the same time, a common faith did pervade the entire conference and created the taken-for-granted atmosphere of all the discussions. What was this faith? Since it provided the accepted starting point, no one paid much attention to it. Still, I wish to analyze this common faith as the theological dimension underlying the entire conference.

The participants shared a common unwillingness or even inability to accept the world as it is because they believed that it was meant to be different. They believed, moreover, that this world could be changed. This faith was present with such a density that one could touch it with the hands. It was a faith one could breathe. This common faith is of course a form of traditional Christian faith. According to Christian teaching, the world is indeed under the judgment of God, it is sinful yet meant to be different; despite its sinfulness it is still divinely destined to salvation; and because of God's redemptive work in Jesus Christ, Christians hold that fulfillment of the divine promises is becoming a reality, however provisionally, in human history. I call this "the common faith" not only because it was the shared conviction of the participants at the conference (a few exceptions I shall mention further on), but also because it combines in an important way doctrinal trends taken from the Catholic and Protestant traditions.

The biblical faith understood in the Catholic tradition has always included the conviction that the grace of God *truly transforms* human life. God's redemption brings creation marred by sin to the fulfillment of its own inclination. In traditional Scholastic language, "grace perfects nature." Against the Reformers' emphasis on the abiding sinfulness of life, the Council of Trent insisted that the sanctification produced by divine grace was an actual transformation of the human being. In the Catholic tradition, God has always been understood as a divine mystery, operative from within people's lives as the source from which they reach out for truth and justice. The metaphysical system of the Scholastics provided a framework in which the divine causality in human life (as *causa prima*) enabled people to become the causes of their own historical destiny (as *causae secundae*). Admittedly, the weight of this theological tradition in the Middle Ages and in modern times was applied to the transformation of *personal* life. It is applied by contemporary Christians also to that of the *social* reality constituted by persons and their interrelationships.

The Protestant tradition has some difficulties here. Can human life be significantly changed? This is a great problem for Lutherans, and it is not always clear whether sanctification as understood in the Calvinist tradition implies a constitutive transformation of human life. These difficulties have to do, I think, with a peculiarly Protestant view of divine transcendence. (We shall return to this topic later.) Yet the common faith I have described embodies a critical dimension characteristic of the Protestant tradition. Protestants have always been greatly impressed by the sinfulness of the world. Protestants were more ready than Catholics in the sixteenth century to submit intellectual systems, ecclesiastical institutions, and all cultural expressions to an evangelical critique. They were unwilling to make positive affirmations in regard to human life unless they first measured it by the gospel norm. The radical inability to accept the world as it is because it is meant to be different and the trust that it can be changed—"the common faith" in our terminology—combines Catholic and Protestant trends in its perception of the gospel. I have called this the common faith, moreover, because it is sometimes shared with people who do not call themselves Christians.

This common faith deserves further attention. It made the Detroit conference a theological conference even when traditional theological subjects were not at the center of people's attention. It is interesting to contrast this common faith with the shared convictions present at other kinds of meetings. What is the common spirit, for instance, at ordinary, academically-oriented theological conferences? At such meetings there is the personal faith of the theologians; each theologian in her own way lives and thinks out of her understanding of the gospel. But there is usually no shared explicitation of what this faith implies in regard to society, its sinfulness, and its future. I suppose that the socio-historical dimension of divine revelation only emerges in people's consciousness when they are profoundly disturbed by the injustices in the world, when they find themselves struggling against the destructive trends in their society, and when out of this socio-political engagement they begin to perceive the message and the promises of Jesus in a new way.

At the Detroit conference this common faith was also shared by sociologists and economists. They, too, read and analyzed the society to which they belonged out of the convictions that it was unacceptable, that it was meant to be different, and that it could be changed. This differs strikingly from the presuppositions that dominate at professional meetings of social scientists and most university departments of sociology and economics. The majority of social scientists still defend the value-free nature of their research and their scientific conclusions. But is not the perception of reality in some way linked to our place in history? Should not scientists clarify for themselves the values and images out of which they perceive society? At Detroit, at least, they shared a common conviction.

The common faith was shared by some people at the conference who did not think of themselves as believers. But since they were involved in struggling against the oppression inflicted on their historical communities, they not only refused to accept the world as it is but also hoped that it could be significantly changed, even if they felt no need to ask questions about the hope that was within them.

The Latin American Theologians

The first group to address the conference was composed of the Latin American theologians who had been invited. Many of them were known to the participants through the English translations of their books and articles. Present among them were Juan Segundo, Hugo Assmann, Beatriz Couch, Enrique Dussel, José Miranda, José Míguez Bonino. (Gustavo Gutiérrez arrived later during the conference.) The group decided to speak as a community on the subject of liberation theology. They wanted to present the analysis of their historical situation and their theological reflections as the product of a common struggle and a shared intellectual process. Instead of arguing out the differences between them, they wanted to give witness to theology as a collective enterprise. What emerged very clearly was how their approach differed from customary academic theology. Theology, understood in terms of personal scholarship and achievement, tends to become the possession of the individual thinker: At universities and divinity schools theologians argue out the right and wrong of their positions. Academic theology usually presents itself as individualistic and competitive. The Latin American thinkers, as well as the other Christian groups who addressed the conference on subsequent days, sought a different approach to theology. While the Latin Americans differed among themselves, especially when it came to deciding with what struggling political group in their countries the Christian communities should ally themselves, they still regarded themselves as a community of thinkers reaching out for the truth in solidarity.

The Latin American theologians acknowledge their total inability to accept the world as it is because they believe that it is destined to be different. Because of this, their epistemology differs from that of traditional philosophy and theology. They refuse to regard truth as the conformity of the mind to a given object. Such a concept of truth only confirms and legitimates the world as it now exists. The world, for these theologians, is not a static object which the human mind confronts and attempts to understand; the world is, rather, an unfinished project which is being built by the people who make it up, and its reality tomorrow and in the future depends in part on what these people think and do. Knowledge is not the conformity of the mind to the given, but a dimension of this world-building process. Our perception of society affects our action and hence inevitably enters into the making of the future. Truth then cannot be measured by conformity to the given. The norm of truth must be taken from the kind of world knowledge helps to create. If concepts legitimate an evil world and help it endure, they cannot be called true even if they could be verified by the application of scientific method. But if concepts enable people to perceive the oppressive structures in the present and discover the trends in history that seek to transform and overcome these structures—this, too, is a scientific task—then they contribute to the process by which the world becomes more truly human. The true and the good are inseparable.

The Latin American theologians applied this epistemology to the revealed truth of Christianity. What is revealed to us is God's judgment on an evil world and God's gracious presence to the world as source of transformation and new life. This revelation took place at particular moments in time, in particular historical situations; it dealt with the concrete circumstances of a historical people. To understand what this revelation means today—and this is the task of theology—Christians must listen to God's Word addressing them from within their concrete historical situation, with ears shaped by their own collective struggle. Truth, divine truth, then is not the conformity of the mind to a divine message uttered ages ago, but the discernment of present evil judged by this message and the discovery of the redemptive movement in history promised by this message. The norm of theological truth, then, is not drawn from an analogy with classical philosophy; it is drawn rather from its role in the ongoing process of world-building. Divine truth is redemptive. The norm of theology is taken from its weight and power in history. God's truth, mediated through Christian faith, enters into the transformation of the sinful world in accordance with the divine promises. In the vocabulary of the Latin American theologians, the norm of truth in theology is "liberating praxis." Christian truth is the perception of the world mediated by Jesus Christ that leads to the divinely promised transformation.

The Latin American theologians explained this viewpoint as if it were foreign to the North American intellectual tradition. But since American pragmatism is a left-wing Hegelianism of sorts, since contemporary process thought regards knowledge as part of the process of world-building, and since the critical sociology of our day evaluates the perception of society in terms of its legitimating or transforming effects, the Latin American epistemology was not strange to North American ears. Catholic theology, it is true, has been in contact with left-wing Hegelian thought only in recent years through its dialogue with Marxism and post-Marxist criticism.

To understand the meaning of the Christian faith, the Christian community must come to a correct understanding of its concrete historical situation. Conversion to God implies self-knowledge. This principle also applies to communities. They too must come to a correct collective self-understanding. The assessment of the evil powers which oppress people in their concrete situations is, therefore, an essential part of theology, for without it the meaning of divine revelation cannot be grasped. The Latin American theologians called this part of theology "social analysis." What they meant by this was mainly an economic analysis of their people's oppression.

In presenting this analysis to the conference Latin American theologians and social scientists worked together. They explained in some detail how the economic dependence of the Latin American countries on the system of corporate capitalism, with its center in the North Atlantic community and more especially in the U.S.A., has not only led to the impoverishment of the mass of the population in city and country but also affected the cultural and educational institutions and through them the consciousness of the people in general. With the help of their national bourgeoisies, the Latin American countries supply raw material and cheap labor to the international economic system. Yet the major part of the profit goes to the owning classes in the developed countries. The economic system, in search of cheaper production costs and wider markets, has generated a new imperialism, the heir of the old political colonialism. According to this analysis, the further industrial development in Latin America, based on capital controlled from the North and following the "Western model" of production for profit, contributes some wealth to the national bourgeoisies and vastly enriches the economic life of the northern countries. The center of the system inevitably enriches itself at the expense of the periphery. The Latin American thinkers insisted that the success and prosperity of the Northern democracies were dependent on the ongoing exploitation of Third World countries. Yet the exploitative dynamics between center and periphery operates even within the developed countries. The industrialized areas enrich themselves at the expense of the outlying regions. Even in these countries, the exploited classes afflicted with poverty and insecurity will grow while the class of those who derive enormous benefits from the economic system will shrink in size. A point in history has been reached, according to this social analysis, when South and North America have become a single interconnected economic unit. The multinational corporations transcend national boundaries, they make decisions without loyalty to any national community, and they acquire power that exceeds that of many national governments. The fate of all countries has been conjoined. Who protects this corporate capitalism? Since the owning classes in the Northern nations, especially in the U.S.A., derive most of the benefits from the present system their governments are willing to protect and use various forms of power in the world, especially in Latin America, to crush the movements of people who seek to sever their destiny from capitalist economy. The speakers stressed as a point of important theological significance that the Latin American peoples cannot escape their oppression and have access to food and the necessities of life unless the whole world is changed. Change at the periphery today demands the dismantling of the center. What follows from this is that when North American thinkers analyze the ills and injustices in their own countries, they should not confine their view to the conditions at home but take into consideration the total picture, the economically interconnected world. Any analysis of the oppressive trends in society must be "holistic."

To make this point before a North American theological audience was, in a sense, the main reason why the Detroit conference had originally been planned. I already mentioned that this original intention had been significantly modified by subsequent developments. But even when the perspective shifted from economic to other forms of oppression and it seemed almost impossible to arrive at a holistic approach, the struggling groups agreed that the meaning of Christian faith and theology emerges in a community only as a reflection on their struggle and only through a clear analysis of the structure of their oppression. Engagement precedes reflection. In the words of Gustavo Gutiérrez, theology is never *actus primus*, it is always *actus secundus*. It is the reflection on the struggle for emancipation. Theology cannot be produced from any historical position whatever. It can be done only by Christians identified with a movement dedicated to the emancipation of oppressed people. This viewpoint distinguishes liberation theology from customary academic theology.

The key word in this connection is "praxis." What does this strange word mean anyway? The English word "practice" refers to any action that applies a particular theory. Praxis, on the other hand, is practice associated with a total dynamics of historical vision and social transformation. Through praxis, people enter their historical destiny. Since praxis changes the world as well as the actors, it becomes the starting point for a clearer vision and a more correct understanding of history. Praxis is the precondition of knowledge, even though in turn this knowledge issues forth into a new praxis. The dialectics of truth begins with praxis. The Latin American theologians explained that for the Christian communities involved in a common struggle the dialectics of praxis and truth is guided by the vision of God's promised reign and the forward movement of history guaranteed by God's revelation in the passover of Israel and the resurrection of the marginalized and crucified Jesus. Even the Latin American theologians who regarded themselves as Marxists understood the logic that moves human history through the class struggle to a universal emancipation as guided and assured by the redemptive presence of God to the world.

Let me say a word about what the Latin American thinkers called "social analysis." Why did they use this word in the singular? When we turn to the social sciences, we actually find many different analyses of society and its ills. The Latin Americans used the word in the singular because they define their approach in opposition to the dominant social science (functionalist or positivistic) which presents itself as value-neutral but which, in their eyes, legitimates the existing order and contributes to its stability. The Latin American theologians have opted for a conflictual sociological model, making use of a Marxist-style class analysis, which brings to light not the stability but the contradictions present in the social order and orients the imagination toward the transformation of the present system. In this perspective, social science and emancipatory commitment cannot be separated. There are obviously different ways of making a class analysis, there are diverse schools of Marxist and post-Marxist social thought; and in fact when the Latin American theologians decide on the practical course of action to be adopted in their countries, they differ considerably in their analysis of the situation. But in the face of the dominant social science approach, they feel united in the use of a critical method and the emancipatory commitment and hence use the word "social analysis" in the singular. The differences between them do not shatter their solidarity. Since the left under political pressure tends to splinter into small, competing, and often sectarian groups and thus weaken its impact on society, the Christian left in Latin

America wants to avoid this splintering. They believe that the Christian symbols out of which they define themselves contain resources that enable them to wrestle against the divisive tendency.

The Black Theologians

The struggle of the black community in the U.S.A. was represented by a group of speakers including well-known theologians such as James Cone, Herbert Edwards, Major Jones, Deotis Roberts, and Preston Williams. Their ideas were familiar to many participants from their publications. The typical U.S. American liberation theology is black theology. Black theological thinkers, participating in and reflecting on their people's struggle for freedom, have developed (without the epistemological preoccupation of the Latins) a critical analysis of the oppression in which they live in the U.S.A. and of the legitimation of this oppression mediated by the culture and religion of the nation. They have repudiated traditional theology as white theology, that is to say, as being vitiated by a largely unconscious ideology which makes the black people invisible, which marginalizes their problems, which sacralizes the white man's history in America, and which serves as a defense of white racial supremacy. The god of white America is not the true God, nor is the lord of the white churches the Jesus in whose name alone there is salvation. Black theology affirms God's victory in the exodus from slavery and God's ultimate triumph in Jesus as the repudiation of the gods of the dominant cultures, whatever their theological names may be. Black theology has developed its own original language of negation, not derived from Hegel and Marx but from the Scriptures themselves. We must negate the world before we can find the true God. The model for the inversion of history is not class conflict but the divine promises that the first shall be last and the last first.

The black theologians were confident that their religious tradition provided power and vision for their people's struggle for freedom. In this regard their experience differed considerably from that of other Christian groups struggling for emancipation. Most of these saw the oppressive trends right in their own religious traditions and therefore had to subject them to a radical critique. This was certainly true for the Latin Americans. Since the Catholic church had been largely identified with the dominant classes, first with the colonial rulers, then with the seigneurial system, and finally with the national bourgeoisies, Catholics had to submit their religion to an ideological critique before they found access to its liberating core. The blacks insisted that theirs was a different experience. Their faith had always been in the God of the black, in the true Lord over the white masters who subjugated them, who promised them freedom and empowered them to persevere in the struggle. While there were traces in black preaching that promised the people "pie in the sky," pacified their angers, and fostered their passivity, these did not constitute the dominant trend. The lived religion and its most authentic expression in the spirituals expressed the soul of the black movement for freedom in America. The black theologians were therefore content with the traditional evangelical images of divine transcendence. On this issue an important controversy broke out later at the conference. The Latin American theologians in particular preferred to think of God as transcendent mystery *present in history* as ground and dynamics of the forward movement toward the promised liberation. For the blacks, the divine Lord *over and above history* was reassuring even in the perspective of liberation. For if this Lord is higher and stronger than the pharaohs of oppression, there is hope for the people's freedom.

It is worth noting that the black theologians also presented themselves as a community. They differed in many ways among themselves, but to demonstrate their solidarity in a common struggle and to illustrate how their theological approach differed from current academic theology, they adopted a common stance. Why should they allow the highly rational conceptualization characteristic of the Western tradition to dominate their thinking? Blacks, they said, prefer to think in terms of stories and metaphors; and since the Bible itself was written in this style, they preferred to keep their theology more specifically black. The competitive model of truth, found in the Western academy, makes the effort to clarify various positions an argument between many thinkers, each wanting to be right; but if truth is uttered in metaphors and stories, it may be more helpful to adopt a cooperative model of truth which allows different perceptions to be clarified by understanding them as perspectival contributions to a collective self-understanding. A similar critique of Western intellectuality was made by the Christian women on the subsequent day.

Yet the black theologians had to formulate their disagreement with the Latin Americans who had spoken to the conference on the first day and whose critical economic analysis had dominated the subsequent discussions. The blacks felt that a class analysis is not enough. The name of the oppression under which they suffer is racism, and while racism is related to economic exploitation and class identification, it cannot be reduced to economic oppression. The blacks complained that the holistic approach recommended by the Latin Americans subordinated and underplayed the problem of racism. It was no accident that in their talks the Latin American theologians had not paid much attention to the racial inequalities in their own countries. The blacks feared, moreover, that arguments over the economic system might divide the black community and weaken them in the face of the white majority. For the blacks the primary enemy is racism; and since the Latin Americans defined as principal enemy the economic imperialism of the Northern nations, especially the U.S., the blacks could not declare themselves in solidarity with them.

What emerged was a conflict of different views, grounded in different concrete historical struggles, which the conference had to confront again and again. The common faith that the world in which we live is meant to be different and destined to be changed was unable to create perfect solidarity; but it did keep the differing groups in an ongoing conversation, first in public and later in small groups. Their historical struggles were different, but as Christians they were unable to let go of one another. They belonged together, even if their common faith could not at this time be translated into solidary action. In the words of a Latin theologian, the blacks suspect Latin theology of being too white, and the Latins suspect black theology of being too American. What does the black community want? Freedom and power to participate in the American empire? Or freedom and power to make the world the home for all peoples? There was no need, however, to read the statement of the black theologians as a defense of American power. What they wanted to affirm in the strongest language was simply that any separation of a class analysis from the analysis of race makes them suspicious. For if this separation takes place, then they, the blacks, shall be bypassed in terms of the more universal problem and hence remain where they have always been, at the lowest rung.

At the same time it would be unrealistic for the black community to look away from the link between racial and economic oppression and for the sake of supposed unity omit to analyze their own community in terms of class identification. Since the black community is in fact divided according to class, an unwillingness to see this would only make the community more vulnerable. It was pointed out in the discussion that black Americans successful in education, commerce, and organization are easily lured away from their communities to white institutions where they learn to identify with the interests of their colleagues of equal status and income. This institutional trend often leaves the black community without leadership. Such issues of class may prevent a black neighborhood from becoming a strong and vital community producing its own leaders.

The Forgotten People

After the presentation of black liberation theology on the third day, the important shortcoming of the conference came to the fore, a shortcoming related to the shift that had taken place in its essential purpose. As I explained at the beginning of this article, at first the conference intended to introduce a team of Latin American theologians to groups of U.S.A. theologians, and it was only after the critical recommendations of the preparatory study groups that the Christians invited to the conference became more representative. Present at Detroit were the Latin American theologians in good number; present were theologians and representatives of the black community and Christian thinkers involved in the women's movement. The blacks and the women could rely, as much as the Latin Americans, on a fully developed liberation theology. Invited to the conference were also active Chicano groups, Puerto Ricans, representatives of the native peoples, and Asian-Americans. But upon arrival, these groups found that they had no opportunity to address the full assembly. This omission was due to the change in the nature of the conference, which had been inadequately assimilated by the organizers. Since originally the accent had been on theology and since the last mentioned groups are only beginning to reflect on the Christian meaning of their struggle and have not worked out a full-blown liberation theology, they were not assigned adequate space. The organizers saw the mistake and regretted it. Fortunately the Spanish-speaking U.S. Americans got hold of the microphones and made their presence heard, and thanks to their active participation in the full assembly and the discussion groups, they communicated their message well and made an important contribution to the conference. Even the silence of the native peoples gave eloquent witness to the ambiguity of the American enterprise.

Let me add at this point that the organizers of the conference tended to identify North America and the U.S.A. so that they forgot —Americans often do—that there was a country in the North called Canada. When Canadian Christians were invited it was too late to organize study groups in preparation and formulate a Canadian contribution to the topic. Several Canadians attended the conference as sympathetic observers. It would have been worthwhile to introduce the conference to the complexity of the Canadian historical experience, so different from the U.S. American one, and to report on the Christian reflection on the struggle for justice in Canada, especially as found in Protestant theologians of the thirties and in Catholic thinkers of Quebec over the last fifteen years. But to have insisted on a

Canadian presentation at the conference would have silenced even more the less affluent peoples. The Canadian Christians who attended the conference as sympathetic observers resolved to create a network of theologically-concerned persons to reflect on the struggles for freedom and justice in Canada, including the Quebec people, the heirs of the British tradition, the more recent immigrants, now English-speaking, from Europe, Asia, and the Caribbean Islands, and of course the cruelly humiliated native peoples.

Let us return to the Chicanos. The Chicanos do not regard themselves as an ethnic minority in the U.S.A.; they think of themselves as a conquered people whose land, language, and culture came under the control of the U.S.A. in 1848 with the Treaty of Guadalupe Hidalgo and who have come to live as exiles in their own territories. They regard themselves as mestizos, Spanish and Indian, and when they speak of themselves as a race, *la raza*, they refer to the synthesis of two distinct anthropological races produced by a common history. While the Chicanos have clung to their cultural heritage, their poverty kept them from developing themselves; many even lost the hope of ever rising from the lowest level. Among the small groups, guided by courageous leaders, the struggle for self-possession has always continued. Over the last decade, largely inspired by the blacks' determination to change their situation in America, Chicano activists have begun a movement to bring together the people dispersed among several states of the Union and organize them in a common cause. In this emancipatory struggle the Chicanos have discovered that their church had largely identified itself with the dominant culture and the ideals of white Anglo-America. While they constitute a large minority in the Catholic church, in some areas even a majority, they have practically no hierarchical representation. The Chicanos regard their Hispanic-Indian form of Catholicism as their authentic religious heritage which they have defended against the Anglo spirit demanding efficiency and mastery even in religious matters. These men and women refuse to abandon their own form of the Catholic religion, which to outsiders often appears superstitious but to them signifies their closeness to nature—the earth and their bodies. This nature is the place where God is present to them. This closeness to nature they contrast with an Anglo-Christianity, even in its (Irish) Catholic form, that is principally concerned with the domination of nature—the earth and the body. The Chicanos feel that the ecological wisdom of ancient Indian religion survives in their Catholic faith.

The firm but gentle protest of the Chicanos brought out more than any other event the radical impossibility to generalize about movements of liberation and the theology which may accompany them. Even the black theologians found themselves accused that, by dividing the United States into two groups, the white oppressor and the black oppressed, they made invisible other oppressed groups in the country, such as the Chicanos. Could it be that out of this inadequate perception of reality the blacks were unable to find ways of cooperating with Chicanos in the parts of the country where they share a common position of oppression? But then, should these two disadvantaged peoples argue in front of a white audience? Is not disunity among the disadvantaged, bred by the psychology of oppression, an element that strengthens the power of the oppressive system? The suggestion was made that the two peoples, the black and the brown, enter into conversation by themselves, without white listeners. It is to be hoped that such a network of conversations between black and Chicano groups will be created as a result of this conference.

The Chicanos had messages for various participating groups. They expressed their disappointment with the Catholic theological community which, instead of being a voice reminding America of the forgotten Catholic people, tends to overlook their existence altogether. Catholic theologians carry on their theological reflections as if all Catholics in the U.S.A. were identified with a specifically European tradition. Could not a greater awareness of the Chicanos on the part of theologians lead to a more pluralistic and hence more authentic vision of the Catholic church and become a lever for wrestling for a more decentralized church organization? At this early point of their struggle, the Chicanos are still looking for visibility in the country. The symbols and structures of their own church tend to disguise them rather than proclaim their presence.

Of importance was also the Chicanos' reaction to the leadership offered by the Latin American theologians. These latter theologians appeared as sons of successful people, well educated and well spoken, possessing an articulate intelligence associated with university life. We are different, the Chicanos said; we are just beginning to acquire a greater number of educated leaders; we are more simple people; we are still closer to the level on which we were held by the oppressor. If we permit you to be our leaders, they said to the Latins, we shall be in the situation in which we have been for so long, unable to find our own words to express our situation and incapable of devising modes of action that correspond to our present needs and our past experience. Even the confident, holistic economic analysis proposed by the Latin Americans posed a problem for the Chicanos. The analysis may be correct in principle, the Chicanos said, but if we receive from you the key for understanding our own subjugation before we reach the maturity to argue with you from a basis of equal education and equal confidence, we will not move toward a liberated form of self-possession. Our struggle is our own. Other people can help us by being in solidarity with us, but the leadership and direction of the movement must come from ourselves, however tentative these may be at the beginning.

These conflicts were important; they were painful to the participants; but they were also deceptive. They allowed members of the conference, especially those belonging to the dominant culture, to let these disagreements relativize unduly the plight of the oppressed peoples and make one critique to take off the edge from the other. We often tend to balance contrasting positions in the creation of a single, complex picture and thus permit our mind to reconcile—and thus falsify—what remains as yet objectively unreconcilable in history.

The conference listened to other voices. What do academic theologians know of the Puerto Ricans' struggle to find themselves as a people and of the Catholic participation in this movement? At best we think of Puerto Ricans as the underprivileged poor in New York City for whom the church must provide pastoral care. But of centers where Catholic activists carry on theological reflection we know very little. And what do we know of the Christians among the native peoples who participate in their emancipatory struggle and who discover the complicity of the Christian churches in the subjugation of their brothers and sisters? How can these Christians relate themselves to the ancient Indian wisdom? Who listens to their theological reflections? Who lends an ear to Asian-Americans who try to understand their struggle for emancipation out of their Christian faith?

The Emancipation of Women

On the fourth day of the conference, Christian women presented their theological reflections on the struggle for emancipation. Again they presented themselves as a community. Their very mode of dealing with their subject provided a critique of traditional academic theology. Several women, including well-known scholars such as Sheila Collins, Alice Hageman, Beverly Harrison, and Rosemary Ruether, sat on the chairs that had been put on the platform in front of the auditorium. Each of them contributed to the presentation from her own perspective. The experienced scholars among them had the self-discipline to give equal space to others. The women in the audience who wanted to add their own reflections were asked to take a chair on the platform. To make room for a new speaker, a woman who had already spoken would empty her chair and move back into the audience. This style of critical reflection tried to replace the highly competitive understanding of truth, proper to academia, with a more cooperative understanding that makes room for contributions from various perspectives as long as they are born of the emancipatory struggle. Why should it always be necessary to cut the flesh of living reflection with the knife of scientific reason? A more contemplative reason may be able to gather the insights based on a variety of experiences and discern in them, despite possible conceptual discrepancies, a shared movement toward truth. The highly individualistic context of research and reflection in the male world of academia often persuades the thinker that the truth is his. Actually the entry into truth is a communal process.

The women insisted that sexism, that is, the subjugation of women as women, is a distinct form of oppression. It is historically interrelated with economic and racial oppressions and hence can never be found in pure form; still, it is an oppression *sui generis*. Sexism is very ancient, it is part of the patriarchal culture we have inherited; it is woven into the very consciousness of our civilization. Unless the historical struggles against economic exploitation and racial injustice become conscious of the ancient sexist heritage, they will not greatly change the lot of women. The speakers remarked that the published works on Latin American liberation theology and U.S. American black theology do not mention the subjugation of women at all. In Latin America this should be an important issue since an oppressive *machismo* dominates the entire culture. At the same time, in presenting the elements of their liberation theology, the women made it clear that they did not identify themselves with the middle-class women's movement, especially as it appears in the mass media, where women often seek new freedoms for themselves in terms of the individualistic and competitive nature of contemporary culture. Only too often do successful women seek new opportunities by asking other women, often black women, to assume a servant role for them. The feminist theologians at Detroit did not want to separate their liberation struggle from the struggle against other forms of oppression.

Contrary to the popular view, modern industrial capitalism did not improve the situation of women in society. Beverly Harrison briefly summarized her research in this field. The new dominant class, the bourgeoisie, created the ideal of "true womanhood," that is, the image of the spiritual, passive, nonproductive woman who defines herself wholly in terms of her husband and children. Since the new industrialism had destroyed the family home as a unit of production and made men work in offices and factories away from their dwelling places, what took place was strict separation between the public and the private spheres. The public sphere of industry, commerce, politics, and education belonged to men, and the private sphere of home and religion belonged to women. Women were excluded from public responsibility and participation in the productive process. The nineteenth century women's movement in the Anglo-Saxon world was the reaction of spirited women against this form of genteel but paralyzing subjugation. At the same time, while society upheld the ideal of true womanhood for the successful classes, working class women were condemned to live in conditions of oppression: hard work, insecurity, utter poverty, and often humiliation. To this day, the poor women in our society are torn apart by the actual conditions of their lives as workers and the image of "true woman" which the mass media and the instruments of culture communicate to her.

Sexism is ancient in our culture. It is woven into the very consciousness we have inherited. The split between spirit and body in human self-understanding and the subsequent quest to achieve the mastery of the spirit over an unruly body created a consciousness which allowed men to identify themselves with the spirit while projecting the body image on women. Since in patriarchal society the negative side of any dualism is projected on women, the women's movement must wrestle against every kind of dualism in the perception of reality. Women must therefore be critical of the place of rationality in Western culture. Here reason rises above and triumphs over the web of life; here reason is aggressive, competitive, and vindictive; it is "the trump card against matter." In a less alienated world, reason might actually emerge out of life, promote its unity, direct the forward passage of this life toward maturity, and be "the very lifeblood of matter."

Women's liberation theology must eventually question the dualistic theism which seems to dominate biblical religion. Dualistic consciousness expresses itself in perceiving God as the master over the earth and thus in making God the supreme image protecting the mastery of men over women and legitimating other forms of domination in society. The women at Detroit were at one in rejecting the view of divine transcendence that has prevailed in Christian thinking, especially in popular religion, Catholic and Protestant, and found a particularly strong expression in Protestant evangelical and neo-orthodox piety. Dualistic theism may not be universal in the Christian tradition: In the ancient church some thinkers spoke of God as ground and matrix of existence. Thomas Aquinas thought of God as *ipsum esse subsistens,* and in modern times Paul Tillich understood God as ground of being. The women were not certain whether these traditional attempts to understand divine transcendence as the mode of God's presence (or immanence) in life and cosmos were helpful at this time. They wanted to wait for a while, experience the transformation of society, and then see whether a more adequate way of speaking of divine transcendence will emerge.

Divine Transcendence

The question of divine transcendence became important at the conference at a later point, after the lecture given by a Protestant theologian. While this lecture acknowledged the oppressions in society, saw God's judgment on the sinful world, and recognized the need to struggle against economic, racial, and sexist exploitation, it was delivered in a tone of evangelical piety that annoyed many members of the conference. The theologian had expressed his sympathy for black theology, especially—it was felt—because of its emphasis on the lordship of God. People vehemently criticized the tenor of his lecture. They felt that he had spoken of liberation so easily and so globally that he escaped concreteness and thus bypassed people's actual struggles. They felt, moreover, that he clung to the story of Jesus as if the manner in which this story is communicated to us and understood by us could not be subject to ideological distortions and hence was not in need of being critically examined. Finally, it was the view of divine transcendence that offended many participants. The lecture gave the impression, though the text did not specifically say so, that God and Jesus were available to Christians wherever they were situated, just by turning inward in their hearts. According to the theologies of liberation proposed by Latin Americans, blacks, women, and other struggling groups, God is not available to people in any position whatever, but only as they identify themselves with the historical struggle against evil and injustice.

What took place at the conference was a clash between two views of divine transcendence. In the course of this argument the theologian who had given the lecture was misunderstood and treated, I think, unjustly, but the clash brought to light a significant difference between two kinds of Christian spirituality, an issue crucial in the development of contemporary theology. Traditional piety in the Protestant and Catholic churches visualized God as the supreme Lord over and above human history. This God was available to believers as they reached out to him, inwardly or upwardly, beyond the actual, historical situation in which they lived. God's transcendence was here unrelated to history. It was, as it were, at right angles to history. Contrary to this, the spirituality associated with many forms of contemporary theology holds that God's transcendence is mediated in and through history. Believers encounter the divine by involving themselves in the struggle for humanization. Since the transcendent mystery is operative in the promised transformation of human life, personal and social, it is here, in *active* engagement and *contemplative* presence to this engagement, that believers encounter the living God. The "non-historical" understanding of divine transcendence, so the Latin American theologians insisted, makes God the eternal protector of an existing order and religion and guardian of status quo; the "historical" understanding of divine transcendence, on the other hand, reveals God's presence in history as source of its redemptive transformation. God is present in people's struggles for their emancipation. The idea that the transcendent divine mystery is immanent in human life and the cosmos is in keeping with the major trends in Catholicism; the idea is more difficult to assimilate in the Protestant tradition, except in the trends influenced by Hegel. The idea is clearly opposed to the view of divine transcendence entertained by neo-orthodoxy, which still exercises a strong influence on American Protestantism, even when preachers have consciously repudiated it.

Black theologians, as I mentioned above, unashamedly affirm God as the Lord of lords. They do not fear that such a view of God will legitimate the existing order. Why not? The meaning of religious language depends in part on the socio-political situation of the people who utter it. When oppressed people invoke God as the Lord of lords, they mean that God is more powerful than the pharaohs of the world. But when the king's men who lord it over their subjects invoke God as the King of kings, they legitimate their king's rule as the one who governs in the name of God. What follows from this is that when a theme of black theology is taken over into white theology, it changes in meaning. If in the dominant culture God's self-communication is understood as taking place in the sacred space, apart from and superior to human history, then the historical struggle for justice and social change is only of secondary and derived importance. The really real is then quite independent from the political order. This is a common view in white America. But if religion is used to trivialize history in this way, it becomes an ideology for the successful classes. In the biblical perspective it is clear, however, that the Holy One of Israel reveals herself in the liberation of her people. Any attempt to separate divine transcendence and human liberation, as we find it for instance in the Hartford Appeal, is against the authentic understanding of Christian teaching.

No Doctrine of Total Depravity

Where did the theologies of the struggling peoples leave the white male participants of the conference? It is a temptation for Christians, especially if they are heirs of a doctrine of total depravity or the utter sinfulness of the human being, to fall into masochistic self-accusations and indulge in protracted convulsions of guilt. Some participants occasionally fell into this trap. They were willing to identify themselves remorsefully as enemy and oppressor. A few men even wanted to get together to develop a theological theory appropriate to their own situation. This was strange; for the important point made at the conference was that traditional theology (and social science) was precisely the theory appropriate to the white man's situation. The wish of the few to sit together meant that they had not yet fully grasped the message of the conference that this is exactly what the American world is: the few white males sitting together and planning society. The more common response of the white participants was the determination to be in solidarity with the struggling peoples, to act in new and untried ways, to enter upon new experiences, and eventually to produce religious reflection from this perspective.

Certainly, to the extent that we are sociologically identified with exploitative institutions, we participate in the social sins of our communities. We even continue to derive advantages from our privileged position. The injustices in the world and our social participation in them produce a painful realization. This makes us sad; sometimes it burdens us with great sadness. But this does not send us on "a guilt trip." It should be clear that we do not find ourselves where we are through personal guilt. The last thing the struggling communities want is to see us indulge in masochistic self-denunciations. While we are sociologically identified with our class and country, we have the freedom personally to identify ourselves with the poor, to find actions that give body to this identification, to perceive the world in a changed manner, and eventually to think thoughts and develop theology that actually promote the transformation and liberation of God's world.

Gustavo Gutiérrez tried to clarify the task of Christian theology, wherever it may be developed, as the systematic effort to reread history from the viewpoint of the rejected and humiliated. This effort defines the Christian left, in this sense I have used the term in the title of this article. Normally history is written by the victors. The successful classes mediate their self-understanding to the entire nation through lore, culture, and the telling of history. But what would happen, for instance, if Canadians were willing to reread their history from the viewpoint of the native peoples? They would discover dark sides of their own culture, related to their material interests, which normally remain unacknowledged and unrecognized. It is the task of Christians in Canada to integrate these repressed elements into the Canadian self-understanding and to seek modification of the material interests which produced the oppression of the native peoples in the first place. One does not have to be a Christian to reconsider one's cultural self-understanding in terms of the oppressed communities. But Christians ought to do this. Gutiérrez specifically demanded that the Christian churches, in fidelity to the humiliated and crucified Jesus, identify themselves with the poor of the world and thus, by relying on the divine promises, come to a proper theological perception of world history. Such a rereading of history is not a purely intellectual task. One cannot identify with the world's poor abstractly and in general. The poor are concrete, historical classes, peoples, and sections of humanity, and hence identification implies solidarity with their struggles. Here too, then, theology must be reflection on praxis. We learn from the story of Jesus that history is changed not by the powerful but by the weak. The current that transforms history comes from below, from the underclasses, and moves society toward greater freedom by subversion. "God has put down the mighty from their thrones, and exalted those of low degree; God has filled the hungry with good things, and sent the rich away empty."

In a recent pastoral letter, the Canadian Catholic bishops, seconded by the other Christian churches in Canada, were willing to look at the development of the Canadian North from the viewpoint of the native peoples and gave voice to the voiceless by demanding that any plans of government and industry to exploit the natural resources of the North must be worked out in consultation with the native peoples. These peoples must at all costs be allowed to protect the land which is the matrix of their survival.

Since the foundations of the white settlements in North America were commercial and expansionist, since the new colonies, whether French or British, were extensions of European empires for the benefit of the rich, and since even the American Revolution did not challenge the inherited system but only shifted the center of profit-making, it is possible to read American history purely and simply in terms of conquest and exploitation. A document, "The American Journey," distributed to the participants prior to the conference, did this brilliantly. Economics was the driving force for the creation and development of the American republic. The author had been willing to reread American history in terms of the humiliated communities. Many participants, however, felt that this was not the whole story. The spiritual and cultural aspirations of the early settlers and their descendants were not simply ideologies legitimating the exploitative and expansionist nature of the American enterprise. They were also the endeavor of a people in a new historical situation to create a civilization for themselves, reflecting the values of their religion and their vision of a new humanity. In other words, a rereading of history in the light of the humiliated communities should not—this, at least, is my position—make one overlook the cultural symbols of the past that at this time could produce a new imagination and provide impetus and direction for radical social change. The Latin Americans, to give an example, may be fully justified in looking at the North American journey simply in terms of their dependency and exploitation, for it is in their own Latin American history that they hope to discover positive cultural symbols to strengthen their solidarity and inspire their common struggle. But U.S. Americans of the dominant culture, while acknowledging the repressed side of their people's past, must search for more in American history than for the sources and patterns of exploitation. They must try to discern in the American experience symbols of new life which can become at this time the sources of a new national self-understanding and an impetus to costly social change.

Do we know that symbols of reconstruction are present in a people's history? One theologian at the conference felt that our present trouble is linked to the demonic nature of the entire Western enterprise. By linking the quest for understanding to the quest for mastery, the progress of Western civilization inevitably leads to the domination of weaker peoples and the destruction of the earth's surface, whether this be through capitalist or communist empires. Most members of the conference, I think, rejected such a doctrine of total depravity. It went against the "common faith." But are there persuasive arguments to show that present in any people's history are cultural elements that provide strength and direction for a movement of social reconstruction? At this point some participants turned from Marx to Durkheim. According to the sociology of Emile Durkheim, the social institutions with which people are identified generate cultural symbols, values, ideals, and ultimately even religion, which reflect not so much what society actually is—this would be the Marxian view—but what society wants and aspires to be. The collective self-understanding of a people, generated by reflection on the great moments of their history and by experienced closeness at the time of crisis, contains symbols that transcend ethnocentric ideology, judge the actual situation of the society, and provide images for possible social change. There is no national history without hope. This is the context in which a discussion of Robert Bellah's contribution to the U.S. self-understanding would have been useful.

Let me also present a theological argument against the doctrine of total depravity, applied to a culture or a nation. According to the Catholic tradition at least, wherever people struggle for their self-understanding and cooperate in the creation of a representative culture, the mystery of God is present to them. God's victory in Jesus Christ assured the universality of divine grace. There is no culture from which God is wholly absent. A purely demonic enterprise can not endure for long: The Nazi reign only lasted twelve years. Present in the culture of any people are the dream of the promised land and the yearning for the peaceful community. There are hints of sacramentality in the experience of any nation. In my view, it is the task of critical theology to discover these hints. For if the pressure for social change comes upon a people, in this case the American people, purely from without, without connection with their own historical experience, they must reject it as a foreign influence. If an entire nation is to reconstruct its social life, the driving force must be fidelity to its own history.

Marxism

At the Detroit conference the term "Marxism" was constantly used. It is not easy to know what people mean when they use this word. Marxism could refer, for instance, to the system of ideas found in the writings of Karl Marx. Marxism, I suppose, could also refer to the various political institutions that call themselves Marxist, be they Communist empires and Communist countries or be they the Communist parties in the West, e.g., those of France and Italy. But Marxism could also refer to the development of Marx's ideas by subsequent thinkers who adopted Marx's perspective but carried forward his thought. From this point of view, Marxism is a complex and often divergent intellectual tradition, constituted by the systematic attempts of various scholars or even schools to use principles derived from Marx to come to a better understanding of society and its history. It was in this latter sense that the word Marxism was used at the conference.

I should remind the reader that a certain Cold War rhetoric has created the image of Marxism as a uniform and fixed system of ideas, institutionalized in identical ways in Communist countries and Communist parties. Catholic thinkers, in particular, tended to speak of Marxism in a reified way—very much as we used to speak of "Protestantism" as a single reality, defined by a few principles, thereby dispensing ourselves from studying the actual currents of the historical phenomenon. In the Catholic church, a new approach to the study of Marxism has been generally accepted only after Pope John's recommendation in *Pacem in Terris*.

In order to clarify the use of the word "Marxism" at the Detroit conference, let me introduce a distinction made by Yves Vaillancourt during one of the discussions. Marxism can be understood (1) as a philosophy, (2) as a plan of political action, and (3) as an instrument of social analysis. The Christians gathered at Detroit did not speak of Marxism as a philosophy. For them the dynamics of history was ultimately revealed by God in the history of Israel and the person of Jesus Christ—even if they should hold that this dynamics moves through class conflict and dialectical reconciliation. Nor did the participants generally speak of Marxism as a plan of action, except a few members from Latin America who were discussing the strategies of liberation in their countries and the search for suitable political allies. The constant references to Marxism at the Detroit conference understood it almost exclusively as an instrument of social analysis.

The Latin American theologians, as I mentioned earlier, showed that Christian theology, in an attempt to come to an understanding of its historical situation, must engage in a social analysis that brings to light the sins of the world, that is, the contradictions within the inherited system and the oppression which they produce. While there are a variety of Marxist social theories, it is possible to define a social analysis as "Marxist" if it focuses on the economic system as the key factor of oppression, if it makes class analysis the central and indispensable element for understanding the social situation, in terms of the interests of the class that owns and controls the major industries. Marxist social analysis at Detroit did not refer to any kind of Marxist "orthodoxy." Who is still interested in Marx's analysis of early industrial capitalism or his theory of surplus value? What contemporary Marxist analysis is interested in are the contradictions of modern, corporate capitalism and their link to the recurring economic crises, to the expansionist policies of the capitalist world, to the creation of dependent territories with impoverished masses, and to the spread of poverty and unemployment even in the industrialized capitalist countries. Are the disturbing events we read in the newspaper accidents of history, or are they related to the economic system that we have inherited?

If Marxism is understood as an instrument of social analysis, it is easy to see that Christians can learn from it, and that if they make it an essential element of their theology of liberation, they may even be willing, in this sense, to call themselves Christian Marxists. In similar fashion Christians have called themselves Christian Platonists and Aristotelians without endorsing the elements of these philosophical traditions irreconcilable with the Christian faith. Yet how useful the Marxist analysis is for understanding the whole of U.S.A. society is a matter of dispute. Since the racial and ethnic identities are so strong in the U.S.A. that they form cohesive patterns which mediate, and in some cases impede, the formation of economic classes, a Marxist social analysis must be highly qualified and nuanced if it is to shed light on the oppressive structures in such a nonhomogeneous society.

Nevertheless the kind of critical social analysis, called Marxist in the sense defined above, has been used by Christians in many parts of the world to formulate their social positions. It is my contention that with Pope Paul VI's *Populorum Progressio*, this kind of analysis has entered Catholic social teachings. Let me give an example of Marxist social analysis (as defined above) drawn not from papal documents but from a recent pastoral letter on Powerlessness in Appalachia, written by the Catholic bishops of the region. (The pastoral is available from the Catholic Committee of Appalachia, 3-1A S. 3rd Ave., Prestonburg, KY 41653.)

Why are the people of Appalachia always oppressed, the Catholic bishops ask? When the mines were working and the people had jobs, they were exploited; when the mines closed, the people were unemployed; and now that many mines are open again, the people's exploitation is not really changed. What is the reason for this? The bishops insist that it does not lie in a lack of generosity on the part of the more successful people in the area, nor is it due to any bad will on the part of the men who run the large corporations. What is involved here is a systemic evil. The principles operative in the large corporation that determine the fate of Appalachia—and the rest of the world—are at odds with the well-being of people. The letter mentions two such principles. The first is called "technological rationalization": This means that in the planning of the operation by the decision-making board all factors of production are considered in terms of their contribution to the total process. Each factor is technologically perfected to make it more efficient in the operation of the whole. These factors include the laborers. The policies made by the board of directors in regard to the workers are produced by the same logic that determines the decisions in regard to all other factors of production. Decisions regarding people are made as if they were things. This is the principle of technological rationalization. The second principle mentioned in the pastoral letter is called "the maximization of profit." This is not a reference to personal greed or lack of charity. It refers, rather, to a principle of planning and decision-making. It simply states that when the board of directors is confronted with various plans of action and development, they will study them carefully, compare them one with the other, and eventually choose the plan that promises to maximize the profit of the company. It is fidelity to this principle and not lack of personal virtue that causes these corporations to make decisions regarding people and their environment that have such devastating effects on Appalachia. The Catholic bishops go so far as to say that Appalachia is here a symbol of the country and the world. The analysis applied to understand powerlessness in Appalachia provides the key for understanding the exploitation in other parts of the U.S.A. and in the Third World. The theology of captivity, movingly developed in the bishops' pastoral letter, is based on what at the Detroit conference was called "Marxist" social analysis.

Let me add that the pastoral letter makes it clear that it does not recommend Marxism as a plan of political action. It does not advocate the public ownership of the giant corporations. It insists, rather, that these corporations are not the only power in the land. There is political power, and its task is to restrict and restrain the activity of these corporations. What is needed, therefore, is that the people dedicated to justice organize, reach out for political influence, and demand that the government protect the well-being of the poor and the integrity of the environment. The letter adopts a reformist position. Still, the radical analysis of the ills of society will make people dream of an alternative economic system where production is determined by the realistic needs of people in society and not by technological rationalization and the maximization of profit.

Theologies of Liberation

Throughout the conference it became clear that one should only speak of liberation theologies in the plural. Each such theology is based on a community struggling for freedom in a concrete historical society, and while they share in a common faith (as I described it at the beginning of this article) they do not wrestle against the same enemy and hence for the time being remain somewhat distinct in their efforts. The participants agreed that there were several forms of oppression, especially those of class, race, and sex, and that these are always interstructured in ways that are historically different in different societies. This point was most clearly expressed by Rosemary Ruether. It could well be that for some peoples the economic oppression is the central, overriding element, to which all other oppressions are subordinated. These people could not be faulted if other groups, struggling out of their situation, regard racist or sexist oppression as the principal enemy. What each group should do in their own place, however, is to examine the forms of oppression which appear secondary and come to a clearer understanding of how these are interstructured with the principal oppression. In some incipient way, then, all liberation theologies reach out for what the Latin Americans called the holistic view.

The participants also agreed that there is no overarching theology of liberation, of which each particular theology is just a special case. Some members even asked the theologians of the dominant culture not to elaborate a general theory of liberation. It would be idealistic (in the bad sense of the word) to suppose that theology could reconcile social movements and mediate between various forms of self-understanding which are grounded on conflicting material conditions and interests. At the same time, since the participants wanted to remain in conversation and discover the historical relationship between their various emancipatory struggles, they actually strained to find a universal language for their respective conditions, a language which would not neutralize or suppress but rather protect and strengthen that particularity of their struggles. For the time being, however, if I understood the drift of the conference correctly, the participants wanted to speak of liberation theology only in the plural.

Theologians of the dominant culture in America are unable to produce a liberation theology. The Latin American theologians even asked them not to use liberation theology as a new toy to make their classes more interesting. Liberation theology is born out of a concrete struggle, and hence when it is presented outside of this context, its very meaning is transformed. This does not mean, of course, that there is no liberating, intellectual task for the theologians of the dominant culture. By opting for solidarity with the marginalized sections of society, especially in their own country, they are able to develop a critical theology, that is, they are able to discern in the inherited religion the ideological trends and liberate the customary theology from its identification with the structures of domination. These theologians are able to come to a more Christian understanding of their society by rereading its history from the viewpoint of the oppressed peoples and develop what Rubem Alves has called "a theology of captivity." The above-mentioned pastoral letter on Appalachia and several pastoral letters on social issues written by the Canadian Catholic bishops have produced important elements of such a theology of captivity. Difficulties in theology, Gutiérrez said at the Detroit conference, used to be only difficulties in theology: We have come to realize today that many difficulties in theology cannot be resolved prior to significant social change.

Since American theology, which here means white, male American theology, did not make a very impressive showing at the Detroit conference, some participants were overly dejected and spoke of the bankruptcy of our theological resources. But is it surprising that we do not have a theology that can deal successfully with the contradictions of our society? Theology cannot perform miracles, Yves Vaillancourt said at one discussion: Since theology can only move a little ahead of the actual historical situation, how can we expect theology to be an instrument of reconciliation when we are in fact divided by objective factors of history? Had American theologians of the dominant culture presented themselves as the self-confident interpreters of the struggles of their country, that would have been the great deception.

Before closing this article, I wish briefly to mention three more related points. First there is the ecclesiological implication of liberation theology. The Latin American theologians insisted that their reflections, though well researched and hence academic, were based on the reflections of the struggling Christian communities in their own countries. The blacks too spoke of the meaning of the gospel as it emerges in living congregations. The women admitted that when they first discovered the weight of antifeminism in their religious tradition, they were estranged from Christianity. It was only later, in consciousness-raising groups, that they discovered the meaning of *ecclesia*. It was this experience of struggling community, of shared insights, shared burdens, shared confidence, that gave them access again to the meaning of the gospel. There was common agreement that liberation theologies are not the product of single thinkers. They are reflections of communities involved in struggle.

But why should struggling people be concerned with theology at all? What does religion have to do with the quest for emancipation? This question was asked several times by participants who did not regard themselves as Christians even though they shared what I have called the common faith. One sociologist, Michele Russell, said that she could understand why middle-class people who involved themselves in the struggle of the poor were in need of relating themselves to a transcendent. This was for them the source of motivation. But she could not understand why the poor or the oppressed themselves were in need of such a reference. She thought that the struggle itself would provide community, vision, direction, and inner strength. This question presupposes, of course, that religious experience is in the long run dispensable. But is this true? Most of the participants had not asked themselves this question at all. They thought of religion as a dimension of life that would participate in all the significant events of their existence, and hence also in their struggle for emancipation. But when asked the question, they were willing to attempt a tentative answer. Some said that their faith provided them with a vision beyond the concrete aim of their emancipation and a critique of the means used in the collective struggle. Others stressed that the Christian call to love prevented the collective aims of the struggle from overshadowing the meaning of personal destiny. Christians who experience their religion as a constant obstacle to their social engagement will soon abandon it, yet such a decision in no way solves the question out of what symbols they want to define their lives and with what faith they will move into the future.

I wish to make a final remark on the ubiquity of sociology at the Detroit conference. Many of the arguments that emerged among the participants were in fact classical arguments in the history of sociology, even if the participants were not aware of this. Karl Marx and Max Weber were both present at the conference. The unwillingness to understand society purely in terms of an economic analysis was expressed in terms that recalled Weber's criticism of Marx: Class and status, not just class, must be analyzed to understand the power structure in society. The marginalization of blacks and women, for instance, is the low status assigned to them, which then affects their economic life and acquires class significance. I mentioned earlier that Durkheim was not absent from the conference, especially among the participants interested in the cultural factors through which people define their identity. Curiously enough, Max Weber's analysis of alienation and powerlessness through expanding bureaucratization was hardly dealt with. It was mentioned once by a few workers, present at the conference, involved in wrestling against the bureaucratization of their unions. The absence of the Weberian analysis was regrettable, for it supplies a critique applicable to capitalist as well as socialist societies. Incidentally, I might add that present at the conference were a group of workers as well as representatives from Appalachia.

All in all the conference was an important theological event. Inevitably it bore the mark of the confusion characteristic of our time. A tidy conference in a broken world is possible only if the real problems are forceably kept outside. What the conference did was to help the groups present to see the viewpoints of other struggling communities and to reach out for a commitment to their own position that *in some way includes* the concern of these others. Such an inclusion, however partial, anticipates what the Latin theologians called the holistic view. While the historical conditions for achieving a holistic view are not present at this time, the conference helped the various groups to stretch their self-understanding and initiate some action toward a more total vision of humanity, free and reconciled. The conference facilitated the creation of many networks of research and cooperation among various groups as the *praxis* dimension of the week-long conversation.

SECTION FOURTEEN

The Follow-Up
of the Conference

The organizing committee attempted to be faithful to the "process" of the Detroit conference, adapting to the requirements of the grassroots groups. Accordingly, at the end of the conference the participants elected a new committee, with greater representation from the various ethnic and social groups, to coordinate the follow-up.

This committee drafted a proposal entitled "The Contextualization of North American Theology." The title itself expresses a change in perspective: There is no longer any attempt to "apply" liberation theology in North America; nor is the attempt simply to discover the "meaning" of liberation theology in the North American situation. Rather the goal is to contribute to a new theology that emerges from the historical, social, and religious context of the North American experience.

The following document is a synthesis of the objectives and the methodology of the follow-up.

431

43

Contextualization of North American Theology

The future of North American theology concerns many people today, especially those who are preoccupied with the concepts of pluralism and the contextualization of theology. We hear about Latin American, African, and Asian theologies. What we call Western theology has been largely, if not exclusively, a European theology.

This seems for many Christians the right time to develop more authentic North American theologies. Otherwise Christianity in the United States will lack the prophetic voice required of it by the ecumenical demands of today and the future.

The context would include many different aspects and issues, one of which, by itself, is far-reaching: The U.S. dominates a large part of the world in economic and technological power. There must be a critical Christian word addressed to the great human issues that arise just from that fact.

The American dream has been increasingly challenged in recent years. For many North Americans, U.S. history expressed in religious symbols is a covenant of freedom and democracy; for some people at home and many in the Third World, it is an enterprise of oppression, domination, and imperialism.

North American theology has to be concerned with the deeper questions of how to speak of Christ in the midst of the ongoing moral crisis of the U.S. It is necessary to recover the tradition of idealism and struggle against oppression in our own history, both secular and religious, and work toward shaping a theology for the future.

There are many perspectives for such a task. Since theology is not the Word of God itself, but a reflection on that Word from the present perspective, the question of the future of theology has to deal with all the claims of Christ over contemporary realities. Politics, language, mass media, education, ecology, urbanization, behavioral sciences, and technology affect the language and mission of the Christian communities.

The aim of this program is to explore one aspect of the "context" of the reality in which Americans live: the dynamics of power and powerlessness in the present American experience. To understand the meaning of the Christian faith, the Christian community must come to a correct understanding of its concrete historical situation. Conversion to God implies self-knowledge. This principle also applies to communities; they must come to a correct collective self-understanding.

The political experience of the U.S. involves two levels: international responsibility, and the domestic complexity and variety of forms of domination and oppression. A North American theology will be different from European theology or Latin American theology. But it is urgent to have a correct understanding of the will of God for our present and our future. God is calling American Christians to conversion, and our obedience to the Lord demands a critical evaluation of the uses and abuses of U.S. power.

A NEW METHODOLOGICAL APPROACH

This program will explore new theological methods. The experience of the work in Detroit indicates three:

The Experience of Ordinary Christians

Theologizing no longer means simply studying sources and ideas in the seminaries or universities. That is not enough. Theology has to spring from the experience of all Christians, both academicians and nonacademicians, who are trying to discover Christ in the Scriptures and in their own lives. There will be a special effort to relate to the experience of oppressed people who are struggling for their liberation here in this country and abroad.

This North American theology will be done primarily, though not exclusively, by groups of the oppressed themselves and will arise out of their own particular experience of oppression. The assessment of the evil powers which oppress people in their concrete situation is an essential part of theology, for without it the meaning of divine revelation cannot be grasped.

Theology and Social Sciences

It is clear for theologians today that theology has to use sociology and psychology to explain the world. But it is not clear how the social sciences are an integral part of theology as are philosophy and other traditional disciplines. Besides that, it is necessary to demystify the so-called value-neutral analysis of social scientists who interpret the U.S. reality.

The task of developing a structural analysis of the U.S. is increasingly seen as integral to theological reflection, suggesting a promising new methodology in North American theology.

Theory and Practice

There has been a change in the understanding of truth, in the sociology of knowledge in general and in theology in particular. Thinking is not now considered prior or superior to action; rather, it takes place in action. The Christian religion was founded not on a word, but on the Word made Flesh. Faith is no longer simply "applied" or "completed" in action, but for its very understanding (and this is theology) faith demands that it be discovered in action.

It is necessary to relate Christian theory and historical practice, faith and praxis. Some theologians are talking of a theology defined as critical reflection on historical praxis. Practice refers to any action that applies a particular theory. Praxis is practice associated with a total dynamics of historical vision and social transformation. Through praxis, people enter into their historical destiny. Since praxis changes the world as well as the actors it becomes the starting point for a clearer vision of God in history.

This program will explore this new way of knowing and its implications for theological reflection. Instead of talking about studying theology it seems better to begin "doing theology"—that is, to discover the meaning of revelation in the midst of experience and the struggle for change and conversion.

THE OBJECTIVES OF THIS PROGRAM

1. To develop new modes of theological reflection that take seriously the different social, ethnic, and racial realities. The program will help further to advance a black theology, a Hispanic theology, a feminist theology, and a reconceptualization of theology among the

dominant groups, following the criteria of the real context of the U.S. experience.

2. To incorporate as themes of theology our own heritage, the challenge of the Third World and the racial, social, and structural complexity of this country.

3. To explore new methodologies in theology, dealing with the relationship between truth and practice, faith and praxis, ideology and faith.

4. To follow the developments of similar efforts of contextualization in other continents, especially in Latin America, Africa, and Asia.

5. To insert the discoveries of this effort into the mainstream of United States theology through seminaries and universities, so this program will not be necessary after the five years for which it is planned.

THE CONSTITUENCIES, STRUCTURES, AND ORGANIZATION

The conference in Detroit was conceived as one moment in an ongoing process of action and reflection which began about a year prior to the week in Detroit and would continue in a deepened and expanded form.

For some months prior to the conference about sixty "reflection groups" around the country prepared for it. To some extent the conference program and format were a product of the combined reflection and analysis of many different groups of people.

This continues to be the model of action and reflection for the follow-up. People who attended Detroit and others who did not attend but who are interested will continue this program of action, reflection, study, and prayer. Theologians, Christian social activists, directors of theological education, social scientists, and racial/ethnic minorities who accept the criteria for participation will be part of this new theological endeavor.

Contributors

HUGO ASSMANN: Brazilian theologian, university professor of communications in San José, Costa Rica

GREGORY BAUM: Professor of theology at St. Michael's College, Toronto, Canada.

PHILLIP E. BERRYMAN: North American theologian working in Guatemala with the Friends Service Committee

LEONARD BOFF: Teaches Christology in Petropolis, Brazil

ROBERT MCAFEE BROWN: Professor of Ecumenics and World Christianity at Union Theological Seminary, New York

MARY BURKE: Staff member of the Center of Concern, Washington, D.C.

JOHN A. COLEMAN: Jesuit priest teaching theology at the Jesuit School of Theology in Berkeley, California

SHEILA COLLINS: Theologian active in the feminist movement; author of *A Different Heaven and Earth: A Feminist Perspective on Religion*

AVERY DULLES: Teacher and writer, working at the Woodstock Theological Center in Washington, D.C.

ENRIQUE DUSSEL: Historian from Mendoza, Argentina, teaching in Mexico City

HERBERT O. EDWARDS: Member of the Department of Religious Studies of Duke University Divinity School

MANUEL FEBRES: Puerto Rican social scientist; former teacher at the New School for Social Research in New York

RENNIE GOLDEN: Divinity school student in Chicago; co-adminstrator of Adult Education Program for blacks and Latinos

GUSTAVO GUTIERREZ: From Lima, Peru; best known of the theologians of Latin American liberation theology

SR. ANNE MARIE HARNETT: Sister of the Holy Names of Jesus and Mary teaching at the Academy of the Holy Names, Albany, N.Y.

BEVERLY HARRISON: Associate professor of Christian Ethics at Union Theological Seminary, New York

MONIKA HELLWIG: Professor of theology at the Catholic University of America, Washington, D.C.

FREDERICK HERZOG: Faculty member at Duke University Divinity School, Durham, N.C.

JOSEPH HOLLAND: Staff member of the Center of Concern, Washington, D.C.

JAVIER IGUIÑIZ: Sociologist from Lima, Peru, teaching History and Development at the University of San Marcos in Lima

DIEGO IRARRAZAVAL: Chilean theologian working at the "Bartolomé de las Casas" Theological Institute, Lima, Peru

BEATRIZ MELANO COUCH: Professor at ISEDET (Instituto de Estudios Teológicos), in Buenos Aires, Argentina

JOSE MIGUEZ BONINO: Protestant theologian teaching at ISEDET (Instituto de Estudios Teológicos), Buenos Aires

JOSE PORFIRIO MIRANDA: Biblical scholar from Mexico; author of *Marx and the Bible*

J. DEOTIS ROBERTS, SR.: Black scholar and professor of Christian Theology at Howard University, Washington, D.C.

SR. JEANNE ROLLINS: Franciscan Sister working on a Swinomish reservation in the state of Washington

ROSEMARY R. RUETHER: Theologian and feminist, professor of Historical Theology at Howard University, Washington, D.C.

MICHELE RUSSELL: Afro-American freelance teacher and writer; on the editorial staff of Feminist Press; member of Association for the Improvement of Minority Employment in Detroit

JUAN LUIS SEGUNDO: Jesuit theologian from Uruguay; director for many years of the "Pedro Fabro" Center and author of the five-volume "Theology for Artisans of a New Humanity"

SERGIO TORRES: Roman Catholic priest from Chile; Executive Secretary of "Theology in the Americas: 1975"